THE HAUNTED FIFTIES

1953–1963

By I. F. Stone

A NONCONFORMIST HISTORY OF OUR TIMES

THE
HAUNTED
FIFTIES

1953–1963

I. F. STONE

With a Foreword by Arthur Miller

LITTLE, BROWN AND COMPANY

BOSTON   TORONTO   LONDON

To my sons, Jeremy J. and Christopher D.

Grateful acknowledgment is given to John Rackliffe
for his help in compiling this collection.

Library of Congress Cataloging-in-Publication Data

Stone, I. F. (Isidor F.), 1907–
    The haunted fifties, 1953–1963 / I. F. Stone; with a foreword by
Arthur Miller.
        p.   cm. — (A nonconformist history of our times)
    Includes index.
    1. United States — Politics and government—1953–1961. 2. United
States—Politics and government — 1961–1963. 3. United States —
Foreign relations — 1953–1961. 4. United States — Foreign
relations — 1961–1963. 5. World politics — 1955–1965.   I. Title.
II. Series: Stone, I. F. (Isidor F.), 1907– Nonconformist history
of our times.
E835.S82 1989
973.921—dc19   88-39721
                                                                        CIP

MV-PA

*Published simultaneously in Canada
by Little, Brown & Company (Canada) Limited*

PRINTED IN THE UNITED STATES OF AMERICA

Foreword

Somewhere in his monumental *Democracy In America,* de Tocqueville notes the odd contradiction between the desire of the American to hew out his destiny without outside interference, and his fear of holding opinions that might isolate him from the majority. The American has always been happiest alongside the winners, and a dread of the accusing finger of the hostile crowd has never been far from mind.

For the mass production of pariahs there has probably never been a time in our history to compare with the fifties. To have kept his head in that hurricane of corrupted speech, ritualized patriotism, paranoid terror, and sudden conversions to acceptability, a reporter needed something more than his wits and investigative talent and a gift for language; he had to have faith. A confident, tolerant America was inconceivable in those times, but I. F. Stone's endurance, I believe, depended on a certain profound faith in just such a return to common sense, fairness, and social conscience.

Looking through his pieces now, more than thirty years later and in a very different American climate, one is struck by their amazing cheerfulness. In terrible times dry, cynical despair is always a secret temptation, and it is often masked by the revolutionary's yen for a cleansing destruction. Stone never departed from the facts long enough to embitter himself with some windy apocalyptic diversion; he was in love, it seems, with the patterns, the mysteries, the promise of the evidence of his intelligence and his senses. I know that in the fifties to find his *Weekly* in the mail was to feel a breath of hope for mankind. If his work never reached beyond a numerical minority, it nevertheless was an inspiration to countless numbers of students, reporters, teachers, and editors who felt, as I did, that he spoke for freedom and truth in a delusionary time.

ARTHUR MILLER
July 1988

Contents

AUTHOR'S PREFACE

A WORD ABOUT MYSELF

I am, I suppose, an anachronism. In an age of corporation men, I have been an independent capitalist, the owner of my own enterprise, subject to neither mortgager nor broker, factor nor patron. In an age when young men, setting out on a career of journalism, must find their niche in some huge newspaper or magazine combine, I have been a wholly independent newspaperman, standing alone, without organizational or party backing, beholden to no one but my good readers. I am even one up on Benjamin Franklin — I have never accepted advertising.

The pieces collected in this volume are from a four-page miniature journal of news and opinion, on which I was a one-man editorial staff, from proofreader to publisher. This independence, like all else, had its price — the audience. My newspaper reached a relative handful, but the 5,000 readers with whom I started grew to more than 70,000 in nineteen years. I was in the black every one of those years and paid off the loans which helped me begin, without having to appeal to my readers or to wealthy friends to keep going. I paid my bills promptly, like a solid bourgeois, though in the eyes of many in the cold-war Washington where I operated I was regarded, I am sure, as a dangerous and subversive fellow.

I have been a newspaperman all my life. In the small town where I grew up, I published a paper at fourteen, worked for a country weekly and then as correspondent for a nearby city daily. I did this from my sophomore year in high school through college, until I quit in my junior year. I was a philosophy major and at one time thought of teaching philosophy, but the atmosphere of a college faculty repelled me. While going to college I was working ten hours afternoon and night doing combination rewrite and copy desk on the *Philadelphia Inquirer,* so I was already an experienced newspaperman making $40 a week — big pay in 1928. I have done everything on a newspaper except run a linotype machine.

I had become a radical in the twenties while in my teens, mostly through reading Jack London, Herbert Spencer, Kropotkin and Marx. I became a member of the Socialist Party and was elected to the New Jersey State Committee of the Socialist Party before I was old enough to vote. I did publicity for Norman Thomas in the 1928 campaign while a reporter on a small city daily, but soon drifted away from left-wing politics because of the sectarianism of the left. Moreover, I felt that party affiliation was incompatible with independent journalism, and I wanted to be free to help the unjustly treated, to defend everyone's civil liberty and to work for social reform without concern for leftist infighting.

I was fortunate in my employers. I rarely, if ever, felt compelled to compromise with my conscience; even as an anonymous editorial writer I never had to write something I thought untrue. I worked for a succession of newspaper people I remember with affection: J. David Stern and his editor Harry T. Saylor on the *Camden Courier-Post,* the *Philadelphia Record* and the *New York Post;* Freda Kirchwey of *The Nation;* Ralph Ingersoll and John P. Lewis of the newpaper *PM;* Bartley Crum and his editor Joseph Barnes of the short-lived New York *Star;* and Ted O. Thackrey of the *New York Post* and the New York *Daily Compass.* Working for them was a wonderfully rewarding experience and I learned much from all of them. From 1932 to 1939 I was an editorial writer on the *Philadelphia Record* and the *New York Post,* then strongly pro–New Deal papers. In 1940 I came to Washington as Washington Editor of *The Nation* and have been here ever since, working as reporter and columnist for *PM,* the New York *Star,* the *New York Post* (for a short interval) and the New York *Compass.* When the *Compass* closed in

November 1952 and no congenial job seemed likely to open up, I decided to launch a four-page weekly newsletter of my own.

I succeeded because it was what might be called a piggy-back launching. I had available the mailing lists of *PM*, the *Star* and the *Compass* and of people who had bought my books. For a remarkably small investment, in two advance mailings, I was able to get 5,000 subscribers at $5 each. I was my own biggest investor, but several friends helped me with loans and gifts. The existence of these highly selective mailing lists made it possible to reach what would otherwise appear to be needles in a haystack — a scattered tiny minority of liberals and radicals unafraid in McCarthy's heyday to support, and go on the mailing lists of, a new radical publication from Washington. I am deeply grateful to them.

It speaks well for the tradition of a free press in our country that even in the heyday of McCarthy it was possible for me to obtain my second-class mail permit without trouble. I had then been working in Washington for twelve years as correspondent for a succession of liberal and radical papers. I had supported Henry Wallace in 1948. I had fought for the civil liberties of Communists, and was for peace and coexistence with the Soviet Union. I had fought the loyalty purge, the FBI, the House Un-American Activities Committee, and McCarran as well as McCarthy. I had written the first magazine article against the Smith Act, when it was first used against the Trotskyites in 1940. There was nothing to the left of me but the *Daily Worker*.

Yet I was able to get second-class mail privilege without a single political question. I encountered old-fashioned civil service courtesy and political impartiality in the post office, and the second-class mail privilege when I started was my bread and butter. The difference between the second-class rate and the cheapest third-class rate was the equivalent of my salary.

My idea was to make the *Weekly* radical in viewpoint but conservative in format. I picked a beautiful type face, Garamond, for my main body type, and eschewed sensational headlines. I made no claim to inside stuff — obviously a radical reporter in those days had few pipelines into the government. I tried to give information which could be documented so the reader could check it for himself. I tried to dig the truth out of hearings, official transcripts and government documents, and to be as accurate as possible. I also sought to give the *Weekly* a personal flavor, to add humor, wit and good writing to the *Weekly* report. I felt that if one were able enough and had sufficient vision one could distill meaning, truth and even beauty from the swiftly flowing debris of the week's news. I sought in political reporting what Galsworthy in another context called "the significant trifle" — the bit of dialogue, the overlooked fact, the buried observation which illuminated the realities of the situation. These I often used in "boxes" to lighten up the otherwise solid pages of typography unrelieved either by picture or advertising. I tried in every issue to provide fact and opinion not available elsewhere in the press.

In the worst days of the witch hunt and cold war, I felt like a guerilla warrior, swooping down in surprise attack on a stuffy bureaucracy where it least expected independent inquiry. The reporter assigned to specific beats like the State Department or the Pentagon for a wire service or a big daily newspaper soon finds himself a captive. State and Pentagon have large press relations forces whose job it is to herd the press and shape the news. There are many ways to punish a reporter who gets out of line; if a big story breaks at 3 A.M., the press office may neglect to notify him while his rivals get the story. There are as many ways to flatter and take a reporter into camp — private off-the-record dinners with high officials, entertainment at the service clubs. Reporters tend to be absorbed by the bureaucracies they cover; they take on the habits, attitudes and even accents of the military or the diplomatic corps. Should a reporter resist the pressure, there are many ways to get rid of him. If his publisher is not particularly astute or independent, a little private talk, a hint that the reporter seems irresponsible — even a bit radical — "sometimes one could even mistake him for a Marxist" — will do the job of getting him replaced with a more malleable man.

But a reporter covering the whole capital on his own — particularly if he is his own employer — is immune from these pressures. Washington is full of news — if one story is denied him he can always get another. The bureaucracies put out so much that they cannot help letting the truth slip from time to time. The town is open. One can always ask questions, as one can see from one of my "coups" — forcing the Atomic Energy

Commission to admit that its first underground test was detected not 200 miles away — as it claimed — but 2600 miles away. This is the story of how I got that story — one example of what independent news gathering can be like.

The first underground test was held in the fall of 1957. The *New York Times* report from the test site in Nevada next morning said the results seemed to confirm the expectations of the experts: that it would not be detected more than 200 miles away. But the *Times* itself carried "shirttails" from Toronto, Rome and Tokyo saying that the shot had been detected there. Since the experts (viz. Dr. Edward Teller and his entourage at Livermore Laboratory, all opposed to a nuclear test ban agreement) were trying to prove that underground tests could not be detected at a distance, these reports from Toronto, Rome and Tokyo piqued my curiosity. I did not have the resources to check them by cable, so I filed the story away for future use.

Next spring, Stassen, then Eisenhower's chief disarmament negotiator, testified before the Humphrey Disarmament Subcommittee of the Senate that a network of stations a thousand kilometers (or 580 miles apart) could police a nuclear test ban agreement and detect any underground tests. Two days after his testimony the AEC issued its first official report on the Nevada explosion for publication the following Monday. This said that the Nevada underground explosion had not been detected more than 200 miles away. The effect was to undercut Stassen's testimony. If the Nevada blast could not be detected more than 200 miles away then a network of stations 580 miles apart would not be able to police an agreement. I recalled the *New York Times* report of the previous fall, dug it out of a basement file and telephoned the AEC press office. I asked how the AEC reconciled its statement in the report about to be released that the blast was not detected more than 200 miles away with the reports from Rome, Tokyo and Toronto the morning after that it had registered on seismographs there. The answer was that they didn't know but would try to find out.

In the meantime I decided to find me a seismologist. By telephoning around I learned there was a seismology branch in the Coast and Geodetic Survey, where I duly found a seismologist and asked him whether it was true that Tokyo, Rome and Toronto had detected the Nevada underground blast. He said that he did not believe the claims of these three foreign stations but he showed me a list of some twenty U.S. stations which he said had certainly detected it. One of these was 2600 miles north of the test site in Fairbanks, Alaska, another was 1200 miles east in Fayetteville, Arkansas. I copied the names and distances down. When he asked why I was so interested, I said the AEC was about to release a report for the following Monday claiming that the explosion was not detected more than 200 miles away. When he heard the AEC angle, he became less communicative. I had hardly got back to my office when the phone rang; it was the AEC press relations man. He said "We just heard from Coast and Geodetic. There must be some mistake. We'll reach Nevada by teletype in the morning and let you know." When the Joint Committee on Atomic Energy later investigated the incident, the AEC claimed it was an "inadvertent" error. No agency in Washington — not even State Department or Pentagon — has a worse record than the AEC for these little "errors."

No bureaucracy likes an independent newspaperman. Whether capitalist or communist, democratic or authoritarian, every regime does its best to color and control the flow of news in its favor. There *is* a difference here and I'm grateful for it. I could not operate in Moscow as I do in Washington. There is still freedom of fundamental dissent here, if only on the edges and in small publications.

For me, being a newspaperman has always seemed a cross between Galahad and William Randolph Hearst, a perpetual crusade. When the workers of Csespel and the 1956 Hungarian Revolution put a free press among their demands, I was thrilled. What Jefferson symbolized for me was being rediscovered in a socialist society as a necessity for good government.

I believe that no society is good and can be healthy without freedom for dissent and for creative independence. I have found among the Soviets kindred spirits in this regard and I watch their struggle for freedom against bureaucracy with deepest sympathy. I am sorry, when discussing our free press with them, to admit that our press is often almost as conformist as theirs. But I am happy that in my own small way I have been able to demonstrate that independence is possible, that a wholly free radical journalist can survive in our society. In the darkest days of McCarthy, when I often was made to feel a pariah, I was heartened by the thought that I was preserving and carrying forward the best in America's traditions, that in my humble way I stood in a line that reached back to Jefferson. These are the origins and the pre-conceptions, the hopes and the aspirations, from which sprang the pieces that follow.

I. F. STONE

The Haunted Fifties

*

Overture

NOTE TO THE REST OF THE UNIVERSE

Within two years you may see a flaming ball rocket up from the earth's surface and swing into position in an orbit around it. Do not regard the spectacle with complacency. These satellites will grow larger and more numerous; men will go up with them. Voyages to the moon will follow. After that the distant realm of planet and star will lie open to Man.

Beware in time. This is a breed which has changed little in thousands of years. The cave dweller who wielded a stone club and the man who will soon wield an interstellar missile are terribly alike. Earth's creatures feed upon each other, but this is the only one which kills on a large scale, for pleasure, adventure and even—so perverse is the species—for supposed reasons of morality.

Should you start a secret mission of inquiry, you will find that the sacred books on which the young of the various tribes have been brought up for thousands of years glorify bloodshed. Whether one looks in Homer, or the Sagas, or the Bible, or the Koran, the hero is a warrior. Someone is always killing someone else for what is called the greater glory of God.

This is not a creature to be trusted with the free run of the universe. At the moment the human race seems to be temporarily sobered by the possession of weapons which could destroy all life on earth except perhaps the mosses and the fungi. But the planetary rocket may revive recrimination. The currently rival tribes, the Russians and the Americans, fear the other may use the new device against them. They may soon be transferring to outer space the hates that in every generation have brought suffering to the earth. It might be wise to stop them now, on the very threshold of the open and as yet unpolluted skies.

AUGUST 8, 1955

1: *The Eisenhower Era Begins*

FROM MINK TO GENERAL MOTORS

Amid the glittering wives of Eisenhower's many-millionaired Cabinet even the wife of "the plumber" was opulent. Mrs. Martin Durkin, the new First Lady of the Labor Department, was to appear at the Inaugural Ball in a bouffant gown by Countess Alexander, of toast-brown Chantilly lace, with a ten-yard sweep of skirt. The wife of the new Secretary of the Treasury barely managed to outpace this proletarian splendor by wearing "huge clips . . . of rubies and diamonds." The political tone of the festivities matched. Thanks to the vigilance of Representative Busbey, of Illinois, Aaron Copland's *A Lincoln Portrait* was dropped from the Inaugural Concert as "un-American." At the Inaugural Reception, Adolph Menjou struck a suave blow for the free world when he turned his back on Soviet Ambassador Georgi Zarubin, who had asked to be presented, no doubt for purposes of infiltration.

There was a surprise in the Inaugural Address. In his farewell to the faculty of Columbia, Eisenhower had said he was breaking a release date to give the assembled professors a passage of special interest from his forthcoming Inaugural. "As long as we preach with conviction and teach with integrity," Eisenhower read, "that is the true defense against communism." The implications were reassuring, but the sentence was dropped from the Inaugural, as Eisenhower dropped a similar passage on a famous occasion during the campaign. The Inaugural as revised carried not the faintest suggestion of a plea for academic freedom, or civil liberty of any kind. The word freedom was often used but only in the general sense in which it always appears when a new war is being whooped up. Eisenhower said "freedom is pitted against slavery; light against dark" but this is an immemorial metaphor. As far back as the earliest tribal wars over stolen ax handles, the issue has been freedom against slavery. The Inaugural was a gaudy composition, febrile and synthetic. Its prose style was not quite as purple as MacArthur's but it was sometimes almost as banal as Ridgway's. Those who listened for concrete ideas listened in vain. All the clichés which make one despair of negotiation were there. "Appeasement" was "futile." We shall never "try to placate an aggressor by the false and wicked bargain of trading honor for security." Eisenhower was bathetic when he said "in our quest of honorable peace, we shall neither compromise, nor tire. . . ." The quest will be very tiring if he thinks peace can be achieved without compromise. Eisenhower seems to be tired already. "In the final choice," he said at one point, "a soldier's pack is not so heavy a burden as a prisoner's chains." Eisenhower is all set to march.

Just where is not clear. Eisenhower is no fire-eater, but seems to be a rather simple man who enjoys his bridge and his golf and doesn't like to be too much bothered. He promises, from what was observed of him by the press on his campaign train, to be a kind of president *in absentia,* a sort of political vacuum in the White House which other men will struggle among themselves to fill. In the meantime Congress, impatient as ever, wants something done about Korea. It would like to widen the war but without enlarging the risk, and at the same time to reduce the military budget; all it wants is a miracle. There are indications that something is up. One does not send one's Secretary of State and Mutual Security Director abroad immediately after Inauguration for a junket, nor just to "gather information." Not much information can be gathered when one plans as Dulles and Stassen do to visit seven countries in nine days. A rapid-fire round of visits at this pace is made for predigested take-it-or-leave-it propositions. If the Korean war is to be widened in search of trick solutions some quick high-level negotiation is necessary.

Eisenhower's path to the White House door is already strewn with time bombs: Truman's mischievous farewell praise for the presidential press conference, which Eisenhower so much fears; the order handing tidelands oil to the Navy; Senator Morse's bill challenging Eisenhower on his promise to erase "every vestige of racism" from the capital. The most explosive of all was that laid in the Wilson case by the obtuseness of his own followers, giddy with victory. Who could have dreamt that big business would prove so crass as to drive a Byrd and a Duff into opposition? The appointments to the Defense Department could hardly have been more brazen. General Motors, largest defense contractor, got the top job and the deputyship. The Army Secretary is head of a firm which does a $125,000,000 business with the Army. The Air Secretary is a heavy holder of motor stock. The Navy Secretary is a Texas oil man. A law which goes back to 1863 makes it a crime for an official to act for the government in transactions in which he is "directly or indirectly" interested. Charles E. Wilson has $2,500,000 in General Motors stock and $600,000 more due him in the next four years providing he does nothing "inimical" to GM's interests. Pending for action by the new Secretary of Defense is an application from GM for an increase in profits on its contracts. Wilson and his associates expect the law to be waived in their favor and Wilson sought to dismiss the ethical problems by telling the senators, "What is good for General Motors is good for the country and what is good for the country is good for General Motors." The remark recalls that outburst by George F. Baer in the coal strike of 1902 when Morgan's man rejected pleas for arbitration by saying that the rights of labor in this country would be protected "not by labor agitators, but by the Christian men to whom God in his infinite wisdom has given the control of the property interests of this country." That brash assertion of property's divine right to rule brought a Bronx cheer from the country even in 1902. No Administration ever started with a bigger, more revealing or more resounding pratfall. Eisenhower will be haunted by General Motors as Truman was by mink.

JANUARY 24, 1953

CHALLENGING THE LEFT: "BACK IKE FOR PEACE"

At the risk of complete and total leftist excommunication—from the ADA straight across the board through the Communists to the Trotzkyists—I want to put forward a daring slogan in the difficult and precarious weeks ahead: "Back Ike for Peace."

Those who live in a dream world may well believe that Eisenhower as President of the United States need only press a button to oust Syngman Rhee, recognize Red China, restore Formosa to the mainland, put Chiang Kai-shek in the laundry business and ensure peace forever by a quick talk with Churchill, Malenkov and Mao Tse-tung. In that dream world, Eisenhower is to be treated with suspicion until a global peace has been signed, sealed and delivered.

Others on the Left are as giddy as a punch-drunk fighter who has had too many blows on the head. They are suddenly certain that the United States is so weak and unpopular with its own Western allies that it *must* make peace in Korea and call off the cold war.

But those with some conception of political realities must see the enormous odds against which Eisenhower has slowly been pushing toward peace in Korea. A powerful wing of the Republican party is against a settlement. The American military bureaucracy has been and continues to be opposed to a settlement. The military if given its head is quite capable of stretching out the talks for another year. There was an ominous ring in the happy announcement from Panmunjom as we went to press: "Remember this is not the armistice agreement. It deals with the prisoner of war issue only." The military are prepared if permitted to split hairs for many months more on the exact location of the cease-fire line and on the question of airfield construction during a truce.

As peace comes closer, Syngman Rhee and Chiang Kai-shek, the principal beneficiaries of the Korean war, grow more desperate. Eisenhower last week barely managed to get Senate leaders to withdraw an appropriations rider which would have had the effect of taking the United States out of the United Nations if Communist China were admitted. Syngman Rhee counts on the support of the same forces in his intransigeance. The significant point in Rhee's attitude is that he nowhere calls for peaceful unification of Korea by elections under UN auspices; now, as in August 1950 when a truce seemed imminent and such elections were being seriously discussed, he fears an unfavorable verdict at the polls.

It is a mistake to believe that Eisenhower has to contend only with a few wild men and reactionaries. A peacefully unified Korea would be the natural cornerstone of an overall settlement in the Far East, but such a settlement would require the recognition of Communist China and its admission to the UN. But even in the labor movement this would command little support. John L. Lewis last week declared that admission of Communist China would be the death of the UN. George Meany of the AFL warned against Soviet peace moves as leading toward "a new Munich." A joint statement

by the CIO, AFL and UMW to the forthcoming Stockholm conference echoes all the rightist shibboleths about "appeasement" and
"liberation." The leadership of American labor is close in spirit to
that wing of the Republican party for which Knowland spoke last
week when he called for the "calculated risk" of war with Russia if
the Korean truce talks fail.

Where then can forces be mobilized to support the drive for
peace in Korea and to block a new intervention if Rhee sets the war
going again? Eisenhower himself is the focal point of a big business
group which wants peace. Their voice was heard in the Senate on
June 3 when Senator Edward Martin, Republican, of Pennsylvania,
said he had always been a strong supporter of military preparedness
but that he had become convinced that under present conditions "it
is almost impossible to provide sufficient money to assure an adequate defense," and that "if the present armament race continues
all the nations of the world will go bankrupt."

Senator Martin spoke in support of a disarmament resolution
introduced that day by another Republican businessman, Senator
Flanders, of Vermont. This resolution, co-sponsored by an impressive list of senators from both sides of the aisle, would instruct the
President to "develop a plan for the transfer of resources and manpower now being used for arms to constructive ends at home and
abroad." This echoes the suggestion put forward by Eisenhower in
his speech to the American Society of Newspaper Editors. A recent
Gallup poll shows 65 percent in favor of diverting defense funds to
world reconstruction. This was essentially FDR's idea and Wallace's,
as it was later McMahon's. Despite the ugly clamor of hate in the
press, it always seems to strike a favorable response. This popular
response is most encouraging for what it tells us about the innate
kindliness and good sense of most of our fellow Americans.

I suggest that this resolution and the President's efforts for
peace in Korea provide points around which the peace forces in this
country may again rally popular support. Truman-Acheson "total diplomacy" sought to make "peace" a subversive word and succeeded
in reducing peace agitation to negligible proportions. Here is a
chance to break out of the repressive strangle, to raise the peace
issue in a context in which people will not be afraid to discuss it.
I suggest that "Back Ike for Peace" is a slogan hard to beat. I also
suggest that unless in every town and city of this country people

begin to talk of peace and call for peace, the bright hope dawning over Panmunjom may yet be suddenly eclipsed in a new and more terrible and wider war.

JUNE 13, 1953

HOW IKE EARNED HIS AFTERNOON OFF

In England the equivalent of our State of the Union message is couched in the form of an Address from the Throne. Everyone knows that this is a fiction, and no one wastes time trying to infer from it the *Weltanschauung* of the reigning monarch. But much nonsense is generated here when the President, instead of being a governing personality, is like Eisenhower a figurehead. In England, the Address from the Throne is fashioned by the Prime Minister, representing the majority party. Here, however, the President being both Chief of State and Head of the Government, there is no Prime Minister. When the President does not govern there is no way to figure out who, if anybody, was responsible for the State of the Union message and the policy decisions reflected in it. Who is "Eisenhower," that is, the Eisenhower in whose name all this is spoken? No one really knows.

The press, being almost entirely Republican, the President has an overwhelming claque. The respectable pundits never permit themselves to see that this (Washington's best-known and best-kept secret) is a king as naked of ideas as a newborn babe. Nobody must be more surprised than the likably unpretentious and modest Eisenhower himself to read next morning in, let us say, Walter Lippmann, just how profound he was the day before. The reality peeped out in that Associated Press dispatch which reported that after delivering the message, Eisenhower was given the afternoon off to play golf, like a small boy allowed to go and play after doing his required stint at Sunday School. "His doctor and the whole White House staff told him to get out on the golf course," Presidential Press Secretary James C. Hagerty related, "and get some relaxation." For a man who hates to read as much as Eisenhower does, reading these 7800 words (aloud yet) must have been work enough for one day.

The message appears to be a rather ill-organized patchwork of bits and pieces from various departments, nauseatingly larded with the wholly artificial religious sentiments now considered *de rigueur* in all American state papers and designed firmly to anchor God on our side in the cold war. The opening section sounded as if it came straight from the State Department; its self-righteous rhetoric is the kind to which we have been accustomed since 1947 and it is amazingly devoid of anything new. The next section must have been drafted in concert by two opposing wings at the Pentagon, with the Treasury as referee. It does at one point warn against "undue reliance on one weapon" (to keep the Army and Navy happy) but it pretty clearly reflects a decision to depend on nuclear weapons and air power. The Treasury, therefore, wants to save on the Army and conventional weapons. Here Eisenhower is put up to speaking *in persona propria,* assuring Congress (where the Army lobbyists are stirring up a rumpus) that this "reduction of forces in certain categories" was made at his "personal direction after long and thoughtful study." This is supposed to scare off congressmen.

Justice Department is next in the patchwork, and "continuance of our aggressive attack on subversion at home" is promised. There follows a pep talk on business—we never had it so good, at least that's what Commerce Department seems to have said. Agriculture was allowed to insist on "flexible" prices; Labor was permitted to suggest a ninety-cent minimum wage. Health and Welfare promises a new health plan but without "socialized medicine." Taft-Hartley is to be revised so that employers, too, must sign non-Communist affidavits and public power is to be watered down further via "partnership" with private enterprise. There are the usual words about small business. Something is promised on education, and a plea is again made for some lowering of tariffs. This is "New Dealish" only in the sense that it does not propose to turn back the clock, except stealthily on hydroelectric power. The idea that this will force the Democrats left is equally nonsensical.

"Eisenhower" is as much and no more to the left than were Landon, Willkie and Dewey. In a two-party system, under normal conditions, both parties play as close to the center as possible. This leaves both the Republican right and the Democratic left dissatisfied but since they have nowhere else to go they exercise no leverage. At the moment, while the Republicans are thus "left," the Democrats are "right." In fact some of them are shopping around for a more conservative candidate than Stevenson. There is even talk of Lausche, a Taft Democrat (!) and a Catholic who might garner in disaffected Republicans and McCarthyites.

The Democrats will make capital in the West on power; keep

mum on civil rights for Negroes; do nothing for labor; jump on Reds as hard as Republicans to prove their purity; exploit the discontent over the security program and at the same time kick up a fuss about cuts in the defense budget to show that the Republicans are the ones who are really "soft" about communism. The country, generally as contented as the Borden cow, will take all this without a *moo* as long as business holds up. There may be a change in the spring, however, when the auto industry finds it just cannot sell all those new cars it is making.

JANUARY 17, 1955

2: *John Foster Dulles: Portrait of a Liberator*

No dodger could have been more artful than the new Secretary of State at his confirmation hearing before the Senate Foreign Relations Committee. John Foster Dulles managed to convey the impression when questioned by indignant Democrats that the foreign policy planks of the Republican platform were just rhetoric and at the same time to assure Republicans like Taft that he stood by every word in them. At one point Senator Humphrey came close to hitting pay dirt. He wanted to know what was meant by the charge that the Democrats had abandoned friendly nations like the Baltic states, Poland and Czechoslovakia to communism. Dulles explained that this was a reference to the policy of containment. Humphrey asked whether it wasn't true that the plight of the Baltic states was due to the Stalin-Hitler pact. "Do you recall having made any suggestions at the time," Humphrey queried, "as to how we might relieve the Baltic states?" Dulles, in his best church-warden manner, replied that he had made no recommendation because he was "in private life" at the time.

It is a pity Senator Humphrey did not press the point further. The Hitler-Stalin pact sealed the fate of Poland as well as the Baltic states. Dulles, though a private citizen, did make recommendations on the subject at the time. After the fall of Poland, on October 28, 1939, Dulles made a speech in Detroit at the National Council of the Y.M.C.A. declaring that he "saw neither in the origin of the present war, nor in its objectives 'any affirmative reason for the United States to become a participant.' " (*New York Times,* October 29, 1939.) In other words, he recommended the abandonment of Poland. The origin of the war lay in Japanese aggression against China and German aggression against Poland. The objectives were to clear the way for German exploitation and enslavement in Eastern Europe, and for Japanese in Asia. Neither origin nor objectives troubled Dulles.

Humphrey went all the way back to a speech Dulles made in 1928 to test the Secretary of State's views on foreign trade. But neither he nor any other senator touched on the contrast between the equanimity with which Dulles regarded Axis aggression before the war and the moralistic fervor with which he preaches "liberation" today. The architect of the so-called "peace of reconciliation" with Japan was reconciled from the very first to Japanese and German aggression. A few months after Hitler marched out of Geneva and into the Rhineland, tearing up the arms provisions of the Versailles pact, Dulles was moved to set forth his views on international politics. His little-noticed and long-forgotten article for the October, 1935, issue of the *Atlantic Monthly,* called "The Road to Peace," is recommended reading for Inaugural Week. Dulles then met the international crisis with a defense of the need for force in history which somehow made the *aggressed* rather than the aggressor seem to blame for what was happening in the world. The road to peace, as Dulles saw it, was to give Germany, Italy and Japan what they wanted.

Dulles likes to imply that he is an old Wilsonian but he regarded the League as merely a means of imposing French hegemony on Europe. He opposed the non-recognition doctrine applied by the League and by Stimson "with reference to the situation brought about by Japan in Manchuria"—the phrasing avoided any implication of Japanese aggression. Dulles was against non-recognition because it was "merely designed to perpetuate the status quo." Dulles in those days harped so much on the wickedness of trying to maintain the status quo as to make himself sound almost like a revolutionary. Dulles thought it "at least conceivable" that what the Japanese were doing in Manchuria reflected "a logical and inevitable tendency" which "could not be held in suspense until that hypothetical day when China was prepared freely to acquiesce therein." The circumlocutions were lush but the meaning was plain. The legal footwork was downright brilliant. The defendant, far from being guilty of rape, was the helpless victim of the plaintiff's obstinate reluctance to give consent!

Smooth is an inadequate word for Dulles. His prevarications are so highly polished as to be aesthetically pleasurable. Let us look more closely at how he did it in the *Atlantic Monthly* article. He began by saying that the drift to war was bewildering. "Faced by a situation which superficially seems so inexplicable," Dulles wrote, "we adopt the time-honored expedient of postulating a 'personal devil.' Hitler, Mussolini and Japanese war lords in turn become the object of our suspicion." Not they, but our overheated imaginations were at fault. We must identify the "underlying forces . . . otherwise we are striking at shadows." The true explanation "of the imminence of war lies in . . . the fact that peace efforts have been directed toward the prevention of change."

Dulles made the desire for stability and peace seem somehow selfish. "Those whose lives fall in pleasant places," he wrote, "contemplate with equanimity an indefinite continuation of their present state. 'Peace' means to them that they should be left undisturbed. . . . 'Aggression' becomes the capital international crime." Notice how Dulles put "aggression" in quotation marks. It was "no mere coincidence," Dulles continued, warming up to his theme, "that it is the presently favored nations—France, Great Britain and the United States—whose governments have been most active in devising plans for perpetual peace." There followed an extraordinary sentence, which the German clients of Sullivan and Cromwell must have relished enormously, "If other countries, like Germany, Japan and Italy," Dulles went on, "adhere only reluctantly if at all to such projects, it is not because these nations are inherently warlike or bloodthirsty. They too want peace but they undoubtedly feel within themselves potentialities which are repressed and desire to keep open avenues of change."

It was all so simple when properly understood. Dulles pleaded the necessity for "a sound body of public opinion ready to throw its influence in favor of appropriate periodical changes in national domains"—no doubt as in Poland and Czechoslovakia. Dulles worked himself up into a positive crescendo of righteousness. "Only in such a way," he concluded, "is it possible to end the unnatural alliance which now exists between liberals and reactionaries, both of whom seek to maintain the status quo, the liberals because they mistakenly think this means peace, and the reactionaries because it perpetuates their exploitation of that which they already have." A man capable of such an argument is a genius of a sort, but not the sort one welcomes as Secretary of State.

Dulles is a man of wily and subtle mind. It is difficult to believe that behind his unctuous manner he does not take a cynical amusement in his own monstrous pomposities. He gives the impression of a man who lives constantly behind a mask. Nowhere else did Dulles venture to indicate his real views on foreign policy as openly as in the article for the *Atlantic Monthly;* his 1939 book, *War, Peace and Change,* cloaks his pro-Axis sympathies in heavy abstractions. When that article is coupled with certain indiscreet outbursts in upstate New York speeches during his 1949 Senate campaign against Lehman, the corporation lawyer's real ideological orientation becomes clear. Dulles, who was never moved to denounce the "statism" of Hitler and Mussolini, said in a speech at Elizabethtown that "bloody" revolution might some day be necessary in this country to combat the "statism" of the New Dealers. The rash remark reflected just such a readiness to use force and violence against social reform as produced fascism in Germany and Italy. The benign and "realistic" view Dulles took of Fascist expansion was not unrelated to a sympathy of outlook on domestic policy. His New York attacks in the 1949 campaign on "handouts for teachers" and "handouts for farmers," like his opposition to federal aid for education, are indicative. The "liberation" with which Dulles is concerned is not liberation from dictatorship but liberation from the welfare state.

Barely eight years after the war against the Axis, a Senate committee has unanimously confirmed the nomination as Secretary of State of a man who was and continues to be both pro-German and pro-Japanese. He consistently misconceived and misrepresented the nature of German and Japanese aggression. The Nazi-Soviet pact and the Japanese attack on Pearl Harbor were facilitated by the mental outlook he typified. But no attempt was made at the hearing to explore his views in the past nor was he subject to real questioning as to the policies he proposed for the future. His obsessive hatred for socialism was the kind the Germans and Japanese exploited before and are exploiting again. It is fortunate for this country, Western Europe and China that he was not at the helm of foreign policy before the war. It is unfortunate that he should be now. The same errors may repeat themselves, in a more tragic form.

JANUARY 24, 1953

3: *McCarthy Rides High*

QUIS CUSTODIET CUSTODEM?

The Romans had a saying, *"Quis custodiet custodem?"*—Who will watch the watchman? The wry question applies patly to the case of Joe McCarthy. The Senator who is now the chairman of the Senate's key watchdog committee is the Senator who most needs watching. The report made on McCarthy by the Senate subcommittee on privileges and elections is a monument to the ineptitude of gentlemen in dealing with a brawler who pays no attention to the rules, Queensberry or otherwise. The report, spottily covered in the nation's newspapers despite a very full account sent out (to its credit) by the Associated Press, is the first official full-length portrait of the most brazen operator to appear in the United States Senate since the days of Huey Long.

The new document is the third Senate report which has found McCarthy mixed up in funny business on which action by law enforcement agencies has been asked. A subcommittee of the Senate Armed Services Committee reporting in October, 1949, called for investigation by the Justice and Defense Departments into the campaign to save the Malmédy slayers. McCarthy figured in this as an advocate of strict Anglo-Saxon due process for the SS men who killed 350 unarmed American prisoners and 150 Belgian civilians in the Battle of the Bulge. Nothing happened. The Rules Committee in August, 1951, suggested state and federal inquiry into the financial irregularities and defamatory tactics of the campaign in which McCarthy helped defeat Millard Tydings for re-election to the Senate the year before. Again nothing happened. It is now the honor of the Senate, not McCarthy, which is going down for the third time.

McCarthy cannot complain that he got less than the due process due him. Six times the subcommittee invited him to appear and rebut the charges bravely made by former Senator Benton, six times Mc-

Carthy failed to show up. The subcommittee lacked the nerve to subpoena him.

The picture drawn by the new report is of a man who cannot resist speculation on margin. His activities in and out of the market since 1942 are those of a born gambler. A series of financial difficulties were eased by some odd transactions of which the $10,000 he received from Lustron for a housing pamphlet is the best known. Newly brought to light in this report is the $20,000 note signed for McCarthy by the Washington representative of Pepsi-Cola at a time when the Senator's bank account in Wisconsin was overextended. Pepsi-Cola was then lobbying for decontrol of sugar and McCarthy was chairman of a Senate subcommittee—on sugar!

McCarthy's financial accounts are hectic. From January 1, 1948, to November 12, 1952, he deposited $172,000 in one Washington bank; his administrative assistant and alter ego, Ray Kiermas, deposited $96,000. Of these amounts almost $60,000 deposited by McCarthy and almost $45,000 deposited by Kiermas "has not been identified as to source." The Senator's most successful speculation was his flier in anticommunism. Contributions flowed in after his famous attack on the State Department, February 9, 1950. In the months which followed more than $20,000 was deposited by him in a special account used for donations to help him fight communism. "However," the report says dryly, "no connection could be established between many of the disbursements from this account and any possible anti-Communist campaign." In one case traced by the committee, McCarthy deposited a $10,000 loan to fight communism in a special account, and then withdrew it three weeks later to pass on to a friend for a speculation in soybeans.

Outgoing Democrats and incoming Republicans will live equally to regret that they did not cut McCarthy down to size when they had the chance. With his congenital cheek and the enormous powers conferred upon him by his key Senate chairmanship, McCarthy promises to become Eisenhower's chief headache. McCarthy is in a position to smear any government official who fails to do his bidding. With much daring and few scruples, McCarthy can make himself the most powerful single figure in Congress and terrorize the new Administration. All those mumblings and rumblings about how Communists are "already infiltrating" the Republicans are indicative.

JANUARY 17, 1953

SOAP OPERA HERO

The cast assembled slowly. That swarthy urchin, Roy Cohn, was one of the first to arrive. McCarthy's new staff director, Frank Carr, the former head of the New York FBI office, turned out to be a stoutish young man with a non-benevolent moon face, small heavily-lidded eyes, and a pug nose so tiny it made his profile seem flat; he might have been the model for a toy Piggy-Wiggy bank. Louis Budenz, grayer and more wrinkled, dashed in out of breath, dangling a large brief case, for a quick conference with Cohn, Carr and a big Scandinavian, Karl Baarslag, who had finally proven too much even for the American Legion and is now doing research for McCarthy. The reports had that Monday-morning look. The big room was but sparsely filled. The TV machines were up and the bright camera lights on when McCarthy made his entrance alone, fifteen minutes late. He had his left hand in his pocket and walked with what was meant to be a modest slouch, a self-conscious grin on his face. The gray jailbird complexion, the covert look of a smart fox, were unchanged. In that gravelly voice, bored, impersonal and inexorable, like the detective hero in a soap opera, McCarthy called the meeting to order. The scene was a familiar one—the caucus room of the Senate office building, on a Monday morning in late September. The fall hunting season, Red hunting that is, had begun.

This season McCarthy is out for bigger game, the biggest he has tackled yet. The attack on military intelligence risks a conflict with the Pentagon, far more powerful and cohesive a bureaucracy than the State Department. Back of this attack sophisticated Washington observers see two factors at work. One is the long-time ambition of McCarthy's ally, J. Edgar Hoover, to take over all intelligence, to bring the Secret Service, CIA, OSS and the various intelligence branches of the armed services under his control. The congressional investigating committees and the rightist papers with which Hoover has friendly relations have helped cast suspicion on CIA and OSS before.

The other factor at work is McCarthy's ambition to create a kind of dictatorship for himself within the framework of established government, to make himself the recipient of complaints from assorted crackpots and malcontents, to build up a secret ring of informants within the government, to use their reports in unscrupulous smear campaigns, and to make officials more fearful of him than of their own superiors.

The outlines of the process were visible in this week's hearing. McCarthy has been getting scuttlebutt from Army intelligence, as he does from other agencies. Of the pamphlet *Psychological and Cultural Traits of Soviet Siberia* which he has attacked, McCarthy said, "We had testimony in executive session the other day that a Major Wilson—I think it was a Major Wilson—strongly objected to this, and pointed out this was Soviet propaganda, Communist propaganda, from beginning to end."

Loose charges are taken at face value while official inquiry into them is brushed aside. "He objected so loudly," McCarthy said, "that Army intelligence finally was forced to call a board to pass upon this." The findings are not revealed but "for some strange reason," McCarthy went on, the board thought the pamphlet should still be used. There are implied threats of future exposure to make the timid tremble. "I should point out," McCarthy warned, "it was a civilian who was selected to head this board, and that civilian also is holding a high position as of today over in the Pentagon." His head may be next.

In the Pentagon, as elsewhere, McCarthy is already dealing directly with department heads. The other book to which he objects (among how many hundreds on Russia which military intelligence must use?) is *USSR: A Concise Handbook,* edited by Professor Ernest J. Simmons of Columbia. McCarthy said this had been used until the beginning of this year "and the new Secretary of the Army said he would immediately check to see whether it is still being used."

McCarthy's attack on military intelligence has alarmed circles friendly to him. For the first time, the *Chicago Tribune* and *Washington Times-Herald,* Colonel McCormick's twin publications, have published an editorial criticizing McCarthy. They disagreed with the Senator about the Siberian pamphlet, said his principal objection seemed to be that the pamphlet "does not assert that all people under the Soviet tyranny are opposed to it." The McCormick organs said it was dangerous in war to embrace "false assumptions about the enemy" and that if there were ever a Russo-American war "it would be an error of the first magnitude to believe that every Russian except the top crust of a couple of million party members was disaffected and would turn on the regime at the first opportunity." Colonel McCormick, who has applauded so many Red smears, rose to the defense of Colonel R. S. Bratton, who was in charge of preparing the pamphlet, as an officer of good reputation who had tried in vain to awaken the Department to the danger in the twenty-four hours before Pearl Harbor.

This effort to reason with McCarthy has a refreshing kind of amusement when it comes from the right. But McCarthy is no more concerned with the realities and mechanics of military intelligence than with those of the overseas libraries or the Foreign Service. He is interested in hashing up enough exaggeration, falsehood and alarm to serve the purpose of advertising himself and making others fearful of his power. For this purpose, as so often, he has gone back to the same limited witch-hunt cast of characters and replayed some of the same old cracked records.

OCTOBER 3, 1953

THE SILENCE IN THE SENATE

The Senate, particularly its Democratic membership, presented an appalling spectacle of cowardice during the debate which ended with approval of $214,000 for the McCarthy committee. Not a single voice was raised in support of Ellender's one-man fight to cut McCarthy's funds and force him to confine the Government Operations Committee to the limits established by the Reorganization Act of 1946. Langer defended McCarthy against the charge of duplicating the work of the Jenner committee. Cooper alone suggested weakly that the Senate could not long escape the responsibility of providing some code of fair procedure for these committees. Morse thereupon objected to making any such rules a condition of the appropriation and insisted that McCarthy had made out a "prima facie" case for the funds he asked. This year, like last, Morse put a spoke in the wheels of Ellender's one-man crusade. Most shamefully of all, though McCarthy taunted them with "twenty years of treason," not a single Democrat rose to defend the party and Fulbright cast the only vote against the appropriation. The Fort Monmouth hearings have been thoroughly discredited, yet except for Ellender no senator dared question them. One has to go back to Tacitus and the Roman Senate in its more degenerate days to match what happened here last Tuesday.

Yet the Democrats had a ready answer. On the plane of political campaigning, the Republicans offer "warmed-over spy"—the notion that the New Deal period was one in which America was infiltrated, betrayed and subverted. But when the Eisenhower Economic Report swings into a pep talk for businessmen to counter what have been termed "communistic" efforts to undermine business, what does it cite as "Basis for Confidence"? Insurance of bank deposits, curbs on speculation, jobless insurance, farm price supports, social security, federal aid to housing. These, in the opinion of Eisenhower and his advisers, have made America more immune to depression, more stable. Yet these reforms were the handiwork of those same "traitors." It's an odd kind of subversion that subverts a country into greater stability. And it's even odder to have the men who accomplished this and led America to victory against Hitler called treasonable by a Senator who had the effrontery to defend the SS men who butchered American prisoners after the Battle of the Bulge.

FEBRUARY 8, 1954

A SKEPTICAL ARMY GENERAL

Under the engaging title, "Communist Infiltration in the Army," the McCarthy committee has just made public the transcript of the executive session at which General Richard C. Partridge, G-2, United States Army, was interrogated last fall about that Army pamphlet on Soviet Siberia.

General Partridge seems to have rubbed McCarthy the wrong way from the start. The General said the pamphlet was designed to give as objective a picture as possible of how people in Soviet Siberia felt about the Communist regime and "not give the idea of the Communist government and the situation in Russia as seen from the United States."

McCarthy charged into the fray immediately. "Do you know," he asked, "that this book quotes verbatim from Joe Stalin, without attributing it to him, as a stamp of approval of the United States Army?" General Partridge said he didn't know that it did.

Instead of nailing the culprit by triumphantly producing the offending passage, McCarthy asked, "Don't you think before you testify you should take time to find out whether it quotes Joe Stalin and other notorious Communists?" The witness never got a chance to answer that question. McCarthy himself didn't seem to know just what had been quoted from Stalin and where.

For a senator who aspires to be an unofficial Secretary of State,

McCarthy is in need of briefing. His next question referred to "the Soviet embassy in Moscow." "If you were to learn," McCarthy asked General Partridge, "that the book quotes from Mr. Simmons [Prof. Ernest J. Simmons of Columbia], without showing what part is from the work of Mr. Simmons; that Mr. Simmons wrote work under direct instructions of the Soviet Embassy in Moscow, would you still say it is an honest attempt to give an accurate picture of life in Communist Russia?"

General Partridge insisted stubbornly, "It would all depend on what was said."

The General tried to explain that the main source of the information used in the pamphlet "were returned Japanese POW's." McCarthy didn't give him a chance. He wanted to know again, "Do you think books with authors such as Simmons, identified as a Communist taking orders from the Moscow Embassy when he wrote this, carrying articles by Corliss Lamont, Harriet Moore, Frederick Schuman, do you think that type of book should be used to indoctrinate our military?"

General Partridge insisted that this was not an indoctrination pamphlet, and that McCarthy was talking about the books listed in the bibliography. McCarthy brushed the explanations aside. He wanted to know whether "a book like that should be withdrawn or used to indoctrinate our military." The General was trapped into heresy.

GENERAL PARTRIDGE. I'd want to read the book first.

THE CHAIRMAN [McCarthy]. Even though you know it is put out by Communist authors?

GENERAL PARTRIDGE. It would all depend on what they say.

THE CHAIRMAN. You don't object to Communist authors unless you first see what they say, although he is writing books under the instructions of the Moscow Embassy. Is that correct?

The General was an intrepid fellow, and had led with his chin. McCarthy later in the hearing again brought up the same business about quoting Stalin verbatim, and wanted to know whether the writer of the pamphlet in quoting Stalin "was trying to give a correct picture."

"Whether he did," General Partridge replied incautiously, "would depend on what he quoted. I don't think everything Stalin says is a lie. He is bound to say something true once in a while. I don't know what he quoted from Stalin."

A phone call to the Pentagon last week elicited the information that General Partridge was transferred out of G-2 shortly after the hearing and assigned in January to command the 43rd Infantry Division in Europe. The Siberian pamphlet was "declassified." But copies are not longer available. "It was sent back," the officer on press duty said obscurely. "Sent back where?" he was asked. "I have no idea," was the answer.

FEBRUARY 15, 1954

THE J. EDGAR HOOVER-McCARTHY AXIS

McCarthy is America's most controversial figure. J. Edgar Hoover is its most feared. When Hoover praises McCarthy, that would seem to be page one news. Remarkably little attention was paid by the press last week to the interview the chief of the G-men gave the *San Diego Evening Tribune* of August 22. The *New York Times* buried the story in a three-paragraph "shirttail" to another McCarthy controversy on page eleven of its August 24 issue. For some reason the story did not appear in the *Washington Post* and the *Washington Times-Herald* until two days later on August 26. The *Times-Herald*, ultra rightist and virtually a house organ for both Hoover and McCarthy, buried the story inside, perhaps because someone felt the G-man had been indiscreet.

One aspect of the indiscretion was touched on by an intrepid reporter at Attorney General Herbert Brownell's press conference here three days later. The Department of Justice is supposed to be— and Brownell insisted that it still is—investigating that Senate report of last January on McCarthy's financial manipulations. The investigating of the Department of Justice is done through—the Federal Bureau of Investigation. The head of the FBI in the San Diego interview called McCarthy "earnest and honest." A reporter asked the Attorney General whether he thought it appropriate "for a member of the Justice Department to make a statement evaluating the character of a person whose affairs are under study in the Department."

The Attorney General declined to comment. He said he had not yet seen the full text of Hoover's statement. "I have full confidence and admiration for Mr. Hoover," Brownell added. "I like to stress that whenever possible." Hoover seems to have a similar confidence and admiration for the Senator he is presumably investigating. Both Hoover and McCarthy were registered at the same seaside hotel in La Jolla—by coincidence the G-man said—when Hoover was interviewed. It will take a very brave FBI man to turn in anything unfavorable on McCarthy after the Hoover statement.

"McCarthy is a former Marine," Hoover said. "He was an amateur boxer. He's Irish. Combine those, and you're going to have a vigorous individual, who is not going to be pushed around.

"I am not passing," Hoover continued more cautiously after this bit of positive hero worship, "on the technique of McCarthy's committee, or other Senate committees. That's the Senator's responsibility. But the investigating committees do a valuable job. They have subpoena rights without which some vital investigations could not be accomplished.

"I never knew Senator McCarthy," Hoover went on, "until he came to the Senate. I've come to know him well, officially and personally. I view him as a friend and believe he so views me.

"Certainly, he is a controversial man. He is earnest and he is honest. He has enemies. Whenever you attack subversives of any kind, Communists, Fascists, even the Ku Klux Klan, you are going to be the victim of the most extremely vicious criticism that can be made.

"I know," Hoover said. "But sometimes a knock is a boost. When certain elements cease their attacks on me, I know I'm slipping."

This admission of close relations and declaration of friendship may give McCarthy an advantage Hitler lacked—the advantage of close liaison and support from the secret police of the government he wants to take over.

Hoover's closet is well stocked with skeletons. Many in the capital fear the stray bones he may rattle. Few who criticize McCarthy dare criticize Hoover. Some who criticize McCarthy will go easy if they know he has the G-man's backing. The silence of the nation's editorial writers on this San Diego interview is more eloquent than any comment they could make. There was similar silence in July when at McCarthy's worst moment (he was forced to fire J. B. Matthews) he held a conference with Hoover and hired the head of the New York FBI office, Frank P. Carr, to replace Matthews as McCarthy's staff director. The Hoover conference and the Carr appointment helped to bolster McCarthy at a bad time.

A Hoover-McCarthy axis must also spike the feeble popguns of those faint-hearted liberals whose anti-McCarthy line has been, "Let the FBI do it." This *is* how the FBI does it. The same mishmash of tenuous guilt-by-association, anonymous gossip and slander on which the congressional investigators feed so lushly is exactly the same mishmash the Coplon case turned up in the FBI files.

SEPTEMBER 5, 1953

THE F.B.I. AND THE WITCH HUNT

Certainly the most tantalizing untold story of this whole period is the part played by the FBI in the witch hunt. Senator Fulbright, the only Senator to vote against the McCarthy appropriation, is also the only Senator with nerve enough to talk publicly about it. The Senator told an Associated Press reporter last week that he was no longer giving information to the FBI because he was convinced that the McCarthy committee had access to its files.

In whatever time McCarthy's sudden access of out-of-town speaking engagements leaves for investigation, this is one question the McCarthy committee will not explore. Yet there is evidence which suggests that the FBI has had close, if carefully hidden, links with congressional witch hunt committees ever since the United States Chamber of Commerce in 1946 launched its drive to purge the government, the movies, the air waves, the lecture platform and the arts, sciences and professions generally of "reds" and "pinks."

There are indications that the FBI and the congressional witch hunt committees were synchronized in the thought control drive, that FBI men moved in to staff the committees, and that the FBI's informers and undercover operatives were released to the committees as witnesses when their usefulness as agents had been ended by exposure, failure to obtain indictments, or their appearance in court.

Robert K. Carr ventures some "general observations" on this in his authoritative work *The House Committee on Un-American Activities, 1945-50.* He writes that "a surprisingly large number" of the hearings in the latter part of this period "made public information already well known to the FBI." He notes, "Often the leading witness in such committee hearings was an undercover FBI agent who had infiltrated the Communist movement." Professor Carr concludes, "It is quite apparent that these hearings were designed to serve the purpose of publicizing information in FBI files."

At another point, Professor Carr observes, "The investigative arm of the committee's staff has always regarded itself as a 'little FBI.' Ex-FBI men have provided part of its personnel, and its methods and interests have been comparable to those of the FBI."

When Elizabeth Bentley was first heard by the House committee, in July, 1948, there was an interesting remark made by its chairman, J. Parnell Thomas. "The closest relationship," Thomas said, "exists between this committee and the FBI. . . . I think there is a very good understanding between us. It is something, however, that we cannot talk too much about."

In this same realm of "something . . . we cannot talk too much about" may lie hidden the story of how the committee first managed to obtain Miss Bentley and Whitaker Chambers as witnesses, how it gathered the atomic spy scare information it used in the 1948 campaign after this information had failed to stand up as evidence in legal proceedings, and how it learned of the J. Edgar Hoover letter to Secretary of Commerce W. Averill Harriman smearing Edward U. Condon, then director of the National Bureau of Standards. This, too, played its part in the attempt to defeat the Democrats in 1948.

The head of the FBI "stayed out of politics"—at least publicly—during the Roosevelt and Truman Administrations because such intrusion might have cost him his job; his own antiliberal preconceptions were notorious within the two Administrations. But material from his files, and witnesses from the FBI's private stables, began to help the Republicans smear the Democrats after the war.

The career of Robert E. Lee, our newest Federal Communications Commissioner, may throw some light on this relationship. Lee had risen within the FBI to be administrative assistant to J. Edgar Hoover in 1941. In 1946 Lee was "loaned" (the word is his) by Hoover to the House Appropriations Committee. In 1947 Lee went into the State Department files for the Appropriations Committee and compiled that list of 108 "subversives" which later supplied the material for McCarthy's sensational rehash in 1950.

Those who think there is any difference between FBI and congressional witch hunt standards should study this compilation, including the suspect in whose raincoat pocket were found Russian lessons, the official of whom it was "revealed that . . . he held an office in the American Newspaper Guild," the man who was "a member of the American Civil Liberties Union," the subvert who "apparently belonged to questionable groups in college. His parents are both Russian-born," and the man who signed a petition "requesting right of asylum for John Strachey, well-known British radical"!

Lee's material was culled from the State Department's own files, and not directly from the FBI. It may be doubted whether Hoover or his assistants have been rash enough to allow a congressional committee direct access to FBI files. But when so many of the committee personnel are former FBI men, especially FBI men "on loan," they have contacts through which they can get and check information. They also bring with them a good deal of knowledge. There are many discreet ways a committee can be "tipped off" by the FBI without making any move which would provide an embarrassing record.

This seems to be particularly true in the case of the McCarthy committee. McCarthy seems to have closer liaison with Hoover than any of McCarthy's predecessors in witch hunting. It would appear that just as Hoover's ties were with the Republicans in their fight against the Democrats, so his sympathies today are with the McCarthyite against the Eisenhower wing of the Republican party. If a fresh staff is needed impartially to investigate the Army charges against McCarthy, Cohn and Carr, some other agency should be available to investigate should the possibility of perjury or some other crime arise from the coming inquiry.

A genuine and comprehensive investigation would look into whether the FBI has used the congressional committees as a means of smearing rival intelligence agencies, especially the CIA and those of the armed services. Much of McCarthy's work, in the case of the Army's Siberian pamphlet and in the Fort Monmouth inquiry, seems to have derived from undercover sniping and jealousy. There is also indication that the FBI has used the committees to revenge itself when the loyalty boards of federal agencies or grand juries have failed to take its informants seriously.

How thin and spurious these charges may be was demonstrated by the case of Mrs. Annie Lee Moss. This elderly colored woman was named as a Communist by an FBI undercover agent, Mrs. Mary S. Markward, who claims to have wormed her way into a leading position in the Communist party in the District of Columbia while working for the FBI from 1943 to 1951. What the press generally has overlooked, however, is the light this case sheds on how vindictive the FBI can be and on how sloppily it can collect its allegations.

The charges against Mrs. Moss made by Mrs. Markward were examined on three occasions by loyalty agencies without the latter's presence as a witness and dismissed on each occasion, the last being in 1951 by the Army's loyalty review board. This seems to have rankled with the FBI. The McCarthy hearings brought out that in the fall of 1951 after Mrs. Markward had been produced as a witness in New York's "second echelon" Smith Act prosecution, Hoover wrote the Army, offering to produce Mrs. Markward as a witness against Mrs. Moss. The Army, however, did not reopen the case, but recently the House Un-American Activities Committee (under the ex-FBI man Velde) held executive hearings from which the McCarthy committee snatched it.

It is clear now that had the Army reopened the case to hear Mrs. Markward in person, the results would not have warranted a verdict against Mrs. Moss. A Republican member of the House committee told the press after hearing her and other witnesses in executive session that he did not feel the evidence was strong enough to warrant public sessions. When the McCarthy committee held a public session, the case fell apart under questioning by the Democratic members, McClellan, Symington, and Jackson. Mrs. Markward was positive in naming Mrs. Moss as a Communist until McClellan asked her whether she could identify Mrs. Moss. This was the answer elicited: "I don't specifically recall that I do know her as a person," Mrs. Markward admitted. "I don't recall that I don't know her as a person, either. I just have no specific recollection on that point."

A typical piece of dirty McCarthy business at the public hearing came when he said that while Mrs. Moss would deny membership, five other members of her alleged cell would be called to testify. McCarthy said he assumed they would plead the Fifth Amendment when asked about Mrs. Moss. The implication was damning. Senator Jackson interjected, "As you recall, they did not take the Fifth Amendment in the committee as to knowing her." At this McCarthy said indignantly, "Let us keep the record straight. If we are going to discuss the executive testimony, I would prefer not to."

Cohn thereupon claimed that there were other informants, still in "confidential" status and gave the impression that he had the run of the FBI files.

SENATOR JACKSON. I take it that information is in her FBI file?

MR. COHN. Yes, sir, it is.

SENATOR JACKSON. The Annie Lee Moss FBI file?

MR. COHN. That is correct. There is only one Annie Lee Moss FBI file. We have ascertained that and have been told that the Annie Lee Moss Mrs. Markward is talking about is the Annie Lee Moss that the file deals with, and there is no other.

But when Mrs. Moss appeared before the committee last week in an unforgettable session, she said there were three Annie Lee Mosses in the Washington directory. First Senator McClellan and then Senator Symington went out of their way by sharp questioning to demonstrate their indignation and sympathy and to protest Cohn's putting into the record what some unnamed witness was supposed to have said. McCarthy left early, knowing (after an executive session) what was coming and the acting chairman, Mundt, made no effort to stop the applause that interrupted McClellan and Symington on four occasions when they made points in Mrs. Moss's favor.

The most striking collapse of evidence, and the strongest testimony to sloppy FBI investigating methods, concerned Mrs. Moss's alleged close relations with Robert Hall, formerly Washington correspondent of the *Daily Worker*. It turned out, however, that this connection was limited to one occasion in 1943 when Hall is supposed to have sold a Sunday *Worker* to Mrs. Moss's family. Mrs. Moss did admit knowing a Robert Hall, but insisted that he was a Negro. Hall is a white man and Cohn by his evasiveness indicated an awareness of this when Robert Kennedy, the minority counsel, asked him about it. Kennedy asked Cohn whether Hall was a Negro or a white man.

MR. COHN. I never inquired into his race. I am not sure. We can check that, though.

MR. KENNEDY (with some surprise). I thought I just spoke to you about it.

MR. COHN. My assumption has been that he is a white man, but we can check that.

Hall, when reached by telephone in New York at the *Worker* office after the hearing, said he did not get to Washington until 1946 and was not in the capital during the war. So (1) he was not here at the time, (2) he is a white man and (3) as a one-man bureau for the *Daily Worker* he would hardly have had time to go around selling the *Worker* personally. None of these facts are hard to establish. In all these years and after three loyalty hearings based on FBI information, the FBI either had not learned them or had suppressed them to strengthen the case against Mrs. Moss. No one who heard

her could doubt her honesty. This poor, utterly non-political woman
("Wazzat?" she cried when Symington asked her if she had ever read
Karl Marx) has been cruelly persecuted and ruined by the FBI and
the McCarthy committee in their feud with the Army.

The truth is catching up with McCarthy. Cohn will not survive
the Army's damning memorandum on his interventions on behalf
of Schine. But McCarthy and the FBI man, Carr, will probably out-
last this inning. And in the uproar, all too few will notice the key role
the FBI has been playing in the witch hunt from J. Parnell Thomas
to Joe McCarthy, and will continue to play behind the scenes as one
adventurer succeeds another in the center of the stage.

MARCH 22, 1954

4: *A Few Who Fought Back*

BLEAK LANDSCAPE OF THE RESISTANCE

Chicago

Walsh's Hall at 1014 Noble Street might have been the scene of
the Hunky wedding in Upton Sinclair's *Jungle*. The hall lies in a
Polish area, one of those incomparably dreary Chicago working-
class districts which sprawl out across the bare plain, miles away
from the opulence of Lakefront and Loop. The building is a three-
story walk-up, on the top floor of which is the "hall," a barn of a
place, with a stage at one end and a small, faintly and grotesquely
Moorish balcony at the other. High columns intended to be orna-
mental line the wall on either side; they appear to be ordinary cast-
iron waterpipe stood on end by some plumber aspiring in his spare
time to architecture. The windows are long and narrow. Through
them, even under a cloudless sunny sky, the wintry Chicago landscape managed to look gray and bleak—row on row of ill-matched
dirty brick and unpainted façades with gaps of dismal backyard in
which stood a few forlorn trees.

The hall was freshly hung with blue and white banners—"The
Bill of Rights Belongs to All," "Stop Police State Terror Against
Foreign Born Americans," "Public Hearings on the Lehman-Celler
Bill." On the stage, against the faded green trees of what appeared

to be a set left over from some forgotten performance of *As You Like It,* a big benevolent Brünnhilde of a woman, six feet tall with gray hair, grandmotherly expression, and one of those round unmistakable Russian Jewish faces, was reading aloud Eisenhower's campaign pledge to revise the McCarran-Walter Act. The woman was Pearl Hart, a Chicago lawyer famous through the Midwest for a lifetime of devotion to the least lucrative and most oppressed kind of clients.

This was the opening session of a National Conference to Repeal the Walter-McCarran Law and Defend Its Victims, sponsored by the American Committee for the Protection of the Foreign Born, one of the last functioning Popular Front organizations.

At that early morning hour the seats beside the long wooden tables set up in the hall were but half filled. That such a meeting should be held at all was something of a miracle. The American Committee for the Protection of the Foreign Born is on the Attorney General's list. It is now involved in proceedings before the Subversive Activities Control Board to compel the Committee's registration under the McCarran Act as a Communist-front organization. Its devoted executive secretary, Abner Green, a tall, lean man with the kind of long cavernous face El Greco painted, served six months in jail after refusing to hand over the organization's records to a federal grand jury in July, 1951. The Secretary of the local Los Angeles committee, Rose Chernin, was unable to attend because she is under bond in denaturalization proceedings. The secretary of the Michigan committee, Saul Grossman, who was present in Chicago, goes on trial in Washington this week for contempt of Congress in refusing to hand his records over to the House Un-American Activities Committee.

Despite this, about three hundred delegates from sixteen states had arrived, some from as far as Seattle and Los Angeles, and one hundred fifty more were to follow. They seemed, considering the circumstances, an extraordinarily cheerful lot. But looking at them during the day one was fascinated by several observations. The first was that the audience was a forest of gray heads, almost entirely made up of elderly folk—those who appeared young in that gathering were, when one looked at them more closely, seen to be middle-aged. This is unfortunately true of most radical meetings in America nowadays; it is as if those with their lives still ahead of them are too cautious or cowed to appear at such affairs. What struck one next about the gathering was the absence of foreign accents—with few exceptions one heard American speech indistinguishable from that of the native-born. Assimilation has done its work and relatively few new immigrants are coming in. One also began to notice that though the deportation drive hits the labor unions hard, there were no labor union representatives present, other than men from a few so-called "progressive" locals. The left labor leaders were conspicuous by their absence; the Taft-Hartley oath made their appearance at the meeting of a blacklisted organization too hazardous.

Not so many weeks ago the case of an Air Force officer named Radulovich attracted national attention. He was about to be blacklisted as a security risk because his father and sister were supposed to have Communist views or connections. Edward Murrow put the case into a brilliant TV show and the Secretary for Air finally cleared Radulovich. But this comparative handful of elderly folk in Chicago were fighting a last-ditch battle for a thousand and one other Raduloviches arrested—as the elder Radulovich may be—for deportation. This Committee, just twenty-one years old, is the only one of its kind.

On the eve of the conference, the American Committee for the Protection of the Foreign Born was given the treatment. The local Hearst paper published a smear attack and telephoned the Committee's various sponsors and scheduled speakers in an effort to frighten them off. The campaign failed. Among those who spoke at the banquet in that same hall that night were Professor Louise Pettibone Smith, Professor Emeritus of Biblical History at Wellesley; Professor Robert Morss Lovett, and Professor Anton J. Carlson, the University of Chicago's famous physiologist, who had not intended to speak but changed his mind after a call from the Hearst press. The sight of these three aged academic Gibraltars of liberalism was inspiring, but again it was sad to note that the distinguished speakers —like the audience—were elderly.

An amazingly large proportion of the victims, too, are elderly. In his comprehensive report, Abner Green pointed out that of three hundred non-citizens arrested in deportation proceedings, almost one third—ninety-three in all—are over the age of sixty and have lived in this country an average of forty to fifty years. The kind of sick and aged folk being hauled out of retirement for deportation as a political menace to this country would be ludicrous if it did not entail so much tragedy. Two cardiac patients, Refugio Roman

Martínez and Norman Tallentire, died of heart attacks in deportation proceedings. The economist and writer, Lewis Corey, long an anti-Communist, died September 16 at the age of sixty-one in the midst of deportation proceedings begun against him because he was a Communist thirty years ago. In California, a Mrs. Mary Baumert of Elsinore, now seventy-six years old, was arrested last month for deportation although she had lived here fifty-one years. In Los Angeles on November 4, Mr. and Mrs. Lars Berg, sixty-nine and sixty-seven respectively, were locked up on Terminal Island for deportation to their native Sweden; they have been American residents since 1904. One Finn arrested for deportation has lived here since he was three months old!

As in the days of the Inquisition, the Immigration and Naturalization Service and the FBI are engaged in using fear to recruit informers, even informers against their own kin. A striking case was that of Francesco Costa of Rochester, New York, arrested for deportation to Italy at the age of eighty-three because he refused to provide information to the Justice Department that could be used to deport his son, Leonard, to Italy. A triple squeeze play was brought to bear on Clarence Hathaway, once editor of the *Daily Worker*. When he declined to be used as an informer, denaturalization proceedings were brought against his wife, Vera. Her brother, William Sanders, fifty-five, an artist who had never engaged in politics, was himself arrested after he refused to give testimony against his sister. Sophie Gerson, wife of Simon W. Gerson, one of those acquitted in the second Smith Act trial of New York Communist leaders, was arrested for denaturalization to punish her husband.

By a political Freudian slip, no mention was made at the conference of one of the worst cases of this kind. In the fall of 1952, Earl Browder and his wife were indicted for perjury in her original immigration proceedings and in February of this year Mrs. Browder was arrested for deportation. These punitive actions followed a warning from Bella Dodd to Earl Browder that he had better show some sign of "cooperation." Though the ex-Communist leader in lonely poverty has withstood the temptations of the rewards which would be his were he to sell his "memoirs" to the FBI and the magazines, little consideration has been shown him. This reflects the savage unfairness with which the left treats its heretics, however honorably these heretics behave.

The deportations drive cuts across every basic liberty. Fifteen editors associated with the radical and foreign language press have been arrested for deportation or denaturalization, including Cedric Belfrage of the *National Guardian,* Al Richman of the West Coast *People's World,* and John Steuben of *The March of Labor.* The foreign language editors arrested are elderly folk editing papers which are dying out as the process of assimilation steadily cuts into the number of Americans who still read the language of "the old country." Almost one third of those arrested for deportation are trade union members or officials. Ever since the Bridges cases began (the government shamelessly is about to launch a fourth try), the use of deportation as a weapon against labor militants has been overt and obvious. Cases are pending against James Matles and James Lustig of the United Electrical Workers and against the wife of William Senter, of St. Louis, another U.E. official, now up on Smith Act charges.

One of the leading victims of the current drive, Stanley Nowak, was present in Chicago. After ten years as a Democratic member of the Michigan State Legislature, part of this time as floor leader, he is facing denaturalization proceedings. This Polish-born legislator played a role in the organization of the automobile industry and was first elected to the legislature in 1938 from the West Side area of Detroit, a Ford worker constituency. Similar charges ten years ago ("Communist and anarchist sympathies") were dismissed with an apology by then Attorney General Biddle but have been revived under the McCarran-Walter Act.

The most numerous and widespread abuses have occurred in the treatment of Mexican-Americans. Reports to the conference from Los Angeles pictured terror and lawlessness—the use of roadblocks and sudden raids on areas in which persons of Mexican origin live, the invasion of their homes without warrants, the exile to Mexico of native-born Americans of Mexican parentage. The Mexican-American community is kept steadily "churned up" to maintain it as a source of cheap labor in constant flux. Green reported that during the first six months of 1953 more than 483,000 persons were deported to Mexico—while almost half a million others were being brought in for low paid agricultural work.

The government is using "supervisory parole" to harass and intimidate radicals who cannot be deported because no other country will accept them. Three Communist leaders convicted under the Smith Act, Alexander Bittelman, Betty Gannett and Claudia Jones,

out on bail pending appeal, were summoned to Ellis Island recently.
They were told that they were being put under supervisory parole,
must report once a week, submit to physical and psychiatric exami-
nation, abandon all political activity *and give information under oath
as to their associations and activities.* They are challenging the order
in the courts.

Last March 17 Attorney General Brownell made a particularly
vulgar St. Patrick's Day speech to the Friendly Sons of St. Patrick—
their parents once the target of similar anti-alien hysteria. In this he
announced that ten thousand citizens were being investigated for
denaturalization and twelve thousand aliens for deportation as "subversives." Action on this scale would dwarf the notorious deportation raids of the early twenties.

The suffering in terms of broken families and disrupted lives is
beyond the most sympathetic imagination. As serious is the moral
degradation imposed by spreading terror. People are afraid to look
lest they be tempted to help, and bring down suspicion on themselves. This is how good folk in Germany walked hurriedly by and
shut their ears discreetly to telltale screams. The American Committee for the Protection of the Foreign Born is fighting to keep America's conscience alive.

DECEMBER 21, 1953

MAN AGAINST MYTH

In refusing to tell the House Un-American Activities Committee anything more than his name, address and time and place of
birth, Barrows Dunham has given Congressman Velde and his colleagues just about all they have a right to know about any college
professor. Dr. Robert L. Johnson, president of Temple University, in
suspending Dr. Dunham as head of its philosophy department, says
every teacher has a duty to cooperate "with responsible government
authority to preserve the freedom of our society." But the Velde
witch hunt is not responsible authority. The House committee is
demonstrably irresponsible in its actions. It has no authority to inquire into education. Until these latter benighted years no one ever
suggested that the way to "preserve the freedom of our society" was
to harass and intimidate nonconformists.

The distinguished author of *Man Against Myth* has boldly en-
tered the lists against the most dangerous myths of our time in chal-

lenging the right of the House committee to investigate education. His pusillanimous chief retires to become head of the Voice of America. But some day it will be recognized that the real voice of America spoke through the philosopher he has suspended. Dr. Dunham's *Man Against Myth* won the applause of minds as diverse as John Dewey, J. B. S. Haldane and Albert Einstein. His action deserves the support of every teacher and of everyone who believes in free education. The fight to reinstate Dunham will be a fight to reinstate freedom of education in America.

MARCH 7, 1953

THE CASE OF THE COOPERATIVE TEACHER

The Voice of America last year asked Dr. Julius H. Hlavaty to make a broadcast in his native tongue, Slovak. He thought this might endanger relatives in the old country but agreed. He gave his services free. The script was prepared for him. It dealt with the Bronx High School of Science were Dr. Hlavaty is head of the mathematics department.

Someone in the Czechoslovak colony in New York disliked the idea of a broadcast by Dr. Hlavaty. A letter was sent Senator McCarthy. Last week Dr. Hlavaty came home one evening to hear that Roy M. Cohn, counsel to the McCarthy committee, had just phoned. Dr. Hlavaty was ordered to appear next morning at a hearing in Washington.

Now Dr. Hlavaty, gray-haired, thin-faced, distinguished-looking, was before the committee. The exposure of New York City schoolteachers is no longer a sensation, and there were only a few spectators in the big Senate caucus room. Though the turnout was poor, the senators did their best, like good troupers, to put on a performance. Dirksen, who relishes himself as a golden-voiced orator, was as deceptively dulcet as an inquisitor about to consign a suspected heretic to the secular arm for slow broiling. McCarthy, in that cavernous marble-walled room, seemed to enjoy sounding like the Voice of Doom in a soap opera.

McCarthy wanted to know whether Dr. Hlavaty was "aware" that the Liberal party in New York had broken away from the American Labor party. Dr. Hlavaty was aware of it. McCarthy wanted to know whether he was aware that the ALP had been cited as subversive. Dr. Hlavaty was not aware of it. The ALP is not on the Attorney General's list. It soon appeared that McCarthy was referring to an obscure "citation" by the Tenney committee in California. Was Dr. Hlavaty aware that the ALP was Communist-dominated? Dr. Hlavaty seemed to assent. Triumphantly McCarthy asked him to identify two documents. These showed that Dr. Hlavaty and his wife had registered ALP in last year's election.

As an exploit in entrapment, this was good senatorial sport. It was not clear just what it had to do with the Voice of America. A senator wanted to know if the example set by Dr. Hlavaty's registration might not subvert his students. Dr. Hlavaty tried to explain that he thought election registrations were a private matter. Perhaps the ALP was lugged in because at the morning session Dr. Hlavaty had denied present or recent membership in the Communist party but pleaded the Fifth Amendment for 1948.

Symington of Missouri seemed to think the committee's jurisdiction extended to theology. "As a good American," he asked Dr. Hlavaty, "do you believe in God?" The mathematics teacher said he did. At one point Dirksen went off on a weird tangent. He wanted to know whether Dr. Hlavaty had been identified on the broadcast. He had been. Then Dirksen wanted to know what if the Voice had broadcast Earl Browder? Would this not encourage Communists abroad? "Were you," Dirksen asked pointedly, "known in Czechoslovakia?" Dr. Hlavaty said if he were known at all it was only as a poor boy who left in 1921 and became head of the mathematics department in a famous American high school. Dr. Hlavaty said he thought this was good propaganda for America. Dirksen desisted.

It was only toward the end of the hearing, on intervention by Senator McClellan, that Dr. Hlavaty was finally allowed to explain just how he came to make the broadcast. But McCarthy would not let him read the transcript into the record. McCarthy said the committee knew there was no Communist propaganda in the broadcast. If so, why had Dr. Hlavaty been called? Cohn jumped in to remedy the effect of McCarthy's admission. He asked Dr. Hlavaty whether there was anything *anti-Communist* in the broadcast. Hlavaty admitted there wasn't.

It was painful to watch. There was no allegation of wrongdoing. A teacher was being ruined because he had done a favor for a government agency. A committee sated with victims took him apart indifferently, like a small boy taking the wings off a beetle. Dr. Hlavaty has been in this country thirty-two years. He has been a teacher for twenty-four. He has a national reputation as a teacher of mathematics. He is one of the best-loved teachers on the faculty of the Bronx High School of Science. His chances to avoid dismissal are slight unless students and parents organize to support him.

MARCH 21, 1953

CHARLIE CHAPLIN'S FAREWELL CUSTARD

There are two voices of America. One is the Voice with a capital *V*, which broadcasts in so many languages so many hours a day what we would like people abroad to think about us. The other, the voice with a small *v*, is the inadvertent message of our own actions. This, the real voice of America, broadcast a strange message last week about Charlie Chaplin.

It told the world that the little funny man on whom we were brought up could no longer bear the spirit of contemporary America and had turned in his re-entry permit. It said there must be something seriously wrong with our America if Chaplin could no longer live in it.

The "voluntary" exile of Chaplin is a measure of how America has changed since we were children. He never became an American citizen but Charlie Chaplin was and will remain more truly American than the blackguards and fanatics who hounded him, the cheap politicians who warned him not to come back.

We do not blame Charlie Chaplin for leaving us. Who could blame a comic genius—one of the greatest of all time—for being unwilling to live in a country which seems to have lost its sense of humor? But we ask him not to desert us altogether.

The man who made *The Great Dictator* owes it to us and himself to put into a new film the tragicomedy overtaking America where greasy informers are public heroes, protectors of gambling dens set themselves up as guardians of public morality, and a Senator who is afraid to answer questions about his own financial accounts becomes the great investigator of others. Come to think of it, *The Great Investigator* would be a worthy successor to *The Great Dictator*.

Turn the laugh on them, Charlie, for our country's sake. This capital needs nothing so badly as one final well-flung custard pie.

APRIL 25, 1953

EINSTEIN, OXNAM, AND THE INQUISITION

The background against which Einstein has issued his call for civil disobedience of the witch hunters is encouraging. There are signs of a growing revulsion against congressional inquisition. McCarthy has had the guidance of Father Edmund A. Walsh at Washington's ancient Jesuit university, Georgetown. But at its sister institution in the capital, Catholic University, the principal address at the commencement exercises last week was devoted to warning the graduates against the hysteria fomented by congressional investigating committees. The Archbishop of Washington, the Most Reverend Patrick A. O'Boyle, presided and "some politicians" were criticized for their readiness to "seize upon any issue, real or spurious, to boost their fame and publicity."

There were similar warnings from as unexpected a source at Radcliffe. There the commencement speaker was Senator Stuart Symington, a businessman and a right-wing Democrat from Missouri, himself a member of the Senate Government Operations Committee over which McCarthy presides. Symington has distinguished himself on the committee in the past by asking witnesses some remarkably inane questions about whether they believe in God. Just what their private theological opinions had to do with government operations, the committee's field of authority, has never been explained. But at Radcliffe, Symington executed a quick metamorphosis and turned up as a liberal to warn that the recklessness of the Red hunters could easily turn into "a new reign of terror." Symington's sudden conversion on the road to Cambridge, Massachusetts, was gratifying, though important chiefly as a weather indicator. Symington wants to be President, and is prepared to move left or right with the prevailing winds. Eisenhower's own gratifying remarks at Dartmouth will help turn those winds against the witch hunt.

In this ripening situation, with public opinion slowly being aroused, Einstein's proposal for civil disobedience of the congressional inquisitors has the merit of getting down to rock-bottom. What McCarthy, Jenner and Velde are doing is wrong. It is therefore wrong to submit to them. They are poisoning the air of America and making people in all walks of life fearful of expressing opinions which may be a little "controversial." It is in this way that they are beginning to impose thought control.

The First Amendment says Congress "shall make no law respecting an establishment of religion." This means that it can establish no standard of orthodoxy. Can it inquire into beliefs it may not regulate? There are many Catholics and not a few Protestants who believe that heterodox opinions on certain fundamental religious dogmas create a political danger for the state by leading directly to "subversive" political views. But this connection of political danger with theological error is hardly new. The Pilgrim Fathers fled from just such inquisition in the England of their time and the provision against an Established Church was intended to prevent the development of similar practices here.

A characteristic of the American system is the denial of absolute powers to the government or any of its coordinate branches. No one would argue that Congress may pass a law taking a man's property without compensation or his life without trial. But the notion has grown up that the congressional power of investigation, unlike all other governmental powers, is virtually unlimited. The recent Rumely decision was only the latest in a series of Supreme Court opinions which have held to the contrary, though the court has yet to apply the same protection to the privacy of men's minds that it has in the past to the privacy of their moneyed accounts.

The witch hunt abuses of our time find their support in two fallacies which have nothing to do with the legitimate exercise of the congressional power of investigation. One is that while Congress has no power to regulate opinion it has a right to expose, disgrace and pillory holders of opinions it regards as dangerous, subversive, heretical or un-American. The other is that which permits a committee of Congress to act as a roving grand jury for the discovery and punishment of individual crimes.

A section of the Fifth Amendment to which amazingly little attention has been paid in the current controversy over congressional investigation says, "No person shall be held to answer for a capital or otherwise infamous crime, unless on a presentment or indictment of a grand jury." The purpose was to protect accused persons from having to stand the shame of public accusation and the expense of trial until a grand jury in secret session had determined that there was enough substance in any charge to warrant publicity and trial.

Ever since Martin Dies and John Rankin these congressional committees have announced their determination to act as a peculiar new type of "grand jury," operating in public and more than content to leave the stigma of serious crime by hit-or-miss questioning of the sort that has been well termed a "fishing expedition." Congressman Keating referred to this type of abuse in a thoughtful speech last month to the San Francisco Bar Association. Keating said that an area which "should be scrupulously avoided" by congressional committees "is the domain of law enforcement officers and the criminal courts." Keating pointed out that "Only in the case of impeachment does Congress have the right to determine whether a particular individual has committed a specific crime against society." None of the procedural reform proposals now in Congress would prevent investigating committees from acting as quasi grand juries or as pillories for holders of unpopular opinions.

The *New York Times,* objecting to civil disobedience of the witch hunters, says, "Two wrongs never did add up to one right." The old chestnut, in this sense, is quite untrue. Gandhi made two "wrongs" add up to one right by refusing to pay the British salt tax. Long before Gandhi, an earlier generation of Americans made two wrongs add up to one right by dumping that tea in Boston harbor rather than pay the British tax upon it. The white folk of the North who refused to obey the Fugitive Slave Law were adding the "wrong" of civil disobedience to the wrong of slavery, and these ultimately added up to the right of emancipation. Even more in point is the fact that our privilege against self-incrimination derives in large part from the civil disobedience of John Lilburne, who refused to testify before Star Chamber in 1637 when accused of importing heretical works from Holland and asked to identify his collaborators. The evil of compulsory testimony from which the Pilgrims fled to this country was eradicated by his bravery in refusing to testify at the expense of going to jail for contempt.

The need for such fundamental defiance is illustrated by the objections advanced against it. "One cannot start," the *New York Times* said, "from the premise that congressional committees have no right to question teachers and scientists or to seek out subversives wherever they can find them; what is profoundly wrong is the way some of them have been exercising it." The fact is that one cannot start from any *other* premise without making defeat inevitable. To accept ideological interrogation is to make nonconformist views of any kind hazardous. To permit Congress to seek out something as vague, undefined and undefinable as "subversion" or "un-Americanism" is to acquiesce in a heresy hunt that must inhibit free discussion in America. One man's "subversion" is another man's progress; all change subverts the old in preparing the way for the new. "Un-American" is an epithet, not a legal standard.

The *New York Times* says "it is one thing to fight the investigations because of the manner of their procedure and another to oppose the right of investigation, which has always been one of the fundamentals of our governmental system." Investigations have been fundamental but the kind of investigations utilized in this witch hunt are something new in American life. The first congressional committee of this kind was the Hamilton Fish investigation in 1930, the Red-hunt precursor of the un-American Activities Committee. The idea that a committee of Congress could interrogate Americans on their political beliefs is a revolutionary excrescence not a fundamental of American government in the past.

One need only compare Einstein's approach with Bishop Oxnam's to see how right the great physicist is. One cannot at one and the same time object to investigation of the churches by the House Un-American Activities Committee and the Senate Internal Security Subcommittee and at the same time insist on a hearing before them as the good Bishop has done. To ask for a hearing is to acquiesce in the committee's power, to establish a precedent by which other clergymen may be hauled into the pillory. To defend oneself, as the Bishop did in that famous point-by-point rejoinder the *Washington Post* published last April 5, is to cut the ground out from under any principled objection to the inquisition. To plead that one is not "subversive" by the standards of the committee or of that *ex parte* blacklist drawn up by the Attorney General is to accept their right to establish a standard of orthodoxy and heresy in American political and religious thinking.

No one can "clear" himself or defend himself fairly before one of these committees. James Wechsler's experience before McCarthy should be demonstration enough of that. We are not dealing with men anxious to learn the truth or prepared to act honorably. We are dealing with unscrupulous political adventurers using the Red menace as their leverage to power. To try and explain to them that one is not a Communist is as humiliating as it is useless, unless one is prepared to go over completely to their service.

At the same time these committees regard the invocation of the Fifth Amendment with equanimity. To invoke the Fifth is to brand oneself in the eyes of the public as guilty of any offense implied by the dirty questions these committees put. Those who plead the Fifth in most cases lose their jobs and reputations. This satisfies the committees, for their purpose is nothing less than an ideological purge of radicals and liberals from all positions of influence in American life and the demonstration to others that nonconformity is dangerous.

Great faiths can only be preserved by men willing to live by them. Faith in free society requires similar testament if it is to survive. Einstein knows fascism at first hand. History confirms his statement that "if enough people are ready to take this grave step" of defiance "they will be successful" but that if not, "the intellectuals of this country deserve nothing better than the slavery which is intended for them."

The path pointed out by Einstein is that taken by the Hollywood Ten and the directors of the Joint Anti-Fascist Refugee Committee, all of whom went to jail for contempt. But tactics that did not succeed at a time when the cold war was begun may fare differently now when it is ebbing away. The Supreme Court did not hear those earlier cases and there has never been final adjudication on two major points of attack against the committees. One is whether they violate the First Amendment by inquiring into beliefs and the other whether they violate the Fifth Amendment by arrogating to themselves the functions of a grand jury. Neither point can be tested until someone dares invite prosecution for contempt.

This is the moment to try. Einstein has lent the world prestige of his name to such an effort. I propose an association of American intellectuals to take the "Einstein pledge" and throw down a fundamental challenge to the establishment of an inquisition in America.

JUNE 20, 1953

McCARTHY'S BLUFF, AND TWO WHO CALLED IT

McCarthy has been engaged in a bluff. Last week two witnesses —Harvey O'Connor and Leo Huberman—called him on it. The bluff is this: congressional investigating committees are not the possessors of a universal writ. They may not inquire into any- and everything. The subjects into which they may inquire are limited to those specified in the rule or resolution establishing the committee.

What is McCarthy authorized to investigate? He is chairman of the Senate Committee on Government Operations, known until last year as the Committee on Expenditures in the Executive Department.

The old name indicates the true purpose and authority of this committee. It is a kind of super auditing body. Its name was changed last year but not its authority. It still operates under subsection (g) of Rule XXV of the Senate. This rule gives McCarthy no authority to inquire into the political beliefs and associations even of persons employed by the government, much less of editors and writers not on the public payroll.

McCarthy's two competitors in the witch hunt may lay claim rightly or wrongly to broad powers of inquisition. Velde is chairman of the House Committee on "Un-American Activities," a term vague enough to cover any person or idea the committee may consider objectionable. Jenner's subcommittee of the Senate Judiciary Committee operates under as loose and sweeping a standard—its concern is with "internal security." But McCarthy's lawful province is with "budget and accounting measures" and with the effect of executive reorganizations. His broadest grant of investigating power is to study "the operation of government activities at all levels with a view to determining its economy and efficiency."

This can be stretched to cover the purchase of books for overseas libraries—to ask who bought them and why, even to inquire into their contents. But it gives him no authority to subpoena writers and editors and question them about their political beliefs and affiliations. James Wechsler of the *New York Post* submitted to a nonexistent authority when he allowed himself to be interrogated by McCarthy and gave McCarthy a list of persons Wechsler had known as Communists. Cedric Belfrage and James Aronson of the *National Guardian* let themselves in for the usual smear-by-implication when they pleaded their privilege before McCarthy instead of challenging his authority.

Last week two well-known writers, O'Connor and Huberman, taking their cue from Einstein, declined to plead self-incrimination and thereby challenged McCarthy to cite them for contempt. This was the first time since the case of the Hollywood Ten that writers have challenged the authority of a congressional committee to inquire into political beliefs. Like the Hollywood Ten, O'Connor and Huberman pleaded the First Amendment in their refusals to answer. But the Hollywood Ten were before the House Un-American Activities Committee. These new challenges were to the more limited authority of the McCarthy committee. The two writers refused to answer questions not only on constitutional grounds—the fact that the First

Amendment protects freedom of expression from restriction by Congress—but also on the ground that the questions were beyond the scope of the authority conferred by the Senate on McCarthy's committee.

O'Connor declined to answer any questions as to political beliefs and associations. His testimony has value as news, inspiration and example. The celerity with which McCarthy got the author of *Mellon's Millions* off the witness stand was eloquent.

Huberman in a prepared statement said he had never been a Communist but was a Marxist and Socialist who believed "in working together with others, including Communists, to the extent that their aims and methods are consistent with mine." Huberman said he was stating that much under oath "not because I concede the right of this committee to ask for such information, but because I want to make it crystal clear that communism is not an issue in this case and to focus attention on what *is* the issue—my right as an author and editor to pursue my occupation without interference from Congress or any of its committees."

Huberman was asked over and over again by Mundt and McCarthy to explain how his views "deviated" from those of communism. Huberman declined to answer and declined to invoke the Fifth, declaring himself ready for a judicial test of his right to resist inquisition into his political views. At the end Mundt covered the committee's retreat with a lengthy statement, suggesting that Huberman not be cited for contempt since he had (1) admitted authorship of his books and (2) said that he was not a Communist. This suggests that the committee is unwilling to venture a contempt proceeding against a writer who says he is not a Communist but refuses to answer other questions about his political beliefs or affiliations.

O'Connor's challenge had to be taken up or risk complete collapse of the McCarthy committee's pretensions to indulge in ideological inquisition. The committee has voted to cite him for contempt. A majority vote of the Senate is needed to initiate a prosecution. Should O'Connor be indicted, the stage will be set for a fundamental battle against McCarthy and McCarthyism, in which every American who cares for freedom must support Harvey O'Connor.

JULY 25, 1953

5: *An Attempt to Compel Informing*

WHY THE PILGRIM FATHERS LEFT

Late Thursday, July 9, at the tail end of a weary night session, the United States Senate passed a new McCarran bill. This one might be termed a bill to repeal the Fifth Amendment. It would give congressional investigating committees a means of destroying the last constitutional refuge of "uncooperative" witnesses—that provision of the Fifth Amendment which says no man shall be compelled "to be a witness against himself," the so-called privilege against self-incrimination.

This bill may prove fateful for liberty in America. If passed, it would create an unwilling army of informers. Anyone who has ever had left-wing associations of any kind would lose the last remaining means of refusing to answer questions which might bring others into disgrace in the current American heresy hunt. Going to jail for contempt would be the only recourse left for conscientious objectors to congressional inquisition.

Rarely has so fundamental a legal change been proposed with so little public discussion and understanding. The average member of Congress will see it only as a bill "to make Communists talk." Actually the measure would have the force almost of a constitutional amendment, undercutting a fundamental right which has its origin in the same grievances which drove the Pilgrim Fathers to Holland and then America. The Fifth Amendment privilege arose in the early seventeenth-century struggle against compulsory testimony under oath before those inquisitorial courts of Star Chamber and High Commission with which the English Crown sought to root out political and theological dissent as subversive heresy.

This is another in the series of those "McCarran bills" which are creating a new America, remodeled for conformity, unsafe for dissent, a chrome-plated version of George Orwell's *1984*. McCarran continues to be the principal instrument for the achievement of the United States Chamber of Commerce's blueprint for thought control in America. The new "immunity" bill is in the same pattern as the

McCarran bills which established the Subversive Activities Control Board and set up proto-Fascist regulations over immigration, our own little Iron Curtain.

The bill would compel a witness to give up his privilege against self-incrimination by granting him immunity from prosecution on any matter to which he testified. "The most important thing," McCarran told the Senate, "is to expose the conspiracy. Punishment of individual conspirators is a secondary thing. Actually the mode of punishment in the witch hunt is by publicity—to disgrace and deprive of employment anyone who has had left connections in the past. The "immunity" does not protect from a public smearing.

The so-called "conspiracy" is so tenuous that even the top leaders of the Communist party have been prosecuted for nothing more tangible than "conspiracy to advocate." There is still no way to prosecute a man for support of left-wing causes or past membership in the Communist party. McCarran admitted that most of the victims are guilty of no crime for which they could lawfully be prosecuted when he expressed the conviction that "many witnesses who claim their privilege . . . are improperly asserting that privilege." Fear of frame-up, unwillingness to inform on others and opposition in principle to political interrogation have led many to invoke the privilege, as indeed it was invoked three centuries ago under similar circumstances by dissenters.

For gangsters and criminals, the immunity offered by the McCarran bill would be a godsend. For them, the immunity would be real enough. But for today's political dissenters and nonconformists, the "immunity" would be spurious. This is a device for widening the impact of terror-by-inquisition and enlarging the blacklist.

The Senate's one dependable liberal, Lehman, rose to fight the bill in principle. Lehman said the bill struck at the separation of powers and would "encourage persons to seek to avoid the penalties of crimes by accusing others."

John Sherman Cooper—the only Republican senator to oppose the bill—did not think that the power to compel testimony by granting immunity should be exercised at all by congressional committees. "The granting of immunity," he said, "ought to be under definite safeguards" as "in a court of record" where "a judge or presiding officer guards the interests of the witness and of the government."

Senator Cooper went on to a more fundamental objection. He

agreed that "undoubtedly" Communists used the Fifth Amendment and he saw no reason why any "loyal or good American, or innocent American" should be unwilling to answer questions as to Communist party membership. But he said that while he wanted to protect the country from "subversion," he also wanted "to protect the free structure itself." He said the Bill of Rights protects "the individual who may be guilty, as well as the individual who is innocent" but that only so could "the guaranty of individual rights from oppression" be made effective. "When for reasons of expediency or emergency, we weaken these individual rights and give inordinate powers or emergency powers to any branch of our government," Cooper warned the Senate, "it is the record of history that at last that power will be used wrongfully, or will be used unwisely, or against innocent individuals."

It was left to a right-wing Democrat, Hoey of North Carolina, to make the most sweeping attack upon the bill. Senator Hoey expressed his friendship and admiration for McCarran. He said he usually followed McCarran's leadership. But Hoey said, "I am opposed to the entire bill. I believe we are going right in the face of the Constitution. The Constitution of the United States provides that no person shall be required to testify against himself. We are undertaking to say that a committee of Congress can do what a court cannot do."

"I am in hearty accord," Senator Hoey went on, "with all the purposes to go after the Communists, to investigate and prosecute them, and all that, but . . . I do not believe we should forget the fact that the Constitution is for the protection of all the people. There are other persons besides Communists in this country. I do not believe we should confer upon any committee of the Congress the power to take away the rights which the Constitution gives to every individual and to every citizen."

Only ten senators asked that their names be recorded as having voted against the bill. The lone Republican among them was Cooper of Kentucky. Two right-wing Southern Democrats were among the ten—Stennis of Mississippi and McClellan of Arkansas, the latter one of the three Democrats who resigned last week from the McCarthy committee. "I believe the bill is unconstitutional," McClellan said. The other recorded dissenters were Magnuson and Jackson of Washington, Kerr of Oklahoma, Lehman of New York, Hennings of Missouri, Murray of Montana, Hayden of Arizona.

McCarran's bill to circumvent the Fifth Amendment had finally cleared its first hurdle. Whether it passes the House may depend on how much public sentiment may be aroused to force hearings.

JULY 18, 1953

IN THE FOOTSTEPS OF JOHN LILBURNE

The Senate, which likes to call itself the world's greatest deliberative assembly, never acted more ignominiously the rubber stamp than last Wednesday morning. Without debate, without a record vote, with only one objection—and that an extraordinarily weak one—it voted to end a privilege three hundred years old. On motion of McCarran, by voice vote, it approved S 16 as amended by the House, a bill to compel witnesses to testify against themselves on promise of immunity.

Last year when the original McCarran immunity bill passed the Senate, Lehman and nine other senators asked to be recorded against the bill. Last week the other nine sat silent as a fundamental Anglo-American right which goes back to the Cromwellian Revolution went down the drain. Senators, like Flanders, who wax eloquent on the menace of McCarthyism, failed to see why it made the Fifth Amendment privilege all the more important. The independent, Morse, who was so concerned a week before about due process for McCarthy, was less of a legal purist about his victims; last year he facilitated the passage of S 16, this year he voiced no objection to the House substitute.

The House, which is no great deliberative assembly, and often sounds more like the assembly line in a packing plant, shone by comparison. There last week, though the Democratic leadership voted for the immunity bill, fifty-one Democratic rebels, three Republicans and the House's lone Independent voted against it under the leadership of Celler, the chamber's one consistent civil libertarian.

We are slipping back to the days before the privilege was won when those who resisted Elizabeth's High Commission, Britain's own inquisition, had no alternative but jail or flight when put under oath and questioned about the heretical views of themselves and their families. This is where, when and why the Pilgrim Fathers began to leave for Holland and later for America. They did not choose to be informers. The right the Congress has voted to withdraw was the right John Lilburne went to jail to establish. It will have to be re-established in the same manner by the heretics and freedom lovers of this generation.

There was thus an almost symbolic propriety in the fact that the same day, on the unanimous consent calendar, this same Senate without objection passed two McCarthy resolutions of contempt against two Harvard faculty members, Wendell H. Furry and Leon J. Kamin. Both, declining to plead the Fifth before McCarthy, had admitted past Communist membership but declined on moral grounds to name others. Furry himself had been named before the House Un-American Activities Committee by Robert Gorham Davis of Smith College and by Granville Hicks. Unlike them, he did not choose safety for himself at the expense of others. Furry said that if called before a grand jury which was investigating "actual crime, not just political crime or crime of opinion" he would tell everything he knew. "I will not give them," he told McCarthy when asked for names, "when it involves political persecution only." Kamin said, "My conscience won't let me traffic in the names of former political associates whom I have no reason to believe were guilty of criminal activities."

This is Lilburne's challenge repeated three centuries later, and now again the challenge is not to the judges or the law but to the juries and to the political arena. The fight for the privilege not to be a political informer is with this new legislation back on the bedrock of individual conscience. Furry and Kamin deserve emulation and support.

AUGUST 16, 1954

6: *The Death of Stalin*

A CHILL FALLS ON WASHINGTON

Amid the burst of bad manners and foolish speculation, there was remarkably little jubilation. A sudden chill descended on the capital. If Stalin was the aggressive monster painted in official propaganda, his death should have cheered Washington. Actually the unspoken premise of American policy has been that Stalin was so anxious for peace he would do nothing unless Soviet soil itself were violated. With his death, the baiting of the Russian bear—the favor-

ite sport of American politics—suddenly seemed dangerous. Even
Martin Dies rose in the House to say that while Stalin was "utterly
cruel and ruthless, he was more cautious and conservative than the
younger Bolsheviks." Few would have dared a week earlier to dwell
on the conservative and cautious temperament of the Soviet ruler,
much less imply that this was favorable to world stability and peace.
Now this theme leaked from every State Department briefing. There
was apprehension that after Stalin there might come someone worse
and more difficult to deal with.

The cold war claque was critical of Nehru for calling Stalin a
man of peace, but Washington's own instinctive reactions said the
same thing. The stress put by the White House on the fact that its
condolences were merely "official" was small-minded and unworthy
of a great power. After all, it is fortunate for America that when
Stalin's regime met the ultimate test of war, it did not collapse like
the Czar's. The war against the Axis would have lasted a lot longer
and cost a great many more American lives if there had been a
second Tannenberg instead of a Stalingrad. Stalin was one of the
giant figures of our time, and will rank with Ivan, Peter, Catherine
and Lenin among the builders of that huge edifice which is Russia.
Magnanimous salute was called for on such an occasion. Syngman
Rhee, ruler of a satellite state precariously engaged in fighting for its
life against forces supplied by Russia, demonstrated a sense of fitness
in his own condolences which Washington seemed afraid to show.

It is difficult to pursue dignified and rational policy when official
propaganda has built up so distorted a picture of Russia. Many
Americans fed constantly on the notion that the Soviet Union is a
vast slave labor camp must have wondered why the masses did not
rise now that the oppressor had vanished. The Bolshevik Revolution
is still regarded here as a kind of diabolic accident. The necessities
imposed on rulers by the character of the countries they rule is
ignored. To understand it would be to put the problem of peaceful
relations with Russia in quite a different perspective and to dissipate
febrile delusions about "liberation." The wisest of the anti-Communist Russian émigrés of our generation, Berdyaev, in his *The Origins
of Russian Communism* has touched on the way bolshevism succeeded because it was so deeply rooted in Russia's character and
past. Bolshevism "made use," Berdyaev wrote, "of the Russian traditions of government by imposition. . . . It made use of the characteristics of the Russian spirit . . . its search after social justice

and the Kingdom of God upon earth . . . and also of its manifestations of coarseness and cruelty. It made use of Russian messianism.
. . . It fitted in with the absence among the Russian people of the
Roman view of property. . . . It fitted in with Russian collectivism
which had its roots in religion."

Every great leader is the reflection of the people he leads and
Stalin in this sense was Russia. He was also the leader of something
new in world history, a party: a party in a new sense, like nothing
the world has known since the Society of Jesus, a party ruling a one-
party state. It is this difference which makes nonsense of prediction
by analogy based on the principle of legitimacy in monarchy or the
later history of the Roman empire. Struggle among the party leaders
occurred after the death of Lenin and may occur after the death of
Stalin, but the party itself provides a cement strong enough to hold
the state together despite such struggles. To regard this as a group
of conspirators may prove a fatal error. This is a movement, with a
philosophy comparable to the great religions in its capacity to evoke
devotion, and based on certain economic realities which give it a
constructive function. It has proved itself capable of industrializing
Russia and opening new vistas to its masses, and this is its appeal to
similar areas in Asia. This is a challenge which can only be met by
peaceful competition, for only in peace can the West preserve what
it has to offer, and that is the tradition of individual liberty and free
thought.

It is time in the wake of Stalin's death to recognize two basic
facts about the world we live in. One fact is Russia. The other is the
Communist movement. The surest way to wreck what remains of
capitalism and intellectual freedom in the non-Communist world
today is blindly to go on refusing to recognize these facts and refusing
to adjust ourselves to coexistence on the same planet with them.
Eisenhower in leaving the door discreetly ajar to possible negotiations with Stalin's successor was wise, and the lesser powers should
seize on the sobering moment to urge Washington and Moscow to
get together.

MARCH 14, 1953

FROM MOSCOW: A NEW KIND OF CONFESSION

One of Marx's favorite maxims was "Doubt everything." His
Communist followers have too long operated on the opposite theory.

They have been trained to believe everything they are told, so long as it comes from Moscow and party higher-ups. The beginnings of such an attitude must already have been evident in Marx's lifetime, since Marx is reported once to have said with distaste that he was not a Marxist. A few readers who are Marxists in this un-Marxist sense have protested our astringent observations on the subject of the charges against the Moscow doctors. We thought the charges "too hideous to be credible," urged that foreign observers be allowed at the trials and observed, "The Russian rulers have a way of erecting possibilities into actualities and then staging trials to 'prove' what they fear. Their trials are political morality plays which cynically assume an audience too unintelligent to be impressed by anything less than melodrama. It is not enough to prove that a man is mistaken; he must be displayed as a monster."

In this as in so many other matters a new and cleaner wind seems to be blowing through the Russian capital. Of all the confessions which have marked the Soviet regime's long series of "show trials" back to the twenties no confession is more startling, more unexpected and more worthy of belief than the confession by the Ministry of Internal Affairs that the doctors had been arrested on false charges and held up to the world as guilty on the basis of confessions extorted by "impermissible" means. The international implications are striking enough—these doctors were alleged to have poisoned Soviet leaders on orders of American "imperialism" directed through its "bourgeois Jewish nationalist" hirelings in the American Jewish Joint Distribution Committee and the Zionist movement. If the charges were false in the case of the doctors, six of them Jewish, might not similar charges in the Slansky and other trials have been equally false? There were indications of a wider revision in a *Pravda* editorial which said "careful verification" had established that similar means had been used to slander "an honest public leader, the people's artist of the U.S.S.R., Mikhoels. . . ." This was the Yiddish actor, Solomon Mikhoels, of whom nothing had been heard in some time.

Jewish readers in the Soviet Union must see in that a hope that the new government will put a damper on a campaign against "Zionists" which had led to the suppression of many Jewish cultural activities and pandered to anti-Semitic feeling. The general message at home, however, must be far more startling. The admission that the secret police had committed a deliberate wrong, that confessions had been wrung by "impermissible" means from innocent persons, must seem an almost revolutionary development to thoughtful citizens of the Soviet Union and the satellite countries where people are accustomed to regard the secret police as all-powerful. This is a development far outside the orbit of the paranoid speculations of Washington about the new Soviet "peace offensive." This is a domestic matter, which opens a door that can never completely be closed again. If the secret police used "impermissible" means in this case, what of others? Which means are "impermissible"? Just how were the confessions extorted? What steps can be taken to prevent such occurrences in the future? Most explosive of all is a question which must follow: what was wrong with Stalin's regime that such miscarriages of justice could occur under it? And how many unjustly accused or framed political prisoners may there be in the penal labor camps of the U.S.S.R.?

Russian policy has too long operated on the half-truth that the Soviet Union was ringed with enemies. The new regime if it continues on this path will discover that the Soviet Union is also ringed with friends. Even in "reactionary" circles in the West there is evident an almost wistful readiness to believe that perhaps peace may be achieved. There are other circles, friendly to socialism, with a great respect for the Russian people, which have been shamed and antagonized by much that has occurred since the Revolution. Amid the gigantic achievements obscured by the mists of hateful propaganda, there has also been an indifference to mass suffering and individual injustice, a sycophancy and an iron-clad conformity, that has disgraced the socialist ideal. The atmosphere bred at home by unlimited dictatorship has been reflected abroad in an unnecessary rudeness and crudeness in dealing with other nations. Part of the Soviet Union's troubles has been of its own creation, just as part of our difficulties in dealing with the U.S.S.R. has been of our own making. The world for nations as for men is often a mirror that reflects their own image, returning hate for hate, good will for good will.

There are forces in the world which do not want peace. There are forces which fear socialism and wish to destroy it even at the risk of self-destruction. These forces play their part now in every Western capital and seek to prevent peace from breaking out. But the new Soviet regime will also find that there is a large, a much larger, body of opinion in the West, which can be won for peace and coexistence and humane relationships if the effort is made. The signs of a change at home will do much to harness this potential for peace. Were the new Soviet regime to follow up its confession about the doctors with steps to make such frame-ups less likely in the future, it would awe the world. Russia needs habeas corpus, the right to counsel and the doctrine of overt act as the test of guilt if it is to dissipate the murk of conspiracy on which its secret police has grown great. Internal changes of this kind would go far to dissipate those fears on which the warmongers depend.

APRIL 11, 1953

7: *Churchill Abandons the Cold War*

When the chief architect of the cold war begins to dismantle his own handiwork, that is—or should be—news. But most American newspaper readers still do not realize the significance of Sir Winston Churchill's "new Locarno" speech last week. The bombshell that led to the hasty calling of the Bermuda conference was the most momentous—and the most poorly covered—story in many months. The *New York Times* did not give the Churchill speech in full text. Commentators shied away from a declaration which carried so many unpalatable implications for American foreign policy. The man who wanted to strangle bolshevism in its cradle had suddenly announced that he was prepared to live with it in its prime.

Since Roosevelt's death, Churchill has been the Toscanini of Western foreign policy. The United States has footed the bills, but he has set the themes. It was Churchill who launched the Anglo-American alliance at Fulton in 1946, with that deadly phrase about an Iron Curtain rung down on Europe. It was Churchill who later the same year in Zurich proposed a Franco-German entente and a United States of Europe as a counterpoise against the East. It was Churchill who at Llandudno in October, 1948, struck the opening note of the "liberation" chorus. He wanted to push the Russians back to their old borders. He called for a showdown while the United States still had a monopoly of the atom bomb.

Now, five years later, Churchill has changed his tune. He no longer speaks as if the problem were simply one of dealing with a Russian menace. It is worth listening closely. "We all desire," he

peripheral settlements because these would relax tension and slow up the pace of rearmament. Their idea was to build up such overwhelming power as to make possible peace by dictation or swift victory by atomic blitzkrieg. Here again the new Churchill line undercuts American strategy.

Churchill's view of internal developments in Russia since Stalin's death also diverges strikingly from the official American line. The State Department, its eyes shut tightly, insists that nothing has happened. It is essential to cold war policy to allow nothing to disturb the endlessly inculcated view that the Kremlin always has and always will be occupied by monsters until the evil is finally exorcised by nuclear fission and holy water. But here is Churchill saying unexpectedly and exasperatingly that he regards "some of the internal manifestations and the apparent change of mood" since Stalin's death "as far more important than what is happening outside." He is anxious that "the NATO Powers" do nothing which might "supersede or take the emphasis out of what may be a profound movement of Russian feeling." To imply that reform in the direction of a less Draconian Russian regime is possible without crack-up, war or counterrevolution, to speak as Churchill does of a "spontaneous and healthy evolution which may take place in Russia" is his ultimate apostasy.

MAY 30, 1953

8: *The New Chief Justice*

FROM VINSON TO WARREN

The late Chief Justice was a politician with little concern for the doctrine of separation of powers, given to acting as if he were still part of an Administration team and as self-assured as he was narrow in his judgment of men and events. He went on the bench in 1946 at the very beginning of the cold war, and the decisions handed down by the majority of which he was a part dutifully reflected the prejudices of the period.

Vinson and his colleagues of the majority dispensed degenerate doctrine. This was the Court which denied a hearing in the Holly-

wood Ten and Barsky cases, permitting congressional inquisitors to
breach the First Amendment and use the public pillory to terrorize
the nonconformist. This was the Court which allowed the Bailey case
to stand, branding a government employee disloyal on secret evidence never fully disclosed to her *or* her judges; the Court which
upheld the Taft-Hartley oath and the Smith Act cases, where that
monstrosity "conspiracy to advocate" was validated and the "clear
and present danger" rule abandoned.

The common denominator of this new Truman Era constitutional law was the familiar premise of repressive government in all
ages and in all its various guises—the notion that the supposed
security of the state took precedence over the rights of the individual
and the claims of free inquiry. Here Vinson, on the excuse of struggle
with "totalitarianism," relapsed comfortably into the legal doctrines
of his *bête noire,* Vishinsky. The cosmic joke of the cold war was this
import into America of Russia's traditional spy-mania and constant
obsessions about conspiracy. The story is really a simple one. A
democratic country, trying to lead a world counterrevolution, naturally developed counterrevolutionary constitutional doctrines, revising Madison in the spirit of Metternich. This was the comedy in
which Vinson played his determined role.

It would recklessly invite disappointment to believe that the
substitution of Earl Warren for Fred Vinson as Chief Justice would
bring this ignoble chapter in American law to a close. A community
preparing—or being prepared—for war is a community in which
basic liberties, though they figure prominently in the blowsy rhetoric
of the warmongers, are always disregarded. The law is earthbound
by its inescapable instruments. Judges, like juries, vary but are subject like the rest of us to the emotions which affect the human herd.
Until the climate of opinion changes, the law as interpreted by the
Court under Warren is unlikely to differ sharply from the law as
dispensed under Vinson.

But having said this as hedge against the notorious lottery of
judicial appointment it would be ungrateful not to recognize the
miracle which has saved us from some Republican analogue of Clark
or Minton. Within the limits set by circumstance and opinion, the
Court may sway to one side or another. An Arthur Vanderbilt would
have intensified the worst trends on the Court. An Attorney General
out to curry favor with fanaticism might have persuaded the Presi-

dent to pick a repressionist Chief Justice to preside over a program in which Brownell promises to become another A. Mitchell Palmer.

We do not know for that matter what passed between the Attorney General and the Governor in those private conferences before the appointment was announced. We have no way of knowing whether pledges might have been made by implication. We do know that Warren's position on the loyalty oath at the University of California made him suspect in the eyes of one wing of the party, though the eagerness to push him upstairs and out of the way may have overbalanced anxiety.

It would be naïve to suppose that Brownell did not seek some assurance that Warren would not prove an obstacle to the intensified deportation drive and anti-"subversive" campaign on which the new Attorney General is embarking on the weird theory that he can thereby prove congressional witch hunting unnecessary. But we may comfort ourselves with the knowledge that assurances given before judicial appointment are apt to prove tenuous; they are contracts without an enforcement clause. It still seems a happy accident that produced a Warren in the party of Nixon and Knowland, and determined the award of our highest judicial office as consolation prize to a Republican as respected, humane and liberal as Earl Warren.

There are grounds for hoping that with Warren there will be a moderately liberal 5-4 majority on the new Court. For the Negro, the change from Vinson to Warren is a clear improvement, which should provide a favorable decision in the pending action against Jim Crowism in the schools. But the situation on civil rights in the sense of racial equality reflects the growing political power of the Negro. The situation as to civil *liberties* is strikingly different; here no sizable portion of the electorate demands improvement, the victims are as yet part of a tiny minority of radicals and intellectuals.

If world tension mounts again, with renewed stalemate on Korea and Germany, Warren will certainly not be immune to the currents which made Frankfurter and Jackson captive on so many fundamental issues. But given a fair amount of peace, we have some reason to expect from Warren's past that there will now be five Judges prepared to put a rein on the worst excesses of the witch hunt. Even under Vinson, the Court enforced the elementary safeguards of the Fifth Amendment. Perhaps under this new lineup there may be some hope for the First.

OCTOBER 3, 1953

MAY 17, 1954

For weeks on Mondays, when opinions are handed down, the Supreme Court press room had drawn a full house, including an unusually large number of Negro reporters. Last Monday, after we had all begun to give up hope of a school segregation decision that day, an unusual event occurred. Ordinarily opinions are given out in the press room after word comes down the pneumatic chute that they have been read in the courtroom above. This time the light flashed and there was a different kind of message. The press aide put on his coat and we were all shepherded into the court chamber to hear the opinion read and receive our copies there.

In that tense and crowded marble hall, the Chief Justice was already reading the opinion in *Brown et al. v. United States.* He read in a firm, clear voice and with expression. As the Chief Justice launched into the opinion's lengthy discussion of the Fourteenth Amendment, the reporters, white and Negro, edged forward in the press boxes, alert for indications of which way the decision was going. "We come then," the Chief Justice read, "to the question presented: Does segregation of children in public schools solely on the basis of race, even though the physical facilities and other 'tangible' factors may be equal, deprive the children of the minority group of equal educational opportunities?" In the moment of suspense which followed we could hear the Chief Justice replying firmly, · "We believe that it does." It was all one could do to keep from cheering, and a few of us were moved to tears.

There was one quite simple but terribly evocative sentence in the opinion. For Negroes and other sympathetic persons this packed the quintessence of the quieter misery imposed on members of a submerged race. "To separate them," the Chief Justice said of Negro children, "from others of a similar age and qualifications solely because of their race generates a feeling of inferiority as to their status in the community that may affect their hearts and minds in a way unlikely ever to be undone." So the fifty-eight-year-old ruling of *Plessy v. Ferguson* was reversed and the court ruled "Separate educational facilities are inherently unequal . . . segregation is a denial of the equal protection of the laws."

The unanimous ruling seemed too explicit to be whittled away in the enforcing decree. The rehearing next fall on the form of that decree, the invitation to the Southern states to be heard, offer a period in which tempers may cool and bigots be allowed second thoughts. At the best, Jim Crow will not be ended overnight. The clue to what is likely to happen in most cities, North and South, may be found in a clause of the questions on which the Court will hear argument in the fall.

The Court is to consider whether "within the limits set by normal geographic school districting" Negro children shall "forthwith be admitted to schools of their choice" or a gradual changeover be arranged. Since most Negroes in most cities already lived in more or less segregated Negro sections, these will still have largely Negro schools. It is on the borderlines that mixing will begin; ultimately the pattern of segregated schools will break down with the pattern of segregated Negro housing areas. The ultimate impact must revolutionize race relations and end the system of inferior status and inferior education which has kept the ex-slave a menial.

Among the audience streaming out of the chamber when the Chief Justice had ended, the lawyers for the NAACP suddenly began to embrace each other outside the doors. They had achieved a giant stride toward the full emancipation of their people. The growing political power of the Negro had prevailed over the growing wealth of the Republican party's newest recruits, the Texas oil millionaires. In a showdown, American democracy had proven itself real.

MAY 24, 1954

9: *The Downfall of McCarthy*

REDOUBTABLE GAMBLER

The key to the situation developing in Washington is that, though the Eisenhower Administration wants desperately to appease McCarthy, McCarthy does not want to be appeased.

The statement made by the President at his press conference last week was so cautiously, even queasily worded, that it seemed at first glance ignominious. He said he had never seen any member of Congress guilty of disrespect toward the public servants appearing before it. He was certain that no one in the government wanted to have his utterances interpreted as questioning the debt we owe the officers and enlisted men of the Army. He did, indeed, specifically include General Zwicker in that tribute but he said not one single word to which McCarthy needed to take offense. The statement was designed to save the President's face with his subordinates in the government and the Army and with the decent people in his party aroused by the Stevens affair. But it was also framed to avoid a direct conflict with McCarthy.

Indeed the first reaction among the reporters streaming out of the most heavily attended press conference Eisenhower has held was one of disgust and disappointment. It looked as if the President had backed away from a fight. The weak answer he gave when asked about McCarthy's attack on Dulles in the McLeod affair made it seem to many present that he was joining Stevens in a crawl, and that the State Department could expect as little real support as the Army had been given last week when the chips were down.

It was the bold effrontery with which McCarthy immediately reacted that put the President's statement in a new light. McCarthy was insisting on a fight. He declined to leave the President any way out. He was demanding abject surrender or a fight which would split the Republican party wide open. For while Eisenhower defended the loyalty of the Army, McCarthy was now charging that Peress had been the "sacred cow of certain Army brass"—this implied a conspiracy to shield a Communist. Where Eisenhower had praised Zwicker, McCarthy called him "a stupid, arrogant or witless man." The words McCarthy used—"the fact that he might be a General"— must have seemed a warning to Eisenhower himself.

The most remarkable event of the day was when McCarthy late in the afternoon "relented" and sent out a message that he wished to delete the word "now" from the cheeky sentence which said, "Apparently the President and I now agree on the necessity of getting rid of Communists." McCarthy's nerve commands admiration. Who else would have the brass, after being criticized in the Stevens affair by papers as far right as the *Chicago Tribune* and his own doggedly faithful *Washington Times-Herald,* to claim that he was the victim of an unprecedented mud-slinging campaign "by extreme left-wing elements of press and radio"? This is a redoubtable gambler, playing for the highest stakes. His match is not yet visible.

What is McCarthy's strategy? His own party had been looking to him as its main card in the fall elections. The political strategists of the Administration, Dewey and Brownell, have shown themselves as unscrupulous as McCarthy; Eisenhower has twinges, but overcomes them easily, as was evident from his cowardice on the issue of General Marshall during the campaign. It looked as if McCarthy could have exercised a position of leadership within the party. Did he decide that he did not want to carry the ball for the Eisenhower Administration? Did he feel that with a recession under way the Republicans were bound to be defeated this year anyway? Does he prefer a fight with Eisenhower which can make it possible for him to place the blame for an electoral defeat on the Eisenhower-Dewey conservative Eastern leadership? Does he want to clear his skirts of conservative fiscal policies so he can play a social demagogue's role in a depression? Does he dream of breaking up the old parties and emerging with a movement of his own?

The situation has its advantages for the fight against fascism in America. During the past year a series of events have finally begun to bring home the meaning of the witch hunt to wide sections of the American people. Earlier only a fringe of radicals and intellectuals had been affected. The Oxnam hearing and the J. B. Matthews charges awakened Protestants to the danger; Brownell's Harry White charges showed the Democrats that they were the ultimate target; the shameful inflation of "security" risk discharges by the Administration angered several million government employees and their families; McCarthy's cruel bullying of Mrs. Annie Lee Moss and her respected Negro lawyer has aroused the Negro community; the Peress affair has antagonized the Army and the conservatives. Though the leadership is weak and compromised, the terrain McCarthy has chosen for battle is advantageous. For the first time the possibility of a broad front against fascism is beginning to shape up in America. This is the hopeful side of a week's events that literally threaten the very foundations of the Republic, making it seem quite possible that McCarthy (like Hitler) may one day "legally" assume power in America.

MARCH 8, 1954

THE FIRST WELTS ON JOE McCARTHY

Buds are beginning to appear on the forsythia, and welts on Joe McCarthy. The early arrival of spring and a series of humiliations for our would-be *Führer* have made this a most pleasant week in the capital.

The events of the week are worth savoring. Blunt Charlie Wilson called McCarthy's charges against the Army "tommyrot" and for once Joe had no comeback. Next day came the ignominious announcement that he was dropping that two million dollar suit against former Senator Benton for calling McCarthy a crook and a liar; the lame excuse promised to launch a nationwide "I Believe Benton" movement. Stevenson followed with a speech calculated to impress those decent conservatives who had grown disgusted with the Eisenhower Administration's cowardice in the Zwicker affair.

When McCarthy sought to answer Stevenson, the Republican National Committee turned up in Ike's corner and grabbed the radio and TV time away from him. Nixon was to reply, and McCarthy was out (unless somebody smuggled him into the program in place of Checkers). While McCarthy fumed and threatened, his own choice for the Federal Communications Commission, Robert E. Lee, ungratefully declared he thought the networks had done enough in making time available to Nixon. Next day a Republican, albeit a liberal Republican, Flanders of Vermont, actually got up on the floor of the Senate and delivered a speech against McCarthy. That same night Ed Murrow telecast a brilliant TV attack on McCarthy.

Under Stevenson's leadership, Eisenhower rallied. At press conference he endorsed the Flanders attack, said he concurred heartily in the decision to have Nixon reply to Stevenson, asserted that he saw no reason why the networks should also give time to McCarthy. Like an escaped prisoner, flexing cramped muscles in freedom, the President also made it clear he had no intention of turning Indo-China into another Korea and even had the temerity to suggest that it might be a good idea to swap butter and other surplus farm commodities with Russia.

The White House conference was no sooner over than Senator Ferguson as chairman of the Senate Republican Policy Committee released a set of suggested rules for Senate investigating committees which are no great shakes at reform but would, if adopted, make it impossible for McCarthy any longer to operate his subcommittee as a one-man show. These may be small enough gains in the fight against McCarthyism, but they were bitter pills for McCarthy to swallow.

So far McCarthy's colleagues on both sides of the aisle have been lying low. When Flanders attacked McCarthy, the Senate was as silent as it was some weeks earlier when Ellender of Louisiana made a lone onslaught and Fulbright of Arkansas cast the sole vote against his appropriation. Only Lehman of New York and John Sherman Cooper a Republican of Kentucky rose to congratulate Flanders. Nobody defended McCarthy, but nobody joined in with those helpful interjections which usually mark a Senate speech. When the Democratic caucus met in closed session, the Stevenson speech was ignored. Lyndon Johnson of Texas, the Democratic floor leader, is frightened of McCarthy's Texas backers.

Great issues are rarely resolved by frontal assault; for every abolitionist prepared to challenge slavery as a moral wrong, there were dozens of compromising politicians (including Lincoln) who talked as if the real issue were states rights or the criminal jurisdiction of the federal courts or the right of the people in a new territory to determine their own future. In the fight against the witch-mania in this country and in Europe, there were few enough to defend individual victims but fewer still who were willing to assert publicly that belief in witchcraft was groundless. So today in the fight against "McCarthyism." It is sometimes hard to draw a line of principle between McCarthy and his critics. If there is indeed a monstrous and diabolic conspiracy against world peace and stability, then isn't McCarthy right? If "subversives" are at work like termites here and abroad, are they not likely to be found in the most unlikely places and under the most unlikely disguises? How talk of fair procedure if dealing with a protean and Satanic enemy?

To doubt the power of the devil, to question the existence of witches, is again to read oneself out of respectable society, to brand oneself a heretic, to incur suspicion of being oneself in league with the powers of evil. So all the fighters against McCarthyism are impelled to adopt its premises. This was true even of the Stevenson speech, but was strikingly so of Flanders. The country is in a bad way indeed when as feeble and hysterical a speech is hailed as an attack on McCarthyism. Flanders talked of "a crisis in the age-long warfare between God and the Devil for the souls of men." He spoke of Italy as "ready to fall into Communist hands," of Britain "nibbling at the drugged bait of trade profits." There are passages of sheer fantasy, like this one: "Let us look to the South. In Latin America there are sturdy strong points of freedom. But there are likewise, alas, spreading infections of communism. Whole countries are being taken over. . . ." What "whole countries"? And what "sturdy strong points of freedom"? Flanders pictured the Iron Curtain drawn tight about the United States and Canada, the rest of the world captured "by infiltration and subversion." Flanders told the Senate, "We will be left with no place to trade and no place to go except as we are permitted to trade and to go by the Communist masters of the world."

The center of gravity in American politics has been pushed so far right that such childish nightmares are welcomed as the expression of liberal statesmanship. Nixon becomes a middle-of-the-road spokesman and conservative papers like the *Washington Star* and *New York Times* find themselves classified more and more as parts of the "left-wing press." In this atmosphere the Senate Republican reply to McCarthy's silly "Communist coddling" charges against the Army is to launch a formal investigation of their own through Saltonstall and the Armed Services Committee. This will be the Republican and Army analogue of the Tydings inquiry into the charges against the State Department and will be greeted with the same cry of whitewash by the growing lunatic fringe behind McCarthy.

There are some charges which must be laughed off or brushed off. They cannot be disproved. If a man charges that he saw Eisenhower riding a broomstick over the White House, he will never be convinced to the contrary by sworn evidence that the President was in bed reading a Western at the time. Formal investigations like Saltonstall's merely pander to paranoia and reward demagogy. What if McCarthy were next to attack the President and the Supreme Court? Are they, too, to be investigated? Is America to become a country in which any adventurer flanked by two ex-Communist screwballs will put any institution on the defensive?

McCarthy is personally discomfited, but McCarthyism is still on the march. Acheson fought McCarthy, but preached a more literate variation of the bogeyman theory of history. Eisenhower fights McCarthy, but his Secretary of State in Caracas is pushing hard for a resolution which would spread McCarthyism throughout the hemisphere, pledging joint action for "security" and against "subversion." Nowhere in American politics is there evidence of any important figure (even Stevenson) prepared to talk in sober, mature and realistic terms of the real problems which arise in a real world where national rivalries, mass aspirations and ideas clash as naturally as the waves of the sea. The premises of free society and of liberalism find no one to voice them, yet McCarthyism will not be ended until someone has the nerve to make this kind of fundamental attack upon it.

What are the fundamentals which need to be recognized? The first is that there can be no firm foundation for freedom in this country unless there is real peace. There can be no real peace without a readiness for live-and-let-live, i.e., for coexistence with communism. The fear cannot be extirpated without faith in man and freedom. The world is going "socialist" in one form or another everywhere; communism is merely the extreme form this movement takes when and where blind and backward rulers seek by terror and force to hold back the tide, as the Czar did and as Chiang Kai-shek did.

There must be renewed recognition that societies are kept stable and healthy by reform, not by thought police; this means that there must be free play for so-called "subversive" ideas—every idea "subverts" the old to make way for the new. To shut off "subversion" is to shut off peaceful progress and to invite revolution and war. American society has been healthy in the past because there has been a constant renovating "subversion" of this kind. Had we operated on the bogeyman theory of history, America would have destroyed itself long ago. It will destroy itself now unless and until a few men of stature have the nerve to speak again the traditional language of free society.

MARCH 15, 1954

THE COST OF ANTICOMMUNISM

There was one scene, in the final minutes, before the tense galleries, after three days of debate on McCarthy, with tired and impatient senators crying "Vote, vote," that would have entranced the creator of Babbitt. Capehart, that rotund Midwestern businessman, was on the floor in a final plea to table any resolution of censure. "There have been times," Capehart told a Senate which could not have cared less, "when, if I could have gotten hold of him, I think I would have thrown him out. There have been other times when I thought, 'By golly, there is a great guy.'" Capehart was maneuvering into position to agree with both the pro's and the anti's when he got back to Indianapolis.

It was comic, as comic as Welker's assurance that McCarthy

must be a good man because he loved Welker's children "and he loves the children of almost every other senator." But amid the burlesque, Capehart's main point faithfully reflected the confusions which haunt Main Street. Capehart declared "out of one corner of our mouths" we say we want billions of dollars to fight communism. We say, "We are going to send your boys all over the world. You may have a third world war." Yet, Capehart continued, "on the other hand" we say, "We do not like McCarthy because he is a little too rough and a little too tough with these so-called Communists." How explain that in South Bend or Little Rock?

This is the heart of the Senate's difficulty. This is why for the sixth time in six years (since the Malmédy inquiry in 1949) the Senate is wearily setting up yet another committee to investigate charges against McCarthy with no more prospect than in the past of a decision. McCarthy is resourceful, unscrupulous and wily, but the Senate is full of politicians as deft and clowns as crafty. They would have brought him down long ago if it were not for the dilemma created by our own demonology. If Communists are some supernatural breed of men, led by diabolic master minds in that distant Kremlin, engaged in a Satanic conspiracy to take over the world and enslave all mankind—and this is the thesis endlessly propounded by American liberals and conservatives alike, echoed night and day by every radio station and in every newspaper, the thesis no American dare any longer challenge without himself becoming suspect—then how fight McCarthy?

If the public mind is to be conditioned for war, if it is being taught to take for granted the destruction of millions of human beings, few of them tainted with this dreadful ideological virus, all of them indeed presumably pleading for us to liberate them, how can we argue that it matters if a few possibly innocent men lose jobs or reputations because of McCarthy? Is not this additional cost too slight, are not the stakes too great? How contend for constitutional niceties while acquiescing in the spread of poisonous attitudes and panicky emotions?

Writ in the skies of the H-bomb era is the warning that mutual destruction is the alternative to coexistence. Until there is a national leadership willing to take a pragmatic view of revolution, a charitable and Christian view of the misery that goes with the great rebirths of mankind, a self-respecting view of the example a free America can set and the constructive leadership an unafraid America can give, we cannot fight the drift to fascism at home and war abroad. We cannot inculcate unreasoning hate and not ultimately be destroyed by it ourselves. We who prate constantly of "atheistic communism" forget that this is what all the great teachers of mankind have taught. There is a retribution that lies in wait for the arrogant and the self-righteous. Where is the man big enough to reach the American people with this message before it is too late?

AUGUST 9, 1954

GUILTY

The unanimous report of the Watkins committee represents one of the rare occasions in recent years when the conservative forces in American society have fulfilled their moral and political obligations. One of the main objectives of any Fascist movement must be to break down the interwoven fabric of tradition, dignity and respect which makes orderly government possible. The safeguarding of these inherited values and attitudes should be of special concern to the true conservative. In this respect the six members of the Watkins committee lived up to their responsibility.

The Senate will follow them in censuring McCarthy. There will be a bitter fight, but that fight will serve only to separate conservatives from reactionaries and Fascists, and to show how few senators are in the latter categories. When a Senator George approves and a Senator Jenner denounces, the line of battle is clear. It is not one on which McCarthy can win more than a handful of votes, and the death of Senator McCarran has deprived him of the only supporter who had any considerable sphere of influence in the Senate.

Basically it may be said that McCarthy is being censured only for being a bully and a boor. But the Watkins committee acted wisely in so limiting itself. The life of the Senate depends on free debate, and there can be no free debate without a latitude in which abuses may occur. The Senate has no right to sit in judgment on the ideas of a senator, but it has a right to censure him for conduct which infringes on its honor and dignity. This is the distinction the Watkins committee drew, and the Senate will accept.

The country is indebted to Senators Flanders, Fulbright and Morse for their part in bringing charges, to former Senator Benton who initiated the original investigation into McCarthy's finances, and to Senators Hayden, Hennings and Hendrickson who went through with the original investigation when other senators got cold feet. The questions put by Senator Hennings to McCarthy in November, 1952, are still unanswered by our Fifth Amendment Senator, and we hope they will be pressed in the censure debate and after.

Did McCarthy divert to his personal advantage funds contributed to him for his campaign against communism? Did he use friends and associates "to secrete receipts, income, commodity and stock speculation . . ."? The most important question of all was "Whether your activities on behalf of certain special interest groups, such as housing, sugar and China, were motivated by self-interest."

McCarthy's function has been to terrorize into silence all those in government and out who were critical of Chiang Kai-shek. In this task, he and McCarran were comrades in arms. The McCarran-Jenner committee investigation of the Institute of Pacific Relations, the McCarthy attack on the State Department were the twin instruments of the China Lobby and of those pro-Fascist forces which wished to reverse American wartime policy, to defame the past, to make Franco Spain and a new reactionary Germany our main allies. McCarran and McCarthy and their clerical allies sought and still seek World War III. And though McCarran is dead and McCarthy may be on the skids, the forces which they served are far from defeated. The paranoiac atmosphere they helped create is far from being dissipated.

The McCarthy censure is in a way the fruit of the Republican victory at the last election. Had the Democrats won, the Republicans would have been happy to exploit and follow him in opposition. But once his own party came into power, McCarthy's arrogance, conceit and ambition would not allow him to play a secondary role. He dreamed of being a dictator, and would not suffer patiently the role of a conventional politician. His German-schooled advisers urged the dynamic course congenial to his temperament and so he was forced to gamble on a clash with his own party, with the President he helped elect, with the army and with the conservative forces of American society. The gamble is being lost. The Republicans, having turned on him, must smash him now. Unfortunately they believe that to do so they must prove that they are in no way "soft on communism." The result is Brownellism, and the kind of competition in anti-communism between Democrat and Republican which disgraced the last few weeks of Congress.

Yet in the context of the political fight which this report will precipitate, must not the witch hunt lose a good deal of its steam? Can McCarthy be bumped off without at the same time making McCarthyism a political liability? Isn't the observed lack of interest in McCarthy, the sheer boredom which is beginning to envelop him in the public mind, a boredom which also extends to the witch hunt? Isn't it degenerating into the private passion of a frenetic few? These are the questions which give one hope.

OCTOBER 4, 1954

10: *Fetish of the Fifties: Security*

INCOMMENSURATE EQUATION: JUSTICE AND SECURITY

In the growing uproar over the loyalty-security program, its critics still cling to a comfortable fallacy. They assume that it is possible to reconcile "security" with justice. They speak as if, by some reform of the rules, or better adherence to them, maximum security for the government and fair trial for the individual can evenhandedly be assured. Thus Mr. Walter Lippmann, in criticizing the President's clumsiness in the Ladejinsky case, asserts the citizen's right in such matters "to have the charge tried by due process" without stopping to consider whether due process is possible in such proceedings. How do you try the "charge" that a man once worked for Amtorg or has two sisters in Russia?

If we stop to compare what happens in the trial of a crime with what happens in the trial of a loyalty-security case, we will begin to see that a more fundamental attack on the problem is necessary if the miasma of suspicion is to be dissipated. Here are some of the differences:

1. The matter of proof. A trial deals with something that happened. A loyalty-security hearing deals with something that *might* happen. When a crime has been committed or attempted, objective proof is possible: a body, a cracked safe, a forged check, witnesses, may all be put in evidence.

But when a man is up on loyalty or security charges, nothing has *happened*. The tribunal is not dealing with an act but with future possibilities. It is engaged in an exercise in clairvoyance. It must determine whether a man might commit a crime some time in the future, whether he might steal or sell secrets. There are no ways to prove what a man *might* do. The essence of the loyalty-security procedure is not the trial of a fact but a guess as to future conduct.

2. How any doubt is resolved: In the trial of a crime, even for the most heinous, such as murder or treason, any reasonable doubt is resolved in favor of the accused. As Blackstone phrased the rule, already venerable in his time, "The law holds that it is better that ten guilty persons escape than the one innocent suffer." Law enforcement is thereby made more difficult. But justice to the individual, not the security of society, is the primary concern.

All this is reversed in loyalty-security cases. To bar a man from a job and label him disloyal because in your opinion he might do something bad in the future is by its nature a decision which resolves the doubt in favor of the State and against the individual. "Security" means to take as few chances as possible, even at the expense of injustice to some people who never have committed a crime and never will.

This is vividly illustrated by Fifth Amendment cases. A man summoned before a magistrate and asked whether he had ever committed larceny who thereupon pleaded the Fifth Amendment could not be thrown in jail or even prosecuted. But a worker in the government or at General Electric or Bethlehem Steel who invokes the Fifth Amendment loses his job. No evidence that he ever committed a crime or was ever a radical—the two are equated by now in the public mind—is required. The invocation of his constitutional right is enough to ruin his reputation and his right to work.

Those who defend these standards fall back on a totalitarian logic. David Lawrence protested recently against what he terms a "left-wing drive" to "surround governmental employees with complex procedural safeguards which would supersede the right of the American government to protect its own safety." Mr. Lawrence forgets that much of the Constitution and the common law is devoted to surrounding people of all kinds, including the disreputable, with complex procedural safeguards which supersede the right of government to protect itself. In such restrictions lies the essence of free government.

3. Avoidance: The difference in the two procedures becomes clearer if you ask yourself how you avoid getting into trouble. To

avoid arrest and trial for a crime, one has to obey the law. But what does one avoid to keep out of loyalty-security trouble? One has to avoid political activity. Since you never know what organization may some day be regarded as suspect, better join none. Since almost any cause may some day be regarded as subversive, better keep away from all. Since there are now informers everywhere, including the campus, say as little as possible, avoid the discussion of dangerous subjects. Be careful what books you have in your library and what publications you read. These may be held against you. Safety lies in the abnegation of one's rights.

4. Standards: Here, too, the difference becomes sharp. There is little doubt as to what is murder, larceny, or espionage. These are defined in the law books.

But what is "subversion" or "Un-Americanism"? The latter is an epithet, the former is a wholly relative term. Much that we take for granted today seemed un-American and subversive a century ago —income taxes for example. Much that existed then would seem "un-American" today—for example, the earlier restriction which limited the right to vote to those citizens who owned property. What one man sees as subversion another man sees as progress.

5. The mode of defense: In a criminal trial, the accused is furnished with a bill of particulars. It informs him that the government will allege that a safe was cracked at such and such an address in such and such a city at such and such a time. The accused may then prove he was elsewhere.

But anything remotely approaching a bill of particulars is rare in loyalty-security cases. The accused is usually asked to rebut vague charges of Communist sympathy or association. The task of the defense is to prove a negative.

Even where particulars are furnished, the outcome is not necessarily conclusive. A man may indeed "clear" himself by proving that he never engaged in liberal or left-wing activity of any kind. But what if he did belong to a radical organization? Does that mean that he is a security risk?

The only espionage case turned up in the whole security program is one which would never be suspected by normal "loyalty" standards. Joseph Petersen had no left-wing connections. A Catholic, graduated from a Catholic school, he never belonged to any organization on the Attorney General's or any similar "list." Whatever this code expert did was for a friendly power, Holland, and for no ideological reasons. He could slip easily through the sieve of customary loyalty standards.

On the other hand a Ladejinsky, for all his demonstrated value as an agricultural expert, could never hope to qualify under them for government employment if he were a new applicant. A man who had once worked for Amtorg, with two sisters in Russia, whose name had been on the mailing list of several "front" organizations during the war would never be freshly hired today. The liberals would never dare defend him. The Ladejinsky case shows the advantage of judging a man by what he *does* when employed, by the record he makes rather than by a system based on paranoid surmise.

6. Witnesses: The difficulty is made the greater by the mode of presenting evidence. In a criminal trial, the accusing witness must be produced in court and subjected to cross-examination. The right to confront one's accuser is fundamental. The government may use informers, as in narcotic or smuggling cases, but it cannot come into court and ask for conviction on undisclosed evidence by undisclosed persons on the ground that to reveal them would endanger its sources of information. The conviction can be obtained only on the basis of whatever evidence and witnesses the government produces in open court.

But in loyalty-security cases nothing is more familiar than the submission of allegations from undisclosed informers. The accused has no chance to confront the accuser. Such confrontations in criminal cases often disclose mistaken identity. Cross-examination may uncover perjury. All these safeguards are absent in loyalty-security cases because here again the security of the state, its secrets and informers, is ranked ahead of justice to the individual.

The anxiety over security reflects its widening impact on our society. As more people are drawn into its orbit, more become aware of its injustices. The government is having trouble; the loyalty program, designed originally to purge the government of liberals and radicals, has ended by making people of all kinds afraid to take government jobs. Something has to be done, and the politicians scent popularity in the issue. But they, like all of us, take the lines of least resistance, and talk only of correcting the "abuses" of the security program.

Few will dare to say it now, but the time is coming when the truth will be recognized, a truth which the Framers of our Constitution wove into the fabric of American government. They saw that there could not be freedom without risk, that no stable society could be built except on a foundation of trust, and that when trust was violated—and only then—a man could be punished. They did not think it was the province of government to police men's minds, or that it had a right to punish them unless they committed some wrongful act. They would have been horrified at our growing system of thought police, of guessing-game "law" about prospective crime, and indeed most of all by our obsession with "security."

An administrative official has a right and duty to judge the reliability of a man he hires. But what is proper and necessary in private administrative judgment is improper when erected into a system of universal surveillance and public defamation of character that chokes off free political discussion in ever wider areas and brands men as "disloyal" or "security risks" on the basis of pseudo-judicial guessing as to whether they might possibly some day commit a crime. The loyalty-security program cannot be reformed. Given peace, it will eventually be abolished.

JANUARY 24, 1955

THE ARMY COMMISSIONS FRANZ KAFKA

In the hassle between McCarthy and the Army, no one has bothered to look up the loyalty form used in the armed services. A correspondent has sent a copy to the *Weekly*. The "Loyalty Certificate" (DD 1 Apr 50 98) is divided into two parts, one covering "conduct," the other "associations."

The instructions warn that "concealment of . . . or failure to divulge in full, conduct or associations of the character set forth" may be grounds for court-martial or civil prosecution. "Consequently," they advise, "you must read the following provisions carefully and be sure you understand them."

This is not easy. The form might have been drafted by Franz Kafka. It contains a nightmarish loophole. This says, "Conduct which may be considered as establishing reasonable grounds for invoking appropriate penalties shall include, but is not limited to the following . . ." Similarly the form says, "associations . . . include but are not limited to membership in, affiliation, or sympathetic association with, any . . . association, movement or group . . . having the following characteristics."

This phrase, "but not limited to," makes a blank check of the certification. Who knows for what other conduct or associations the signer may later be held liable? With most documents, it is advisable to see a lawyer. This one calls for a clairvoyant. The final provision adds a touch of wit. "I understand," it says, "the meaning of the statements made in the certifications above." It may be doubted whether the Judge Advocate General himself could sign that honestly.

Even without this legal beartrap, the wording is hazardous. It seems at one point to revive the old common law of constructive treason. One provision covers "writings and acts which can reasonably be considered as intended to encourage seditious or treasonable opinions . . ." This recalls the crime of "imagining" the death of the King.

Another provision proscribes "advocacy of revolution *or* of force or violence to bring about economic, political or social change." This would seem to cover non-violent changes which are "revolutionary" only in the metaphorical sense. Provision (d) also contains an innovation. It refers to unauthorized disclosure, "under circumstances which may indicate disloyalty," of information "of a classified *or* non-public character." What kind of information is not secret but "non-public"? Anything which might embarrass some commanding general?

The final conduct provision is a dragnet. It specifies: "Acting, attempting to act, or knowingly failing to act when such conduct is calculated to serve the interests of another government." One has only to look at the controversy raging over Mr. Dulles's conduct at Berlin to see how impossible a standard this is.

At the Pentagon, I was told that a Form 98 A is supposed to be appended. This names the organizations listed by the Attorney General. But the proscribed organizations are "not limited to" these. The loyalty form covers any organization which can be regarded "as seeking to alter the form of government of the United States by unconstitutional means regardless of practice, advocacy or non-advocacy" of "force, violence *or intimidation*." Our italics underscore another Army innovation—adding "intimidation" to "force and violence." This is broad enough to cover McCarthy, Cohn and Schine. And what are "unconstitutional means" in the absence of "force, violence or intimidation"?

Many lawyers will agree that those like Major Peress who pleaded the Fifth Amendment rather than fill this out were well advised. The form naïvely says that those who invoke the Fifth

Amendment are required to describe "the specific part of any conduct, membership, or association about which claim is made." If taken literally this would require the soldier to reveal what he was trying to keep from disclosing.

Our correspondent writes that at one induction center soldiers were lined up to sign this form *en masse*. When one soldier said he would like to study the form before signing it, he was ordered to sign and given an extra copy to study at his leisure. A Pentagon press officer assured me this could not have happened in the Army.

MARCH 8, 1954

MORALITY: A SECURITY PROBLEM

Last weekend Easter and Passover coincided. These are the two spring festivals of what is so often referred to as Judaeo-Christian civilization. This is the civilization whose values we are getting ready to defend against those who do not believe in God, think the end justifies the means, place a low value on human life, deny the existence of spirit, and do not hold—as we do—that man is sacred because made in the image of his Creator.

The dual occasion provoked an outpouring of sermons. There were even sermons in unexpected precincts. Popular magazines meditated for a moment—in full color—on the meaning of the resurrection. Columnists who prided themselves on being intellectuals wrote (rather ostentatiously) on going to mass or seder. But amid this chorus of piety I did not notice that anyone dealt with what I should have thought an obvious but striking theme. This was the inclusion, among the charges against Dr. J. Robert Oppenheimer, of the allegation that he had opposed the making of the hydrogen bomb on "moral and political" grounds.

I suppose that on the basis of rendering unto Caesar what is Caesar's, the Church could excusably shy away from any comment on the latter half of this indictment.

But the "moral" half of the indictment is another matter. Is not morality the province of Church and Synagogue? Have we not been told over and over again of the dangers which flow from divorcing science from morality and morality from religion? When a scientist is accused of objecting to the H-bomb on "moral" grounds, it begins to sound as if there were circumstances under which the government regards morality as subversive.

We have seen many conversions in our time. What if Dr. Oppenheimer should get up at his hearing and say that after long thought he had returned to the faith of his fathers and now took literally the injunction, "Thou shalt not kill"? What if the hearing board were forced to bar him from all defense work on the ground that he took the Ten Commandments literally?

Or what if Dr. Oppenheimer got up and said that after long brooding he had been drawn to Jesus and become a Christian and felt impelled to live by the injunction, "Love your enemies . . . resist not evil"? What if he were to say that he could not reconcile the making of newer and bigger bombs with his new-found religious belief? How embarrassing if the hearing board were forced to declare Dr. Oppenheimer a security risk because he had become a Christian.

APRIL 26, 1954

THE OPPENHEIMER VERDICT

The underlying assumption of the Oppenheimer verdict is that he and other scientists like him are no longer needed. His past Communist associations and radical sympathies were fully known to General Groves when Dr. Oppenheimer became his right-hand man in the building of the A-bomb. The report of the special hearing board says "a calculated risk" was taken. Indeed the report discloses for the first time that the alternative considered by those in charge of security was "to open up the whole project and throw security to the winds rather than lose the talents of the individual." "What we have learned in this inquiry," the report observes, however, "makes the present application of this principle [of the calculated risk] inappropriate in the instant case." This says obscurely what has been evident for some time from a close scrutiny of official utterance, that the H-bomb is believed to be just about the limit of destructive power which can be safely used. The problem is no longer one of theoretical physics in the discovery of new and vaster weapons, but of applying known theory to the perfection and accumulation of fissionable and thermonuclear weapons.

But this, if true, is only true if one believes that no adequate defense is possible, or even worth exploring on any scale comparable to that expended on the A- and H-bomb. The assumption that men like Dr. Oppenheimer can be dispensed with is interlocked with the assumption that the only real defense is overwhelming offensive power. This, too, is implied by the report. For it says that in "evaluating advice" from a scientist, government officials concerned with military matters "must also be certain that underlying any advice is a genuine conviction that this country cannot in the interest of security have less than the strongest possible offensive capabilities in a time of national danger."

"The strongest possible offensive capabilities" means that nothing is to detract from the main job of mounting the offensive. The psychology of that attitude was made vivid by Oppenheimer himself in the July, 1953, issue of *Foreign Affairs* ("Atomic Weapons and American Policy") when he lifted the curtain a little on a bitter intramural dispute. Oppenheimer reported, "A high officer of the Air Defense Command said—and this only a few months ago, in a most serious discussion of measures for the continental defense of the United States—that it was not our policy to attempt to protect this country, for that is so big a job that it would interfere with our retaliatory capabilities."

To cope with the dangers from the Pandora's box we ourselves unlocked, we must now seek "absolute security" (as the report puts it) and in that search resolve all doubts against the individual and in favor of the State. This is the first premise of totalitarian society. Just how far the shadow of this case may fall when extended by this means will be evident on reflection. All who agreed with Oppenheimer that the H-bomb should not be built must become suspect with him. The Atomic Energy Committee was 3-2 against the H-bomb; David Lilienthal, Sumner T. Pike and Dr. Henry D. Smyth agreed with Oppenheimer. The AEC General Advisory Committee was unanimously against an H-bomb "crash" program. According to the *Fortune* article, of all the scientists only Enrico Fermi of the University of Chicago "forthrightly sided" with the AEC minority, Lewis Strauss and Gordon Dean. Do all these become security risks or at least men whose advice is suspect?

The infection of the heresy reached into the hearing board itself. The one-man dissenter, Professor Ward V. Evans of Loyola University, who thought Oppenheimer's clearance should be restored, said of the scientist's qualms: "Only time will prove whether he was wrong on the moral and political grounds." And what of those men in the Administration, of Secretary of the Treasury Humphrey and Secretary of Defense Wilson and of Eisenhower himself who have been cutting Air Force appropriations and believe balanced forces and a healthy economy important to true defense? The theory made the orthodox standard by the hearing board is not the theory on which this present Republican Administration has proceeded, nor the theory implied in the President's famous atomic message of last winter. Can there be true debate and honest advice, mutual trust and respect, in the atmosphere this report reflects and will in turn deepen?

The impossible search for "absolute security" is incompatible with a free and healthy society. If this is to be national policy, why should anyone be trusted? There is a momentum here which plays into the hands of those who are prepared to be most unscrupulous and extreme in pandering to a growing paranoia. One of the charges against Oppenheimer is that he testified for others who were security risks. Can we, then, trust the long list of men who testified on his behalf? They included some of the most distinguished names in American banking, business, education and science. But will this protect them from a Jenner or a McCarthy? Will the men who smeared General Marshall hesitate before these lesser lights in their struggle to achieve power by panic?

The way is cleared for them by the Draconian rhetoric of the report. "There can be no tampering," it says, "with the national security, which in times of peril must be absolute, and without concessions for reasons of admiration, gratitude, reward, sympathy or charity." This is resonant with the fanaticism of terror; this is the spirit in which Robespierre sent Danton to the gallows, and Stalin condemned Trotzky and Zinoviev. Neither "gratitude" nor "charity" is to stand in the way of "security." The only difference is that the wrinkled face of the counterrevolution, frightened of the future, peeps out from between these fallacious lines.

Why fallacious? Because they carry terrible and familiar hidden assumptions. "Security" is set up as a standard, as if it were a known quantity, easily weighed and determined. But actually where does security lie and who is to determine it? The answer of this report, if read closely, is that the military and the secret police are to be the judges. Not Congress, not popular discussion, not free debate, but the Generals and the FBI are to determine what "security" is and make the rest of us conform to that standard. The society sketched out by this report is a combination of the garrison and police states.

We have come full circle in our constitutional development.

One of the tests set up by this report for a security risk is whether a man is prepared to subordinate his private judgment to that of the security police. In the section on whether a man may be loyal and still a security risk, the report says a proper attitude of mind "must include an understanding and an acceptance of security measures adopted by responsible Government agencies." This implies that the Government knows best and its decision must be accepted. "It must involve," the report continues, "an active cooperation with all agencies of Government properly and reasonably concerned with the security of our country." "Active cooperation" would seem to be a euphemism here for informing.

But this is not all. The report goes on to say that this proper frame of mind "must involve a subordination of personal judgment as to the security status of an individual as against a professional judgment in the light of standards and procedures when they have been established by appropriate process." Finally, the report says, "It must entail a wholehearted commitment to the preservation of the security system and the avoidance of conduct tending to confuse or obstruct." What is thus called for is complete allegiance to the FBI. Anything which might "confuse or obstruct" is to be avoided.

On the altar of security as thus established all else is to be sacrificed. In discussing Oppenheimer's readiness to defend Dr. Edward U. Condon and his continued friendship for certain security suspects, the report says pompously, "Loyalty to one's friends is one of the noblest of qualities." But it adds immediately afterward, "Being loyal to one's friends above reasonable obligations to the country and to the security system, however, is not clearly consistent with the interests of security."

It is because of these friendships that the majority found Oppenheimer a security risk, though loyal. It complains that several times Oppenheimer declined to answer questions by the FBI about friends, declaring the questions irrelevant. It uses an extraordinary phrase to condemn Oppenheimer for this. It says "he has repeatedly exercised an arrogance of his own judgment with respect to the loyalty and reliability of other citizens to an extent which has frustrated and at times impeded the working of the system."

A medieval inquisitor might have used that phrase—"the arrogance of his own judgment." At least an ecclesiastical court would have been setting up over private judgment some system of ancient and venerable tradition. This sets it up against the anonymous judgment of a notoriously unreliable and politically illiterate secret police.

Nothing that ever came from the pen of Edgar Allan Poe quite matches in horror the full report of the special hearing board in the Oppenheimer case. A great scientist, a sensitive man, a loyal and devoted citizen (by the board's own findings) was confronted again with the regurgitation from the sewers of the security files.

But perhaps nothing in the story is more horrible than the defense offered in the dissenting opinion. Professor Evans said there was not "the slightest vestige of information" to indicate that Oppenheimer was not loyal, and added—as if this was the highest recommendation—"He hates Russia."

Not just communism alone, but "Russia," a whole nation, a historic concept, a hundred million people. But where but in present-day Russia could one match the standards, the police-state philosophy, the suspicions of this report? Must a scientist "hate Russia" to be respectable? Is it not his province to try and understand what "Russia" is? Can a Christian nation thus enforce a new Gospel of Hate? Can a nation be really secure which demands blind unreasoning hatred instead of understanding? Is it not likely this way to blunder into war and disaster?

JUNE 7, 1954

LOYALTY AND DOUBLE JEOPARDY

John Paton Davies, Jr., was tried nine times on loyalty charges, and finally cashiered for "indiscretion" on the ninth try. John Stewart Service had been cleared once by a grand jury and six times by the State Department Loyalty Security Board when he was fired—on the eighth try. John Carter Vincent had been cleared three times when he was finally "retired" on the fourth turn round.

Just by the law of averages any government can get any man if it can try and try again. The evil is not limited to government officials. Edward U. Condon, once head of the Bureau of Standards but now in private employment, is being put through the hoops of another investigation after having been four times cleared.

William W. Remington, after being cleared in loyalty proceedings, was tried for perjury. When the conviction was reversed the government tried him again—this time on the ground that he had lied in the course of his first trial.

Harry Bridges, whom the government has been trying to deport since he led the San Francisco waterfront strike in 1934, is now the subject of a fifth try by the government, in the guise of a suit for denaturalization. But substantially it is the same case the government lost four times before.

In various ways, by various subterfuges, the government is violating the spirit if not the letter of one of the most ancient safeguards of the Bill of Rights. This was designed to save people from the pain, expense and risk of being prosecuted, or sued, over and over again for the same offense—until the desired conviction was obtained. Without it, just by the law of averages, any government can eventually "get" any man.

The provision in question is that part of the Fifth Amendment which says no person shall "be subject for the same offense to be twice put in jeopardy of life or limb." This is the famous "double jeopardy" clause which is supposed to prevent the government from trying or punishing any man a second time for the same offense.

Of all the provisions of the Bill of Rights, none is older than this. It was solidly established in the common law as far back as the days when Norman French was still the language of the courts.

Said an early federal decision (42 Fed. 590), "we will find no principle of the common law grounded upon the rock of the Magna Charta more firmly rooted than that no man shall be twice vexed with prosecutions for the same offense." An early state decision (17 Pa. 126) said the "right not to be put in jeopardy a second time for the same cause is as sacred as the right of trial by jury, and is guarded with as much care by the common law and the Constitution."

A committee of lawyers would perform a public service if they made a study of the way this safeguard is being eroded in contemporary political prosecutions, and suggested some means of extending it to loyalty proceedings.

Ostensibly these are purely administrative and carry no penalty and are therefore outside the scope of the "double jeopardy" clause. But in fact discharge for disloyalty is more serious than many types of criminal convictions; lives and careers may be blasted forever.

While the law acquiesces in the fiction that such proceedings are not serious enough to warrant the protection of the double jeopardy clause, apologists for what is happening urge that loyalty proceedings are *too serious* to be accorded constitutional safeguards.

Thus the *New York Herald-Tribune,* approving the Davies

ouster, said editorially, "To provide maximum safeguards against infiltration, subversion and error, doubts of the reliability of a government servant are to be resolved in favor of national security, rather than of the individual concerned."

This view threatens to reverse centuries of struggle. Had it prevailed, there would have been no Bill of Rights at all. The excuse of "national security," the harsh treatment of "subversion and error," the relegation to secondary place of individual rights and justice—these were the familiar standards by which in earlier times heretics were burned for the good of society and their own presumed salvation.

NOVEMBER 15, 1954

THE ARMY AND THE MIND OF YOUTH

The day Eugene William Landy was refused a commission in the Naval Reserve because his mother had once been a Communist a two-volume study of military security cases was presented to the Secretary of the Army by Norman Thomas. While the Landy case made headlines, too little attention was paid the report. This shows the Landy case was no nightmarish accident, but the result of a system of screening in which it is not at all uncommon for the political sins of the parents to be visited on their children when they enter the Army.

The special report on "The Draftee and Internal Security" taken in protest to the Pentagon showed how often in the Army a boy's worst enemy turns out to be his mother. One hundred and ten cases were examined and forty-nine are set forth in detail. In no less than eleven of these, soldiers found themselves branded disloyal because of their mothers. A sample is the allegation served on Case Number forty-nine, "You were closely associated," he was informed, "with your mother, ..., a reported Communist party member, and continue to correspond with her." Soldier boys should check on Mama before writing home.

Mothers are not the only menace. "The Draftee and Internal Security" shows that before wooing a girl it would be well to have *her* family tree examined by the FBI. A mother-in-law, though long dead, may prove as troublesome as a mother. In one soldier's case G2 reported that he had a mother-in-law "who was reported to have been 'lying low as a Communist for a long time' and was supposed to become active in the peace movement again." G2 did not add that the only peace movement in which she could possibly become active again was the Second Coming, since the lady in question was dead. Nor did the G2 summary, the report notes, "include the easily verifiable information that the alleged mother-in-law died in 1940, when the inductee was ten years old and ten years before he met the girl he married!"

The cases show that fathers, grandparents, brothers and sisters, in-laws, boyhood associates, chance remarks at school and books read at college may all come back to haunt one in the Army. Books, indeed, are a special Army bugaboo. Rowland Watts, author of the report, summarizes it by saying, "A careful study of the Army Military Personnel Security program . . . makes it difficult to avoid the conclusion that the ideal draftee is an only child of spontaneous generation who, despite a hermit childhood, has miraculously acquired the ability to read and write English but has never made use of these skills." The habit of reading can be as hazardous as the accident of birth.

The Watts report shows the mindless machinery beginning to grind a nation's youth into conformity. It reveals that all the evils so familiar in the loyalty screening of government employees—anonymous charges, Star Chamber procedures, politically illiterate allegations, suspicion of the slight liberal tendency—have spread to the armed services. The source and sponsorship of the report give it additional weight. Its author, Rowland Watts, a member of the Baltimore bar, is national secretary of the Workers Defense League, which represents the various Socialist, non-Communist and anti-Communist sections of the left. A grant from the Fund for the Republic made the study possible. Kenneth M. Birkhead, national director of the American Veterans Committee, joined Norman Thomas in presenting the report at the Pentagon. It deserves the widest possible publicity and lays the basis for fundamental reform. It also—as its author notes—offers the labor movement a preview of the kind of mentalities and screening procedures to which workers would be subjected if the Department of Defense should succeed in getting the Butler bill for screening labor through the next session of Congress. What happens to the worker's son today may happen to his father tomorrow.

Indeed, as Watts points out, if the Butler bill does not pass, then "an almost as effective, albeit somewhat slower, resolution of the problem from the Army's standpoint is to screen the future labor force of the country as it passes through its hands and render it impossible for those it remotely suspects ever to enter an industrial plant." What the armed forces are doing is to give a less than honorable discharge with a notation showing that doubt about loyalty exists. Such a discharge is a bar to many kinds of employment.

In addition, since draftees move into the reserve for a number of years, they are liable during that period to an undesirable discharge if their political utterances and associations or those of their relatives and wives do not conform to Army standards. "It is inconceivable," Watts writes, "that the Congress intended to delegate to the Army political and social control over every young man subject to the Selective Service Law from the dawn of his mature understanding until he approaches thirty. Yet this is the effect of the Army's application of what it considers to be the law. Through the threat of an 'Undesirable' discharge, it says, 'Conform, not only on active service but for the full term of your developing maturity.'" The stronghold of freedom is doing its best to mobilize an army of the cowed.

AUGUST 15, 1955

LOYAL COASTGUARDSMAN COMES HOME

Mother: Oh, George, it's been *so* long.

George: Doesn't seem unusually long to me, Mother.

Mother: Son, do you know it's been exactly five years, three months and nine days since you were last home?

George: But you remember the wording of my loyalty clearance decision, Mother? That's not too long a time for a boy whose "relationship to his mother has not been close." You wouldn't want me to risk my clearance, would you?

Mother (wiping her eyes): Of course not, dear. But how silly of me, going on like this, when you've brought a nice friend home with you. Won't you introduce him?

George: Well, he's not exactly a friend, Mother. But he was kind enough to come home with me. Just to see that everything was —well, you know . . . I thought it'd be best to have a witness just in case. So I asked our local FBI man if he wouldn't come along. This is Agent Donald Thomas, Mother.

Mother: Well, I'm happy to know you, Mr. Thomas. Won't

you join us at dinner? Just let me straighten things up here a minute. You know I didn't expect you, George, and everything's in such disarray.

George: Mother, what's that you're pushing under the sofa pillows?

Mother: Why, nothing, dear.

George: Let me see it. Give that to me, this instant.

Mother: Oh, dear, it's just some magazine a neighbor left.

George: Mother, it's *The Nation,* and you know it. And you promised me you were going to lay off all that sort of thing.

Mother: I swear I haven't touched anything more radical than the *Ladies Home Journal* since—since that awful time they denied you your commission. This—this just was left here by that neighbor.

George: Well, you shouldn't associate with such neighbors.

Mother (humbly, still tidying up frantically): I know, George. I promise. Anyway, *The Nation* isn't so radical. I bet even Mr. Thomas sometimes reads it.

Mr. Thomas (politely): I've often read *The Nation,* Mrs. Martin—as part of my official duties, of course.

George: Mother, what are these under the table? Are you selling benefit tickets again?

Mother: It's really all right, son. It's just a benefit for that Republican Women's Auxiliary.

George: But you promised, Mother. That's political. And you know one thing leads to another. You promised to keep away from benefits. First thing you know you'll be back helping the foreign-born or something. Oh, you make me so nervous, Mother. And I worked so hard for my commission.

Mother: Now, now. Just sit down and dinner will soon be ready.

George: Mother, I'm sorry but I don't think we can stay to dinner after all.

Mother: Oh, son.

George: Well, I just remembered I have another appointment that's awfully urgent. But I'll be seeing you again soon.

Mother: Oh, George. Don't make it so long this time. I promise . . . you know what.

George: Sure, Mother.

Mother (calling after them as they go down the stairs): And

George, please be careful. I get so worried when I read about those Russian submarines that seem to come up along the coast every spring.

George (firmly): That will do, Mother. *That's* classified.

SEPTEMBER 19, 1955

11: *First Call for a Test Ban*

The picture in our minds of the atom bomb is of something that we have stockpiled in a kind of dark closet, which can be taken out and used if we so choose. But enough is known to indicate that this is misleading, that the atom bomb is not just another new weapon which can be held in reserve like poison gas or germs; it is a revolution in warfare.

There is now a whole growing family of atomic and hydrogen weapons adapted for use in various situations by various branches of the armed services. And if atomic weapons are being adapted to the strategic and tactical needs of the various services, then these services in turn must be adapted to the use of atomic weapons.

If one prepares to wage atomic war, one must recast one's army, navy and air force radically. This means that we are confronted with a decision of policy quite different from taking a bomb out of a stock pile. Once the basic decision is taken to make the next war atomic, many other decisions follow which make the first difficult, and perhaps in practice impossible, to reverse. For the war begins with armies, navies and air forces trained to attack with, and defend themselves against, fission and fusion weapons. The die that may mean the destruction of civilization is not only cast but loaded in advance.

It is against this background that attention should be called to a talk given in London a week ago by Field Marshal Lord Montgomery. With Generals Gruenther and Norstad, Montgomery is one of the triumvirate which commands the NATO forces. He spoke on "A Look Through a Window at World War III." And what he said, according to the London *Times,* was that "at Supreme Allied HQ they were basing all their operational planning on using atomic and thermonuclear weapons in their defense, and this called for a certain reorganization of their forces and in their strategy."

It is sometimes assumed that we will not use nuclear weapons unless the enemy does. But Montgomery made clear in London, as he did in a speech a few weeks earlier at Ankara, that we would use nuclear weapons for defense against attack, whether that attack was atomic or not. The decision has been made, the armed forces shaped, for atomic war.

In the light of these military realities, the renewed debate at the UN over atomic disarmament between the United States and the U.S.S.R. takes on a new significance. This debate is again plunged into another lengthy and arid veto-and-inspection controversy. This controversy—pitched in these terms—is insoluble. For there is no way to convince either side that any system of inspection and control may not be evaded or abused by the other.

The whole controversy in some ways is nonsense. Atomic weapons cannot be made in washtubs, nor launched without the most extensive measures of mobilization, dispersion, and defense in preparation for the retaliatory blow from the other side. As Montgomery said, the purpose of having active forces "in being" in peacetime "would make it impossible for the east to launch an attack successfully without a preparatory build-up of their forces, which we would know about." No iron curtain could hide the preparatory measures required to launch an atomic world war.

Nevertheless there is no way to convince the American public that the Russians might not make and catapult bombs in secret from some hideaway in Siberia, nor convince the Russians that the Americans might not utilize inspection to spy out the prime bombing targets of the U.S.S.R. In this atmosphere to debate veto-and-inspection, as Lodge and Vishinsky now are doing, is worse than hopeless. The world public is lulled into a false sense of complacency by the debate, while the real decisions have already been taken, the military vested interests on both sides built up, a juggernaut created which can move in one way only, the way of the A-, the H- and soon the C-bomb.

It is this which makes the Krishna Menon proposal of last week so crucial. There was a kind of cosmic comedy in the way the United States and the U.S.S.R. hastily joined hands in shelving and thus shutting off General Assembly debate on the Indian proposal for a "truce" in the testing of new atomic and hydrogen weapons. This proposal, which was first made by Nehru last April and endorsed by Indonesia and Burma, alone offers a simple and enforceable way to put a stop to the atomic arms race, to ease tension and thereby to create an atmosphere in which further agreement may become possible. A "truce on tests" is self-enforceable because the new weapons are so powerful that if exploded their radioactivity is detectible anywhere on earth.

India spoke for mankind when its representative challenged the criminal rubbish on our side about using the atomic bomb "only in defense against aggression." Both sides in every war always claim to be *aggressed*. Menon uttered what may prove to be the prophetic epitaph of our civilization when he said use of H-bombs would prove "suicide for the nations who used them, genocide for those against whom they were used, and infanticide for posterity." If there is still a peace movement left in America, this must be its platform. As a first step away from mutual destruction, no more tests.

NOVEMBER 1, 1954

12: *The Drift of Foreign Policy: Sanity or War*

QUEMOY AND MATSU

For the first time in many months the people of this country have a way to make their voice heard for peace. This is to demand public hearings on the Morse-Lehman resolution, and its passage by Congress. So far as we know no newspaper—not even the *New York Times*—has published the text of this historic resolution or of the masterly speech made by Senator Wayne Morse of Oregon in introducing it. We think it a commentary on the pass to which we have come that it is left to a little publication like ours to make available texts so important for peace.

The Morse-Lehman resolution would limit the blank check given the President by the Formosan war powers resolution; it says the latter shall not be construed as authorizing military operations in defense of Quemoy and Matsu; it asks the United Nations to undertake the evacuation of the islands. The Morse-Lehman resolution would also begin to untie Chiang Kai-shek from the United States apron strings knotted by the Mutual Security Pact; the resolution asserts the right of the United States to defend Formosa but adds significantly, "until such time as its sovereign status is determined by peaceful processes."

The Morse-Lehman resolution would thus accomplish two purposes. The evacuation of the offshore islands would at last make possible a tacit cease-fire on the Formosa strait. The status of Formosa would be unfrozen and the way cleared for negotiation to determine its future. Where the Administration has been trying to proceed by threatening China with atomic destruction, the Morse-Lehman resolution would put the Congress on record as directing a return to the methods of diplomacy under conditions which make it possible. This is why the war party is mobilizing to bury the resolution in the Senate Foreign Relations Committee.

The fight for the Morse-Lehman resolution is a fight against something worse than secret diplomacy—and that is secret foreign legislation. With all the fuss about Yalta, no one raises a cry about the private discussions which have been going on behind the closed doors of Senator George's suite at the Mayflower, and in the White House. No one knows what is being said, what commitments are being made, what decisions are being reached—though these may literally mean a Third World War. What FDR did at Yalta is history, but what Dulles tells George in private at the Mayflower may be our fate and destiny. This is a fight to take the shaping of foreign policy out of the hands of a few and return it to the Senate and the people.

The people of this country are being treated as if they were mindless idiots. They are told we must make a clear commitment to Formosa lest the enemy stumble into war, and then they are told we cannot make our intentions clear about Quemoy and Matsu because it is important to keep the enemy guessing! The Constitution says the President is to make foreign treaties with the advice and consent of the Senate, but the Senate has degenerated into the role of rubber stamp for the State Department. The weakness of the Democratic party leadership, and Senator George's gentle but almost dictatorial control of the Foreign Relations Committee has turned the Senate into a complaisant instrument, instead of the partner in policy the Constitution intended it to be. The reality of "bipartisanship" is to create a one-party state in the making of foreign policy.

In the past two months, four fateful commitments in the sphere of foreign policy have been pushed through Congress with less consideration than is often accorded local harbor improvements. The Southeast Asia Pact on February 1 and the German rearmament

accords on April 1 passed the Senate as minor items of an afternoon's work. The Formosan war powers resolution and the Mutual
Secret Pact with Chiang were aired only in secret hearings at which
Dulles and Radford were the chief witnesses and no one was heard
in opposition, though the former was the first blank check for preventive war ever signed by an American Congress. On foreign policy
the Senate is beginning to act like the Supreme Soviet in Moscow
where whatever the government asks is adopted by acclamation. It
is this withdrawal from democratic control of the vital decisions of
war and peace, of life and death for our country, that Senators Morse
and Lehman are fighting on our behalf.

APRIL 11, 1955

TOWARD GLOBAL NEGOTIATIONS

Far more important than any evacuation of Quemoy and Matsu
is the eviction of Knowland and the China Lobby from the driver's
seat of American foreign policy. This is what happened here last
week. With the Secretary of State's press conference on Tuesday,
there has been a complete about-face in American foreign policy.
We may not have been heading for war but we were certainly facing
in that direction. We move now toward global negotiations. In making the shift, Eisenhower called Knowland's bluff. When Knowland
finally broke his silence by summoning the press to his office in the
Capitol Wednesday afternoon, the reporters expected a fighting statement, looked for a dramatic resignation as minority leader. There
under the inevitable picture of Lincoln sat the leading spokesman of
the pro-war faction, pink, ruddy, prosperous and overweight, with
the booming affability of a small-town realtor. What came out was
a toothless rehash of the familiar statements about Yalta and appeasement. Knowland had crumpled.

What has happened here on foreign policy this year is much
like what happened last year on McCarthy. A coalition led by conservatives and supported by both wings of the Democratic party
made it possible for the Eisenhower Administration, indeed forced
it, to take on McCarthy, and to deflate his wild-man minority. A
similar coalition has gone into action and achieved a similar deflation of the pro-war extremists. The Stevenson speech, and Senator
George's initiative, gave Eisenhower assurance of Democratic support if he turned on Knowland and moved toward negotiations.

Knowland, like McCarthy, had also become a personal rival, a contender for the next presidential nomination, one of the few dissident voices in the Republican chorus begging Ike to run again. This is the kind of politics an Army man like Eisenhower understands. He has cut the big humorless Californian down to size.

The State Department had built up three men. It had staked its all in Europe on Adenauer. It had built up Mohammed Ali of Pakistan as the counterweight to the neutralist Nehru. It had made George its "Vandenberg" in the Senate. Last weekend all three allies put the squeeze upon it. Adenauer must have four-power negotiations; the impact on Germany of the Austrian treaty cannot easily be overestimated; the Germans are eager for a try at unification along the same lines. Mohammed Ali had been won by Chou En-lai, and the Pakistani announced that Chou had made a "quite reasonable" offer to settle the Formosa question peacefully. This was not Nehru, this was Ali speaking—it just could not be rejected out of hand. Finally here at home, the gentle and shrewd old Georgian Saturday night failed utterly to take his cue from the Department in his speech to the newspaper editors. Where the Department had icily set out preconditions for talks with Chou, George spoke up for talks without conditions and even referred—horrors!—no less than three times to our Russian "friends."

Back of George speak the really big and sober money men of this country, not the Texas newly rich but the Rockefellers, heavy industry (except for aviation) and most of Wall Street. With him stand the two big businessmen of the Cabinet, Humphrey and Wilson, and the conservative military element at the Pentagon. Eisenhower, basically a peace man and a military conservative, seems to have been carrying on his own "meeting on the Elbe" secretly with Zhukov. The President and this crowd, with an ear to the grass roots and an eye to a stable dollar, would love to face next year's elections on a peace program with a juicy tax cut, and the only way to cut taxes is to cut world tension. Not being liberals or Democrats, they can move toward coexistence without fear of being called pro-Communist. The first problem was to disengage from the China Lobby. Rising popular resistance to war, reflected in both parties, has made this possible.

Dulles had to change his tune or give up his job. The Department's press officers, adept at poisoning the wells of public opinion, had been casting suspicion on the Austrian treaty and throwing cold water on the prospects of negotiation. Dulles got back and after seeing Eisenhower completely changed his stance. He welcomed the Austrian treaty. He accepted the idea of talks with Chou and of an agreement for a cease-fire despite Chiang's opposition. Dulles even said that he felt that Red China unlike the East European satellites had a considerable measure of independence. Saul on the road from Duck Island seemed to have become Paul. Only in his answer to a question about whether the Hammarskjöld mission had helped to make peace talks possible did he show his true colors. Ungraciously Dulles said he saw "no discernible relationship." But Hammarskjöld brought back from Peking the same offer of talks in which the Chinese Communists, without giving up their claim to Formosa, would nevertheless accept a cease-fire. If Dulles hadn't slammed the door hard on Hammarskjöld last January, the American fliers in Chinese jails would now be free.

MAY 2, 1955

MOLOTOV AT SAN FRANCISCO

San Francisco

The curtain raiser for the San Francisco Conference was an unfortunate bit of pantomime. Delegates flying in from abroad found that Eisenhower was running the American government from a secret bomb shelter while Molotov was taking the afternoon off to visit an art gallery. No doubt the contrast was sheer coincidence, any implications unintended. But whoever planned Operation Alert to start just five days before the tenth anniversary meeting of the UN was not very wide awake. Incoming foreign ministers picked up their first American newspapers with their breakfasts to read that millions of Americans were assumed to be killed and some fifty-nine cities assumed to be in ruins as the result of an assumed H-bomb attack, while one of the principal architects of all this assumed carnage was touring the Metropolitan Museum in New York and being as ingratiatingly bewildered as an average Joe by abstractionist painting. The dumb show implied that while the Russians were relaxing we Americans were still driving ourselves wacky, and therefore to be humored rather than trusted by a world in search of peace. The timing was deadly. If the Democrats were in power, J. Edgar Hoover would be sure that somebody in Washington was getting paid off for it with the Order of Lenin, two Armenian rugs and a free pass to the Moscow subway.

In the preliminaries, Molotov got the publicity breaks here at home as well as abroad. To the assembled press waiting for his arrival in San Francisco, all of Madison Avenue's hucksters seemed to have gone over to the enemy. That picture of Molotov in a ten-gallon hat en route was the biggest stroke of genius in press agentry since the late Ivy Lee discovered that the elder John D. could atone for his millions by giving away dimes. The hat on Molotov recalled similar pictures of Cal Coolidge on campaign; both looked like a fifty-eighth variety of pickle in this kind of headgear; the picture suddenly made Molotov seem just another Republican politician ready to pose in anything for a vote. It's going to be hard to keep the cold war going if Molotov starts acting like a brother Elk.

Here in San Francisco Molotov has been accorded movie star treatment. Under gray skies, in the grimy old railroad station at Oakland last Saturday, reporters, photographers, plain-clothesmen and cops swarmed over the platform and the tracks waiting for his train to come in. The limousine driving him off was blocked by reporters until he let down a window and through an interpreter made a statement of greeting. At Monday night's reception for delegates in the Mark Hopkins on Nob Hill and at Tuesday night's glittering affair at the Palace of the Legion of Honor, Molotov's brief appearances stole the show.

Hostile propaganda has boomeranged. The Russians have so long been depicted as monsters that everybody is quite dazed to discover that they are human. Telescopic lenses and cameras watch every move made by Molotov and his entourage in the baronial home they rented in plush suburban Hillsborough. When Molotov finished speaking Wednesday, the Opera House rapidly emptied. Suddenly, for a press and public which craves spectacle, the old Bolshevik has become a character. Of the Big Four ministers, nobody ever heard of Pinay, Macmillan as yet is a name only to the book trade, and Dulles hasn't the popular touch. Perhaps for want of something more exciting, this little gray methodical man, who outwardly seems more like one of Gogol's devoted government clerks than a veteran revolutionary and shrewd statesman, has caught —and is exploiting—popular fancy. Moscow ought to send him on tour. When the papers start calling him "Mollie" the cold war will be over.

But Molotov's success here is not the result of press agentry alone. The General Assembly heard President Eisenhower on Monday, the new British Foreign Secretary on Tuesday, and Molotov on Wednesday. Only the Russian offered more than vague generalities to the hunger for peace which makes itself felt even in this gathering of diplomats, politicians and bureaucrats. Mr. Eisenhower's speech was painfully uninspired. He drew applause only twice, once when he said "we shall reject no method, however novel, that holds out any hope however faint, for a just and lasting peace." The other was for that famous quotation from Lincoln about "the dogmas of the quiet past." Lincoln's words shone like diamonds amid the synthetic and labored phrases ghosted for Eisenhower. As for Macmillan, the new British Foreign Secretary has a genius for banality.

The Opera House was jammed Wednesday morning to hear Molotov. The scene was striking. On the stage, the flags of the United Nations were banked against the black curtain with the gold UN emblem. Dwarfed against that huge backdrop, Van Kleffens, Hammarskjöld and Cordier sat in yellow-back chairs overlooking the rostrum below them. The first floor with its red plush seats was given over to the delegates. Little blue flags marked off the sections and gave the names of the nations represented in each. About 10:30 A.M., when Romulo of the Philippines had finished speaking, Van Kleffens gave the floor to Molotov. A little, stocky, gray-haired man in a gray suit got up from the second row to the right of the auditorium and slowly moved to the rostrum. His voice came across translation headphones in clipped "English English." His own voice in Russian was pleasant, liquid, often forceful but not harsh. The lack of demagogy, the sober tone and earnest manner were impressive, especially after the rather blowsy oratory which is Romulo's stock in trade.

Where Eisenhower was interrupted by applause only twice, Molotov was interrupted by applause five times. The first was when he called for the outlawing of atomic weapons; the second, when he said that China ought to be a party to any discussion of disarmament; the third, when he spoke of the good feeling of the Soviet people toward the American people; the fourth, when he said it depended largely on these two peoples to consolidate peace and security for many years to come; and fifth, when he said this was all the Soviet people desired and that he was confident that this was also the desire of the people of America.

The tone was conciliatory, and though there was little in the speech which Molotov had not said before there was much which the Western powers have yet to answer. The speech was in large part a repetition of the Soviet disarmament proposals of May 10, but these have been dismissed in Washington with scant attention. Earlier Soviet proposals for outlawing atomic weapons were met with the rejoinder that this would leave the Soviet bloc with superior armies. In the May 10 proposals, as Molotov pointed out, the Soviet Union gave in to this argument and "without any modifications" accepted the Western proposals on conventional armies and weapons. The United States, the U.S.S.R. and China would each be restricted to armies of less than 1,500,000 men. In addition the Soviet Union also went further than ever before in specific proposals for inspection and control to guard against surprise attack and to enforce atomic disarmament. These proposals would lift the Iron Curtain. They represent major concessions, yet they have called forth no response.

The San Francisco meeting gave Molotov a world forum in which to make people aware of the Soviet concessions, and in which to force the Western powers to take notice of them. In this sense, the Molotov speech has transformed the nature of the conference. In effect bargaining has begun. Dulles in his speech Friday must make some reply to Molotov's concrete proposals, or lose a round by default in the battle for public opinion. Dulles sought after the Molotov speech to brush it off, but British reactions and those of Belgian Foreign Minister Spaak showed how deeply impressed Allied Western opinion was by Molotov's tone. Real concessions have been made by Moscow to the West on disarmament and as Molotov said "it is up to the U.S.A. and the other Western powers to make the next move."

So far there have only been petty publicity dodges. The United States delegation seems to have feared that Molotov might suggest a ban on nuclear tests in his speech. The night before, Lodge therefore issued a statement which created headlines about a new American "Atom Plan," but this when examined turned out only to be a statement which calls for the collection of data on the effect of nuclear tests. Lodge put forward the dubious proposition that "the best scientific information" says "properly safeguarded nuclear testing, in contrast with nuclear warfare, is not a threat to human health." (Obviously some progress has been made, since Mr. Lodge does not insist that nuclear warfare itself is healthful.)

The other "reply" to Molotov was the Cuban speech. If the purpose of this typical cold war speech about Soviet "slavery" was to embroil Molotov in an undignified quarrel, it not only failed but boomeranged. The result of Dr. Portuondo's speech and Romulo's intervention was to anger Van Kleffens, and to make a bad impression on other friendly delegates. The hearty handshake with which Lodge greeted the Cuban after his speech and the pat on the back given him by Dulles showed their approval. They had gotten a stooge to do what they did not dare do themselves. They may have hoped that Portuondo and Romulo between them might turn the meeting into an anti-Soviet brawl.

Molotov has clearly won the first round. Whether he wins the second and last round of this conference depends on the reply made by Dulles Friday. The resounding defeat in the Senate of the McCarthy "liberationist" resolution shows how united both parties are in support of genuine negotiation; the war party is reduced to pigmy proportions. The Eisenhower Administration could now lead from strength and take the initiative in the search for a settlement instead of merely reacting to Soviet proposals in a half-hearted, negativistic way unworthy of a great power.

JUNE 27, 1955

McCARTHY'S SECRETARY OF STATE

In Washington last week, as in San Francisco the week before, there was a striking divergence in tone between the President and his Secretary of State. The President was hopeful, his Secretary of State astringent, about the outlook for Geneva. Mr. Eisenhower said the chances of solid progress were better than he thought they were two months ago; Mr. Dulles left the impression that the chances had been rendered less promising by a Russian "loss of interest" in German reunification. The President said flatly that he was sure the plane incident over the Bering Strait was a local matter, and not a deliberate act of policy; he even mentioned that the weather was bad and therefore visibility poor at the time of the shooting. His Secretary of State issued a press release saying, "So far, however, we doubt that the [shooting] represents a *considered* policy on the part of the Soviet Union." The word italicized illustrates Mr. Dulles's genius for poisonous ambiguity.

Nowhere was the divergence more evident than in the President's response to a question about the plan for a congressional resolution expressing the hope that the Communist satellite states can achieve freedom. This, always one of Mr. Dulles's fervent themes, elicited a lukewarm response from Mr. Eisenhower. The President would not commit himself; he had said again and again that there could be no real peace until all nations had the right of self-determination, but we were not going to war to free them. This will be a cold douche for Mr. Dulles's East European politicians-in-exile.

Were it not for the President's hopeful words next day anyone would assume from the Secretary of State's press conference last Tuesday that there was no point in going to Geneva unless to demonstrate that there is no hope of peace. The list of subjects on which Mr. Dulles sees no chance of agreement is long enough to cover any feasible agenda except exchange of weather reports. On Korea, he saw no hope of reaching an agreement on unification. Ditto for Indo-China; he stressed the fact that neither the United States nor South Vietnam was a party to the Geneva agreement of last year promising elections for a unified Indo-Chinese regime in 1956. The only place he wants unification is Germany; unless the Russians were prepared to surrender and accept American terms for a unified Reich, they would be demonstrating "insincerity."

Molotov seemed to feel that the Russians had sufficiently proven their "sincerity" in Austria and Yugoslavia, by accepting Western terms on conventional arms and by offering to lift the Iron Curtain to continuous international inspection. "Mr. Secretary," Mr. Dulles was asked, "Molotov said that the next step on disarmament was up to us now. Is it your present thought that the Allies will take some step on disarmament at Geneva . . . ?" Mr. Dulles replied (the rules require that his words be given in indirect discourse) that there will be no specifics discussed at Geneva. If no "specifics" are to be discussed, what will the Heads of State do on that summit? The purpose, Mr. Dulles said in reply to another question, was (we use his words as closely as the rule allows) merely to set up procedures for arriving at results which we both find acceptable in principle! The exclamation point is ours.

The President was applauded at San Francisco for declaring that we would try any method, however novel, that holds out any hope for peace. His Secretary of State seems to be busy shutting off as many avenues as possible to a solution. One proposal has been to sweeten German rearmament with a non-aggression pact between Eastern and Western blocs; Mr. Dulles rejected that idea. Indeed any agreement whatsoever seemed to be ruled out by his remark on the danger of dealing with those whom you don't trust. He wants a rearmed and a reunited Germany allied with NATO, and he reluctantly recognizes that this is linked with the problem of disarmament, but he sees no possibility of arriving at an agreement on disarmament at Geneva because (again the indirect discourse) it is an extremely complicated subject and there are infinite varieties of formulae which might be applied. There are many permutations and combinations which would all have to be explored. . . . Though the latest NATO war games underscore the total deadliness of atomic war, this is not a man in a hurry for peace.

The day before the San Francisco conference Mr. Dulles spoke at the "Festival of Faith" in his favorite religious strain, but one Gospel injunction which never appears in his unctuous homilies is "Blessed are the peacemakers." He belittled Krishna Menon at press conference. His great triumph at the UN gathering was to block a "Declaration of San Francisco" in which East and West would have made a new pledge of peace; the setting would have further relaxed tension. His own speech privately appalled our Canadian and West European friends; this was the same cracked cold war record the State Department has been playing since 1947. The Senate had defeated the McCarthy resolution two days earlier, but Dulles's was a speech tailored to its belligerent specifications. The President, if he is to succeed in his search for peace, must get himself a new Secretary of State. This one is McCarthy's.

JULY 4, 1955

FOREIGN POLICY AND MELODRAMA

The best of us seem to approach foreign policy in terms of melodrama. James P. Warburg, certainly one of our more intelligent writers on foreign policy, warns in a rather hectic letter to the *Washington Post* of the dangers which confront us at Geneva. The peculiar terms in which Americans of this generation tend to see the problems of international relations are reflected in one passage. In this Mr. Warburg says the Kremlin is attempting to create neutral buffer zones in Europe and in Asia "which it no doubt hopes will be susceptible to later seduction or subversion."

Now seduction and subversion are real dangers in some situations. Nellie the Cloak Model, if we recall correctly, was seduced and in the literal sense subverted, i.e., overturned or turned over when the champagne dispensed by the villain had done its wicked work. But can one nation "seduce" another? Can one nation chuck another nation under the chin, ply it with liquor, soften it up with mink stoles? In all their centuries of life side by side, did Germany ever "seduce" France or France "seduce" Germany? The British are pretty devilish fellows, but in generations of occupation they never succeeded in "seducing" India or Ireland.

How far do we carry such silly metaphor? Nations are moved by their interests. They are not light-headed girls. Turkey was not "seduced" by the United States; it needed the counterbalance of American aid against Russian demands on the Straits and the Armenian provinces. Most nations in between the great Powers today need some degree of neutrality to avoid being ground to pieces in a struggle between them. This is what moves Tito and Nehru and U Nu. If a neutral zone were created in Eastern and Central Europe, how could these countries be "seduced"?

"Subversion" is more respectable but no less mysterious. Can one nation "subvert" another? Even Austria had to be occupied by Hitler's armies. Revolutions are not brought about by "subversion." It is not "subversion" but hatred of the French which keeps Indo-China in crisis. It was not "subversion" but generations of wounded self-respect which made Gandhi the leader of India's millions against the British. It was not "subversion" but "a long train of abuses and usurpations" which brought about our own Revolution.

There is involved here more than a manner of speaking. This is a way of thinking, and it affects foreign policy. We may see an example of it in the Hoover Commission report on intelligence agencies, or at least those excerpts thought fit for the not-to-be-trusted public. Let us begin with a sentence which says a great deal more than it was intended to say about current attitudes. "The task force has recognized," the report says, "the incompatibility in method between the practice of diplomacy and more direct and active operations incident to the collection of intelligence and the conduct of cold war." Diplomacy is diplomacy and war is war. But what are these "more direct and active operations incident to . . . the conduct of cold war?"

In wartime the CIA's predecessor, the OSS, could carry on sabotage or assassination as part of the necessity of war. Surely the Hoover task force was not recommending any such lawless tactics in time of peace? But what did it mean by this reference to "more direct and active operations" and by its criticism of the State Department for interfering with "efforts" which "might have brought direct and immediate results . . . that would have justified the attendant political risks"? These cryptic allusions underscore the need for a joint congressional committee to exercise some check over the cloak-and-dagger operations of the CIA, and for this recommendation we should be grateful.

It is a serious matter for the whole world that on the eve of Geneva, of the first meeting of heads of state since 1945, of a meeting which may give the world a chance to avoid the mutual suicide of an atomic war, the Hoover Commission should issue a report complaining that "among some of those responsible for implementation of our foreign policy by diplomacy and negotiation, there seems to exist an abhorrence to anything that might lead to diplomatic . . . complications." Apparently some of us not only believe in the possibility of carrying on foreign policy by "seduction or subversion" but want to practice them ourselves, despite our moralizings about those who believe ends justify means.

Insofar as intelligence is concerned, its collection is hampered by the mentality which sees foreign policy, revolution and history as the product of pulp-fiction conspiracy. Reactionaries always prefer to see the great convulsions of history as bedtime stories; this is comforting and absolves them of responsibility. Mr. Herbert Hoover, I am sure, still thinks he lost in 1932 because of some "subversive" plot; the apple-sellers on the corners were never really visible to his kind of eye. Such mentalities are unfitted for intelligence and dangerous if allowed to carry on cloak-and-dagger operations.

Can there be peace if a huge, unsupervised and unregulated governmental establishment is allowed to act out Hollywood scenarios? How much control can we have of the basic decisions of war and peace when such an agency may create or manufacture "incidents"?

JULY 11, 1955

MUTUAL INSPECTION: JOHN MEETS IVAN

At the San Francisco conference the Syrian foreign minister made a remark which comes to mind as one watches the Soviet farmers in Iowa and the United States farmers in the Soviet Union. He said that more important than the meeting at the summit was the meeting at the base.

When Communist visitors from the Ukraine are welcomed at Kiwanis Club luncheons in Des Moines and capitalistic American farmers are cheered in Kharkov something has been done for peace which is more powerful than any pact or system of inspection. This is, indeed, the kind of inspection the world needs—the kind in which John looks at Ivan and Ivan looks at John and neither sees the horns that propaganda had led him to expect and each says, "Gosh, he's a man, too, just like me."

Nothing is more deadly for the war spirit than the discovery that the enemy, too, is human. This is the most disarming of all disarmaments. So while we are glad to hear that Soviet leaders and American leaders may visit each other's countries soon, we hope there will be more exchange of ordinary folk. Farmers are kin the world over, but so in as genuine a sense are newspapermen and storekeepers (private or collective) and auto mechanics and welders and miners and streetcar conductors. Let us tear down the evil screens on which Russians have seen Americans as lynchers and Americans have seen Russians as slavemasters and visit with our brothers.

AUGUST 1, 1955

13: *The President's Illness*

The President's illness is a world calamity. Dwight Eisenhower has occupied a most peculiar role in American politics. Through him, exploiting his fame as a soldier and his personal charm, the Eastern seaboard moneyed interests who direct the Republican party achieved a number of purposes. They attracted enough of the independent vote to win the 1952 elections from the Democrats, who have since 1932 been the majority party. They put into effect a program which accepted the main accomplishments of New Deal and Fair Deal but sought to establish a climate favorable to big business, notably in the control of basic resources and of fiscal policy. Above all, in the search for a sound dollar, a balanced budget and tax reduction, they moved to end the Korean conflict, to liquidate the cold war, to recognize the world atomic stalemate, and to cut down swollen military expenditures. Only through the foremost American General of our generation could they put some curb on the Pentagon, and only through a General speaking for a conservative party could they begin to negotiate with Moscow and Peking without being accused—in the overheated atmosphere of an America driven slightly wacky since 1947—of "appeasement," or treachery.

To this pattern of political manipulation, Mr. Eisenhower has contributed little, but that little was decisive. He came to the White House uninformed, politically naïve, and almost childishly trusting in the men of wealth who groomed him for the presidency. But he also brought with him certain intangible but crucial assets. A lifetime soldier, he was no militarist. The leader of a victorious coalition in the greatest war of history, he was genuinely a man of peace. His own high rank and long military experience made it impossible for the Pentagon brass to overawe him; he handled them as no big businessman or corporation lawyer could. He had a very modest view of his own capacities but his own swift rise in the Army and success in the war had given him a justifiable confidence in his one great gift —a gift of getting along with people, of solving and smoothing over organizational problems. Hence his faith that he could sit down and talk with the Russian leaders and begin to move toward agreement. Though this faith reflected an oversimplified view of power politics, it supplied a vital missing ingredient, a readiness to confer, a willingness to assume there were human beings with human problems on the other side, too. For the first time since FDR died we had a leadership which was not afraid to negotiate. People at home and abroad sensed this basic good will and hopefulness in Dwight Eisenhower, and trusted him for it; this is why the heart attack brought such world-wide instinctive dismay.

We share this feeling and join in the universal wish for the President's speedy recovery. But no one sees the possibility of a miracle great enough to enable Mr. Eisenhower to bear the burdens of a presidential campaign and another term. And this is serious.

We are proud of the fact that as early as June 13, 1953, in an editorial "Challenging the Left: 'Back Ike for Peace,'" we were the first voice left of center to recognize the President's historic role. Now, as two years ago, the balance of forces for peace is still a precarious one. It was through Eisenhower that the big businessmen in the Cabinet like Humphrey and Wilson have been able to put some brake on the arms race. Sherman Adams and Stassen and Humphrey will have much less of a check on Dulles and Radford with Eisenhower out of the picture in the next few months. The problem of untangling our relations with the Soviet bloc has hardly begun; the difficult knots remain to be untied. Four more years of Eisenhower, with a Democratic Congress, in which Senator George could have gone on playing his wise and healing role, were badly needed. Now, there is no substitute in sight, except in the unlikely event that Chief Justice Warren could be prevailed upon to take the Republican nomination.

At this juncture, the Democratic party, and particularly its liberals and laborites, cannot be relied upon. The two historic events of the past two years—the defeat of McCarthy in 1954 and the deflation of the China Lobby in 1955—were the achievement of bipartisan coalitions under conservative leadership. Only a continuance of such leadership can make possible the adjustments American society must make if peace is firmly to be established and world atomic suicide avoided. We are going to have to recognize Communist China and we are going to have to recognize that the only alternative to a dangerously divided Germany—with both sides arming for what could flare up into a greater Korea—is to permit its neutralization outside NATO in return for unification and free elections. These concessions to reality will be painful because our people have been fed on pipe dreams and paranoid nightmares. The liberals, their spirits rubbed raw by accusations of communism, are much less ready to recognize these realities than are the conservatives and the big businessmen. Those forces which may not want war but certainly make peace more difficult to obtain—the dominant portions of the Roman Catholic hierarchy and the American Federation of Labor—are much more powerful in the Democratic than in the Republican party. The aviation lobby, which fattens on war alarums, depends on leading Democrats. They and their labor allies like the arms race as a means of maintaining employment. Consequently they find it comfortable to believe that if only we arm heavily enough the Kremlin will surrender. Even Stevenson has been sour about Geneva. Despite Senator George, the Democrats are still a cold war party and the prospect of their return to power at this time is appalling.

OCTOBER 3, 1955

14: *The Sickness of the South*

THE MURDER OF EMMETT TILL

Next to the President's collapse, the worst news of the week was from Mississippi. The jury at Sumner brought in two verdicts, not one. The immediate and visible decision was that J. W. Milam and Roy Bryant were not guilty of killing a fourteen-year-old colored boy. The other, unspoken, unintended, unconscious but indelible was a verdict of guilty against all the rest of us and our country.

There are scenes at the murder trial which imprint themselves unforgettably: the Negro reporters, as they walked into court one day after lunch, being hailed by the Sheriff with "Hello, niggers." Mrs. Bradley, the mother of the victim, testifying that she told her son before he left for the South "to be very careful how he spoke and to say 'yes, sir' and 'no, ma'am' and not to hesitate to humble yourself if you had to get down on your knees." Moses Wright—we salute his courage—testifying that when J. W. Milam came to get his fourteen-year-old nephew Emmett Till, he asked, "You from Chicago?" and when the boy answered "yes" Milam said, "Don't you say yes to me or I'll knock hell out of you." Mrs. Bryant's sexy whopper (which Judge Swango to his credit kept from the jury) that this fourteen-year-old boy with a speech defect had grabbed her round the waist, solicited her with an unprintable expression and boasted, "I've been with white women before." J. A. Shaw, Jr., the foreman of the jury, asked by the press what the jury thought of Mrs. Bradley's testimony, replying, "if she tried a little harder, she might have got out a tear."

Emmett Till's broken body, with the bullet hole in the right temple and the gaping hole in the back of the head, as if broken in by a rock, testified to a maniacal murder. Those who killed him were sick men, sick with race hatred. The murder and the trial could only have happened in a sick countryside. Where else would a mother be treated with such elementary lack of respect or compassion? Where else would the defense dare put forward the idea that the murder was somehow "framed" by the NAACP? Where else would newspapers somehow make it appear that those at fault were not the men who killed the boy but those who tried to bring the killers to justice? There is a sickness in the South. Unless cured, there may some day spring from it crimes as evil and immense as the crematoria of Hitlerism.

If Milam and Bryant did not kill Till, then who did? Nobody in the South asks the question, at least publicly. Who was the third man with them? Where are the two missing witnesses? Nobody cares. Mississippi went through the motions, and the motions were enough to muffle the weak conscience of the northern white press. The judge was honorable; the special prosecutor tried hard; who can quarrel with a jury verdict? But the jury was all white, in an area two-thirds Negro. And of what use was an upright judge and a special prosecutor when the case was rushed to trial without adequate preparation or investigation? This was only the final scene of a lynching, hastily covered with a thin veil of respectability by a shrewd governor. The same governor, Hugh White, as chairman of the Legal Education Advisory Committee, has just put forward a six-point program to fight desegregation which calls for abolition of compulsory public schooling and legislation to "prohibit interference with state law under cover of federal authority." Hugh White is himself the leader of Mississippi's racists and nullificationists.

Before the war and the witch hunt, when there were still organizations like the Southern Conference for Human Welfare, there would have been public meetings of protest under mixed auspices. It shames our country and it shames white Americans that the only meetings, in Harlem, Baltimore, Chicago and Detroit, have been Negro meetings. Those whites in the South and in the North who would normally have been moved to act have been hounded out of public life and into inactivity. To the outside world it must look as if the conscience of white America has been silenced, and the appearance is not too deceiving. Basically all of us whites, North and South, acquiesce in white supremacy, and benefit from the pool of cheap labor created by it.

Will the Negro take this latest outrage? Unless Negroes rouse themselves to make their indignation felt in some dramatic way, nothing will be done in Mississippi or in Congress. A. Philip Randolph last Sunday suggested a march on Washington like that which dramatized the FEPC fight before Pearl Harbor. Were thousands of Negroes to converge on the Department of Justice and demand action against the murderers of Till, and of the other Negroes whose recent murders have gone unpunished in the South, such a demonstration would have an impact. The American Negro needs a Gandhi to lead him, and we need the American Negro to lead us. If he does not provide leadership against the sickness in the South, the time will come when we will all pay a terrible price for allowing a psychopathic racist brutality to flourish unchecked.

OCTOBER 3, 1955

THE WHITE RACE: ALABAMA AND ALGERIA

February 6, 1956, was a bad day for the white race. In Alabama and in Algeria, its better elements surrendered to its worst. In Alabama, the State University gave in to hoodlumism and under a shower of eggs and tomatoes expelled its first Negro student. In Algeria, the new French government of the Socialist Guy Mollet gave in to hoodlumism and under a shower of tomatoes and manure accepted the resignation of General Georges Catroux as Minister Resident in Algeria. In the eyes of a world two-thirds colored, watching those demonstrations, the supposedly more civilized white race bespattered itself.

The issues are both complex and simple. The complexities arise because it is impossible to correct one wrong without committing another; the *colons* in Algeria, like the whites in Alabama, fear being swamped in a rising sea of color. The simple, common and fundamental characteristic of the crisis in both places is white resistance to equality because with equality the whites will no longer be able to live off the cheap labor of the blacks and browns. The colored in both places exist in a stage only halfway from slavery.

Peoples and nations are made glorious by those men who are willing to stand up against their own in defense of justice for minority elements. Milton opposing his own Puritans, Voltaire and later Zola defying the French mob, Gandhi living with the untouchables—such are the incidents which give a people honor in the eyes of mankind. But where was Southern chivalry when Miss Autherine Lucy arrived in Tuscaloosa? Worse than the ignorant mob was that scene her first day in class—"She sat alone on the front bench." How wonderful it would have been for the South if a few students, a handful, two or three, even one, had deliberately sat down beside her as a demonstration of human kindness and contempt for the mob mind. The world would have known that in the section which produced Jefferson and Madison the old spirit still flickered.

Perhaps the greatest problem of our time, greater than the transition to socialism, is peacefully to effect the change from a world in which the white race is dominant to one in which it will itself some day be in danger of minority status. The treasures of civilization must be passed on to the half-educated and the primitive. New loyalties which can weld men together irrespective of color must be forged. Fears must be faced and hatreds prevented. In this perspective the British Queen's colorful procession through self-governing Nigeria is a happy portent.

But the way in which the French are losing all hold on half-barbaric North Africa, where they could still perform a civilizing mission, and the way our South drifts to a new outburst of race hate and race war, foreshadow calamity. That French mob cut the ground from under the French-educated Arabs who had still hoped for cultural ties in an equal French union. That Tuscaloosa mob, and the cowardly way the University and Governor Folsom gave in to it, is doing the same to the moderate elements in our own Negro community. The longer that responsible white leadership delays the unpopular step of enforcing educational integration which is now law, the harder it will become, the stronger the mob will grow. This lawlessness is a monster best killed in its cradle. In this country the Tuscaloosa outburst strengthens the case for the Powell amendment; better no school aid at all than aid to those who defy the law.

FEBRUARY 13, 1956

EISENHOWER GOES NEUTRALIST—ON CIVIL RIGHTS

Neutralism has been made a dirty word in American politics. Both parties are against it. We are constantly being treated to homi-

lies from the White House and the State Department on the wickedness of being morally neutralist. But apparently these high principles
only apply to disputes between the United States (right) and the
U.S.S.R. (wrong), in which Pandit Nehru (by refusing to take our
side) demonstrates incorrigibility.

The President at press conference the other day delivered himself of an impromptu message on integration which was afterward
filmed and is being shown in the movie houses. Mr. Eisenhower deplored the extremists "on both sides." We weren't hearing the people
of good will in the South. "We hear the people who are adamant
. . . they even resort to violence," he said, "and the same way on
the other side of the thing, the people who want to have the whole
matter settled today."

If we stop and translate this into realities, we will see that the
President is adopting at home the moral neutralism he deplores
abroad. Let us turn to Clay, Kentucky. There last week a mob of
white miners and farmers massed near the Clay elementary school
to prevent any Negroes from entering. These were the "adamant
people" to whom the President referred. Several school days in a
row they turned back a lone Negro woman who tried to enter her son
of ten and her daughter of eight. Mrs. Louis Gordon finally gave up,
and sent her children to an all-Negro school six miles away. "I just
couldn't continue to take them out there every day," she told reporters. "They were in too much danger." Mrs. Gordon is one of
those people whom Mr. Eisenhower described as "on the other side
of the thing, the people who want to have the whole matter settled
today."

We would like someone to ask the President how he can take
that mob and that one brave Negro mother, and lump them together
as "extremists." The mob opposes enforcement of the law; the
woman asks for her children the benefit of the Supreme Court's
decree. By any standard, isn't the mob wrong and the woman right?
Isn't Mr. Eisenhower's attitude "moral neutralism" of a real and
obnoxious variety?

Is it fair to speak of Mrs. Gordon as wanting "the whole matter
settled today"? Isn't this an invidious way to describe what is happening? The Supreme Court decision is three years old. Unless her
children are admitted "today," i.e., at the beginning of this year's
school term, they must wait another year. And another year means,

for them, as for many colored children in the South, another year of traveling a long extra way from home to school. "Six miles away" is twelve extra miles of travel daily, no small matter for children of eight and ten. Do they walk or ride? And if they ride, who pays their fare? These are bread and butter questions in most Negro homes.

Mr. Eisenhower says we aren't hearing the people of good will in the South. Their voice is not heard because the same mob spirit which overwhelms the Negro also cows them into silence. If the President is afraid to speak clearly, what can they (themselves a minority) say with the mob outside? This is what Adlai Stevenson meant when he told the Liberal party in New York last week that it was the President's duty to create "a climate of compliance." This was what Adlai courageously was trying to create when he told a hostile, often booing, American Legion in Los Angeles the week before that we could not convince other nations that we believe in justice "when mobs prevent Negro children from lawfully attending school."

We were sorry Adlai had to spoil his Liberal party speech by invoking that double talk from the Democratic platform about rejecting "all proposals for the use of force to interfere with the orderly determination of these matters by the courts." There will be no orderly determination without some show of force. A false dichotomy has been set up about force and persuasion. Both are needed. Neither can succeed without the other. But mobs can never be merely persuaded. They will overwhelm the good people of the community unless dealt with firmly. What progress has been made in Kentucky and Tennessee was made because Governors Chandler and Clement to their credit called out the militia to show that they meant business. And both Governors were able to act because of the political realities in these border states, which differ sharply from the Deep South in two ways. The Negro votes in Kentucky and Tennessee. Both have a two-party system.

In the one-party Deep South, where the Negro if he votes at all has no real choice, integration has not made a dent. All those fancy compilations only hide the fact that outside of the western fringe of Texas, which is more western than southern, the only progress is in the border states. Everywhere from Virginia on, the South is preparing to nullify the law, to resist it, and there are too few places where Negroes have been able even to file suit. Unless some firm moves toward enforcing compliance are soon made from Washington, the lines may harden for a long, long fight in which the South, its destiny and its good people, will more and more come under the control of the worst elements and poison the political life of the whole country. Behind the school struggle is the shadow of a conflict as grave as slavery created. The South must become either truly democratic or the base of a new racist and Fascist movement which could threaten the whole country and its institutions. On this, more than any other issue, fresh leadership in the White House is urgent.

SEPTEMBER 17, 1956

15: *The Free Mind at Work*

THE VINDICATION OF OWEN LATTIMORE

If Owen Lattimore was not a perjurer, then Joe McCarthy and Louis Budenz are; it is a pity there is not some way to make the Senator and the FBI informant stand trial. It is also a pity there is no way to make the government pay damages when it puts a man to endless agony and heavy financial cost, then decides to drop the charges against him. The Department of Justice ought not to be allowed to engage in gambles of this kind at other people's expense. The perjury charge was an obvious phony from the start; the government did not dare indict him for denying McCarthy's charge that he was the top number one Soviet spy in America or Budenz's unwilling identification of Lattimore as a Communist under pressure from Robert Morris, then counsel for the McCarran committee.

Why did Brownell decide to drop the charge? For one thing he had just picked a Justice Department official, Warren E. Burger, to fill the vacancy on the Court of Appeals here. Had the government asked for a rehearing of the latest 4-4 decision, Burger would have had to disqualify himself. Though not in the Criminal Division, Burger helped map legal strategy in the Lattimore case. A second factor is that Simon Sobeloff, the Solicitor General, who refused to argue the Peters case in the Supreme Court, also had a low opinion of the Lattimore prosecution. Thirdly, chances of a successful appeal to the Supreme Court were slim. Finally, the Chief Justice is a powerful Republican and his general attitude toward the witch hunt may have had some influence. It is not hard to imagine someone saying at the White House, "When is Herb Brownell going to stop making a fool of himself in that Lattimore case?"

The moral and psychological effect of the victory cannot be overestimated. It will strengthen resistance to the witch hunt; give teachers elsewhere more courage; strike another blow at the fading repute of all who ganged up at the China Lobby's behest on Lattimore. The legal effect is to discourage investigating committees from carrying on ideological inquisitions. A man's opinion of whether he follows the Communist party line or not cannot be made the basis of a perjury indictment. The fight will not be over until Lattimore has been reinstated in his teaching job at Johns Hopkins; its president says that is up to the trustees, who meet in September. Justice will not have been done until he is teaching again. And for this victory a salute and thanks is due the Lutheran conscience of brave Judge Youngdahl and the devotion of Lattimore's lawyers: to Thurman Arnold, Senator O'Mahoney, Abe Fortas, Paul Porter and their associates. They had the honor to fight and win one of the historic battles for intellectual freedom in America.

JULY 4, 1955

HARVEY O'CONNOR: FULFILLMENT OF A RESPONSIBILITY

Harvey O'Connor made history here today. He was the first witness in all these years of the witch hunt to take the stand in his own behalf on a trial for contempt. When the Assistant United States Attorney, William Hitz, Jr., moved in for the kill and asked him whether he had ever been a member of the Communist party, O'Connor turned to Federal Judge Joseph C. McGarraghy and offered to answer the question if directed by the Court. But the Judge, to everyone's surprise, declined to do so and disallowed the question when Hitz later tried to ask it in a different form. O'Connor, in the first trial of a First Amendment contempt case since the Hollywood Ten (whom Hitz also prosecuted), thus found himself the beneficiary of a judicial ruling which enabled him to demonstrate readiness to answer the question without risking the hazards of a perjury prosecution.

Though McCarthy himself appeared as a witness in the case, it was O'Connor who stole the show. The Senator looked older and fatter, his wife younger and svelte, when they turned up in the courtroom yesterday. Two years ago McCarthy's appearance as witness in a federal court would have drawn a moderate-sized mob. But there were only about a dozen spectators on hand when the trial opened yesterday. Except for one stout bailiff, who looked as pleased with Joe as if he were DiMaggio, the audience seemed only mildly interested when McCarthy was sworn in.

The Senator shows the effects of his fall from glory. His head has grown, his figure thickened, as if he had passed his change of life, and stood on the threshold of old age. He looks with his too eager smile like a man who feels that he has become disreputable, secretly agrees with the verdict passed upon him, but wishes people would like him anyway. He who made so many people infamous and drove them out of respectable society now stoops slightly, as if under the weight of a similar fate. On the witness stand, prompting the prosecutor and offering information which had not been asked, he seemed to forget that he was a witness in a courtroom, and no longer an all-powerful committee chairman. But he showed undiminished agility in crookedly inserting slander wherever given the least opening and had several times to be stopped, benevolently but firmly, by the Judge. He nevertheless managed in his once familiar style to call O'Connor "a long-time paid functionary of the Communist party." The "paid" was a touch of the old genius.

Judge McGarraghy, the newest member of our federal bench, a Taft Republican, upheld the defense when the government sought through McCarthy to show that it had reasonable grounds to ask O'Connor whether he was a member of the Communist "party" or "conspiracy." Both questions were asked in 1953 and it was on the refusal to answer the second that contempt was alleged. Defense counsel objected that this would allow McCarthy to put into evidence at second hand any informer scuttlebutt in his committee files.

When McCarthy was on the stand, "the old Acheson State Department" seemed again to be on trial. The Senator said when O'Connor was summoned as a witness in July of 1953, his subcommittee was investigating "the extremely vicious anti-American propaganda" on the shelves of United States overseas libraries. For the first time, McCarthy actually specified which of O'Connor's books were on those shelves: his books on the Astors, the Guggenheims and the CIO Oil Workers Union. He made no complaint about their contents, however, insisting that whether such books "were anti-American or not" their purchase for overseas libraries added to the prestige of Communist authors and through them "swelled party coffers."

At one point McCarthy and Hitz seemed to be treading a line designed to avoid any charge of censorship or ideological inquisition. But under cross-examination by van Arkel (O'Connor's lawyer), McCarthy testified he believed books which "unfairly" portray American historical figures should be purged from overseas library shelves. Van Arkel then asked, "How about books blaming Roosevelt for Pearl Harbor?" McCarthy met that one head on. "I personally think he was responsible for Pearl Harbor," McCarthy reacted angrily, "so I'd hardly exclude those books."

In demeanor, appearance and tone, O'Connor presented a striking contrast to McCarthy. A distinguished-looking man, with graying mustache and ruddy face, O'Connor spoke in quiet unaffected accents, as if in man to man talk with the Judge. He said the McCarthy committee had shown no interest in the content of his books, that he had nothing to do with their purchase by overseas libraries, and that he thought it the duty of a citizen to cooperate with any properly constituted congressional inquiry. But O'Connor said he felt that McCarthy wanted only to blacken his reputation as the Senator had many others. "Writers have no special privilege," O'Connor explained gravely, "but we do have a special responsibility to defend the First Amendment." He asserted when cross-examined by Hitz that he did not think any committee of Congress could validly inquire under the First Amendment into political beliefs. He insisted that when McCarthy asked him whether he was "a member of the Communist conspiracy" the Senator was using "as an epithet a term too vague" to be susceptible of proper answer. "My misfortune," O'Connor said, "was that I had written books. If I hadn't written books, I wouldn't have been there. . . . I felt the committee had no reason to roam in the realm of beliefs."

When O'Connor stepped down from the stand late this afternoon, he had succeeded for a few hours in turning his trial into a trial of McCarthy. The atmosphere of two years ago, when McCarthy's shadow was still long and heavy upon the land, had been revived.

The Judge hears final argument tomorrow, and has asked for trial briefs two weeks hence. Whether O'Connor is acquitted or convicted, whether he is ultimately freed or jailed, his appearance in court this week will prove a memorable defense of fundamental liberties.

OCTOBER 10, 1955

BARROWS DUNHAM: ACQUITTAL

The acquittal of Professor Barrows Dunham in federal court here last week was a defeat for the House Un-American Activities Committee and the Department of Justice. The Fifth Amendment was never more sweepingly invoked than by Professor Dunham. When called before the committee two years ago, he refused to do more than give his name, and the place and time of his birth. When he declined to answer questions as to his educational background and occupation, he was held in contempt. The government argued that the answers to these questions were known and could not have been incriminating. But Judge Joseph C. McGarraghy ruled that the nature of the investigation and its setting justified Professor Dunham.

In deciding that Professor Dunham had properly invoked the privilege, Judge McGarraghy in effect overruled the trustees of Temple University in Philadelphia. When they dismissed Professor Dunham, they did so on the ground that he had "misused" the privilege. It would have been more seemly to wait until that question had been decided by the courts. But what happens now that the trustees have been declared in error?

This is a challenge to the academic profession and to the people of the Philadelphia area. A full professor, head of his department, a philosopher of distinction, author of several well-known works, was dismissed from his post, despite tenure, on legal grounds which have failed to be sustained in court. Since the trustees misread the law, justice calls for Professor Dunham's reinstatement.

In that almost empty courtroom last Wednesday (who cares about another professor on trial?), with Committee Counsel Frank S. Tavenner, Jr., on the witness stand, it was an experience to hear him read into the record the testimony of professors who "cooperated" and again to live through the anguished moments our latter-day inquisitors imposed on scholars and teachers, bartering safety for self-respect. Professor Dunham was one of that handful who came through the ordeal with honor in a period when few American intellectuals showed much in the way of guts.

OCTOBER 24, 1955

ALBERT EINSTEIN

Professor Einstein would not have liked a stuffy tribute. My wife and I loved him. He was a charter subscriber to the *Weekly*, and often strained its primitive bookkeeping facilities by renewing when no renewal was due. We and our three children had the great pleasure on several occasions of having tea with him at his home. It was like going to tea with God, not the terrible old God of the Bible but the little child's father-in-heaven, very kind, very wise and yet himself very much a child, too. We feel that we have lost a friend.

If our dim understanding of his work has any validity, we thought of it as a lifelong search for a new and greater unity in physical phenomena, and the re-establishment of the possibility of law in the universe. A world made up only of statistical probabilities offended his profoundest instincts; he was like Bach or Beethoven, striving for new harmonies, but with the tools of mathematics and physics. There were times when one felt his infinite zest in the search that was his life, though he sadly called himself a has-been last time we saw him, which was last August.

The man who sought a new harmony in the heavens and in the atom also sought for order and justice in the relations of men. As the greatest intellectual in the world of our time, he fought fascism everywhere and feared the signs of it in our own country. This was the spirit in which he advised American intellectuals to defy the Congressional inquisition and refuse to submit themselves to ideological interrogation. In that position he was interpreting the First Amendment as Jefferson would have done.

Professor Einstein—if I read him rightly—felt like a failure rather than a success: he died without quite achieving that unified theory he sought. But his was a beautiful and satisfying life, and nothing would have pleased him more than how many—and such diverse —people remember him with affection, especially the children of the neighborhood in Princeton who recall the cookies he gave them.

In that Olympus where he goes to dwell with his few peers, this is something all his own. Newton and Copernicus and the misty Pythagoras, too, could sweep the heavens with their grasp—but none

of them were remembered by so many humble friends, for so many
simple human kindnesses. In this realm, far beyond politics and
physics, Einstein reigns alone in warm human memory.

APRIL 25, 1955

16: *National Suicide as a Form of Defense*

The real reason Washington rejects Atomic Energy Commissioner Thomas E. Murray's proposal for a world H-bomb demonstration is not for fear of what it might do to Them but for fear
of what it might do to Us. The basic decisions of atomic warfare have
been made from the beginning without consulting public opinion. At
first from necessity and later from considerations of military security
and finally from fear and habit, atomic decisions have been and are
being made in secret, without popular consultation.

Democratic processes have been one of the first victims of nuclear fission. The decision to try and make the bomb and the decision
to drop it on Japan were, of course, made privately. So was the decision to go ahead and make the H-bomb; had it not been for a slip
by former Senator Ed Johnson of Colorado the public would never
have known of it. Finally the decision to use "tactical" atomic weapons, and to refashion the armed services for atomic warfare, has also
been made by the inner circles of the government without debate in
Congress or elsewhere. The current Sagebrush military maneuvers in
Louisiana show how far that transformation has gone.

The atomic thunderbolt is no longer a final weapon to be held
in reserve for use only under the gravest circumstances on presidential decision, but *the* weapon around which all our military planning
and training now revolve. Though atomic warfare means national
suicide and humanity's final holocaust, the decision to engage in it
has been made. We have been consulted as little about it as if we
lived under a dictatorship.

Only once has there been a great national debate on atomic
policy and that came when the aroused atomic scientists descended
on Washington like a flock of Paul Reveres to raise the alarums
against military control of atomic energy. That great debate, right

after the war, was made possible because (1) Congress had to be consulted if an atomic energy act were to be passed, and (2) the atomic scientists had not yet been frightened away from political activity by the loyalty-security mania. In this case political activity meant an attempt to fulfill the highest moral responsibilities in the society to which they had made so fatal a gift. But that was before the onset of the cold war, and since that time the government has succeeded by one means or another in shutting off real debate.

Every attempt by the Russians from the Stockholm peace petition to the latest Molotov proposals for a world pledge against atomic warfare has been hooted down. Discussion of foreign policy has been made to seem somehow unpatriotic; talk of peace, suspect. Mr. Acheson's call for "total diplomacy" in January, 1950, merely put this into a vivid and sinister phrase; it sought at home the same kind of "disciplined" attitude toward foreign policy on which dictatorships pride themselves. Oppenheimer's ordeal, of which the atomic scientists knew long before the public, provided the scientific elite with a chilling object lesson. The decisions were to be made by our "betters"—though these self-appointed "betters" included some of those generals with prognathous jaws and Neanderthal minds who adorn the covers of our news weeklies and wield the power of world, life and death through our ever-ready Strategic Air Command. The reality has been the subordination of the best scientific minds to military control through the rich carrot of military research grants and the heavy stick of possible loyalty proceedings. In a period when no general ever makes a speech any more without giving God a plug, and self-righteous moralizings ooze from every political pore, real morality has been completely abandoned in our imbecile fascination with these new destructive toys. The atom is our totem; the bomb our Moloch; faith in overwhelming force is being made into our real national religion.

The Pentagon and State Department have feared public debate lest it interfere with the task of recasting our armed forces, our moral standards and our minds. There is evidence that this remolding process is far from complete and irreversible. The latest Gallup poll shows that peace far outranks every other problem in the public mind (42 percent answered peace—the farm problem, which was next, drew only 8 percent). To hold an H-bomb demonstration in the Pacific, as Mr. Murray proposes, with the world press and all other governments represented, would be not merely to frighten Them but to awaken Us out of our lethargy.

Thanks to Mr. Murray, we are now authoritatively warned that the atmospheric and soil contamination from large thermonuclear explosions is a far graver menace than had hitherto been supposed; apparently there is a limit to the safe amount of thermonuclear explosion even without war. A new substance, radioactive strontium, not hitherto present in the air or earth, has been created and released. Its contamination continues long after the blasts. As it passes from the soil into food and the human body, it can create bone tumors and fatal effects. Commissioner Murray says that estimates of how much radioactive strontium can safely be absorbed "have changed almost wildly" in the past year. A year ago it was said that we had little to fear because the amount would have to increase by one million times; now the estimate has been reduced to ten thousand times. Mr. Murray thinks this figure will be lowered. His four fellow commissioners, in rejecting his proposal for an H-bomb demonstration, significantly fail to deny these figures. Their official statement merely says that until further study has been made "it is impossible to be definite about the genetic effects." This is quite different from the statements of a year ago that fear of radioactive fall-out was exaggerated. Why should these matters be cloaked in secrecy, the decisions on them made without popular discussion?

The lack of real debate has allowed a thick deposit of dubious ideological fallout to contaminate the public mind. A whole series of doubtful propositions have been rubbed in by official statement and their echoes in a well-coordinated press. There is first of all the notion that but for the bomb the Russians would have overrun Western Europe after the war. This is highly doubtful in view of the terrible wounds they still had to heal from the last war, the enormous headaches occupation of Western Europe would have added to their problems, the civil war it would have provoked and the world war it would have unleashed.

America has twice been plunged into world war unprepared, and twice won despite that initial handicap. The Russians are not fools; they do not underestimate the huge industrial capacity and human resources of the American people. It is, I believe, the most dreadful nonsense to say that they would have overrun Western Europe if we had not had the bomb. The same is true, in my opinion, of the equally prevalent notion that there would be world war today but for fear of our bombs. The Russians and the Chinese have enough to do at home; and even without the bomb, war with America would ruin them for a generation. Then there is the newer notion that we must not give up nuclear warfare because only the bomb counterbalances the "hordes" at the disposal of Russia and China. But this completely overlooks the fact that these "hordes" now have the A-bomb and the H-bomb, too. So we no longer have an advantage. Would it not be better for both sides to see if some means cannot be found to ban nuclear warfare for humanity's good?

In the past, certain terrible weapons have been held in reserve by both sides, and neither have used them; poison gas is an example. It is one thing to have the bomb in reserve. It is quite another to equip whole armies with atomic weapons so that they are no longer able to fight any other kind of war. That is what we are doing. We are thus deciding in advance that a new war shall be a war without mercy and limit. The notion that atomic war can be limited; that atomic weapons can be used, as Eisenhower once said, like "pistols," fosters the most dangerous misconceptions. Once such a war begins, neither side dares hold back its worst and biggest bombs, though this may mean total mutual destruction.

Atomic war means national suicide. The ultimate delusion of the atomic era is the notion that national suicide is a feasible means of defense; how apparently sensible and sane men could drift into such beliefs will astound future historians, if there are any. All this has been underscored by the Sagebrush maneuvers. They have shown how easily radar defenses can be jammed by an attacking air fleet; we can wreck Russia's cities but Russia can wreck ours. And the whole human race may be ruined by the aftereffects. Is it not irrational, then, to decide for atomic warfare when atomic warfare means mutual suicide? Should such a decision be made without the fullest national and world debate? How much security is there in plans for defense which could do no more than assure our dying people that the enemy was dying, too? The Strategic Air Command can destroy the enemy, but it cannot defend us.

To set off on the path of atomic warfare is to set off on a path from which there is no return, toward a goal where there can be no victory, into a hell where none could survive. Until now the worst wars have been, to some extent, limited—if not by human intention and hatred, then at least by human capacity to destroy. But this war, the war we have been trying out in Operation Sagebrush, the atomic war must become unlimited war, against Us as well as Them. On those whom the bombs spare the radioactive dusts will fall, gently and impartially as the rain.

NOVEMBER 28, 1955

17: *U.S.S.R.: The Twentieth Congress*

THE MEANING OF KHRUSHCHEV'S REVISIONS

The striking thing about the Khrushchev speech to the Soviet Communist Party Congress is that he begins to admit that the danger of thermonuclear war and the consequent necessity of peaceful coexistence are incompatible with the older Marxist-Leninist view of violent revolution. For violent revolution—and this means civil war—in almost any important country between the two rival great powers would bring on intervention and make world war very difficult to avoid. One need only imagine what would happen were revolution to break out in India or in Italy, threatening to overturn the world balance of power, to see that if the Russians seriously want peace they must at the same time change the tactics of the world Communist parties for whom Moscow is the new Rome.

So those who want world peace, and see mankind's destruction in a new war, must welcome the signs of a shift in Muscovite doctrine. Khrushchev departed from Lenin, though not necessarily from Marx's later thinking, when he denied that force and civil war were the only paths to socialism, when he continued the new policy of friendliness to the once reviled Social Democrats, and when he even suggested (a real heresy) that "the parliamentary form" might be used (Lenin said it had to be smashed) and converted from "an organ of bourgeois democracy into an instrument of genuine popular will." This until yesterday was "rightist opportunism."

In this context perhaps the most interesting observation made by Khrushchev came when he spoke of the possibility of using parliamentary forms "for the transition to socialism" and then added, "For the Russian Bolsheviks, who were the first to accomplish the transition to socialism, this way was excluded." This begins to recognize that the conclusions drawn by Lenin from Russian experience, where parliamentary forms under the Czars were delusive, do not necessarily fit other countries where parliamentary forms and democratic government have often been the vehicles of peaceful social change and reform. The reader should also notice in this connection that Khrushchev speaks of "the right-wing bourgeois parties" as being bankrupt, which implies that left-wing "bourgeois" parties may be allies in "the peaceful transition to socialism."

The Khrushchev speech is not to be read merely as a new encyclical in Communist political theology. At this very moment the future of France and Italy may well depend on the attitude taken by their Communist parties; they hold the balance of power in the former, and may soon do so in the latter. Despite socialist fears of Communist duplicity, a new Popular Front may be necessary in France to meet the North African crisis and the new Fascist threat visible in Poujade. In Italy the pro-Soviet left Socialists of Nenni have been seeking alliance with the left wing of the Christian Democrats. Some such coalition may be necessary to unite all those in Italy who want social reform against tomorrow's danger of a new Italian fascism.

Such coalitions could only be stabilizing influences if the Communists in France and Italy can provide some assurance that their support would be something more than a Trojan horse from which first to capture and then liquidate (as happened in the "popular democracies") their non-Communist liberal and Socialist allies. Socialist fears of a Communist alliance are all too well founded in recent East European experience. Add the sudden shifts to which the Communist line is subject and the slavishly abject dependence of the Communists on Moscow and you begin to see the real dimensions of the problem. Yet unless there is some way to unite the various kinds of people in Italy who want social reform, whether Catholic, Republican, anticlerical, Socialist and Communist, fascism may easily revive since fundamentally nothing in poverty-stricken Italy has happened since the war except to shore up the rotten foundations.

The French situation is not the same but just as critical. The North African revolution deeply touches French national pride; without North Africa, she sinks into a third-rate power, facing a resurgent Germany. The white colonists see the fruits of a generation's labor endangered by a primitive and barbaric tide. To get them to give up what they have, to conciliate the miserable Arab masses, and to reconcile them if possible to a new equal life with and within France is the greatest task which has faced French statesmanship since Napoleon. In the national bitterness of failure, a new fascism may make its thrust. But can Frenchmen unite to fight it, if they must fear that part of their ranks may break away at any time on orders from a foreign source? This is the question which haunts Mollet and Mendès-France.

The international perspective is as difficult. A growing instability in France and Italy, coupled with an increase in Communist power in both countries, would make relaxation of tension between East and West impossible. Khrushchev admits that if good relations are not established between Moscow and Washington, there is no way to cut down the arms race and a tension that must grow more warlike. Yet such good relations will be impossible to achieve if there are crises in France and Italy. This is what makes Communist policy in both countries so important to peace, and this is what makes Khrushchev's revisions of Communist doctrine in the direction of peaceful change and social democracy so important.

The question which the Khrushchev speech does not deal with is how he can reconcile this responsible attitude toward West European problems with a Middle Eastern policy which rests on arms shipments into so tense an area. The policy of peace cannot be reconciled morally or politically with the kind of dangerous fishing in troubled waters which Moscow pursues in the Middle East. There Russian policy encourages war, and discourages those who would like to see stability created by removing the area from great Power rivalry.

Finally Khrushchev's discussion of the Beria affair and liberty within the Soviet state must put liberals and Socialists on warning against too close a Communist embrace. The Communists still have a lot to learn. Khrushchev is still talking the kind of coarse demonological rubbish in which he engaged at Belgrade on meeting Tito. If Beria, the highest G-man of the Soviet State, were an imperialist agent —and we leave this kind of poppycock to party stomachs—then the whole secret police system stands condemned and a first essential under communism as under any other society is to give the individual *rights he can enforce against the police and the state*. The injustices Khrushchev so conveniently blames on Beria are the same ones which Beria blamed in the same terms on *his* predecessors. Yet when Khrushchev says that "experience has shown that enemies of the Soviet state attempt to use the slightest weakening of Socialist law for their foul subversive activities" he is talking the same witch-hunt language we know so well in America and opposing fundamental reforms to make new Berias impossible. All the reforms Khrushchev mentions are mere purges from the top in the secret police apparatus—not the basic reforms in criminal procedure promised after Stalin's death and the exposure of the doctors frame-up. The demonology still reflected in Khrushchev's speech must be gotten rid of if a decent society is to be created. Here, too, the Communists must learn from the best traditions of the West if there is to be progress toward world peace and stability. In this respect, too, revision of "Marxism-Leninism" is overdue.

FEBRUARY 20, 1956

HISTORIC MOMENT IN THE SOVIET UNION

To the objective observer in the uncommitted lands of the earth it must have seemed last week that the United States of America and the U.S.S.R. were beginning to exchange political systems. In Russia, *Pravda* for the first time gave authoritative confirmation of the anti-Stalinist views Khrushchev was reported to have expressed. *Pravda* accused Stalin of "monstrous" excesses in his latter years. Stalin's terror began with the murder of Kirov in 1934, a murder which Trotzky blamed on the Soviet secret police. The murder frightened Stalin into a series of executions and political trials which made a farce of the 1936 Constitution. But now comes word from Leningrad, where Kirov was party leader, that at the Kirov museum in that city the murder is no longer blamed (as in the Great Soviet Encyclopaedia) on "a Trotzkyite degenerate," but only on "an enemy of the people," identity and motive unknown. A new view of Kirov's murder must lead to a new view of the left and right opposition to Stalin and that in turn to a new attitude toward the right of opposition.

This historic moment when the Soviet Union is turning toward political and intellectual freedom could be a moment of triumph for America. It is a moment for magnanimity in foreign policy and for example in democratic behavior. Instead we saw an act of frantic folly—the nationwide "income tax" raids on Communist party headquarters, the padlocking of the *Daily Worker*. The spectacle of the American giant rearing in fright before such a mouse as the harried

Communist movement in this country must make us look ludicrous abroad. It must make us seem to be in the grip of forces much like those which ruled Russia under Stalin—an intense fear of "subversive" ideas, an insane suspicion of the opposition, a readiness to use any device to destroy opponents. In our milder fashion, we are continuing the practice of the "purge." Though so far only Communists have gone to jail, thousands of others have been reduced to second-class citizenship, defamed, "exiled" internally (as in Russia), deprived of reputation and livelihood, held up to public contumely. This was Stalin's way with the opposition, and it is now ours. When the Russians come to the point of evicting Stalin's mummy from the Kremlin, perhaps they will send it here to the more congenial atmosphere of Brownell-era Washington. We might in turn send them the Jefferson Memorial; it may inspire them, at the moment it only embarrasses us.

APRIL 2, 1956

18: *A Visit to Moscow*

THIS RIVAL GIANT

I had six wonderful days in Moscow and three in Warsaw—all that my limited means and tight printing schedule would allow. I managed with a dozen words of Russian, an Anglo-Russian dictionary, and a mixture of English, French, German and Yiddish to speak with many people, officially and unofficially, through organizations and casually, in the streets, parks, theatres, cafés and restaurants. I visited a *kolkhoz*, a collective farm just outside Moscow, and I had a long interview with one of the Soviet jurists who is helping to revise the criminal code. I talked with Soviet journalists, with Communists and non-Communists. In Moscow I found people friendly and eager to talk but still afraid; Warsaw, on the other hand, was astounding in its frank speech. I had hoped by visiting Warsaw on my way back to sample the atmosphere of a satellite capital and see how it differed if any from Moscow. The differences were amazing, and provided unexpected perspective on the new developments in the Soviet world. I had no briefings at the United States Embassy either in Moscow or Warsaw, and only casual contacts with fellow Americans—I wanted my own fresh impressions rather than the second hand and I decided to write them after leaving Russia rather than trust to the precarious mercies of the often arbitrary and frustrating censorship which still exists there. And I want to report, for what little it may be worth, what I managed to see and hear and observe on my own.

The people of Moscow and the *kolkhoz* outside it were a perpetual revelation. Beneath the monolithic dictatorship of a monolithic party in a country hermetically sealed off for a generation from any foreign news or contact of which the regime did not approve there was evident a wide variety of personality and viewpoint. Though I never had the feeling of complete frankness in any conversation in Moscow (unlike Warsaw), I heard enough to feel that all those years of control and molding had not produced a real uniformity of opinion. I found smooth careerists whose yesmanship was as slick as anything in Hollywood, devoted Communists with hopelessly rigid blinkers, and cynics who gave one the feeling of laughing up their sleeves at the monotonous patter of the dull, verbose and obscure Soviet press. There are fanatics whose faces turn black at the slightest criticism, deeply thoughtful and discontented people bursting to talk but still fearful, and a few men of truly cosmopolitan views neither ignorant nor contemptuous of the West but devoted to their country and the building of socialism. I saw a young man blush when he admitted he was a Komsomol, as if that were a form of time-serving, and finally say to me in mixed Russian and German after a painfully slow conversation and as if this were the ultimate distillation of his generation's experience, *"Ili schweigen ili gefängnis"* (either silence or prison). And there was still a pall of fear over the few Jews with whom I managed to speak in Moscow.

But these were the intellectuals, the elite, the governing circles, the students, the engineers, the technicians, and they are only a very small part of Russia. The first vivid impression stepping out with excitement into the streets that first morning, even in the heart of Moscow, was that this was overwhelmingly and unmistakably a peasant country. The shiny cars, the smart policeman, the overwhelming massiveness of streets and buildings, the strange yellow walled palaces, the huge Bolshoi Theatre on the right and the fragment of old medieval wall on the left, the New York style advertising signs selling vitamins and taxi service, the bookshops jammed with technical works in many languages the swift-moving purposeful crowds—none of this struck one so forcibly as the observation that this was a land of peasants, of East European peasants, the real peasants, only a few steps from serfdom. I had seen them only once before, in a market place in Belgrade, but they were unforgettable—gnarled creatures, almost like trees, leathery, worn by weather and hardship, tough, patient and submissive but stubbornly and subterraneously enduring beneath that submissiveness. Here the streets were filled with them, and they did not look at all like those pictures by Sovfoto in which all the faces are washed shiny and smiling. They looked as if they could use soap and water. They were poorly dressed, often in the padded quilt jackets familiar as far east as China, the women with kerchiefs, many with boots, and mostly lean. Where there is fat it is the fat of women whose diet is too largely bread.

This city of Moscow, their capital, is strange and immense as their country, endlessly fascinating as the people are but unlike them more than slightly repellant. It is not Europe, it is not Asia, it is Russia as America is America; Europe and Asia have affected both but the product is new, *sui generis.* And it is easy to understand why Peter left Moscow in disgust to build himself a new capital as a window on the West, and why the Pan-Slavist reactionaries of the nineteenth century dreamed of making it Russia's center again. For despite that marble subway and the new skyscrapers—the overlay of Communist Babbittry engaged in making Moscow the best biggest and Bolshoi-est of all cities, just like America only better is their dream—the old Holy Moscow lies heavy and inescapable on the new world center of atheist communism. No city could be more incongruous, jumbled, conglomerate; so bedraggled with the past as it struggles toward the future. The Czars and commissars alike built to strike the visitor with awe at its immensity; everything at first sight seems huge, even monstrous, almost Egyptian. Then as one looks closer one sees a general slovenliness like that of a peasant giant with his shirt tails out of his pants. Elderly crones like caricatures of womanhood endlessly dibble-dabble at the dirt of the streets with wisplike brooms. The buildings are flaked, poorly painted, in need of repair. Between new apartment houses and skyscrapers one sees the old-fashioned Russian log houses like the quaint illustrations in old editions of Pushkin, and in the courtyards behind them are glimpses of slums squalid beyond conception.

The Czars liked size, and so did their successors. The old yellow-walled palaces impress with strangeness rather than beauty, and the new skyscrapers and apartment houses are overlaid by doodads and petty ornament and pretty pastel bits of color. The new university is a kind of Soviet Empire State Building, impressive and striking but a little boring. "Socialist realism" in architecture is about as vulgar and ostentatious as Miami and just about as socialist; the opulent new Moskva Hotel would fit perfectly into the Florida resort if it were not built in such a heavy, old-fashioned, dark kind of way. The taste is the taste of the *nouveaux riches*. In architecture, painting and sculpture, this revolutionary society is utterly non-revolutionary, sterile and tasteless. The visual climax are those neoclassic statues of athletes with—not just loincloths—but full underdrawers of stone on them, and the bits of cloth so prudishly carved across the navels of the Graces. In this, too, Moscow is the most mid-Victorian of capitals.

But all this modern overlay seems surface. The heart and soul of Moscow is still the Kremlin. The eye, the footsteps, are drawn back constantly to the brick-walled medieval battlements of this old fortess town on a bluff which still dominates Moscow militarily and —one feels—spiritually. The Kremlin is a huge place, big enough for the armed trading town it once was, set in the heart of Moscow. The Kremlin is a vast museum and as vast a cemetery and at the same time the center of government, a capital which is also a Mecca. The devout from all over the Soviet Union turn their steps toward that black, square, modernist mausoleum just outside the Kremlin walls where Lenin and Stalin lie embalmed side by side like modern Pharaohs to be venerated by a people profoundly necrophile. It is the character of the Kremlin as a tomb that is so unexpected and revealing. If Stalin's portrait is still everywhere, and his body lies undisturbed in state, this is easier to understand after one has visited the Kremlin church in which Ivan lies beside the son he killed and Peter is interred near the son he had executed—for being a "reactionary" as my Komsomolka guide explained. The Russians are used to crimes in their rulers; they are a people like Job. They seek patiently in suffering to find some meaning in the inexplicable cruelties of Heaven.

Red Square with the brooding Kremlin, the gay candy-stick pillars of that child's delight, St. Basil's, the modernist mausoleum as black, stark and strange as something out of a science-fiction nightmare, and the big department store across the way—what could be more jumbled, more incongruous, more confusing! I believe that some day Communist Russia will abandon Moscow as Peter did, and for much the same reasons—to escape the dead hand of the past, to open fresh windows on the world. But all this paradox and piety is Russia. On a Saturday afternoon I stood in line with the patient to see Lenin and Stalin, and the next day I saw the same devotion in the solemn beauty of the Russian Orthodox mass as it was being celebrated in Moscow's crowded churches. It is the Russian people to whom one feels drawn with love, still half-barbaric, deeply religious whether as Christians or Communists, capable of much senseless cruelty, and of the deepest devotion. This Russia, Holy Russia in a new sense to the world's left intellectuals, is unmistakably backward, no model for the future, Byzantine, slavish and submissive, still enmired in the past, but a giant from whom, given peace, there will be giant accomplishment.

MAY 7, 1956

NATASHA'S READY ANSWERS

On our way back from our visit to the Kremlin, I asked Natasha, my tourist guide, whether she had any questions to ask about America. She wanted first to know why Paul Robeson could not get a passport. I said I had criticized the government's action in refusing him a passport. She then wanted to know what I thought of the condemnation of the Communists in the United States. I said I had criticized that in public speeches and in my paper. She asked whether many people agreed with me and I said unfortunately not many did. When she looked triumphant, I asked her a question. "How many people in this country," I asked, "would be willing to defend the right of oppositionists to speak against the government?" To this she had a ready answer.

"We have no oppositionists," replied Natasha.

"But suppose you did?" I insisted.

"How could we have oppositionists?" she said. "A man cannot be an oppositionist for himself alone."

"Tolstoy was an oppositionist on his own," I countered.

"No," Natasha replied, "he spoke for the people."

"But the people were voiceless," I replied, "until a few such men had the courage to speak for them."

"Well," Natasha said, "if we had oppositionists, someone would defend their rights."

To illustrate she began to tell me about her trade union.

"In our union," she said, "some people are timid but most of us speak up. Why the other day we even got the reinstatement of a fellow worker who had been fired."

"We have unions in America, too," I said, "and they often get workers reinstated."

"Yes," she said, "but in America unions cannot strike."

"That's not true," I said, "there are lots of strikes in America."

"No," she said, "under the Taft law, workers cannot strike."

"That's not true," I argued. "The effect of the Taft-Hartley Act has been very much exaggerated. We have strikes all the time."

"But union leaders are afraid to call strikes," Natasha insisted, "because they may be heavily fined."

"There have been fines," I said. "But that has not stopped strikes."

By this time we were back to the Metropol and the conversation was over. Natasha looked at me with condescension as a benighted heathen. The idea that something she had read in her party press might possibly be wrong obviously never occurred to her.

I got a different sort of question about America and a different reaction from a Red Army officer. I saw him sitting by himself in a café. I walked over and asked, *"Sprechen sie Deutsch?"* He answered in German, "A little." He spoke no English or French and communication was difficult. He was a friendly man, with clear intelligent eyes, and the face of a kindly person. He wanted to know—after I told him I was an American journalist on my first visit to Moscow—how many rooms the ordinary worker has in the United States. This was his first question. I said in a city like New York even well-to-do people might have small apartments but that in many cities like Philadelphia workers owned their own homes, and that these were five- or six-room homes. He did not look at me with pity as a victim of capitalist propaganda. He looked pleased, as if I had told him something which buttressed his own convictions. I asked him why there were still so many pictures of Stalin around and he said this would soon pass away. He said Russia was "going back to Lenin," and that many bad things had happened under Stalin. He looked incredulous when I said I liked Moscow. Trying hard to express his feelings in his inadequate German, he said—as if in a few words he was distilling the product of long thought—*"the peasant here has a hard life."* He said, "I am a soldier but I believe in peace." Then he pointed to his uniform and said, "I cannot speak freely." He paid for his drink and left.

I visited two government buildings, the offices of Tass, for copies of speeches made at the Twentieth Congress, and a Ministry of Culture office on Zhdanova Street where the Soviet Information Bureau publishes its Daily Review of the Soviet Press. In both there were uniformed police guards inside the door and no one could get by the guards without showing a pass with a photograph on it. Workers coming down the elevator on errands in the lobby showed their passes each time they passed the policeman. It reminded one of the Pentagon in wartime Washington.

I went to the Ministry of Culture because I wanted a translation of the full text of a long editorial which *Pravda* published on April 5. The fragmentary reports I had seen of it in the foreign press on my way to Russia were disturbing. What was most disturbing was the vagueness of the editorial. I talked to the official in charge of translations at the Ministry of Culture. I told him after reading the text that I could not make head or tail of it. "Suppose," I said, "I were a Soviet citizen, honestly trying to understand what was permissible free speech and what was slanderous and antiparty and therefore impermissible, how could I find out from this editorial? It would only leave me confused and afraid." His answer was that all these matters referred to in the editorial had already been explained at party meetings. "Anyone who attended these meetings will know what the article means," he said. "But," I insisted, "what is the use of a newspaper article which can only be understood if the reader attends a private meeting to hear the explanation?" His reply was that this was an internal party matter. "In your country," he said, "there is free discussion—no," he interrupted himself, "that is not a good word— in your country problems are first discussed in the press but in our country they are first discussed in party meetings and in factory meetings and then we decide how much should go into the press." The talk was held in the English translation bureau, and some of his fellow workers had a hard time trying to keep a straight face during this conversation.

The Russians like their contacts to be organizational. They like visits by delegations rather than individuals. Organization contacts relieve the individual of responsibility. If a visit turns out badly, the fault lies with the organization. In addition, contacts between delegations facilitate that exchange of slogans, safe generalities and non-political pleasantries which the Russians prefer to real talk, which may become dangerous. If you reach a man directly in his office, he will call in a colleague to take part in the conversation, and provide a witness to the talk.

I succeeded in starting impromptu discussions with Russians everywhere. I was not rebuffed once, and this—other foreigners told me—was a complete change from a few years ago when it was simply impossible to talk with Russians at all except on strictly official business. But I never succeeded in making a date with a Russian for a further talk alone. One man I met through an official organization for a group talk seemed most intelligent and most eager for real discussion. I asked him if he would come to my hotel for tea next day and continue our talk. He said he would like to and that he would call me up and let me know. A half-hour before the appointed time he telephoned to say he couldn't come because his wife had a bad cold but he would call me within the next day or so and make another date. I never heard from him again.

I had a talk with two journalists on a well-known Soviet publication which circulates widely abroad. One man, a top editor, was well-tailored, slick, and intelligent but not an attractive type; he seemed very much like the Hollywood intellectuals in the film industry, a born yes-man, with a sharp nose for any change in the wind. One felt that he would never stick his neck out for any man or any principle. He was well-stocked with glib answers for the freedom of the press questions he expected from foreign journalists; what these glib answers boiled down to was that the "capitalist" press faithfully echoed the line of its government, too. The existence of some independent voices and of some independence even in the conservative and conventional press was conveniently passed over. The other man, a subordinate, was more independent-minded. I asked whether Soviet writers and journalists in the future would have more freedom but I never did get a clear answer.

"It would be wrong," said the first journalist, "to say that writers felt restricted. The young people were a new Soviet generation which expressed what it sincerely had been feeling. Now that the party thinks it necessary for writers to be more independent and to write more naturally and from within, they will do so. But it would be wrong to say they were restricted."

"So," I suggested, "it is a question of changing the habits of writers?"

"Yes," was the answer, "and of revising some conceptions."

Then he added what I thought was a most appalling commentary. "Our writers," he said, "thought that to criticize our life was not their affair. They thought only to be happy and not to criticize."

When I asked whether there would be more freedom of speech, the first man said there had always been free speech in Russia. But when I asked whether any Soviet journalist had criticized the earlier attitude toward Tito or the "doctors' plot" he shifted his ground and said that the press in America or England on a subject like the German problem all followed the same line, too. "Our newspapers," he said, "defend our line, too."

I said this was not entirely true in the West. I said the *New York Times* had criticized the padlocking of the *Daily Worker* just before I left. I said I had criticized the "doctors' plot" in my own paper because I felt there was something fishy about it. I asked whether in the future, if there were a similar frame-up, some Soviet journalist would criticize it, too.

"If you ask us about the 'doctors' plot,' " the journalist explained, "now we know. The facts were distorted and invented by the Beria gang. Now that the facts have been made known, we have attacked the 'doctors' plot.' But you have to know the facts."

He never did answer my question about the future. When I cited the fact that one man, like Zola, could force open the Dreyfus case in France, I struck no response. The idea of getting the facts on one's own and of opposing the government in a political or criminal prosecution was completely foreign to his mentality. I felt not merely opportunism but genuine submissiveness in his attitude.

The other journalist seemed to feel that something more was needed to satisfy my questions. "We lived in a besieged fortress," he said. "I am now forty-two. All of my generation were accustomed to believe in the security agencies because these were our shield against real enemies. When we heard of measures taken by these agencies, we were sure they must be true. No revolution ever had so many enemies as ours.

"Now," he continued, "we know that these revolutionary bodies like the security police can also make mistakes. The result is a new atmosphere. Our party and the government have hardened their control over these agencies and put new and good people into them to improve them."

I suggested that one way to "improve" the secret police was to give the individual citizen more rights against them, to establish safeguards like our habeas corpus against the police.

"In the West," the second journalist explained, "it was different. You had a very long experience and got used to defending yourselves against the bourgeois state. But here from the beginning it was a people's state and there was no practical need for such protective procedures. The last few years, however," he conceded, "have showed the need for some such safeguards."

On the question of Tito, the second journalist also had something interesting to add. He said, "Only a small number of our people ever went abroad. We had no way to judge for ourselves. Now that thousands are beginning to go abroad and see for themselves, it will help to prevent such mistakes in the future."

Everywhere I found Russians went out of their way to be helpful as soon as they learned I was a foreigner, and there seemed to be no prejudice against me when I said I was an American. I got to the Bolshoi Theatre just as the performance was starting and the ushers were closing the doors. I didn't know where to go or what to do and was on the verge of being shut out when I told an usher, *"Ne panamayou parusski"* (Don't understand Russian). He at once caught on that I was a foreigner, found me a vacant seat in the darkness and then after the first scene came back and took me to my proper place.

I went to two performances in Moscow. The first was at the huge Bolshoi Theatre where a ballet named *Laurenciana* was being played that night. I liked the enormous, brightly-colored theatre, the gay sets, the music and the audience, which was enjoying itself. But I found the ballet itself conventional, and the story corny; peasant boy saves peasant girl from advances of arrogant knight in medieval village. I was so bored I left after the first act. I didn't think it half as much fun as just walking the streets and looking at the people.

The other performance was a sheer joy. I saw *The Girl with the Fluttering Eyelids,* a satire on Hollywood, done at the puppet theatre of Abrasov. It had been on a triumphant tour in England, and someone should bring it to America. I had never seen anything like it before—a full-length play written for puppets, and the puppets specially designed for the play. The satire was terribly clever—I heard later that our Ambassador Bohlen had enjoyed it immensely. In one scene there are three puppet stenographers taking dictation at once from three collaborating writers in the best frenetic Hollywood manner. An elderly usher who spoke English kindly explained the plot to me before the play began; it was a take-off on *Carmen*. But after the second act, when I saw the smugglers being executed with a flame gun and I asked her to explain, she suddenly went dead on me. She hadn't seen that act, she didn't know what had happened, she practically couldn't speak English any more. I gathered later that Abrasov was satirizing the Marshall Plan and American military policy in that scene. The usher was afraid of offending me if she explained.

I believe that subconsciously or unconsciously every American in Moscow must feel a slight uneasiness, even a little anxiety. These are our rivals and imitators; the subway and the skyscrapers and even more so the booster spirit reflect their desire to imitate, to overtake and to surpass our own country. It is easy to see on the surface how far they yet have to go, and to sneer at their *nouveau riche* vulgarity as the nineteenth-century English visitor sneered (in much the same worried spirit) at the new brash giant growing up in America. But to see the building going on and the beautiful new department stores, to read the speeches of the Twentieth Congress and the stupendous figures of the new Five Year Plan, is to feel that this new rival is a giant, a gauche and slovenly giant whose manners it is easy to ridicule, but whose capacity for huge strides is not to be discounted.

MAY 14, 1956

THE SOVIET CRIMINAL CODE

In his *History of Russia,* Bernard Pares tells us that the efforts of Nicholas 1 to help the peasantry "were prejudiced from the outset because the work was wholly entrusted to the bureaucracy and kept secret from the population, whose support was therefore never enlisted." The bureaucracy was hostile to the reforms and Nicholas "met with continuous resistance, which even went so far as the omission from new editions of such statutes as established peasant rights." This passage comes to mind when one discovers how secretive the present regime is about reforms in the criminal code.

One of the most important things one learns in the Soviet Union today is that the average Soviet citizen is considerably less informed than the foreign visitor about the changes being made in Soviet criminal law and procedure. The most striking instance of this is the abolition of the dreaded "Special Board" of the MVD.

When I interviewed Professor Sergei A. Golunsky, a member of the commission now at work on the revision of the Soviet criminal code, and asked him what changes had been made to give Soviet citizens greater protection against the secret police, the first thing he cited was this abolition of the Special Board. This Board had power to condemn without trial, on the basis merely of documentary charges by the MVD and without even seeing the accused. Professor Golunsky said this had been abolished in September, 1953.

What I did not learn until later was the extraordinary secrecy in which this reform was shrouded. It first became known to outsiders last August when Professor Harold J. Berman of the Harvard Law School visited the Soviet Union. When he asked Soviet jurists about the Special Board they told him it had been abolished but that the decree had never been published. Professor Berman said no one could explain why the decree was kept secret. He mentioned abolition of the Special Board in a talk he was invited to make before the Institute of Law in Moscow. But when newspaper correspondents tried to report the abolition in their dispatches, the censor refused to permit transmission of the news.

Although Professor Berman on his return wrote of this decree in last December's issue of the *Harvard Law School Bulletin,* it was not until this month that the Soviet censor allowed mention of the abolition of the Special Board. On May 4, in describing a talk which a group of visiting French Socialists had with Anatoli Votin, president of the Soviet Supreme Court, correspondents were allowed to report that Votin read the text of this decree to the visitors and that it had never been published in the Soviet Union. The only known news of it in the Soviet Union was a two-line reference in last January's issue of *Sovetskoye gosudarstvo i pravo,** the monthly law journal published by the Institute of Law of the Academy of Sciences. This is, of course, a technical not a popular publication. Even there, despite the intense interest the reference must have aroused among Soviet lawyers, the text was not published.

* Soviet State and Law.

As striking an example of the failure to inform the ordinary Soviet citizen of the changes being made or considered in criminal procedure occurred a few days before my interview with Professor Golunsky. This same law journal, *Sovetskoye gosudarstvo i pravo*, in its April issue carried an editorial criticizing Vishinsky and convictions by confession. A kind of grapevine seems to operate in Moscow when the regime wants it to, and this editorial in an obscure legal journal at once found its way into the hands of foreign correspondents. I raised the question with Professor Golunsky. I said the editorial was very encouraging and that full accounts had been cabled abroad where millions would read about it but that the average Soviet citizen would not know about it since the story had not been carried in the Soviet press. He had no explanation to offer.

By any standards, both these stories were sensationally important news. Only two months earlier, in his speech to the Twentieth Communist Party Congress, Voroshilov had declared that "a big role in the struggle for socialist law belongs to our press" and urged the need "for widely propagating Soviet law among the entire population." Even without such urging, "Special Secret MVD Board Abolished" and "Vishinsky Technique of Conviction by Confession Attacked" would have been legitimate eight-column lines across page one of *Pravda* and *Izvestia*. Since these are papers closely controlled by the Soviet government and the Communist party, one wonders why neither story was printed. Are these changes in law and attitude encountering the same undercurrent of resistance in the Soviet bureaucracy that the peasant reforms of Nicholas encountered in the Czarist bureaucracy?

One of the principal reasons I wanted to visit the Soviet Union was to learn what had happened to the revision of the criminal code promised after Stalin's death and whether new safeguards were to be enacted to make the excesses and injustices of the Stalin period impossible. The newspaper reader abroad sees frequent stories about reform of criminal procedure in Russia based on articles like that in *Sovetskoye gosudarstvo i pravo* and in interviews accorded foreign visitors. But these articles and interviews do not reach the ordinary reader in the Soviet Union. He must judge by what he reads in the press, and the picture as his press reports it is a confusing one.

More than three years ago, on March 27, 1953, after the death of Stalin, a general amnesty was declared. The same day it was announced that the Ministry of Justice had been "instructed to draft appropriate proposals" for the reform of the criminal code and to present these to the Presidium of the Supreme Soviet within thirty days. Since then, beginning with Beria's exposure of the "doctors' plot" as a frame-up and culminating in Khrushchev's recent "secret" speech attacking the crimes and injustices which occurred under Stalin, there have been a series of exposés. Excesses by the secret police have been denounced and victims rehabilitated, but that promised revision of the criminal code has not yet been forthcoming, and the outlook for law reform is still confused. There is much talk of reform, but the emphasis is on a shake-up in the personnel of the secret police and on providing stricter supervision from above rather than in attacking the problem by providing new specific guarantees for accused individuals. The Soviet citizen hears attacks on Beria and Stalin and on "the cult of personality" but he hears little about concrete reforms to provide new checks on the secret police. On the contrary he still hears much that stresses the need for continued security surveillance and builds up that same atmosphere of suspicion on which police excesses thrived during the Stalin years.

An example is provided by Khrushchev's speech to the Young Building Workers on April 11. "The capitalists," Khrushchev said, "are well able to defend their capitalist world and its exploiting order of things. They know how to organize their intelligence service and smuggle their spies and saboteurs into our country. . . . We must be able to recognize the enemy, to see through all his tricks in good time." If capitalist spies and saboteurs may be lurking everywhere, a vigilant and powerful secret police is necessary. This was Stalin's view. Khrushchev's does not seem very different. In that same speech to the young building workers, immediately after this reference to "tricks," Khrushchev said, "We must strengthen in every way the security of our state, be vigilant and nip in the bud all enemy activities. In criticizing the weaknesses and errors that have been made in the course of our advance, we must first of all see to it that this criticism strengthens the Soviet system." Criticism must be "constructive" but who is to determine whether a specific criticism is constructive or only an enemy activity "in the bud"? Khrushchev went on, "Our enemies hope that we will relax our vigilance and weaken our state security service. No, this," he said, "will never happen! The proletarian sword must always be sharp, must always ably protect the gains of the revolution, the working class, the working people." (Prolonged applause.) This sounds remarkably like Stalin.

Under Stalin differences of opinion were constantly being translated into this kind of melodrama. It was in this atmosphere that the excesses and injustices now exposed were bred. But let us listen again to Khrushchev, this time in his speech to the Twentieth Party Congress, and the same accents may be heard. "The imperialists," Khrushchev told the Congress, "had placed special hopes on their old agent, Beria, who had perfidiously wormed his way into leading posts in the Party and the Government."

If the 'imperialists" are so devilishly clever that they can put an agent into the very highest circle of Soviet government, how can one live at peace with these imperialists, how can one trust them, indeed (for this kind of poisonous nonsense boomerangs) how can one trust the highest officials of the Soviet government itself? This picture of Beria "perfidiously" *worming* his way "into leading posts in the Party and the Government" is not calculated to create that calmer atmosphere in which a repetition of Stalinism may be avoided.

For more than twenty years, according to Soviet leaders themselves, their secret police apparatus has been headed by a series of traitorous monsters. Yagoda, Yehzov, Abakumov and Beria in turn were removed, disgraced and executed as foreign agents and frame-up artists. As each man fell there were shake-ups in personnel, victims were rehabilitated, reforms were promised. Yagoda came in as a reformer in 1934 when the old OGPU was abolished and the NKVD established; this was supposed to symbolize a shift from the older system of revolutionary terror to one of "Socialist legality." In 1939 Beria was assigned to "purge the purgers" and to correct wrongs done by the NKVD under Yagoda and Yehzov. The new leaders have executed Beria and told their people that during the last twenty years of his life Stalin was responsible for monstrous crimes. The main instrument of these crimes was the secret police, operating in a legal system which gave their victims none of the elementary safeguards we know in the West.

In any country where public opinion could express itself freely the result would be the abolition of the secret police and a reform of the whole legal system. But in Russia today, when one really tries to find out what is happening, the results are still vague and meager. The highest officer of the new regime, the new party leader, Khrushchev, is ambiguous on the subject. "Experience has shown," he told the Twentieth Congress, "that the enemies of the Soviet State attempt to use the slightest weakening of Socialist law for their foul, subversive activity." He wants to "raise revolutionary vigilance among the Soviet people and strengthen the State security agencies."

Discussion of the promised new criminal code at the Party Congress was left to the much less important speech made by Voroshilov, and he devoted only five paragraphs to it. He said that a new criminal code and a new code of criminal procedure were being drafted which would help to "safeguard the rights of citizens." But although Voroshilov spoke of the need for "immense activity in educating our cadres" in Socialist law, he did little "educating" himself. He did not touch on any of the rights to be safeguarded—on the right to counsel, on the right to know why one was arrested, on the right not to be subjected to prolonged interrogation in prison pending trial. Nor did he speak of the need for revising those terrible areas of Soviet criminal law in which treason and counterrevolutionary crimes are so broadly defined as to invite injustice and make dissent of any kind dangerous. Like Khrushchev he was specific on only one point, and that point stressed better supervision from the top.

"In accordance with the directives of the Central Committee of the CPSU [Communist Party of the Soviet Union]," Voroshilov said, "the Presidium of the Supreme Soviet of the U.S.S.R. has approved a new Instrument of the Procurator's Office in the U.S.S.R. Based on the Leninist teaching on the role and tasks of the Soviet Procurator's Office, the instrument is a clear program of activity for the office, confronts it with the task of being principled and irreconcilable in the struggle for strict observance of law by all establishments, responsible persons and citizens of the U.S.S.R."

This bit from Voroshilov is Communist gobbledygook, and will be recognized as such by intelligent Soviet readers. Judging by past history, the Procurator's office is no substitute for a good criminal code. The Procurator's office is a peculiar Russian institution, founded by Peter the Great. The Prosecutor General was intended to be the cleansing arm and inspecting eye of the autocratic sovereign, an Inspector General with power to inquire everywhere and to punish whatever infractions of law he uncovered. The institution reflects the desire of a centralized autocracy for efficiency in administration—that, rather than justice for individuals, has been its emphasis under the Communists as under the Czars before them. All the excesses of the last twenty years occurred not only in spite of the Procurator General but with his fervent collaboration. Vishinsky was Procurator General during the worst of the thirties and one need only go back and read his idyllic description of the office in his *Law and the Soviet State* (1938) and check it against what we now know, to see how little confidence can be reposed in assurances that the powers of the Procurator have been "restored." Reliance on the Procurator General is no substitute for a system in which accused persons through private counsel and within the framework of strictly defined crimes can defend themselves in open court.

Everything about my interview with Professor Golunsky was charming. I was even charmed with the nice lady at VOKS who arranged it after telling me that the Soviet Union did not have a secret police "not in the sense that you foreign newspapermen think" and after explaining to me that while the new government had admitted many "mistakes" in this field it had not said that past policy was wrong. (It was not till later that I began to realize how faithfully these fine split hairs conformed to the official line.)

Professor Golunsky gave me no such double talk. He turned out to be a tall, slim, aristocratic-looking man in his fifties, a legal scholar with a cosmopolitan outlook and a thorough grasp of British and American law. He teaches law at Moscow University and it must be a privilege to be one of his students. I listened to him with pleasure and I came away with respect. If Russian scholars of his type had a free hand I believe one would see a welcome evolution within the framework of socialism back toward freedom of expression and a fundamentally safeguarded criminal law. And I am not at all sure, in the light of the swift and sensational developments since Stalin died, that there may not be a clean break in this direction one of these days. I think we Western intellectuals can help that process by resolutely refusing to mistake shadows for substance, and by insisting on real changes as the price of the rapprochement the new regime desires with the liberals, Socialists and independent leftists of the West.

But what my interview with Professor Golunsky showed me was that the Soviet Union still has a long way to go. The only two concrete reforms he could name were the abolition of the Special Board and the newly revised law of last year "strengthening" the Procurator's Office. The new code of criminal law and procedure still seems to be bogged down. In March, 1953, definite proposals were promised in thirty days. Last fall Professor Berman was told the new law would be ready "about February." It was now May of 1956, and it was clear from my talk with Professor Golunsky that many good decisions were still in abeyance but that at least one bad one had already been made. The bad one is that there will be no revision of the notorious law of counterrevolutionary crimes.

The day the Soviet Union repeals this law will be the day the world will know that the new regime really means business. The first paragraph is enough to give its flavor and show the blank check it gives the police. "Any action is considered counterrevolutionary," the law says, "which is directed toward the overthrow, undermining or weakening of the authority of the Workers' and Peasants' Soviets, or of the Workers' and Peasants' Government (whether of the U.S.S.R. or of a constituent or autonomous republic) . . . or toward the undermining or weakening of the external security of the U.S.S.R. or of the fundamental economic, political and national gains of the proletarian revolution." This is sweeping enough to put any critic in jail, or frame any opponent.

Among the questions still in abeyance is whether accused persons shall have the right to have counsel present during their interrogation before trial. The question of the point at which private counsel may participate is not yet settled, though it will be an improvement over present practice where the counsel does not appear until the case is brought into open court. The question of when a man can have counsel is important. As Professor Golunsky explained, in ordinary cases the police will still be able to hold a man for thirty days before trial and in extraordinary cases for three months. This will also be an improvement since in practice the secret police have been able to hold a man as long as they liked without trial. But even one month, much less three, of unrestricted interrogation may be enough to break a man or force a false confession à la Vishinsky. (The new Yugoslav code provides for eight hours uninterrupted rest during every twenty-four hours in which a prisoner is held for interrogation by the police.) All trials will be public except those involving sexual crime or military or diplomatic secrets —the latter may prove a dangerous exception.

The new criminal code will be a test of the new regime. To make the vindication of injustice depend upon the Procurator General will be to allow the central autocracy to decide what rights shall be enforced and who shall get justice. To grant greater rights to the individual would be to weaken the central power and to make it possible for individuals unjustly treated to enforce their rights in the courts against the State as they can in Western countries. Without revision of the definitions of treason and counterrevolution, freedom of discussion will not be achieved. The Soviet bureaucracy and leadership are obviously reluctant to go that far, but ferment at home and criticism from abroad may yet force them toward fundamental reforms.

MAY 21, 1956

THE LEGACY OF STALIN

The way home from Moscow has been agony for me. I have been reading furiously in Russian history and a little in Russian law and in past Communist controversy in an effort to evaluate what I have seen. The deepest questions of history and morality are raised by Russia, the terrible intermingling of good and evil in the evolution of society, history's endless riddle of whether-it-might-have-been-otherwise. My knowledge is inadequate, my ignorance is vast, my only credentials are that these conclusions represent what one man has seen and felt.

All sorts of advice has poured in on me from my friends, and from what I know my friends would say. All the inhibitions of expediency have been urged upon me, the inhibitions of the most worthy expediency—the fight for world peace. But I hate the morass into which one wanders when one begins to withhold the truth because the consequences might be bad—this is, indeed, the morass on which the Russian Communist State is built. I am not wise enough, and perhaps no one else is either, to know how much truth may wisely be given the public with our eye-droppers. I am only a reporter and one does not go to Moscow every day. This is what I think, not what I believe may wisely be told the reader. It may be wrong but it is not synthetic.

I feel like a swimmer under water who must rise to the surface or his lungs will burst. Whatever the consequences, I have to say what I really feel after seeing the Soviet Union and carefully studying the statements of its leading officials. *This is not a good society and it is not led by honest men.*

No society is good in which men fear to think—much less speak —freely. I don't care how many tons of steel the Russians produce. It is not by the volume of its steel but by the character of the men it produces that a society must be judged. The kind of men Russia has produced is the kind which must always be wary, quick to sense any change in the wind and adjust to it, careful never to give way to the anguish of seeing injustice, always guarding one's tongue, alert to survive at whatever cost to one's neighbor.

This society is a paradise only for a rather stupid type of Communist party member, good but sharply limited. If you believe everything you read in the papers, lack imagination, and feel no need to think for yourself, you can be very happy in the Soviet Union and engage in useful devoted work. Or you can shut yourself up in a scientific laboratory and work on your own scientific problems and close your eyes and ears to what is going on outside or maybe even to your unlucky colleague next door. But for the journalist, the writer, the artist, the thinker, the man who cares deeply about the basic questions of humanity and history, the U.S.S.R. has been a hermetically sealed prison, stifling in its atmosphere of complete, rigid and low-level thought control. In this atmosphere has been bred a whole generation of sycophants, and yes-men, and writer-politicians.

It is impossible to imagine unless you have been there what it means to live in a country in which you do not know what is going on outside. The Soviet press is matchless for turgidity and obscurity; it prints only what the men at the top think people ought to know and it is written by uninspired hacks scared to add a thought of their own lest they get into trouble. I invite readers to check this for themselves by reading three authoritative expositions of the new line— *Pravda's* article of March 28, "Why Is the Cult of the Individual Alien to the Spirit of Marxism-Leninism?" (It can be found in full English translation in the March 30 issue of the now defunct Cominform weekly, *For a Lasting Peace, for a People's Democracy*); *Partiinaya Zhizn's* article of March, 1956, "Wherein Is the Harm of the Cult of the Individual?" (English text in the April 12 issue of the Soviet Information Bureau's *Daily Review of Soviet Press*); and *Kommunist's* article of March, 1956, "Fully Re-establish and Develop Leninist Standards of Party Life" (English text in the April 4 issue of the *Daily Review of Soviet Press*). They are as alike as if all three were the results of a party briefing at which the writers took down the words from on high in as verbatim a manner as possible. The same thoughts, the very same phrases, reappear in the same kind of repellent gibberish.

When you ask in Moscow where foreign papers can be purchased, the answer is that your bookstall in the hotel carries all kinds of foreign papers. But when you watch the stall in the Metropol or the National or the Savoy (the three Intourist hotels) all you see are the East European and Chinese Communist party publications and that completely empty waste of paper, the *Moscow News*. I don't know what it was like when Anna Louise Strong edited it, but there is certainly no news in it today. I could not even buy Western Communist papers like *L'Humanité*. When I picked up a copy of the London *Daily Worker* in the Prague airport on the way back, I got the full flavor of what I had experienced in journalism. The London *Daily Worker* seemed like a bright, newsy, *real* newspaper after the Soviet press. In Warsaw, they have begun to sell Western "capitalist" papers. It will be a sign of real change when this happens in Moscow. It is indicative that a Communist intellectual with whom I discussed this problem in Eastern Europe admitted to me that he "couldn't live" without the *New York Times*. It was a confession and a tribute. Whatever the shortcomings of the Western press, there is no comparison between it and the Soviet press. Out of the variety of news and opinion in the Western press one can sift even the most unpopular truths. To read the Soviet press one has to become expert in decoding a peculiar kind of party language, developed to hide the facts rather than to make them public.

Again I invite readers to check this for themselves. I cite as an example the dissolution of the Cominform, a major news and political event of the Soviet world. The full text of the joint statement by the Bulgarian, Hungarian, Italian, Polish, Rumanian, Soviet, Czech and French parties explaining the dissolution may be found in the final, April 17, issue of the Cominform bulletin, which is on sale in New York. The front page also carries an article on the dissolution snappily entitled "For the Further Development and Strengthening of the International Communist Movement." I challenge anyone to read these two pieces of drivel and find in them any real explanation of why the Cominform was dissolved.

This is why I am compelled to conclude that the present leaders of the Soviet Union are dishonest. I mean dishonest with their own people, not only with the non-party masses but with their own Communist party members. If they want to make a clean break with the Stalinist past, they can best demonstrate it by telling their people what they are doing and why. How can you have "democratic centralism" in the Communist party, i.e., free discussion within the limits of party discipline (what Lenin meant by the phrase), when the party members themselves aren't told what is going on?

I cite as a major example the Beria business. No one outside a very small circle at the top really knows why Beria was executed. Those who study the tortuous, veiled and contradictory language of the various statements published in the Soviet press will find themselves completely confused. Only persons rendered permanently idiotic by complete submergence in party-line literature will take at face value the charge that he was a British or imperialist agent. This is how Stalin operated; he never met an opponent on the ground of honest discussion; first slander and then the firing squad were his answers. And *everybody* turned out to be a foreign agent!

Now, if the charge was meant seriously, why didn't the new rulers demonstrate their intention to operate differently by presenting their evidence against Beria in open court? Why was he tried secretly and so swiftly executed? Was not the treatment of Beria in the true Stalinist tradition? And nothing was more truly Stalinist than the obscure and slanderous verbiage of the various statements on Beria.

I cite as another major example the attack on Stalin himself. Nobody yet knows just why and how it was decided to go so far in the denigration of Stalin. After his death, the press began to play him down. But in 1954 and again in 1955 his picture appeared with Lenin's on the front page of the November 7 issue of *Pravda,* celebrating the anniversary of the Revolution. Zhukov in Red Square paid tribute just last year to the party of "Marx-Engels-Lenin-*Stalin.*" As recently as last December 21, *Pravda* published a 2,000-word article on the 76th anniversary of Stalin's birth, an article full of the most lavish praise of the dead dictator in Marxist theory and in practice, in industry and in agriculture. The language was that of the Stalin cult.

What happened between the end of December and the Twentieth Party Congress in February? Indeed why did Khrushchev confine himself to generalities about the "cult of leadership" in his report to the Congress on behalf of the Central Committee February 14—only to make a savage attack on Stalin at a secret session eleven days later, on February 25? Why was it secret? Why did Communist newspapermen leak the gist of this secret session deliberately to other newspapermen in Moscow? Why was the Soviet censor so "sticky" about passing these reports until after they had leaked from abroad? No one knows. Indeed it is amazing how little anyone knows of what really goes on in Moscow.

What one does see is that somehow the attack on Stalin has the same crass, crude air as Stalin's own attacks on his own victims. Stalin had a series of scapegoats on whom he blamed the abuses of his regime in his periodic relaxations. His successors act the same way. Their scapegoat was Beria and then Stalin himself. By blaming all the evils of the regime on the dead dictator, they may hope to increase their own popularity. But to blame the evils of Stalinism on Stalin is obviously inadequate. It is not merely that they were his accomplices; their cowardice is understandable. It is that Stalinism was the natural fruit of the whole spirit of the Communist movement. The wanton executions, the frame-ups, the unjust convictions and exiles—these would not have been possible except in a movement whose members had been taught not only to obey unquestioningly but to *hate*. The average Communist was prepared to believe anything about anyone who differed with him in the slightest; the liquidation of the opposition was not just a duty but a savage pleasure. And if "errors" were occasionally made, these were the unavoidable sacrifices of the revolution. This was the spirit the Communist movement bred. Stalin embodied that spirit. To change it one must do more than hang Stalin in effigy, or defame him in self-serving panic as Khrushchev is doing.

The more one studies Russian history the more one sees how deep were the roots of Leninism in Russian radical thinking of the nineteenth century as well as in Czarist habits. Lenin was fashioned by the weight of many generations. But whether Lenin was right or wrong and whether so complete a dictatorship was really necessary is beside the point. The point is that the Revolution has succeeded; socialism in Russia is there to stay; capitalism will never be restored; even among the escapees the only major criticism is of collectivization. Russian industrialism, despite Russian slovenliness and that callous waste of men and manpower one feels in Russia, has advanced on giant boots, thanks to economic planning. Now Khrushchev, in revealing the extent to which the abuses had grown under Stalin, shows that these are not figments of hostile propaganda. ("Multiply all you have read abroad by ten," a Communist said to me, "and you will get the dimensions of Khrushchev's revelations about Stalin.") The problem has been posed by the new regime itself. How is a repetition of these terrible evils to be avoided? How indeed are they to be wholly eliminated?

It is in seeking the answer to these questions that I found Russia and its leaders most disappointing. These are the very competent managers of a great industrial empire; their speeches at the Twentieth Congress show their grasp of concrete industrial problems. They get down to brass tacks in studying steel output or railroad management. But they do not show the same spirit at all in grappling with the evils they have themselves exposed. These Socialist industrialists, these lifelong Marxists, drift off into vague mysticism and into worship of personality. When a system breeds monsters, as they say their secret police system has bred monsters for twenty years, then something must be wrong with the system. If Yagoda, Yehzov and Beria were all monsters, should not the ordinary citizen be given greater protection against the police in the future, greater rights of his own? Should not the public be educated to understand the reason for these rights and their existence? Should not the press be encouraged to criticize when it suspects frame-ups? The questions which confront Russia today under communism are like those which confronted the framers of our own Constitution. Individual rights are no less, perhaps more, necessary under communism than under capitalism; the coercive power of the new State is greater. These questions are not yet even being discussed in Russia.

Instead we come across a lot of vague talk about "collective leadership." But Stalin as well as Lenin talked of collective leadership and its virtues. And what does collective leadership mean? Again I urge the reader to examine the basic documents for himself. An eleven-man Presidium may be just as wrong as a one-man dictator. *Pravda* said April 5, "Throughout its history the Party's policy was and remained a Leninist policy." *Pravda* says the Party's policy has always been "correct." (A revealing Bolshevik word; it implies an absolute standard of measurement, like a yardstick; how can this wooden mentality be reconciled with the rich, complex and dynamic views of a man like Marx?) But what sense does it make to say that the Party has always been correct when you admit that for the last twenty years of Stalin's life he used the Party as his vehicle for all kinds of injustices and abuses? Obviously the Party was incorrect when it allowed itself to be frightened into silence, acquiescence, collaboration and submission by Stalin. The Party and the Central Committee for these people are mystical concepts; the whole is different from its parts; the leaders may be rotten and the members cowardly but put them together and they are miraculously the bearers of the future! Instead of rights, guarantees, free discussion, Russia is told to repose faith in the Central Committee, that is in the eleven-man Presidium, in "collective leadership."

The speeches of the new leaders are wholly inadequate to the correction of the evils they have exposed. So long as there is only one party, and it has a monopoly of government and controls all expression, there cannot be freedom. Russia is strong enough, secure enough, to move away from the one-party system. We have two parties which do not differ in essentials; they could have two parties, too. Their society is stable enough for stable politics. The kind of one-party rule which may have been necessary to achieve the Revolution has become a positive hindrance; this is the real lesson of the revelations about Stalin.

I came away from Russia with the strong conviction that Khrushchev is more crude and vulgar than Stalin, and will if given the chance take over completely. I believe his colleagues have forced him into the attack on Stalin and talk of "collective leadership" to prevent a return to one-man rule. In the process they have intensified the ferment which began with Stalin's death and set in motion events whose momentum they may not be able to control. The new policies have opened Russia's windows on the West and given us a chance to resume contact with this huge and wonderful segment of humanity. In the interests of peace, and of peaceful change in Russia, we ought to strive to keep the windows open, and to help along the process which may some day carry Russia forward from the current relaxation to freer institutions. I believe not only her people but her rulers want peace; and I believe that given peace they will slowly liquidate Russia's terrible backwardness and unholy past.

But this process will not be helped by indulging in delusions, or by quickly forgiving and forgetting Stalinism in the belief that Russia has now fundamentally changed. Changes there are, and given the natural extremism of the Russian temperament, no one knows how much further they may go tomorrow. But we will not help the Russian people by letting this crowd of leaders soft-soap us; in any free country, after similar revelations, a whole new set of men would have been swept into power as earnest of real change. Nor will we help ourselves, and our power to fight for a better world and a better society, by joining hands with the poor deluded house-broken Communist parties of the West. They remain Russian puppets; they will jump back through the hoops as soon as they get new orders. Their members cannot be freed from intellectual bondage until the parties themselves have disintegrated. Nothing has yet happened in Russia to justify cooperation abroad between the independent left and the Communists.

MAY 28, 1956

19: *In the Fresher Air of Poland*

The first thought which came into my mind as I drove into Warsaw from the airport was, "I'm in Europe again." Some of the apartment house fronts on the streets through which we passed recalled Paris; others, Italian *palazzi*. The people in the streets were not only better dressed than in Moscow but looked *chic*. At the airport limousine station I was met by a Polish gentleman who spoke English with an Oxford accent rendered subtly different by an undertone of the softer and slower intonations of the Slav. He had the grand manner whose impress the lordly Polish aristocracy have left on their country, a manner more seignorial than anything to be encountered in London or Paris. There were still terrible scars and ruins amid the newly rebuilt areas—apartment house fronts sheared away as if by a giant hand, exposing the rooms within in all their pitiful vanished intimacy. I was taken to the Bristol Hotel, which escaped the war with little damage since it was the German headquarters. All foreigners now stay there. It gave one a strange feeling to check into the rooms from which SS and Wehrmacht directed the deliberate extermination of so many millions of human beings.

The Bristol, small and provincial, was quite a contrast to the enormous caverns of the Metropol in Moscow, but the Bristol was in better repair, and the furnishings were modern. The prices, at four zlotys to the dollar, were fully as expensive as Moscow, and I copied down a few at breakfast. Coffee was 8 zlotys, $2; ham and eggs were 12 zlotys, $3; tea cost 65 cents a glass and a pat of butter, a quarter dollar. There were a half-dozen Chinese in the dining room, but though they spoke English I never succeeded in talking to them. The newspaper stand at the Bristol, like that in the Metropol, carried only Communist publications, but the Bristol had Western as well as Eastern Communist papers. There was *Le Drapeau Rouge* from Belgium, *L'Unità* from Italy, *L'Humanité* from France and an old copy of the New York *Daily Worker* as well as *Pravda, Neues Deutschland* and *Rude Pravo*. But I soon learned that the great event on the intellectual front in Warsaw was that for two months at five main cafés it was now possible to read the *Manchester Guardian,* the *London Times, Le Monde, L'Information* and *L'Express*. A limited number of copies were also on sale daily at the bookstalls, adjoining these coffee houses. I went to one of them, a big coffee house in the Central European tradition, its walls lined like a library with newspapers and magazines neatly racked for the use of its customers. There were as yet no American publications except the *Daily Worker* and *Masses and Mainstream*.

Warsaw is now the first Soviet capital in which foreign, i.e., "capitalist," papers can be read in the coffee houses and bought on the bookstalls. Only those who know Central Europe will fully appreciate what this means. On the Continent, where intellectuals customarily read several languages, people read foreign papers far more than they do in the United States, and a visit to a café in Prague or Vienna was a chance to get a quick bird's-eye view of the world press. I am sure that nothing so irritated the Czech intellectuals with the Communist regime in that country as that they could no longer read the *London Times* or even the *New Statesman and Nation*. They still can't in the Prague coffee houses. The appearance of Western papers in Warsaw symbolizes better than any other single event the change taking place in Poland, and the difference between Warsaw and other Soviet capitals. I expected to find some slight variations. I found instead a completely different atmosphere. I have nowhere in the world, East or West, not even in Tito's Belgrade in 1950, heard Communists talk as they are talking in Warsaw, without Communist clichés or party cant, and a good deal more freely than in the loyalty-purge-haunted government circles of Washington. My visit to Warsaw was a revelation and a pleasure.

I am sure that Poland remains in many fundamental ways a satellite of Moscow, but there is nevertheless an atmosphere in Warsaw, a change in the government and a spirit in the Polish press which goes far beyond the regimented de-Stalinization in Moscow or the obedient but tepidly cautious imitations dutifully arranged in East Germany, Czechoslovakia, Hungary and Bulgaria. Germans will goose-step in any direction, the Czechs are as submissive as Russians, the Hungarians have been politically devitalized by one dictatorship after another since World War I. But the traditionally and historically rebellious Poles—invited to speak up by Stalin's detractors—have answered with a loud and enthusiastic roar.

Polish Communists talk a language one does not hear elsewhere. "We have our own McCarthys," said a Polish party journalist at lunch; no Russian, no American Communist, would admit that there were "McCarthys" among his comrades. "You can't knock Marxism into people's heads with a hammer," a second-echelon party functionary told me in describing the difference between the Polish and the Russian approach to the peasant problem. Even during Stalin's heyday Poland avoided the "Bolshevik logic" he applied to the peasantry with such singularly disastrous results—as Khrushchev now testifies in discussing the Russian farm problem. "The Socialists have good reason to mistrust us," said another Polish Communist in discussing the desire to revive the Popular Front, "we have to prove to them that this time joint action will not mean their political liquidation." A Polish official, discussing the Gomulka affair, said, "We disagreed with Gomulka before and we disagree with him now. But we never thought him a traitor. Our secret police are experts at faking evidence. They produced all kinds of material incriminating Gomulka. It had a fishy smell but we didn't know how to disprove it. At least we didn't stage a trial and force a confession and kill him and we're proud now that we can release him." No Russian official would admit, simply, that the secret police were expert at faking evidence. I got no double talk in Warsaw.

The week I was there, that which began on April 23, saw the first meeting of a Communist parliament in which there was real debate, real differences of opinion and real criticism of the government. This was no Supreme Soviet, invariably unanimous even in condemning its own past. The Sejm meets in a building of chaste simplicity, refreshing after the Byzantine baroque of Moscow; plain Doric columns surround the huge semicircle of a skylighted chamber in which the delegates convene. It was built by Pilsudski in 1928 and reconstructed in 1946-47. The lovely white building contains no "icons"—no busts or paintings of governmental leaders; Poland, unlike Stalin's Russia and Tito's Yugoslavia, never really had a "personality cult." The day I was there the session of the Sejm looked about as bored and desultory as a normal session of Congress in Washington; the press galleries looked equally "normal," i.e., bored. The discussion during my visit was on science and the schools. A deputy, Zofia Zemanek, boasted that higher education in Poland had outstripped Britain; that while there were only 30 higher school students per 10,000 in Britain, there were 52 per 10,000 in Poland. Even in this a new note was struck. The official summary quoted her as saying "a certain degradation of science had been evident in the past few years. Schematism and vulgarization had led to the ossification of science which, deprived of broader contacts with foreign countries, *without polemics,* could not develop properly." (Italics added.)

There was no dearth of polemics at the session. The Prime Minister, Cyrankiewicz, invited them in his opening address. He welcomed "the sound wave of criticism" sweeping over Poland, said it meant that "every conscious citizen is becoming an activist," and he demanded a new attitude on the part of the government toward the Sejm. "Undoubtedly," Cyrankiewicz said, "we will have to break with the practice by which the overwhelming majority of legal acts come into life in the shape of decrees, without previous discussion at Sejm committees." The Sejm was no longer to be a rubber stamp. Instead, like any normal legislature, it was to exercise "control over the organs of the executive power and the activities of the Government." Such control was "a no less essential factor in consolidating the rule of law." But in order to do so the members of the Sejm "must have access to sources of information" and in this respect "the situation was bad in the past." Questions from Sejm members had been treated in the past "as an irritating nuisance." He promised an end to such practices. "Cooperation with the Sejm will be, and must be, a fundamental rule for all organs of Government."

Cyrankiewicz is one of the Socialists who joined with the Communists in the formation of the "United Workers Party," indeed the last one left in high position. His speech had a non-Communist flavor in its discussion of civil liberties. He thought "the vigilant reaction of public opinion to each violation of binding laws and civil rights can be of great assistance" in maintaining "the strict observance of the rule of law." He said debate was taking place in Poland in a society "where there still exist class antagonisms and where the class enemy undoubtedly is still active." But the lesson he drew from this echoed the rationale of classic liberalism. He said that "in the atmosphere of political activisation, when in the course of this great debate the political armor is growing more perfect, when the maturity of the masses is certainly growing at a double rate, while complaints and grievances are being revealed and, thanks to this, can be overcome, the enemy is finding it increasingly difficult to operate. . . . Of what importance," he asked, "are insinuations, slanders, gossip, whispering campaigns and intrigues at a time when all of us are openly exposing all shortcomings and errors . . . ?" Strikingly absent was any implication that "democracy" was to be limited to the Party, much less that it was to be channeled within "correct" limits of "Marxism-Leninism," Russian style.

The week before the Sejm opened, the government had already begun to activate this policy by providing real information to the parliamentary committees; for the first time in Polish postwar history, these committees began to discuss and work on pending legislation. When the session opened, the deputies were not slow to take advantage of the cue given them by the Prime Minister. A newspaperman deputy, Osmanczyk, launched a vigorous attack on press policy. He said too much space was consumed by "tremendously long official statements" and so-called "original articles telling us the same thing in slightly different words." He protested that the government was "still providing mere droplets of information for the press, meted out according to the various strata of the population—the larger the circle of readers, the smaller the droplet." This is a perfect description of Soviet press policy. Another deputy, Drobner, once a left-wing Socialist, assailed the system under which the Sejm passed decrees "as if at a military command—get up, sit down, get up again, sit down again, and make ourselves the laughing stock of the community."

Two Catholic deputies spoke up on behalf of non-Communist Catholic opinion. Deputy Horodynski said millions of believing Catholics were helping to build socialism and protested "the false division of the nation into Marxists and Catholics." The former Count Lubienski, a member of Pax, the Roman Catholic organization which supports the regime, asked that Catholics be allowed to set up their own youth organization or that the Communist Youth

Union be transformed into "an organization of young people embracing various world outlooks." This challenge to the monistic and monolithic character of a Communist regime drew replies from two deputies. One, Gwiazdowicz, dwelt on the hostility of the clergy to the people and the anticlerical traditions of the peasantry. The other, Deputy Helena Jaworska, accused the clergy of intolerance and of exercising pressure on young people. She said young people were free to join the official Youth Union or not as they pleased and that persuasion was the only method of ideological influence it used. The tone of this debate, the fact that it took place at all, was significant. It was equally noteworthy that five Catholic deputies voted against the bill to legalize abortion. There was unanimity—but it was genuine—in the approval accorded the amnesty under which thirty thousand political prisoners are being freed and compensation will be paid the wrongfully imprisoned. And there was unanimity within the Sejm as well as without in the summary dismissal of Radkiewicz, former head of the secret police; of the public prosecutor, and of the chief military prosecutor. Most indicative of all was the decision to restore the full civil rights of all who fought in the rightist Polish Home Army during the last war.

It was a pleasure to find Jewish cultural life flourishing in Poland. There is a Yiddish press and a Yiddish theatre—indeed the Jews of Poland even during the last days of Stalin suffered no such period as befell the Jews of the Soviet Union, a period in which Jewish artists and writers were liquidated, and Jews themselves made targets of public scorn. In this respect, too, the Polish record is the best in Eastern Europe and notably better than in the neighboring Czechoslovakia with its Slansky frame-up and the long imprisonment of the now freed Israeli journalist, Mordechai Oren. The leaders of the Jewish community in Warsaw speak with none of those apprehensive inhibitions one feels in the Jews of Moscow even today, and it was an encouraging experience to start up a conversation with a stranger at a bookstall, to find that he was a Jew and to walk about Warsaw with him talking Yiddish.

For me the high point of my visit to Warsaw was to see what the Poles are doing to rebuild their capital. Before leaving it the Germans systematically destroyed what was left, house by house and building by building. The Poles are rebuilding the old Warsaw *exactly as it was*. The ancient market, the old churches and monuments are being reconstructed in precise and loving replica of the past. The new apartments are being built and planned to fit in with the old; Poland is an architect's paradise and socialism is demonstrating its great advantage in this heroic task of rebuilding and resurrecting the old city treasures. No effort is being spared to make Warsaw rise again from the ashes of Germany's wanton malevolence. In this resurrection of their beloved and lovely capital, the Poles demonstrate a national will to live that must stir all who believe in courage and in indestructible spirit. Their one big architectural problem is what to do with that huge Soviet super-duper Roxy theatre, that stupefyingly huge and tastelessly opulent Palace of Culture and Science which Stalin gave them. The problem of how to make it fit into the quiet elegance of Warsaw seems to be an insoluble one.

Poland was the first of the Soviet satellites to react vigorously to the downgrading of Stalin. Just four days after Khrushchev's speech attacking the dead dictator, a speaker on Radio Warsaw called for greater freedom of thought and declared that Poland had been too long "spoon-fed on an insipid, messy hash of slogans. . . . Today everyone must realize that he has not only the right but the duty to think and to express his thoughts. . . ." Every Communist leader there goes out of the way to assure the visitor that this does not mean a break with Moscow, that on the contrary the new line will make it easier for Poland to remain in friendly alliance with the Soviet Union. The Polish leaders feel that the old policy of trying to play an independent role between Germany and Russia is bankrupt, that Poland must for its own safety stand with the U.S.S.R. But they are determined to find a way within these limits to a freer society. For them this does not mean the restoration of capitalism— or that mixture of feudalism, fascism, clericalism and capitalism which was prewar Poland—but they see no reason why socialism cannot be combined with freedom of thought and security of the person. This is a struggle to liberate Poland which deserves sympathy from all Liberals and Socialists abroad. And in my opinion it may far better than Tito's Yugoslavia provide model and inspiration elsewhere in Eastern Europe.

JUNE 4, 1956

20: *The Presidency, 1956*

WHO IS EISENHOWER?

The problem which tantalizes us political scientists here in Washington is trying to determine just who *is* President. Some days it seems to be Hagerty. Other days it seems to be Sherman Adams. Occasionally Leonard Hall acts as if he were the leader of the Administration as well as the party. The armed forces keep complaining that the Secretary of the Treasury has taken over, and several times the man at the desk in the Executive Mansion has clearly been Herbert Brownell. Eisenhower himself turns up on the more ceremonial occasions, when he is in town.

All this leads us to suspect that the real explanation of the Nixon mix-up is that Stassen must have consulted Eisenhower on one of those days on which somebody else was President, probably Hagerty. This seems to us a much more plausible hypothesis than that advanced by our distinguished colleague, John O'Donnell in last Wednesday's *Daily News*. "Probably," O'Donnell wrote, "as those closest to Ike in the Cabinet and on Capitol Hill now insist, the President realized that he had made an error last Friday when Stassen told him that he was going to urge Herter as a replacement for Nixon. . . ." We believe the error was Stassen's; he just didn't notice that the little brass plate bearing the legend "Mr. President" was on one of the desks in the outer lobby that day.

The effect on the average voter, who tends to be old-fashioned, may be unsettling. Untrained in philosophical abstractions and unable to grasp the advantages of a pluralistic approach to the presidency, he may feel it would be safer just to elect one man to the job in November and have done with it. Herter's reaction to Stassen's nomination may help further to confuse and disaffect him. Not only do none of these Republican Presidents, all nominally Eisenhower, seem to know how to run their own official family, but now this fellow Herter seems to be getting ready to run for Vice-President by nominating Nixon for the job. And wasn't there something in the papers about Nixon reciprocating by nominating Herter in return?

It's bad enough not to be quite sure at any given hour just who is President, but what if come November we were no longer sure who was Vice-President either?

JULY 20, 1956

THE GOP'S OWN PERSONALITY CULT

We found ourselves happy during that climactic session at San Francisco that the proceedings were not being telecast to Moscow. The startled Soviet viewer might have imagined that the United States had taken over the cult of personality. That parade of "little people" seconding the nomination of Dwight D. Eisenhower would have recalled the mass meetings at which steel workers and collective farmers bounded for a moment out of obscurity to hail the boundless virtues of one who had now best be nameless. There was a Mrs. Schneider from Texas telling why "we mothers" loved Ike; a coach from Notre Dame who said Ike always made "the right play at the right time"; a little businessman from Louisiana who put his hand over his heart and said he "wholeheartedly" accepted every jot and tittle of Ike's platform; a worker who said of Ike, "It makes you proud just to look at him"; a nice Jewish lady from Boston who hailed him as "the best President we ever had" and quoted her beloved rabbi on something we did not catch, probably Ike's astounding grasp of the finer points of the *Mishnah*. Not since Stalin passed away has any people had such a paragon for leader.

It would all have seemed too familiar to a viewer in Moscow, right down to the virtues of "democratic centralism" in which the opposition is allowed to cut its own moral throat in public before being sent to the sub-Arctic gold mines. There was Comrade Stassen grateful for the favor of being allowed to second the nomination of Comrade Nixon against whom he had long been plotting, probably at the instigation of a foreign power, since no evidence of domestic support had been uncovered. There was Comrade Knight joyfully dancing the *kupak* for Nixon at the head of the California delegation, probably in the hope that he would only get a ten-year sentence. There was Joe Martin's indignant roar, "Who does he want to nominate?" when a foolish comrade from Nebraska tried to disrupt democratic unanimity by nominating somebody else. The only other subversive note, injected before anyone was quite aware of what he was saying, came in the invocation offered by the Episcopal Bishop.

His prayer for Eisenhower was a sly one. "Grant him," he intoned, "an added measure of insight and understanding." This shows the danger of allowing political freedom to the clergy.

Our favorite character among those sedately tumultuous Republicans was uncovered by a Diogenes for CBS. In the wings he found a bevy of lightly spangled nymphs from a nearby night club waiting with Nixon banners. (At the last moment their enthusiasm seems to have been cruelly repressed because they never appeared on the floor.) When he asked one of them, "Are you Republican?" she tee-heed uncertainly and said "Yes," obviously a girl with quite a memory span. But next to these lovely politicos were two Chinese children waiting with Nixon banners and when the CBS man asked one of them, "Who are you demonstrating for?" he answered in honest bewilderment, "I don't know." The delegates on the floor were better informed. They knew the names. But of the reality behind "Eisenhower" and "Nixon," the real capacities, the real intentions, the real men, the *"dinger an sich"*?

There must have been no more than a dozen men on that floor who really knew the labors of propping up an old soldier into a statesman, of interrupting golf and bridge to get papers signed, of painfully briefing him in the mysteries of the tariff, and straightening him out on the farm problem. There may have been even fewer who knew the real story which reached its climax when Eisenhower and Stassen called off that anti-Nixon campaign like two small boys shamefacedly caught by teacher. As Eisenhower told the reporters, "Well, you will remember for quite a little while, I didn't know that Mr. Nixon was going to run again, he took quite a considerable time after he and I first talked it over, to make up his mind. . . ." Suppose Ike had been left at the last moment without a running mate? No doubt this anxiety explains his announced willingness to interview any applicants for the job in San Francisco. The help problem in the White House is terrific.

This Republican convention, though it did move somewhat slowly, and often seemed a concert interspersed with political speeches, had its memorable moments. There was that boast from Dewey, just a hundred years after Lincoln, the glad tidings of a new emancipation, "Guatemala is now free." There was Herter, plodding with gentlemanly desperation through those encomiums of Nixon. If ever anybody had a psychosomatic sore throat it was the Governor of Massachusetts nominating another man for Vice-President when he would rather have stayed in bed with a nice case of pneumonia. There was Martin shouting to the only rugged individualist who had turned up in years at a Republican convention, "You take Joe Smith and get out of here." And there was Martin at press conference earlier in the day dismissing questions about Ike's health as "rather morbid." There was Ike telling the press that Stassen would second the nomination of Nixon and asking the reporters, "Is it today?" and adding (possibly after a whispered assist from Hagerty), "Yes—this afternoon." And Ike being asked whether he thought it was "possible to nominate a stronger candidate than Mr. Nixon" and answering, "Well, I wouldn't know."

The strangest spectacle of all at this convention was the appearance on the platform of a darkly handsome man who looked like a young Italian tenor, but turned up to speak rather than sing. The absence of jowls, the high intellectual forehead, the frizzly hair-do and the graceful manner made him seem altogether alien among the GOP's solid citizenry, taking time off from real estate and embalming for politics.

Only a day before, James Reston in the *New York Times* had reported, perhaps tongue in cheek, that Eisenhower would now be able to articulate his thoughts better because Emmet John Hughes of *Time-Life-Fortune*—the drafter of the "I shall go to Korea" speech in 1952—had rejoined him temporarily as a ghost writer. Here was Hughes being introduced to make a speech on his own as an "independent" for Eisenhower, and taking himself quite seriously, the young idealist given his chance to tell off those politicians at last. Though obviously in no danger of losing his job for addressing a Republican convention, Hughes was determined to prove his independence. He leaned hard and tactlessly on Negro rights, made a posthumous attack on McCarthy, and drew a deadly blank when he said there was a danger that loyalty was being confused with conformity. It wasn't so much what he said as how; this evident foreigner seemed somehow sincere. The convention was first puzzled, then bored. The scattered applause said clearly that it couldn't care less. Hughes, laboring hard against the palpable indifference, mopped his brow and hurried out as if in search of a stiff drink and a friendly Democrat. The experiment in letting a ghost talk had failed. This was no place for an egghead, even one on the payroll.

Of the 1952 slogan about corruption, Korea and communism, the first and third have been muted. There is a truce on corruption, since Dixon-Yates may easily cancel out mink and deep freezes. Communism was noteworthy by its almost complete absence. Joe Martin was alone and old-fashioned in speaking of the "indelible stain of corruption and communism" and even he explained to the press afterward that he did not mean the Democratic party. Knowland and Nixon have given the party a clean bill of health. "There is only one party of treason in our country," Knowland said, "and that is the Communist party." Nixon said of those people in Chicago, "I'm sure they are all loyal Americans." The tide of reaction is receding and the Democratic party is legal again. What the Republicans are running on this year is Korea—Korea and prosperity. Ike is the man who ended the war in Korea without starting a new one, the man who proved we could have prosperity without war. This was the theme song of the convention, woven into almost every utterance. And unless Ike turns ill before November, it may prove potent enough—and true enough—to win.

AUGUST 27, 1956

21: *Hungary*

THE WORKERS RISE AGAINST THE WORKERS' STATE

For those of us who have all our lives regarded socialism as our ideal, it is humbling to see that the leading role in the convulsions sweeping Eastern Europe is being taken by the working class, and by the factory workers in particular. Those to whom socialism in the nineteenth century most appealed, the workers, the idealist students, the intellectuals with a conscience, these are the elements at the head of the risings in Poland and Hungary today, as they may be tomorrow in Czechoslovakia and the Soviet Union. It is not the ghost of the dispossessed bourgeoisie nor the resistance of the incorrigible peasant to whatever threatens his hold on the land; it is the reaction against Marxism-Leninism by those very elements it sought to serve and to inspire. These risings in the middle of the twentieth century are a caricature of what happened in 1870, in 1905 and in 1917. The workers rise against the workers' state. The epic of the Paris Commune and the Moscow Soviet is played out again in reverse.

It is instructive to notice that workers may be aroused to the same kind of fury against their Socialist managers as against any capitalist oppressor. This will not surprise those of us who have been in Eastern Europe and caught that aroma of ruling class complacency which the party apparatus exudes whether in Stalinist Russia or Titoist Yugoslavia. The men who devoted their lives to the emancipation of the oppressed are too often and too soon succeeded by men who now take it for granted that *they* shall have the Cadillacs, the *dachas,* the more spacious apartments, the fine linen and the servants. Sometimes it is even the same men. This would not have surprised the great anarchists of the last century; from Bakunin to Kropotkin, they foresaw that a Socialist bureaucracy could also oppress and exploit. There was an echo of their warnings in a contemptuous reference which Gomulka made in his speech to the Polish Central Committee on October 20. He spoke of those in the leadership of the Communist party who "felt more strongly linked with their comfortable posts than with the working class." It is the bureaucrat, the bureaucrat with secret police and censor at his disposal to protect that comfortable post, who is the universal focus of the long pent-up anger among the masses in the Soviet world. More fundamental than the economic problem is the moral and institutional problem implicit in this picture; men will suffer want together in the pursuit or defense of an ideal. It is an unjust inequality of sacrifice, a high-handedness among those who claim to serve them, that embitters and provokes. No condescending stereotypes about "bourgeois democracy" can hide the giant lesson of events—the worker needs the secret ballot, the opposition party, "due process" of law and the free press fully as much under socialism as under capitalism. Otherwise he has merely changed bosses.

The new bosses, sure of their jobs, secure from criticism, fearful only of purge from above, may mess up an economy and hide their own incompetence from view. Gomulka in that same speech acidly analyzed the reality behind the boast that in 1955 at the end of the Polish Six Year Plan the output of coal—the key item of the Polish economy—was 20 million tons higher than in 1949 at the end of the Three Year Plan. This is the sort of figure that is customarily trumpeted abroad as evidence of success. But Gomulka showed that more than 14 million tons of this increase was due to overtime work, that output per worker per working day in coal mining had dropped 12.4 percent in 1955 as compared with 1949, and 36 percent as compared with 1938. "The economic policy in relation to the mining industry," Gomulka said, "was marked by unpardonable thoughtlessness. The system of work on Sundays was introduced, and this could not but ruin the health and strength of the miners, and at the same time made it difficult to maintain colliery installations in proper working order. The practice was also introduced of employing soldiers and prisoners in some of the collieries. . . ." This glimpse of the actual conditions in Poland's most important industry tells us more than any abstractions of why it became politically necessary to put a man like Gomulka at the head of the Polish regime, indeed it explains why the regime and the Russians needed Gomulka so badly that he could bargain and insist on his own terms.

When I was in Warsaw last spring, the same people who boasted that they had resisted Russian demands for a "show trial" of Gomulka and saved his life were as insistent that Gomulka would never come back in the party or the government. Obviously they, like the Russians, underestimated the strength of the tide set in motion by the Twentieth Congress in the Soviet Union and over-estimated the power of the party apparatus to keep the popular upsurge of hope within the safe bounds of comfortably vague fulminations against "the cult of the individual." I felt then that Poland, because of its spirit and traditions, would (rather than Yugoslavia) take the lead in the Soviet world toward more concrete changes. It is clear now that economic disintegration and popular discontent had been growing to the point where a Gomulka in Poland and a Nagy in Hungary had become urgent necessities. They were necessary as symbols of some real change. No one, perhaps not even Gomulka or Nagy, really know what they stand for in terms of a program; both are perhaps too old in Communist party ways really to understand the cry for freedom. But their political power in this juncture arises from the need of the masses to see at the head of the government someone whose sincerity has been certified by persecution, whose spirit has been purged by suffering. Above all in Warsaw as in Budapest the masses wanted someone who had suffered at the hands of the Russians and their stooges and could therefore be trusted to express wounded national sensibilities against the occupying Power and the Russian-style Communist bureaucrat.

This is the 1848 of communism. In 1848, the February Revolution in Paris set off a chain reaction across Europe against that hated combination of secret policeman and priest which was symbolized in the Holy Alliance and Metternich. Within a few months half the thrones in Europe had been overturned and constitutions exacted from the remainder by a revolutionary bourgeoisie sick of the decayed alliance of feudalism and clericalism. A century later we see a similar rising, this time by the working class in Eastern Europe against a similarly ubiquitous secret police enforcing a new sacred dogma and maintaining a new lay priesthood in power under communism. Poznan and Poland have ignited a new revolt under far more difficult circumstances, though remarkably alike in surface detail. Thus in the boasted age of atomic bomb and jet plane, the urban mob, the student rally, even the barricade make their reappearance and exert their power. Tito, who led the first revolt against Stalinism, now holds back; it is his own heretic, Dedijer, who hails the Polish revolutionaries. The Yugoslav and Russian bureaucrats discover a mutual interest in putting the brakes on this revolt against bureaucracy, and in Budapest for the first time the demonstrators demand an end of the one-party system—a historic moment. For without a legal opposition, there can be no real reform of communism, no real democratization.

Danger besets this new revolution on every hand. There is the danger of sliding back into an East European morass of black clerical reaction supported by the West, as Horthy and Pilsudski once were. There is the danger that Russia, fearing the loss of its new *cordon sanitaire* in Eastern Europe, may intervene more openly, precipitating international consequences. There is the danger that the Russian rulers, unsure of themselves, divided in their counsels, may turn back from their hesitant dip into liberalization and restore Stalinist harshness, fearing that the revolutionary ferment may even reach and arouse the long submissive and terrorized workers and intellectuals of the Soviet Union. Polish revolt has often sparked Russian uprising. In Moscow alone there is no Tito, no Gomulka, no Nagy, to symbolize a real break with the past; there alone Stalin's collaborators survive in power. What if Trotzky had never been exiled and murdered, what if Bukharin had never been liquidated! What a different picture there might be in Moscow today! How differently Russia could deal with its rebellious satellites and protect its legitimate interests if they saw in Moscow new faces they could trust!

OCTOBER 29, 1956

THE SOVIET GOVERNMENT SMASHES SOVIETS

We wonder how many readers, scanning the news from Budapest, remembered that "Soviet" means council in Russian and that Soviets originated in the workers' councils which sprang up in the factories of Moscow during the Revolution of 1905. The workers' councils whose dissolution the Soviet government and its feeble Hungarian puppet have been trying to enforce with blood and fire are the direct descendants of those workers' councils through which the Communists first came to power in 1917. These factory councils proved as powerful against the Kremlin and Kadar as they once were against the Czars and Kerensky. December, 1956, will be remembered in the history books as the time when a government which calls itself Soviet turned its guns in panic on Soviets. In this vivid scene perished the delusion that mistook a dictatorship of bureaucrats and gendarmes for a working-class utopia. If events are to be gauged by their impact on men's minds, this was the most important event of the year, outranking even Khrushchev's posthumous attack on Stalin. Whatever happens inside Hungary, its workers have succeeded in bringing about a new revolution.

Yet for those of us who look back with filial piety on our ideological forebears and who glory (despite Walters and Eastlands) in the tradition of our country, it was a joy to see in this new revolution far off upon the Danube the rebirth of our own Jeffersonianism. One of the two major demands of the workers' councils in their ultimatum to the Kadar government was the right to establish a labor press, free from control by the government. The Sage of Monticello, a philosophical country gentleman, always distrusted the urban proletariat but he would have felt an immediate kinship with the workers of Budapest. They acted out of old and festering grievances in the spirit of Jefferson's often repeated emphasis on a free press as the primary safeguard of liberty. The workers of Budapest destroyed another Stalinist delusion—that the Soviet system (as embodied in the Stalin constitution) is "even more democratic" than ours because it not only guarantees a free press but makes available presses "free" to the workers. Outside Poland, nowhere in the Soviet zone can a worker get anywhere near that dangerous weapon, the press, and in Russia it has been a long time since any protesting worker dared print even a mimeographed leaflet.

In the wake of this new revolution, still convulsing and spreading in East Europe, even making itself felt in Lithuania, there reappears in reverse another well-known phenomenon of politics. In the twenties, though it preached world revolution, the Stalin government cold-shouldered and soft-pedaled the revolutionary movement, first in Germany and then in China, when it looked as if revolution were at last possible. This was the "sell-out" in which Trotzkyism was born. Today we are seeing a similar tendency on the other side. Faced at last with the possibility of that "liberation" they so long preached, Mr. Dulles and his friends in West Germany are soft-pedaling the anti-Communist revolution. From the NATO meeting in Paris we are told that Bonn has given its agents in East Germany strict orders to avoid anything which might lead to an insurrection there; Mr. Dulles's emphasis on "morality" as the sole weapon is regarded as a signal to Moscow that it can crush the new revolution without fear of our intervention in its behalf.

Just as Stalin once feared that revolution in Germany and China might lead to war with the West, so the West now fears that the new revolution in Eastern Europe may lead to war with Russia. In both cases revolutionary phrases evaporated when it became a question of taking risks to fulfill them; crisis showed Dulles like Stalin was a cautious conservative, not an adventurer. This is understandable when nuclear weapons are poised for action. We merely note the reappearance of a pattern. But already from the bombed-out cellars of Budapest one may hear the same anger and disillusion with Washington that betrayed German and Chinese revolutionists once felt with Moscow.

DECEMBER 17, 1956

22: *The Eisenhower Doctrine*

GRAND DESIGN

The phone rang in that sunny State Department office, and the pleasant elderly woman in charge answered. "Oh, it's very quiet here this week," she assured her caller. The President was golfing in Georgia, the Secretary of State convalescing in Florida. The Undersecretary of State, when not commuting between them, was unavailable; Mr. Herbert Hoover, Jr., the only Undersecretary of State who has never held a press conference, saw no reason to hold one now. From Georgia, America's ranking active statesman, James Hagerty, opined that the situation seemed to have improved; he must have been watching the fairway. In devastated Budapest, the general strike was in its second month; ninety thousand Hungarians had fled. The whole Soviet world was tensed for the next outbreak. A new war seemed to be brewing in the Middle East, this time between Iraq and Syria. In Egypt, the bulk of the UN police force was still stalled at the Abu Suweir airfield. Europe was running out of gas, and England and France were swept by anti-American feeling. But it was quiet here in Washington. Ambassadors desperately seeking some line on policy were shunted off to assistant secretaries who knew no more than they did. The sign on the doorknob read plainly, "Do not disturb." The leadership of "the free world" was resting.

This picture is not to be written off merely as the result of illness or incapacity. Inaction, too, can be a form of action, and reflect fundamental long-range policy. To glance back at the events of the past month is to see that the government's behavior, as distinct from its utterance, assumes a pattern. The pattern in Europe is to act as if there were a sphcres-of-influence agreement with the Russians. When the United States does not even protest the abduction of Imre Nagy and drags its feet on Hungary at the UN, as first Dulles and then Lodge did, it signals to Moscow that we have adopted a complete hands-off policy toward Eastern Europe, perhaps in the hope that the Russians will thus be more ready to keep hands off the Middle East, where our material interests lie. Those of us who complained that the United States missed a chance to help Eastern Europe by challenging the Russians to withdraw their armies if we withdrew ours from Western Europe were misled. Judging by its behavior, the United States is not interested in the "liberation" of Eastern Europe; it is not prepared to give up its forward bases in Western Europe as the price of forcing a Russian withdrawal. Washington is set on West German rearmament, still hopes to force unification on its own terms, fears that a withdrawal might leave Germany free to make a deal with the East. American policy is satisfied to have Europe divided into two zones. To revise these plans because Budapest rose against the Russians may seem sentimental nonsense at the Pentagon.

A similarly hard-boiled view may be discerned beneath the rhetoric about the UN and the "rule of law" in the Middle East. Policy there is made by oil and its premise is to win the friendship of the Arabs. We are prepared to defend England and France in Europe but not in the Mediterranean. There we conceive of them as "through" and feel that the sooner their hold is liquidated the faster a new stability can be created. The American oil industry would like to take over the whole area; it is not worried about the Russians, it feels that it has both the markets and the marketing facilities without which Arab oil is valueless. When Israel attacked Egypt, the first intention was to demonstrate American friendship for the Arabs by a special session of Congress and sanctions against Israel. The intervention of England and France upset these plans, but in insisting on their withdrawal "forthwith" we are pursuing essentially the same line. Once Britain and France are out, dollars can be used to cement a new kind of colonialism; the Moslem world from Casablanca to Karachi can be brought into the American sphere of influence; it is anxious to enter the sunny orbit of the Treasury. And if Russia acquiesces, we can help her smooth out the difficulties in Eastern Europe. This is the grand design visible behind the unruffled, almost smug, surface of Washington. The trouble is that it may underestimate the explosive nature of the situation, the unsteadiness in the Kremlin and the temptations of the Middle East.

DECEMBER 3, 1956

A READINESS TO POLICE THE WORLD

The statesman whose future memoirs we would most like to read at this moment are those of Nehru. No one in the world could have been more surprised when what is pompously being called the new Dulles or Eisenhower Doctrine emerged in the wake of his pleasant trip to Washington. If the tenor of the inspired stories which preceded and accompanied his visit was any clue to those long hours he spent with Mr. Eisenhower at Gettysburg, he must have been startled to learn on returning home that the upshot to their exploration of the subtle and complex problems of the Middle East was only to be another dose of Dr. Dulles's favorite household remedy, the threat of massive retaliation.

In retrospect the Washington he visited must appear to Pandit Nehru a Potemkin's Village, hastily erected to flatter and impress. He was greeted as an Eastern Sage and consulted like a wise Elder Brother. The United States had cut itself loose in the Suez crisis from Anglo-French colonialism and abjured power politics. Our reliance was to be on the United Nations and on the moral force of mankind. The grand design being unveiled in private talks with influential correspondents was, as the London *Economist* reported on December 15, "a very different matter indeed from the traditional concept of 'filling a vacuum' with military bases, alliances, puppet governments, or even economic subsidies." India's neutralist Prime Minister was cast for a key role and it was hoped that "a man like Mr. Nehru might be able to talk sense to a Nasser where the British Navy could not."

Everything was done to make a peacemaker feel at home, and to erase any impression that American policy was too prone to wave its shootin' irons. There was one set of inspired stories saying that a major premise of American policy was now the fear that the unsteady Kremlin if too hard-pressed might resort to war in desperation. Another, only a few days before Nehru's arrival, said there had been approved a new and hopeful plan to break the disarmament impasse. The Bulganin letter of November 17 was to be seized upon for negotiations looking toward an immediate reduction in armed forces, a thinning out of NATO and Warsaw pact troops, and even an attempt to limit and control development of the dreaded intercontinental ballistic missile. Mr. Nehru must have felt that he was coming to a capital at last prepared to welcome his message. It is easy to imagine the charming naïveté and engaging sincerity with which Mr. Eisenhower discussed these hopes for peace with his visitor during that long day together on the farm.

Those whose ears are attuned to the realities of Washington began to realize the very next day that Mr. Eisenhower might have been receiving Pandit Nehru in a dream world. They were alone together on December 17. On December 18 Mr. Dulles held his first press conference since his operation. From his answer to that very first question about the Bulganin message ("there is no plan"), it was clear that the State Department was clinging firmly to its own version of what the French call *"immobilisme."* On disarmament, on satellite policy, on Germany, there was to be no change. The answers all reflected the same cold war state of mind, relying on containment and "situations of strength" to force further Soviet retreats without the necessity for any new initiatives in diplomacy. As for our own allies in NATO, Mr. Dulles was almost contemptuous in the brisk way he made it clear that we could not obligate ourselves to consult them.

This was the spirit in which Mr. Dulles earlier proclaimed massive retaliation, and those who now reread his answers at that press conference will better understand the new "doctrine" being unveiled on the Middle East. The Dulles or Eisenhower Doctrine is like the Truman Doctrine before it, which Mr. Dulles also helped to formulate, a unilateral declaration of readiness to police the world by overwhelming force. The reappearance of the stale formula discloses again that while Mr. Eisenhower reigns, he does not govern; Mr. Stassen, his favorite, may have the President's ear but Mr. Dulles firmly holds his arm. The successive revisions of the reply to Bulganin and its emergence as a quick brush-off shows who is the boss.

It is not the reliance on threat of force which makes the "new" approach to the Middle East appalling. It is that the problems cannot be resolved by force. The "new" approach is really only the old lazy-minded abdication of diplomacy by those who are supposed to be our diplomats. It dodges the crucial problems of Arab-Israeli peace and a Suez settlement while covering this failure with the loud affirmation of the obvious. It takes no new declaration to make clear that a Soviet attack on the Middle East means war; that has been clear from the first and explains why Stalin backed down on Iran. The only excuse for this is cynical. It is that Congress cannot be made to acquiesce in loans for the Middle East except by a war scare and the Red menace.

If so the price paid is a heavy one. We dismiss the Arabs as a vacuum; downgrade Israel to a minor regional nuisance; announce that the Middle East is to be our preserve after helping to force our bitter Western allies out of it; ditch the UN just when it was hoped that it might begin to work. Even by oil company standards, this is not wise or adequate policy. More dangerous than that vacuum in the Middle East is the vacuum here in Washington.

JANUARY 7, 1957

THE MOTE IN MINE OWN EYE

The terrible observation in the world crisis is that nations, peoples, and individuals take the law into their own hands when they feel that their really vital interests are at stake. To listen to the debates at the UN, one could well believe that humanity was celebrating international hypocrisy week. One of the great discoveries in industry was that of interchangeable parts. Listening to the oratory, one could speak of interchangeable moral phrases. What the Russians said in condemnation of the British in Egypt was exactly what the British said in condemnation of the Russians in Hungary. Russia thought the conditions Britain and France attached to their acceptance of the cease fire "incompatible with the national sovereignty of Egypt." Insert the word "Hungary" and you see what we mean.

Since every man is a microcosm, in whose heart may be read all that sends armies marching, I must admit I am no better. Because so many bonds attach me to Israel, I am ready to condone preventive war; I rejoiced when my side won. Though I preach international understanding and support for the UN, I found all the excuses for Israel that warring nationalisms always find to excuse breaches of the peace. Should they wait until the enemy is strong enough to attack them? Is it not mere prudence to anticipate the blow? What better time to save Israel than in concert with Britain and France, on the eve of the American election, and before the winter rains made the Negev and Sinai impassable for tanks? Israel's survival seemed worth the risk to world peace. And this is how it always is and how it starts, and I offer up the mote in my own eye.

The Russians and the Egyptians say Israel was the aggressor, and so it was. But what were all those MIGs for, which Moscow poured into Egypt in exchange for its precious cotton? What was Nasser doing when he boasted that he would soon exterminate Israel? . . . And from the Arab side I can hear the recriminations about the homeless refugees it was their sacred duty to revenge and put back into repossession. The quarrels of nations are as difficult to unravel as those of children, but the pistols are no longer toy.

If only we were all saints like the Indians, breathed deeply, and meditated on the infinite wisdom of certain sacred syllables. . . . We are grateful for Nehru. But the old Adam lives in him, too. He is a Kashmiri. Kashmir's high lovely vales are home to him. Nehru, like the rest of us, finds abnegation easiest at a distance. He can be altruistic about Sinai and Budapest. But when Kashmir is at stake? Nehru has just arranged for a puppet "constituent Assembly" (dissident members in jail) to declare Kashmir part of India, though Nehru himself once promised that he would abide by a plebiscite's decision between India and Pakistan. In Kashmir a Hindu minority has long ruled a Moslem majority and a plebiscite would mean that Nehru might rule an India with its most beloved portion, his home, torn from it. . . . So are we all.

What the Russians are doing in Budapest is so dreadful that even the Indian, Icelandic and American Communist parties protest. Moscow is ready to do anything in order to keep in its "zone of security" governments politically satisfactory to it. But haven't we just finished a campaign in which the Republicans boasted of the quick way we toppled the Arbenz government in Guatemala? Moscow doesn't want anti-Russian and anti-Communist governments in Eastern Europe. We in the Caracas agreement tried to ensure that no anti-American and anti-capitalist governments could be formed in our hemisphere. How we honor brave fighters for freedom . . . until they shoot down *our* tyrant friends, as recently in Nicaragua.

The fact that H-bombs now exist and that a new war may ruin the earth—this is forgotten when vital interests are touched, when it seems a matter of life and death for one's own. This is the fatal phrase, "one's own." Perhaps it will take a new menace from outside the planet to make men feel at last that all who inhabit it are their own.

But beware of these fine phrases. I too, like the rest of them (and maybe even you), am a hypocrite.

NOVEMBER 12, 1956

23: *Mental Climate of the Fifties*

FREEDOM OF THE PRESS: A MINORITY OPINION

The main obstacle to the creation of a well-informed public is its own indifference. In every country with a free press, thoughtful papers which conscientiously try to cover the news lag behind the circulation of those which peddle sex and sensationalism. This is as true in Paris and London as in New York; and if Moscow ever permits a free privately-owned press, *Izvestia* and *Pravda* will fall far behind any paper which prints the latest on that commissar's love nest.

The second obstacle is that most papers are owned by men who are not newspapermen themselves; publishing is a business, not a Jeffersonian passion, and the main object is as much advertising revenue as possible. Thus it happens that between the attitude of the publishers and that of the public, most papers in this country print little news. And this, except for local coverage, is mostly canned, syndicated, and quick-frozen.

The third obstacle is that this has always been and is now more than ever a conformist country; Main Street and Babbitt—and de Tocqueville long before Sinclair Lewis—held a faithful mirror to our true nature. It doesn't take much deviation from Rotary Club norms in the average American community to get oneself set down as queer, radical, and unreliable.

Against this background, it is easy to see why the average Washington correspondent is content to write what he is spoon-fed by the government's press officers. Especially since the press is largely Republican and this is a Republican Administration, there is little market for "exposing" the government. Why dig up a story which the desk back home will spike?

It was this astringent view of our profession and its circumstances which I found lacking in the newspapermen's testimony which opened the investigation launched here by a special House subcommittee on government "information." The most perceptive of the witnesses, and one of our very best reporters, James Reston of the *New York Times,* put his finger on the vital point when he said that worse than suppression was the "managing" of the news by government departments. But the news is "managed" because the reporters and their editors let themselves be managed.

The State Department is an outstanding offender. Very often, for example, newspaper readers get not so much what actually happened at the UN as the "slant" given out in the corridors afterward to the reporters by a State Department attaché.

The private dinner, the special briefing, are all devices for "managing" the news, as are the special organizations of privileged citizens gathered in by State and Defense Departments for those sessions at which highly confidential (and one-sided) information is ladled out to a flattered "elite."

As a reporter who began by covering small towns, where one really has to dig for the news, I can testify that Washington is in many ways one of the easiest cities in the world to cover. The problem is the abundance of riches. It is true that the Government, like every other government in the world, does its best to distort the news in its favor—but that only makes the job more interesting.

Most of my colleagues agree with the Government and write the accepted thing because that is what they believe; they are indeed—with honorable exceptions—as suspicious of the non-conformist as any group in Kiwanis.

Though the first day's witnesses included the best and boldest of the regular press, no one mentioned the recent deportations of radical foreign language editors and of Cedric Belfrage of the *Guardian*. No one mentioned the Communist editors and reporters prosecuted—*for their ideas*—under the Smith Act. No one mentioned the way McCarthy "investigated" James Wechsler. Surely thoughtful men, as aroused as these were over the future of a free press, might have given a moment's consideration to the possible danger in such precedents. Did they feel it would be indiscreet to go beyond respectable limits? That such fundamental principles are best left for orations on Zenger and Lovejoy, both conveniently dead?

NOVEMBER 14, 1955

THE FIRST AMENDMENT AND THE TWENTIETH CONGRESS

The curtain has just rung down on another scene in the comic ballet over at the Subversive Activities Control Board. Last spring the Supreme Court returned to it the case of the Communist party. It was returned on the ground that the testimony of three perjurers had been used in arriving at the order requiring the party to register as subversive. The three were Paul Crouch, Manning Johnson and Harvey Matusow.

The board has now stricken the testimony of all three from the record, and reaffirmed its decision. This was hardly a surprise, since the board operates under a statute—the only one of its kind—which virtually gives the name and address of the culprit to be convicted under it.

The Communist party, in a new delaying action, had asked the right to present evidence that since the Twentieth Congress there no longer was a world Communist movement as defined in the Act, and that it was now independent of Moscow.

The board declined to hear the evidence and ruled that the reality of the change could only be tested "in the crucible of time." This was like sending a man to jail with the consoling observation that time would tell whether he was guilty or not. If due process is still due process, we think the board will find this case thrown back in its lap by the courts.

We ourselves don't see what the Twentieth Congress has to do with the First Amendment. Whether the Communist party is or is not a faithful echo of Moscow is something to be hammered out in free political controversy, not to be decided by calling in the cops. The new legal issue begs the question. Can the Government in a supposedly free society label certain parties and their publications "subversive," make them wear a yellow badge and reduce their members to second-class status? Can such registration be reconciled with the Bill of Rights? The question which concerns us is not whether Stalin is dead but whether Jefferson still lives.

Two New York newspapers used the same metaphor last week in deploring a decision by the State Commissioner of Education that ex-Communist teachers cannot be dismissed for refusing to inform.

The *Journal-American* found the decision "intolerable" because in the public school "Communist poison can be injected subtly into the minds of the young." The *World-Telegram* argued, "Suppose you were a teacher and saw somebody slipping poison into children's lunch boxes? You'd report that person. Now is there any less reason to report somebody slipping poison into children's minds? Make no mistake about it—a Communist teacher can do exactly that by slanting practically any subject."

This metaphor implies that while other teachers grow prematurely gray trying to drum such comparatively simple matters as the multiplication table into the heads of their little charges, Communist teachers have some mysterious means for slipping the complex subtleties of Marxism-Leninism unobserved into the same tender skulls. One method seems to be analogous to intravenous injection—they "slip" it into the child mind. Another seems to be by means of a diabolic gift only Communist teachers are assumed to possess, since they can do this "by slanting practically any subject."

We pause, avid for more detail, over that "practically any subject." How do they do it in Latin? By blaming the conjugations on capitalism? Or in geology? By hinting that the rocks are bigger in the Soviet Union?

AUGUST 20, 1956

ON THE DEATH OF TOSCANINI

All the obituaries of Toscanini told how he had defied Mussolini and refused to play the Fascist hymn, *Giovannezza,* choosing exile rather than knuckle under. But of all the newspaper writers who applauded the Maestro's bravery, who was brave enough to note that we ourselves do not encourage our artists to be Toscaninis? We do not use the bludgeon and castor oil, as the Black Shirts did, to enforce conformity. We have milder methods for frightening people. We put them in the pillory before the Senate Internal Security Committee or the House Un-American Activities Committee. We make them unemployable. If Toscanini had dared criticize this American variant of *Fascismo,* we would probably have driven him into exile as we did Chaplin, or kept him here under "house arrest" as we do Paul Robeson, punishing him by refusing to let him perform abroad. Our artists have been taught that it is safer not to mix in politics.

In this sense, not to mix in politics is not to mix in life, to be but half a man; to look the other way when other men are treated unjustly; if there are crematoria, not to hear the screams; to abdicate. How can one be a true artist, striving unattainably to express the deeper meanings, as Toscanini did, and be but half a man? Can a eunuch make love? Toscanini in this was like Einstein, and it is something to remember that the greatest conductor of our time, like the greatest physicist, was an anti-Fascist; both chose exile rather than submission. But where are the younger men to follow them?

In the United States, as in the U.S.S.R., the artists, scientists and intellectuals are encouraged to take part in politics but only as the State orchestrates it. There they are encouraged to criticize Western imperialism, here to speak out against Soviet oppression in Hungary. There the first question they ask you is about Paul Robeson, but it is considered bad taste to ask them about the Soviet Robesons, the dissident artists and writers who ended up in sub-Arctic labor camps. Here we are allowed to celebrate the way the writers and newspapermen resisted in Budapest, staking their lives on the demand for free expression. But I did not notice any of our newspapermen demonstrating outside the half-empty courtroom in Washington last Friday where Robert Shelton of the *New York Times* was found guilty of contempt for invoking his First Amendment rights before the Senate Internal Security Committee, and Mary Knowles the librarian was given 120 days in jail for the same offense.

There is a numbness in the national air. There was no hostile mob outside the courthouse. There were no sympathizers massed within it. Every day we are told that freedom is the precious possession we must be ready at the drop of a bomb to defend with our lives against Them, but nobody took an hour off from work to come down to the courtroom and see whether maybe the First Amendment was in danger. Our reflexes have not been conditioned to associate the First Amendment with the Freedom on which the Pentagon puts a big capital F; the Bill of Rights is not conspicuous in the briefings of the Strategic Air Command. Indeed, as the sophisticated may whisper to you, that stuff about the First Amendment is "commie talk." *Real* Americans don't talk that line. It's "commie" here and "bourgeois" there. This is the shadow of what Orwell saw coming.

Our country is supposed to be the citadel of private conscience against State power. But when Mrs. Knowles's lawyer, Henry Sawyer III, a Philadelphia city councilman, spoke with passion of the Christian and Quaker tradition against informing, of early Church Council edicts against those who turned their brothers in, of the Quaker printer William Bradford who in 1689 was the first man in the New World to invoke the privilege, his moving words seemed to find a wall rather than an audience in the owlish rotund man on the bench with the dark-rimmed spectacles. It was only when Sawyer pleaded that if Mrs. Knowles had submitted to the authority of the committee it would have meant informing on the father of her son that the Judge was moved, but in the other direction. Judge Rizley broke in to say that he had seven children and eleven grandchildren and that his sons and sons-in-law had been engaged all over the world in the Army, the Air Force and the Marines in resisting communism. The Judge told Sawyer, "I just can't bring myself to say to her that she should not serve some time." Mrs. Knowles made an appealing figure as she stood there awaiting sentence, thin and wan in a trim suit. The Judge made a great show of being troubled, but he sentenced her to four months. No harm would have come to her, he said, if she had only answered the committee's questions. "Suppose," he asked, again referring to his sons and sons-in-law, "*they* refused to obey the command of their country?" Does a civilian owe the same duty to the State as a soldier? Is a citizen to be commanded in a free society? Was not Mrs. Knowles, too, a soldier in her way, standing on a battlefield colder and lonelier even than the 38th Parallel, in defense of something precious in America?

The Judge does not regard the Internal Security Committee's powers with niggardly eye. Mrs. Knowles had told the committee she was not a Communist, that she had not been associated since 1947 with any organization on the Attorney General's list, that she had no knowledge to impart of any unlawful act, and that she was after all not a government employee but worked in a private library belonging to a Quaker group. The Judge brushed all this aside, as had the committee. Its real target in hauling her before it for the second time in September, 1955, was the Fund for the Republic, which has given Plymouth Meeting five thousand dollars for its courage in continuing to employ Mrs. Knowles. The committee, like the Inquisition, regards the uncowed spirit as an affront. It would if it could wipe out every center of resistance.

Shelton's case was similar. He, too, was an innocent bystander, a case of mistaken identity caught in the cross fire of the committee's attempt to smear the critical *New York Times*. Shelton's counsel, Joseph L. Rauh, Jr., made a vivid court record, though the only witness called was Jules Sourwine. He was the committee's counsel when it launched its investigation of newspaper business a year ago and is back as assistant counsel, after an ignominious defeat in Nevada politics where he hoped to become a United States senator.

By tart questioning, Rauh showed that America's greatest newspaper was the focus of the committee's abortive inquiry into Communist "infiltration of the press." Only witnesses whose silence or testimony might reflect upon the *New York Times* were called in open session; no other newspaper was investigated; Shelton himself was called by mistake. One of those precious informers who cannot even get names right had Shelton mixed up with another (non-Communist) newspaperman of the same last name. Prosecutor William Hitz, Jr., defended this light-hearted method of serving subpoenas by advancing the theory that the committee has power to pick up any "man on the street" and haul him up for interrogation on his political views, whether or not there is "probable cause" (as the criminal law requires) to believe that he has pertinent information. This was substantially upheld by the Judge.

Perhaps the most alarming aspect of the Shelton trial was the Judge's magnanimity to the *New York Times*. The Judge observed that the court was prepared to take judicial notice of the fact that no one had accused that paper of being communistic. When judges begin to take judicial notice of whether papers are subversive or not, it is time for thoughtful editors to begin to worry. A free press was never supposed to operate, like a trusteeship, under the watchful eye of the courts. Or of Congress. Judge Rizley added that his generous offer of a clean bill of health to the *New York Times* did not mean that Congress doesn't have power to investigate it. Indeed the resolution establishing the Senate Committee on Internal Security, like that establishing the House Committee on Un-American Activities, is so broad and vague that it can investigate anyone whose ideas it considers dangerous. It is not Judge Rizley's reasoning but the resolutions on which attack must be made.

A second *New York Times* employee, Seymour Peck, goes on trial next week, also for contempt of the Senate Internal Security Committee. A different kind of judge, Luther Youngdahl, presides over his trial but the outcome is unlikely to be very different. Conviction of contempt is all but a foregone conclusion in that and in the case of a third *New York Times* man awaiting trial. The newspaper announced that Shelton's status as an employee will remain unchanged until final disposition of the case. But what does that mean? Will the three lose their jobs if they lose on appeal? Will the *New York Times* finally treat as disreputable characters men who are risking a great deal in defense of the freedom of our profession? Do we only honor Peter Zengers when long dead? When will the *New York Times* take the offensive?

What if a new McCarthy appears? What is to keep him from subpoenaing a whole brigade of *New York Times* men and smearing that paper with the hue and cry of loose Red charges? Newspaper business is full of ex-liberals and ex-radicals with past utterances and associations easily exhumed and exploited against the background of an alleged Communist conspiracy to infiltrate the press.

Against this background it is painful to report that the American Newspaper Guild has done nothing to help the newspapermen caught in the committee's web, and that the *New York Post* seems

to be the only big paper in the country which is treating this affair as
it deserves. The *Post* sent its brilliant columnist, Murray Kempton,
to cover the Shelton trial; it carried a strong and serious editorial on
the implications of the verdict. But when are other editors going to
react?

We urge editors also to look at the new revised *Guide to Subversive Organizations and Publications* just published by the House
committee. It has added to the blacklist *The National Guardian* and
Jewish Life, along with the vanished Progressive party. Let them
ask themselves whether we are going to allow the fungoid growth of
an atmosphere in which it begins to be taken for granted that a congressional committee—or any other agency of government—may
decide which publications are subversive and which are not. Now, in
this lull, when reaction ebbs and the battle would be easy, is the time
to wipe out this excrescence on a free society.

JANUARY 28, 1957

24: *Ike in Action*

THE EASY WAY OUT

The problems of the world are so complicated that it is a pity
people's minds have to be further confused by the kind of chrome-
plated generalities and warmed-up helium which filled the President's
Inaugural Address, as it did his State of the Union message. The
style had the sheen of good advertising copy; it subordinated realistic
discussion to selling. The new arms budget, highest ever in peacetime, was sold as "the price of peace." The world scene was pictured
again as cold war melodrama: the struggle of us goodies against
them baddies. The world is indeed divided, but division cannot be
blamed entirely on Them. Our friends, Syngman Rhee, Chiang Kai-
shek, and Diem, are also dividers; ready, like the Communists, for
unity at any time, but on their own terms. The President spoke of
"tragically" divided Germany, but it is a tragedy that rests very
lightly on Dr. Adenauer and our big business friends in the Reich.
They are in no hurry to assume the economic and political problems
of the impoverished, socialistic and Protestant East zone. We say

we don't like a world divided, but the countries like India which feel that way and try to stand aside from the general division of mankind we stigmatize as "neutralist," a bad word. We say we don't like a divided Europe, but in both addresses, as at press conference last week, the President showed remarkably little interest in trying by diplomacy to achieve the withdrawal of the Russians. But who expects sensible discussion of detergents in soap copy? Better just to say, "It floats."

The trouble with continually picturing our side as 99 44/100 percent pure is that it creates a public mind totally unprepared for the give-and-take necessary to heal the discords of an imperfect world. We are so used to hearing about the "free world" that we forget that most of our allies in that free world run regimes as dictatorial and as bloody but often a good deal less constructive than those of the Communist states. Most of Latin America, virtually all of the Middle East, are governed by dictators dependent for their maintenance on armed force, which we supply under "mutual aid" (shade of Kropotkin!). When the President spoke of "the building of a peace with justice in a world where moral law prevails" he was talking in the kind of rhetoric which unfits free men for tackling real problems. The corollary of all those rosy words is that until we reach this pie-in-the-sky state of virtue we must continue to arm to the teeth. We are all for justice, but it can only be achieved slowly, by charity, and patience. What is the just solution—to take only problems divorced from the Communist issue—in North Ireland, or Algeria, or Cyprus, or Palestine, or Kashmir? No solution to these old and tangled feuds is possible which will not be unjust to somebody. The President's oversimplified self-righteous rhetoric may drum up emotions for war. It will never prepare men to compromise for peace.

Dwight Eisenhower is a man who shies away from a scrap, and gravitates naturally to the path of least resistance. This is evident in dealing with our most acute domestic problem, that of race relations. It was characteristic of him in the State of the Union message to advocate a program of school aid "uncomplicated by provisions dealing with the complex problems of integration." Mr. Eisenhower is all for Law, with a big capital L, until he runs up against a law difficult to enforce. At press conference last Wednesday he looked relaxed and confident until Robert Spivack of the *New York Post* asked him about the appeal by Southern Negro leaders that he come South and use his influence to stem the rising mood of violence. He was at a loss for an answer, consulted with Jim Hagerty and then replied lamely that the request had been referred to the Justice Department for study. We can just see the lights burning there far into the night.

That instinctive fondness for the easy way out is charting the course of the next four years. We wish there was comfort to be found in the symbolism of the attack made on Mr. Eisenhower at the very beginning of his second term by the Council of State Chambers of Commerce. The council, like his own Secretary of the Treasury, objects to the huge budget and its renewed and New Dealish spending. But this welfare state to which Eisenhower is turning comes coupled with the garrison state; Humphrey represented the big business influence which was against New Dealism but was also for relaxation of world tension to cut arms spending. The weakening of his influence is therefore no unmixed blessing. Ahead of us lies renewed cold war and arms race, sugar-coated by social welfare measures. But the major share goes to the Pentagon; the blueprint is to make all the world outside the Soviet zone our protectorate and beneficiaries. Mr. Eisenhower has emerged as a Truman Democrat, dependent on the arms race as the WPA of our prosperity, and facing inflation with essential equanimity.

JANUARY 28, 1957

THOSE BULL SESSIONS WITH ZHUKOV

We were fascinated by Eisenhower's account at press conference of his wartime ideological bull sessions with Zhukov. The President said, "I was very hard put to it when he insisted that their system appealed to the idealistic, and we completely to the materialistic." It is indicative that the only freedoms Eisenhower stressed, as he recalls, were commercial: "A man can earn what he pleases, save what he pleases, buy what he pleases." Nowhere did the President mention the right to think as one pleases. Eisenhower saw freedom in businessmen's terms, the freedom of the market place. Limited to those terms, the system is wide open to Zhukov's reproach in the classic Socialist-Communist tradition, "Everything that is selfish in man you appeal to him. . . ."

Ideologically Ike was as ill prepared and naïve as the average G.I. His account of the conversation is in striking accord with the portrait drawn by a writer in the summer issue of the quarterly *Dis-*

sent, summarizing the findings of the research branch of the United States Army in its volumes on *The American Soldier* in World War II: "The American soldier emerges from this collective portrait as a man without serious commitment. He fought because he *had* to; meanwhile he looked out for himself as much as he could. The resistance to ideology, stemming partly from the American dream of individual success which not even the depression had been able to destroy, was now re-enforced by military experience. Soldiers fighting for democracy found themselves serving under a tremendously authoritarian military caste which they justifiably despised."

The only effective answer to Zhukov was that communism in practice had become not a brotherly society working for the common good, but an authoritarian hierarchical system run by a bureaucratic caste, on the basis of unquestioning obedience by subordinates. But these are also the characteristics of armies.

It is not surprising that a professional soldier like Eisenhower failed to criticize communism effectively for habits of regimentation he had been trained all his life long to accept as virtues. The civilian ideals he defended were abstractions with which he had too little experience. Even now, years later, as President, the freedom that comes at once to the surface of his mind when he is asked to answer a question "off the cuff" at press conference is the freedom to make money. This is, indeed, the only Magna Charta capitalism prizes; the rest is tolerated as oratorical eyewash.

JULY 29, 1957

25: *Toward the Preposterous War*

MISGUIDED MISSILES

What was so appalling about the Bermuda conference was not the meagerness of the results but the mendacity of the final communiqué. In putting their names to it, Eisenhower and Macmillan testified to a cynical contempt for the intelligence of their own people. The real agreements in the joint statement were not new and the new agreements were not real. The decision to give Britain nuclear missiles was reached in the Wilson-Sandys talks at the beginning of February, and the decision to join the military committee of the Baghdad Pact was made several weeks before Bermuda. The "accords" reaffirming support for the reunification of the Germans in the sweet bye-and-bye, and of sympathy for the Hungarians will only infuriate both; these phrases mask the old lazy-minded unwillingness to do anything for either people by negotiation and diplomacy. As for the Middle East, the best commentary on those accords was the one-word answer of Secretary Dulles at press conference last week when asked whether any instructions had yet been given United States vessels on where and to whom their Suez tolls are to be paid. His answer was "No." If no decision has been registered on that elementary a point, what reason is there to believe any have been arrived at on the more complex issues?

The joint communiqué was most floozy where the problem was most grave, that of responding to world-wide anxiety about nuclear tests. All Eisenhower and Macmillan offered was a willingness to register with the United Nations advance notice of their tests and "permit limited international observation" if the Soviet Union would do the same. The rest was only a joint reiteration of the sham "intention to conduct nuclear tests only in such manner as will keep world radiation from rising to more than a small fraction of the levels that might be hazardous." This, as the ordinarily pro-Eisenhower *Washington Post* pointed out, "accepts the optimistic view that the tests are doing no harm, although no one really knows and . . . is designed to sanction new British thermonuclear tests as well as to dignify the double talk about the American 'clean' bomb." The truth is that the United States seems to be doing exactly what AEC Commissioner Murray warned against in his address last November to the Catholic Association for International Peace: "We allow weapons technology to control the weapons program . . . and the stockpiled results of the weapons program to control military policies." We continue testing to make "better" if not larger bombs; we give no real thought as to whether they can ever be used without world suicide; but since the stock piles grow bigger we "economize" by equipping our own and allied armies with them in a kind of mindless momentum which could carry us all toward the final catastrophe.

For the British people the communiqué must be doubly disappointing. They had hoped that Macmillan would win some of those concessions on freer trade with China which Eisenhower promised Eden to study fourteen months ago. Apparently Macmillan was unable to persuade Eisenhower to join him even in the most generalized accord looking toward the lightening of cold war restrictions on trade between East and West. The other eloquently blank space in the communiqué was the absence of any reference to Britain's desire for military retrenchment, particularly in regard to her occupation forces in Germany. Instead the statement said that in the interest of "mutual economy" certain guided missiles would be made available to Britain by the United States. But it is doubtful that this will prove an economy to either; missiles are expensive to produce and expensive to man. This gift will cost Britain many millions of dollars in additional arms expenditure. Other costs may prove more serious. Britain, living beyond its income, needs relaxation of world tension in order to reduce her arms burden and increase her trade. To establish nuclear missile bases capable of bombing Moscow will be to step up tension. The British people ask for bread, and we give them guided missiles.

Nothing could be more misguided than these missiles we intend to put into mass production and then parcel out among our allies. They may make the drift toward war irreversible; they will certainly make it harder to be certain that small wars do not expand into the big one, as the missiles fall into more and more hands. We are indeed acting as if war were inevitable. We are establishing forward bases, deploying our navies, preparing bases for our air fleets. We are waging economic warfare. We are digging deeper all the terrible divisions of the world—of Germany and Europe; of Korea, China, Indo-China and East Asia; and by joining the Baghdad Pact, of the Middle East. We have set our faces against any negotiation with the other big power of the world; we have downgraded disarmament to a minor side show no one takes seriously. Everywhere this process is impoverishing mankind; wasting manpower and materials with which a start might be made on the world's poverty. With the arms race and the cold war comes creeping inflation; it makes its appearance even here in the highest peacetime budget of our history. The voice of Nehru pleading for Russo-American negotiation is drowned out in our press; every effort of the Russians to negotiate is howled down. This is not responsible conduct. Eisenhower said last year that war is now "preposterous." But if war is preposterous, should we not shore up the precarious foundations of peace instead of piling up and handing out ever deadlier arms?

APRIL 1, 1957

THE RESPONSIBILITY OF THE SCIENTIST

The central point at the Nuremberg trials was that no man, soldier or civilian, could absolve himself from guilt for crime on the plea that he was obeying orders of a superior. The question now is whether the world scientific community will continue to work on the perfection of methods for slaughter which may extinguish human life on this planet. This is what every scientist must face up to in his own conscience. The answer he gives will determine whether he is a man, in the full sense of the word, responsible as a man should be for the fate of other men, or a tool.

One section of the world scientific community has given an answer. The declaration of the eighteen German atomic scientists that they will take no part in the production, testing or utilization of nuclear weapons is an event of magnitude in the realm of history and morals. The scientists of Germany, who know from bitter shame what it means to have collaborated in mass murder on orders of the State, are the first to answer "no" to the process which would turn the earth itself into a vast crematorium. If there is no echoing answer from America and Russia, from Britain and France, the World War against fascism will seem in the eyes of German youth a lie. For the best minds of East and West will seem to be marching past them, too, in goose-step, weakly absolving themselves of responsibility, shrugging their shoulders, with the old feeble Germanic excuse, *"Ich bin nur ein kleiner Mensch."* The greatest minds of our generation will indeed seem little men.

Dr. Albert Schweitzer, from deepest Africa, has added his noble voice, appealing as did Bertrand Russell and Albert Einstein with nine other scientists two years ago for an end of preparation for nuclear war. But the Germans, among them one German Jew, Max Born, who returned to Germany, have done more than make an appeal. They have set an example. The text of their declaration, which no paper in the United States has yet printed (a fact itself significant), is important in that it answers the nonsense being spread by military propaganda that small, tactical, "baby" bombs can somehow safely be used. They point out that these baby bombs are the equivalent in firepower of the bomb which fell on Hiroshima, no harmless military toy. The declaration deserves to be widely circulated, if only to combat the delusion that tactical atomic weapons are somehow safe, and have effects which can be limited to the immediate battlefield.

The declaration itself is part of a chain reaction set off by the new British White Paper. If Britain must have the H-bomb and place primary reliance for defense upon its possession, then so must Germany and if Germany, then France; and if France, then Italy; and if Italy, then Israel; and if Israel, then Egypt. . . . When every power, great or small, can brandish these ultimate weapons, the chances of setting off the ultimate conflagration will be increased many-fold. The Bonn *General Anzeiger* of April 13 wondered why the German scientists should suddenly have pledged themselves not to take part in the production of nuclear weapons, since the Paris treaties for German rearmament forbid their production in the Reich. There is speculation in the German press that the German scientists spoke up because tacitly the Western powers have already agreed that this restriction will be waived. Imagine what Hitler would have done if he had had this weapon, imagine what a new Hitler would do with it, and one can understand why the German scientists at the first hint of this decided to speak. We honor them for doing so.

APRIL 29, 1957

MILITARY MINUET

Comment on the Soviet intercontinental ballistic missile has avoided the most obvious of its consequences. This is the destruction of the Eisenhower "open skies" proposal. The idea was that continuous aerial inspection of the bases from which a strategic blow could be launched would eliminate the fear of a nuclear Pearl Harbor. In this improved atmosphere, reduction in arms would become feasible.

But the debut of the long-feared ICBM opens a new era. Inspection is no longer the key to relaxation of tension. Airfields may be spotted and policed from the air, but ICBM launching sites may be widely scattered and easily hidden. A strategic strike requires measures of concentration and unusual movement; these can be observed. But widely separated ICBM launching sites may be activated quickly and unobtrusively, underground. In addition, most important of all, is the time difference. The fastest bombers would take at least six hours to reach their targets; an ICBM can make the trip in thirty minutes. This would be the maximum warning time even with perfect inspection, assuming that a country devilishly determined on sudden war would be high-minded enough not to seize inspectors and inspection posts at the zero hour.

The Pentagon will not be sorry to see the end of the "open skies" proposal; one has only to read the discussion of inspection in Henry A. Kissinger's well-informed *Nuclear Weapons and Foreign Policy* to gather how astringently the armed services have always regarded it. But politically the collapse of the aerial inspection approach is serious. From a public relations standpoint, the "open skies" plan was all the United States had to offer world opinion in competition with the Soviet's "ban-the-bomb" campaign. So long as we could go through the endless palaver of perfecting a 100-percent certain aerial inspection plan, we could avoid the issues of testing and nuclear warfare.

Meanwhile the Pentagon could go on with its dream that we were so far ahead technologically that we could soon re-establish something like the atomic monopoly we enjoyed in 1945-49 and *then,* if necessary, negotiate disarmament. The State Department, for its part, hoped that from the pressures of the continued arms race it could exact a Soviet surrender on Germany. All these hopes have now been exploded. Whatever the full truth about the Soviet ICBM, it is clear that the Russians will soon have that "ultimate weapon" in working order, apparently before we do.

The outlook is not hopeless *if* public opinion as a first step can force the military at least to give up their insistence on further testing, if not their reliance on nuclear weapons. We have already achieved the fabrication of a hydrogen warhead small enough to be used on a missile, and a ban on tests will not block development of an ICBM. Further testing means (1) that other nations will soon have nuclear weapons, thus making control all the more difficult, and (2) further pollution of the atmosphere by fall-out. Of this problem of pollution, one can only say two things with assurance: (1) that there is a wide and uncomfortable margin of ignorance around current estimates of both the somatic and genetic dangers, and (2) that since 1931, long before the perilous atomic nucleus was unlocked, scientific estimates of the safe limits of radiological exposure have proven too optimistic, and have steadily been revised downward.

The latest warning in this area is that given by two scientists of the Naval Radiological Defense Laboratory in San Francisco at the meeting last month of the American Institute of Biological Sciences; they estimated that in less than fifteen years the concentration of strontium 90 in humans as a result of nuclear weapons set off through 1955 may reach the danger point. An agreement on testing is feasible because monitoring stations five hundred miles apart would be enough to detect violations as low as the kiloton range. If this could be negotiated apart from the Rube Goldbergian complications and conditions of the whole Western package plan, a great step forward would be accomplished.

What is required is what any bureaucracy hates most to do —some new thinking. It was difficult enough for the Eisenhower Administration to find in the "open skies" proposal a common denominator low enough to reconcile Pentagon and State Department. To find a new formula, especially one which involves real negotiation, would be even more difficult. The newspapers generally also take the line of least resistance—their panacea is to step up the arms race, but this route leads only to bankruptcy, moral and financial, and to war. As for the military, always worried lest the public "relax" and Congress cut appropriations, they probably see the Soviet ICBM as a not unmixed blessing, since it must raise fear and tension.

The military's favored nostrum at the moment is the one Kissinger puts forward in his brilliant but poisonously delusive book. This is that, with both sides fully armed for mutual suicide, we must now prepare to wage limited nuclear war. The same men who say peaceful coexistence is impossible will now tell us that we can go into a kind of military minuet with Moscow, politely agreeing to fight nuclear wars but only on a limited scale and for limited objectives.

SEPTEMBER 9, 1957

26: *The Mind of Nikita Khrushchev*

IS THIS MARXISM?

Thoughtful intellectuals on the left would do well to study carefully the text of the interview Khrushchev gave Turner Catledge of the *New York Times* (May 11). The interview shows a man of great shrewdness, with a peasant's vividness of speech, but with an outlook on society not very different from Stalin's.

Earlier Marxists saw the dictatorship of the proletariat as a painful temporary necessity, but this man's world, like Stalin's, is a simple world of blacks and whites, in which those at the top decide which is which. Censorship, in this view, is as Khrushchev told Catledge a "rational use of a means at the disposal of society not to waste . . . ink, paper and paste on information that only creates harm." The permanent censorship has been the ideal of the closed society since Plato.

Khrushchev said that as Marxism-Leninism grew more "fashionable," it would become more important to oppose "pseudo-Communists" in order to "keep the theory clean." The metaphor with which he tried to explain was revealing. "We can compare it to the Army," Khrushchev said. "When a company is marching all in step except one man he should try to keep step or . . . drop somewhere in the tail until he learns to march correctly." That was also the way the cult of the individual and all the terrible abuses connected with it happened. Men were taught they all had to march as one; to keep step. Between the censored press and the regimented people none dared question Stalin.

How could such a man have downgraded Stalin? It is clear that Khrushchev hated Stalin. It is not clear that he hates Stalinism. Indeed it has been clear for some time that he has begun to regret that attack on Stalin and is anxious to rehabilitate the dictator in order to reconstruct the shaky foundations of the dictatorship. He is getting ready to deny that he ever spoke at all. "I don't know what you mean by the text of my speech," Khrushchev said when Catledge referred to it. "There was a text apparently fabricated by the United States intelligence service. But this publishing house, headed by Allen Dulles, has no great standing in our eyes."

This is the Bare-Faced Super-Whopper. Khrushchev does not yet dare deny that he attacked Stalin. Too many millions know that he did. He does not say, as an honest man might, that the published text was wrong in this respect or that. It is all a fabrication by the CIA.

Stalin was a very great man, so Khrushchev now says, though admitting his faults were considerable. But when Catledge asked what these were, Khrushchev said they were the faults mentioned in Lenin's testament. But these were all personal faults. Here is the leading figure of the most important Marxist country in the world, where dialectical materialism is gospel, and he attributes all the failings of several decades to one man's personality defects. Is this Marxism?

Khrushchev did say it is "impossible for one man or one party to exercise the exclusive right to interpret Marxism and Leninism." He speaks of a "collective interpretation." But how does this arise in the absence of free discussion? Where does this collective consciousness, like the *sobornost* of Russian Orthodox theology, lie? In the magic of some new communion, in some new priesthood? Is this not mysticism? Is it not nonsense, the nonsense of a self-deifying bureaucracy?

Lenin, though wiser and kinder, was also in some respects as simple-minded. But this is not socialism as it was envisaged by Marx and Engels. They saw in it a more perfect democracy, not rule from the top by a self-chosen few. Marx and Engels would never recognize a Marxism that purported to be a self-contained system embracing the totality of truth, from which correct answers could be obtained on any subject by turning on the top spigots in the hierarchy. This rigid, naïve, dogmatic view is the very opposite of that rich, complex and dynamic concept of social change which Marx and Engels developed in the tradition of English philosophical materialism.

The Khrushchev mentality is the mentality which—as Tito revealed—thought Rakosi an "honest revolutionist" as easily imposed on Budapest as flim-flam is imposed on Moscow. With this mentality in command, one can expect further eruptions in Eastern Europe and ultimately in Russia itself, and one can expect the further degeneration of the world Communist movement as it dutifully swallows Khrushchev's new CIA whopper, as it once swallowed Stalin's assurance that Lenin's testament was only a Trotskyite invention.

When the Continental Congress in 1774 tried to win Canada to the revolutionary struggle against England, it explained in a *Letter to the Inhabitants of Quebec* why certain rights were being insisted upon. Of freedom of the press, it said that this was a means "whereby oppressive officers are shamed or intimidated into more honorable and just modes of conducting affairs." Two centuries later this takes on new meaning in the struggle against Stalinism. If freedom of the press had not been so completely crushed by Lenin and Trotsky at the very beginning of the Bolshevik Revolution, Stalinism would never have come into being. It is not in censorship, or in dogma handed down from above, in a continued goose-step, that Russia and East Europe can avoid the evils Khrushchev himself exposed last year.

MAY 20, 1957

NO COMPETITION IN IDEAS

The Khrushchev interview was a major event for all who desire a relaxation of international tension. The Columbia Broadcasting System performed a public service by it. Khrushchev's performance was strikingly superior to Chou En-lai's when interviewed some months ago by Ed Murrow. Though the Chinese Communists have shown themselves more flexible theorists than the Russians, Murrow got nothing from Chou En-lai but slogans and propagandistic rantings. Khrushchev deserves credit for seizing what Chou En-lai missed, the opportunity to emerge as a human being for an American audience. This humanization of the leaders and people on the opposite side is the first essential toward peace. Will the Russians reciprocate by ending the shamefully mendacious current "smear America" campaign in the Soviet press?

There was nothing new in the Khrushchev interview, but then there rarely is in any interview with a top-rank leader. But he said some things which need to be said, and which he as a Russian had a right to say to an American audience. He had a right to complain of the generals and admirals in our own country who make entirely too many speeches "saying in how many hours the Soviet Union can be destroyed by the power of the United States." He was making a good point when he said that the trade embargo we impose on the Soviet bloc "does little damage to us. On the contrary, it compels us to make an extra effort and produce things at home which would otherwise have been brought from your country."

Next in importance was the picture of Khrushchev himself which emerged from the hour-long interview. It was the picture of a shrewd manager in a Socialist society, himself passionately concerned about his own major assignment—an increase in food output.

He was agile in evasion where he did not want to meet the issue, and he is obviously a man of ability. He can also be as tricky—and transparent—as a peasant haggling over a pig. When, for example, Khrushchev said the Soviet armed forces had already been reduced by 1,800,000 men, B. J. Cutler of the *New York Herald-Tribune* asked him how many men remained. His answer was that he didn't know the question would arise and therefore had not asked the Minister of Defense and didn't know. This was not very clever.

With this peasant slyness goes a conventional Communist mind. He foresees competition in production but not in ideas; his remarks on jamming the Voice of America show how naturally he takes to the sophistries of Soviet censorship.

When Daniel Schorr of CBS asked him about the recent statement by Peking which *Pravda* republished on the contradictions which arise under communism between the masses and the leaders, Khrushchev denied that there were any such contradictions in Russia. This will evoke a discreetly silent but unmistakable horse laugh among those who read it in Russia. (No doubt this is why the Soviet censor struck this question and answer out of the version released in Russia.) Finally, after all that happened in Poland and Hungary, Khrushchev can say, "We have no intention of imposing our ideas on anybody" and predict that the Kadar regime in Hungary "will flourish for ages to come."

But we see nothing ludicrous in Khrushchev's challenge to test his assertions by mutual withdrawal of troops from Europe. If we believe that most of the East European satellite regimes rest ultimately on Red Army bayonets, would not mutual withdrawal liberate these regimes?

The real reason for resisting this proposal is that United States diplomacy is not concerned with East European liberation but with building up German military power in alliance with the West to the point where the Russians and Poles might be forced to accept a territorial revision which will again open Slavic East Europe to German expansion. The atomic pistols are being cocked in the hope of some day frightening the Russians into just such a surrender. This is the key to the barren vagueness of disarmament talks.

JUNE 10, 1957

27: *The Liberal Court of Earl Warren*

THE COURT TURNS BACK THE CLOCK

While the Senate last week was burying McCarthy, the United States Supreme Court buried McCarthyism. The decisions in the Schware and Konigsberg cases do more than decide that radicals have a right to practice law. The decisions turn their back on an era in which the mere allegation of leftist sympathy or affiliation was enough to put a man outside the pale. A striking example will illustrate how unmistakably the Court has turned back the clock to an earlier and saner period. One of the charges on which the New Mexico Board of Bar Examiners refused to permit Rudolph Schware to take its tests for admission to the bar was his arrest and indictment in 1940 for recruiting volunteers to aid the Loyalists in Spain. The Supreme Court says, "even if it be assumed that the law was violated, it does not seem that such an offense indicated moral turpitude. . . . Many persons in this country actively supported the Spanish Loyalists," and it adds coolly, "In determining whether a person's character is good the nature of the offense which he has committed must be taken into account." This has a positive Rip Van Winkle-ish flavor; it awakens from a twenty-year sleep the forgotten attitudes most thoughtful Americans shared at the time; it expunges two decades of carefully nurtured nightmare.

The words were those of Mr. Justice Black, but no longer speaking in last-ditch isolation for Black and Douglas dissenting. Here he spoke for a majority which included not only Chief Justice Warren and our new (Catholic) Justice, Brennan, but even— *mirabile dictu*—Mr. Justice Burton. Indeed the "right wing" of the Court, Justices Frankfurter, Clark, and Harlan, saw no reason to dispute the majority's judgment in respect to Schware. Their concurring opinion indicates the change in atmosphere as strongly as does the majority decision. The circumstance which they found "controlling" was the fact that the New Mexico Supreme Court, in upholding Schware's exclusion from the bar, laid its main stress on the fact that Schware was admittedly a member of the Communist party from 1932 to 1940. The New Mexico Supreme Court said it felt that "one who has knowingly given his loyalty to such a program and belief for six to seven years during a period of responsible adulthood is a person of questionable character." Even the three Justices on the right find this "so dogmatic an inference as to be wholly unwarranted."

A few years ago, when McCarthy was riding high, it is difficult to imagine the Supreme Court even agreeing to hear the Schware and Konigsberg appeals. The mingled facts and allegations would have made them seem too disreputable to deserve judicial intervention. Beside his past membership in the Communist party and his indictment for recruiting volunteers for Spain, Rudolph Schware had used a false name as a labor organizer, and had been arrested several times for "criminal syndicalism" during the 1934 general strike in California. Normally—or at least by the standards which had become normal during the cold war decade—this would have been regarded as more than sufficient to show bad character and therefore disqualify for admission to the bar. Raphael Konigsberg's record was as bad, if not worse, from this point of view, because his political derelictions were more recent. California's rules require that an applicant for admission to the bar must establish the fact that he is of good moral character and does not advocate violent overthrow of the government. Konigsberg had been identified as a Communist by an informer before the State's own (Tenney) Un-American Activities Committee. He had refused on First Amendment grounds to answer any questions put by the bar examiners as to his political beliefs and associations except to swear that he did not believe in violent overthrow. And he had written a series of editorials during the Korean War for a publication called the *California Eagle* which no one would ever have mistaken for pieces by Walter Lippmann. Indeed the editors of the *Daily Worker* might well have rejected some of them as on the intemperate side.

The selections given in the briefs for the State Bar of California show that Mr. Konigsberg was not slavishly devoted to the cause of understatement. "Not all the criminal gangs in American history put together," he wrote in one editorial, "were as great a danger to our country's welfare as are the generals who today urge that American youth be trained as 'killers'. . . . None of the murders have been so sinful as a Dulles who uses religion to champion the anti-Christ. None such a threat to our security as a United States Attorney General who denies us the right to bail and tells brother to spy on

brother." Another selection was headed, "The Cesspool" and sub-
headed "Traitor! Traitor!" It was succinct, if not calm. "Betrayal is
in the air," he wrote. "Judges with impunity violate our constitutional rights. . . . Stool pigeons are the new national heroes. . . .
The President violates his oath of office by dragging us into war."
Another selection said, "To consider loyalty to America as identical
with Truman, Dulles & U. S. Steel is, to me, the ultimate in sacrilege.
. . . Lynchers of Americans and engineers of the doctrine of guns
over butter." Obviously Mr. Konigsberg is not one to use his First
Amendment rights sparingly. The horrified bar examiners found
these selections not only heretical politically but "morally deficient."
His own intrepid attorneys, Edward Mosk and Samuel Rosenwein,
must have wondered whether the Justices of the Supreme Court
would not hastily pull the bedcovers over their heads after reading
these selections and deny Mr. Konigsberg a hearing.

The majority seems to have regarded these brash utterances
with a sense of humor that has been lacking here for some time.
Indeed Mr. Justice Black exhumes from the record and cites in a
footnote, with an almost audible chuckle, an editorial in which Mr.
Konigsberg in his machine-gun prose centered his fire on the Supreme Court for refusing to hear the Hollywood Ten and said this
made "that high tribunal an integral part of the cold war machine
directed against the American people." Mr. Justice Black for the
majority finds that these editorials "fairly interpreted only say that
certain officials were performing their duty in a manner that, in the
opinion of the writer, was injurious to the public. We do not believe
that an inference of bad moral character can rationally be drawn
from these editorials. . . . Courts are not, and should not be, immune to such criticism. Government censorship can no more be
reconciled with our national constitutional standard of freedom of
speech and press when done in the guise of determining 'moral character' than if it should be attempted directly." It has been a long
time since a majority of the Supreme Court regarded radical utterances with such Hyde Park calm.

The majority, as if celebrating a kind of field day after the long
winter of judicial evasion and abnegation, has no time for craftsman-
like legal conservatism. "The State argues," Mr. Justice Black says,
"that Konigsberg's refusal to tell the examiners whether he was a
member of the Communist party . . . tends to support an inference

that he is a member of the Communist party and therefore a person of bad moral character. . . . Obviously the State could not draw unfavorable inferences as to his truthfulness, candor or his moral character in general if his refusal to answer was based on a belief that the United States Constitution prohibited the type of inquiries which the committee was making. On the record before us, it is our judgment that the inferences of bad moral character which the committee attempted to draw from Konigsberg's refusal to answer questions about his political affiliations and opinions are unwarranted." This gives new weight and dignity to claims of First Amendment privilege.

It is always hazardous to draw straight lines from general propositions in current cases to the outcome of other future cases. But it is hard not to be hopeful about a court on which a majority of the members (the newest judge, Whittaker, took no part) regard so astringently views, facts and allegations which until recently would have been damning. The two appellants, Schware and Konigsberg, though men with honorable war and civilian records, would have been crucified by a McCarthy. Liberals, middle-of-the-roaders and conservatives alike on this Court seem prepared to take an adult view of past Communist party membership, and a respectful attitude toward First Amendment claims. They seem prepared at last here, as in other free societies, to untangle the real problems of communism from the hobgoblins of cold war demonology. Whatever that evil and unscrupulous adventurer McCarthy died of, a black sense of failure and public rejection hastened his sodden end. His punier successors are likely to contract similar ailments when they ponder on the *Schware* and *Konigsberg* decisions. It looks as if the witch hunt is drawing to its close.

MAY 13, 1957

THE WATKINS AND SWEEZY DECISIONS

If Torquemada had received a Papal edict ordering him to cease burning heretics unless actually caught defacing church property, he would have been no more appalled than the staffs of the House Un-American Activities Committee and the Senate Internal Security Committee by the *Watkins* and *Sweezy* decisions. A deep gloom has settled on both. The day after the Supreme Court handed down its verdict, the Senate committee was supposed to interrogate several long harassed officials of a left-wing union. But its acting chairman, Senator Hruska, meekly consented to a week's postponement on request of defense counsel, Victor Rabinowitz. Mr. Rabinowitz said he needed a week to study the Watkins opinion and to advise his clients. It was apparent that what he wanted to advise them on was whether under this decision it was any longer necessary to answer the kind of questions in which these committees specialize. The House committee later the same day postponed a similar executive session for the same humbling reasons. On both committees, staff members were unusually subdued and polite, as is natural in men threatened by technological unemployment. For while no one here in Washington is sure precisely what the Court's ruling in *Watkins* means, there is agreement on both sides of the fence that it means serious trouble for both inquisitorial committees.

Our own opinion is that June 17, 1957, will go down in the history books as the day on which the Supreme Court irreparably crippled the witch hunt. The Court did not in so many words declare ideological inquisition by Congress unconstitutional under the First Amendment, but it came as close to saying that as is probably feasible. A few more cases may be required to develop clearly the full implications. But when these appear it will be seen that the House Un-American Activities Committee as we have known it for two painful decades is out of business. So, I believe, are the little un-American committees set up by the states in imitation of it. The Internal Security Committee of the Senate, too, will have to behave quite differently if it is to survive at all. The Court under Warren struck four mighty blows last Monday for a freer and saner America. The *Service, California Smith Act, Sweezy* and *Watkins* decisions represent giant steps away from the peculiarly un-American habits engendered in the era which began with Dies and closed with McCarthy. The best thing Chairman Walter can do now is to bequeath himself to the Smithsonian.

We would not blame him and his colleagues if after all these years of witch hunting, they *really* suspected witchcraft. While attention was diverted to chasing random Communists, who had time to suspect citizens as solid as Eisenhower and Brownell? Who would have dreamt that they would pack the Court with Constitution-carrying Republicans? Who could have foreseen five years ago that the first Republican victory in a presidential election since 1928 would give us a Court like this one? Where Walter and Eastland made their mistake is now obvious. They investigated the wrong party.

The discerning noticed some time ago, of course, that poor Earl Warren had fallen prey to possession by a liberalistic succubus beyond hope of exorcism. But Harlan—hand-picked by Brownell—had been regarded as impervious to demoniac wile. Yet it was Harlan who wrote the *Service* and *California Smith Act* decisions. The effect of the former is moral. Mr. Service, eight times cleared, once by a grand jury, six times by loyalty security boards, and once by a Senate investigating committee, was nonetheless fired by Secretary of State Acheson under pressure from McCarthy and a weak-kneed Loyalty Review Board. Mr. Service was McCarthy's first triumph, and one of the China Lobby's earliest targets. Mr. Justice Harlan's ruling was procedural, but in effect it held that once a Secretary of State has set up formal regulations to provide some semblance of due process in loyalty cases, he has waived such powers of summary discharge as were conferred on him by the so-called McCarran riders. He cannot turn around and summarily fire a man who has been cleared by the normal departmental loyalty-security procedures. We congratulate Mr. Service and his faithful counsel, Charles Edward Rhetts, on victory in their long fight for justice.

California's was the first Smith Act case in which the Supreme Court has adjudged the sufficiency of the evidence. The *Dennis* decision dealt only with the constitutionality of the Smith Act. The Pittsburgh case was remanded for a new trial on the informer issue. Here for the first time the Supreme Court was doing what Chief Justice Vinson promised it would some time do when he wrote *Dennis*. It was evaluating the evidence and the conduct of the trial. The result was not only to order the acquittal of five of the California defendants but to set standards for the retrial of the other nine which will make new convictions in future Smith Act trials much more difficult. Much of what Mr. Justice Harlan wrote for the majority (only Mr. Justice Clark dissenting on the result) is fine-spun Alice-in-Wonderland nonsense of the kind bred on courts trying to reconcile with First Amendment freedoms a statute which makes the dissemination of ideas a crime. What Mr. Justice Black and Douglas in their separate opinion assert will some day be the law. But in the meantime it is helpful to have Mr. Justice Harlan insisting that there must be some semblance of "incitement to action" to make a Smith

Act conviction stick. A few more astringent decisions like this one and the Act will die on the vine.

The *Watkins* and *Sweezy* decisions were a triumph for three brave dissenters on the circuit bench, Chief Judge Henry W. Edgerton and Judge David L. Bazelon of the Court of Appeals for the District of Columbia, and Judge Charles E. Clark of the Second Circuit in New York. Judges Edgerton and Bazelon wrote the first opinion here on Watkins, 2-1 for acquittal, only to have themselves hastily reversed on rehearing by the full bench. More important, however, is the fact that Chief Justice Warren in *Watkins* and *Sweezy* has largely adopted the reasoning of that noble and moving dissent Chief Judge Edgerton wrote in 1948 in the *Barsky* case when cold war was just beginning to stow away traditional freedoms in deep freeze. Judge Edgerton was the lone dissenter a decade ago against the decisions which sent the Hollywood Ten, the members of the Joint Anti-Fascist Refugee Committee, Dr. Edward Barsky, Helen Bryan and Richard Morford of the National Council for Soviet American Friendship to jail for contempt of the House Un-American Activities Committee. In those days the victims were still pleading the First Amendment, not the Fifth, but except in the case of Eisler who fled, the Supreme Court steadily denied them a hearing. A footnote to the Warren opinion now dismisses these old decisions as "contrasting views" and cites with honor the Edgerton dissent and that by Judge Clark in the Josephson case, the other dissent in that period which made a fundamental attack upon the House committee.

This line of attack, now adopted by a majority of the Court, is that the legislative power of investigation is limited by the First Amendment, and that a summons to appear in the public pillory of the House Un-American Activities Committee or a similar State body may "abridge" freedoms of speech, press and assembly by intimidation. This way of violating the First and Fourteenth Amendments is made easy by the adoption of vague resolutions sweepingly permitting investigators to make their own preconceptions a measure of orthodoxy and a mandate to harass heretics. Five Justices in *Watkins*—Warren, Black, Douglas, Harlan and Brennan—serve notice that they are not disposed any longer to punish for contempt those who fall afoul of what any current House investigator may consider "un-American." In *Sweezy,* six Justices—Warren, Black, Douglas and Brennan for the majority, Frankfurter and Harlan concurring—serve notice similarly that investigations carried on by such states as New Hampshire to ferret out so-called "subversive" persons will likewise be disapproved by the Court. Where there is the possibility of infringing First Amendment rights, neither Congress nor state legislatures can be sure any longer of having their authority enforced by contempt proceedings unless they spell out carefully by specific resolution just what information they want and why. And the excuse had better be a good one.

The resolution will have to be precise and in addition the witness will have to be told at the hearing (and not later on trial for contempt) just exactly why the question is being asked him and why the information sought is pertinent. The Court does not say in advance that there can be no investigation which does not impinge on First Amendment freedoms. But by forcing Congress and the legislatures to be precise in this way the Court makes it impossible to carry on the witch hunt as we have known it.

We have come to the end of an era. Martin Dies at the very beginning of it made clear that he conceived of the House Un-American Activities Committee as a kind of roving grand jury, acting not in traditional secrecy but in the full blaze of publicity to punish by defamation those radicals who could not be reached by criminal prosecution. Now we have the Supreme Court saying in *Watkins* that Congress is not "a law enforcement or trial agency," and that it cannot expose for the sake of exposure in the area of ideas protected by the First Amendment. The *Sweezy* decision says the same thing as regards investigations by state legislatures. It stresses heavily protection of academic freedom as well as political liberty from such inquisitions, and it also contains a side remark that may sound the end for that type of question which is designed not to elicit information but to break a man morally by making him an informer. "The questioning," Chief Justice Warren said of the interrogation our friend Paul M. Sweezy, co-editor of the *Monthly Review,* resisted in New Hampshire, "indicates that the investigators . . . were not acquiring new information as much as corroborating data already in their possession."

The *Watkins* and *Sweezy* decisions must be read together. They promise a new birth of freedom. They make the First Amendment a reality again. They reflect the steadily growing public misgiving and distaste for that weird collection of opportunists, clowns, ex-Communist crackpots, and poor sick souls who have made America look foolish and even sinister during the last ten years with their perpetual searching under the national bed for little men who weren't there. The full measure of the agony and suffering they have inflicted will never be known. We are grateful to the Chief Justice and to the Court, and we may all be proud as Americans that the great traditions of our country had sufficient strength to overcome them at last.

JUNE 24, 1957

28: *The Black Man's Burden*

NOBODY TO VOTE FOR

More important to the Negro than the right to vote is the right to live without humiliation. The right to vote in the one-party South, where rival Democratic candidates, if any, compete in appeals to racism, has been highly overrated in the Senate debates which are slowly destroying hopes of an effective civil rights bill. The right to sit down undisturbed in a bus after a hard day's work, the right to justice when short-changed or cheated, the right to have one's children begin to grow up without being treated as niggers or even (as the better white folks slur it) *nigras,* these are the rights, these are the everyday agonies, these make the bitter bread of the black man's affliction. All this has been forgotten in the complacent discussions which paved the way for defeat of Part III, the human rights section of the civil rights bill, and may end in emasculating Part IV, its political rights section, with a jury trial amendment.

What is missing from the debate is easily discernible. The Negro has his champions in the Senate but no spokesman. The massive researches of a Douglas of Illinois, the noble humanism of a Clark of Pennsylvania, the legal labors of a Javits of New York, are no substitute for a man who could speak as one who himself knows what it means to be born black. Amid the sterile legalisms and the courtly compliments what is missing are the realities only a Negro can know and only a Negro senator could express. From the gallery, through the eyes of a Negro, there must be a constant anguish in the lily-white scene. The Senate appears not merely as an exclusive club but as a white man's club in which a younger group faces up reluctantly to the task of enacting regulations painful to some of its oldest members. Even through the speeches of those most devoted to the Negro's cause there runs a tone of supplication, apology and tenderness. Rarely has so much exquisite tact been expended on the oppressor by those who are supposed to be rescuing the oppressed.

JULY 29, 1957

NIXON WAS CORDIAL IN GHANA

Amid all the ballyhoo in our press about Vice-President Nixon's visit to Ghana, little attention was paid to two items which will bulk large in the eyes of Africans. The first is that Dr. W. E. B. Du Bois, the greatest living Negro historian, who wrote the story of the black continent from the black man's point of view, was unable to attend the independence celebration. The State Department refused to give him a passport unless he would sign a non-Communist affidavit. The second is that the Reverend Martin Luther King, leader of the Montgomery, Alabama, bus boycott, was unable to get any response from the Eisenhower Administration until he ran into Vice-President Nixon at the Ghana celebration, where the two men "shook hands warmly" for the photographers. The Vice-President travels all the way to the Gold Coast to woo a new Negro nation. In far-off Africa, Dr. King can even get his hand shook. But at home the brushoff greets repeated Negro appeals from our own South for presidential intervention against racism and terror. The place to win Africa's friendship is still Montgomery, Alabama.

MARCH 11, 1957

THE BEGINNINGS OF A REVOLUTION

What we are seeing in the South is something which resembles a revolution. The government is trying to bring about a deeply unpopular change. The moderates have been counseling peaceful resistance, and undermining respect for the agencies of government. The moment has now come when leadership passes to the extremists, who advocate force and violence. The street mobs have begun to take control.

The mobs are only a handful, and those who would resort to violence are still a minority. But that minority has so much power because its aims are the wishes of the majority—to block integration. The power of the mob may be measured by the silence of the South's normal leadership. Except for the Mayor of Little Rock, no public figure has spoken up for obedience to law. No senator from the South, no governor, no member of Congress, no leader of the bar, has dared publicly utter a restraining word. This dead silence may prove to be the inner "eye" of a hurricane.

It is whispered in Washington that unless something is done soon by the federal government the moderates will be destroyed politically. The southern senators only a few weeks ago looked like shrewd and skillful statesmen. Now they appear to be appeasers and quislings. How can they compete with a Governor who calls out the National Guard to prevent integration? The niceties of senatorial footwork would look ludicrous if explained to a southern audience which has just seen *action*.

The best the moderates offered was a long, slow, delaying action. To the extremists this was only a gradual form of surrender. They have taken the offensive in the border states of Arkansas and Tennessee where integration had already begun. They can claim to be pushing integration back, instead of retreating slowly before it. The extremists have outbid the moderates.

The moderates prepared their own downfall. In the state legislatures, the moderates enacted nullification. In Congress all last spring during the civil rights debate, the moderates helped to intensify in the South a pathological state of mind: suspicion of the Supreme Court, distrust of all federal judges, a feeling that alien and esoteric forces were plotting against the South and its "way of life." The moderates, when a little integrity and courage might still have counted, pandered to the view that resistance to law was an almost sacred duty for white southerners, a pious obligation they owed their past. Faubus, the mobs and the dynamiters are only acting out what the moderates taught them.

The mob itself is what mobs usually are, unstable fringe elements, eager for any occasion to vent long pent-up hatreds, hatred of their own ugly selves they spew outward on whatever their social conditioning makes the target. The South has more than the normal quota of such sick souls, as it has more than the normal quota of poverty, ignorance and shiftlessness plus a frontier habit of violence. The average southern white is probably more afraid of the mob than the average southern Negro, since the former fears his own good instincts, which might betray him into "nigger loving" opposition. The latter may regard the mob as an almost normal recurrence of white bestiality which one may avoid without loss of self-respect.

These human scarecrows and juvenile delinquents in the news photos and on the television screens might become a majority overnight. If they can provoke a race riot, if they can make the issue seem starkly North versus South, the United States could find itself in the gravest crisis since Fort Sumter. Every day's delay by the President, whose enormous personal prestige might be put to good use at this juncture, risks irreversible events.

Unfortunately we have a President who is nine-tenths figurehead. A figurehead must be manipulated. There seems to be no one around to tell him what to do, and so he turns up in the same picture pages, happily relaxing on the eighteenth green. "Mr. Brownell also informed the President," the *New York Times* reported almost tongue in cheek, "that a Nashville school had been bombed. Mr. Hagerty said the President's reaction to this had been 'the same as anyone else's would be—he thought it was a terrible thing.'" The gaping walls of the Hattie Cotton School are not as terrible as this gaping vacuum in the presidency.

If the situation were not so deadly serious, one would be tempted to satirize the contrast between the airlift swiftly unloading arms six thousand miles away in Jordan to meet an exaggerated crisis in Syria with the irresolution the government shows at home. The dangers of communism seem to arouse Washington much more quickly than those of racism, though the latter comes up in a form which is a fundamental challenge to law itself.

This is a time to see ourselves as others see us. The ugly hate-filled faces of the whites in Little Rock and Nashville, the bravery of the Negro children and their parents, the minister knocked down and beaten in Birmingham, the poor feeble-minded Negro emasculated by Klansmen just to prove their mettle, are giving the colored majority on this planet a picture of us it will be hard to eradicate. Whether here or in Algiers, the white race just doesn't seem as civilized as it claims to be.

SEPTEMBER 16, 1957

29: *A Stranger Knocks at Heaven's Gate*

With the launching of the first artificial moon into the skies, man stands at last on the threshold of the universe. *Outside* takes on a new meaning. There new worlds beckon a new Columbus. The Infinite, on which mystics brooded, may become the playground of the astronaut and man may roam where God is supposed to have presided.

Like any other stranger, knocking at a new door, Man must nervously adjust his tie and give himself a quick once-over, hoping to make a good impression. The self-inventory is not reassuring. To a fresh eye at the outer world's window, the newcomer may seem a creature of terrifying habits.

Wherever man goes, he brings with him war. His poets glorify it. Each generation's healthiest youth is trained for it. Any difference within the human species is enough to serve as excuse for it. Religion, coloring, national jealousy, capitalist competition for markets, deviations of dogma among Communists—the excuses vary, the behavior remains the same.

One may easily imagine the anxious debates of an interstellar conference called to consider the danger. What if men transplant their feuds, as Spaniards and Englishmen did after crossing the Atlantic? Theological gibberish was imposed by fire and sword on the bewildered Indian. What if the Russians reach the far side of the moon and demand that its creatures eschew bourgeois ideas? What if we Americans, suspicious of uncommitted neutrals, land atom-armed on Mars and insist that the inhabitants adopt free enterprise? The human race may seem a pest which has suddenly appeared out of one small planet, making unsafe the highways among the stars.

Were some flying saucer to land cosmic investigators for a closer look, they would be startled to find that mentally men live centuries apart. Here are men with modern instruments so fine they can plot the course of the most distant suns. Next door to them may live men who turn for guidance, in their daily newspapers, to horoscopes like those cast by Babylonian astrologers millennia earlier. Here walk men brooding on the new multidimensional geometries. Past them in the same streets walk others who cross themselves when they see a black cat. Some men seem the harbingers of a new race; others seem fresh from the cave. Little wonder that so heterogeneous a mass is swept from time to time by outbreaks of madness, from the St. Vitus dance of the Middle Ages to those furnaces into which some human beings shoveled several million others only yesterday. Ours may not seem a wholesome breed for stellar immigration.

A gleaming metal ball hurtling regularly around our planet may be the first signal of intelligent life on earth to observers elsewhere who could not see into the murky depths of our aerial ocean. They might be surprised to learn that the minds which have made such wonders possible nowhere rule the human societies of which they are a part. Whatever the ostensible form of the society, everywhere the cunning govern. Here the ruler may be a Tammany-style politician, there a commissar. The finer minds everywhere are subordinate to the inferior.

The two contenders for mastery of the earth, the "communistic" Russians and the "capitalistic" Americans have this in common. Their rulers equally distrust the "intellectual." The intellectual, like a special breed in a hive, is well-fed so long as he devotes himself to the tasks allotted to him by his masters: the fabrication of new weapons, the inculcation of ideas to keep the human herd submissive. But let him begin to speak his mind, and he gets into trouble. At the least he may find himself deprived of livelihood; at the worst, he may be imprisoned as "subversive" or "counterrevolutionary." The intellectual on both sides is prized and yet suspect, favored but subjected.

It is symptomatic that the foremost mind of our time, the man who found the magic formula that unlocked the atom, was exiled from his German homeland as racially inferior, and regarded in America, though with tolerance because of his greatness, as more than a little subversive, while in the Soviet Union his theory of relativity was taboo as "bourgeois." The rulers everywhere prefer mechanical brains.

Objectively speaking, it would probably be better for the universe if man remained earthbound. In the wake of the first satellite, we give no sign of closing ranks and facing outward as a united species. There is no sudden sense of how petty has become all that once divided us. There is little reverent wonder for the adventures which could lie ahead. Instead there is intensified fear, and a demand to step up preparations for the next war, which must now be fought in the upper skies as well. Missile stocks are up. Nothing has changed but the magnitude of our potential for mass murder.

As the sky fills with satellites and the sky platforms are manned and armed, will Americans and Russians shoot it out in the wild yonder, destroying each other and the world with them? It might be better, after all, if space *were* left to a newer species, bred to live in peace and to take joy in diversity. Our first reactions, like all our past, show how unfit men are for the heavens. We would only stain red the Milky Way.

OCTOBER 14, 1957

30: *Our War Economy*

THE LIBERALS AND THE MILITARY BUDGET

The most striking political phenomena in the past week was the way American liberals abdicated their responsibility in dealing with military spending. One voice was raised here to warn, "while defense expenditures are necessary, they are for the most part a loss rather than a contribution to the national economy. . . . Defense expenditures drain away national resources which would otherwise be devoted to building up the nation's capital structure and improving the people's levels of living." But this warning did not come from Walter Reuther, but from Ralph J. Cordiner, president of General Electric, at the Eighth Annual Armed Forces Day Dinner. The budgetary manifesto issued by the ADA over the signatures of Reuther and fifty-eight other liberals uncritically supported the President's budget. "Three fifths of the proposed budget goes for national defense," was all their statement said on this crucial subject. "Surely we agree that the security needs of the United States must be met despite the cost." It is strange when only a big businessman talks as liberals used to.

Of course the nation's security must be met whatever the cost, but this is question-begging. The real question is whether we are to accept at face value the Pentagon's notion of what the real security needs and the real costs are. Here we need study and leadership on management and on policy. Is the money being spent carefully or wastefully? Are the intelligence and planning behind the military program sound? Are the country's economy and fate being tied to an arms race which can lead only to military domination and perhaps to war? These are questions on which liberals and labor leaders normally spoke out. Today they are silent.

A report filed here last Tuesday disclosed the kind of facts and made the kind of criticism which have normally come from liberals. It said 80 percent of all military procurement and 95 percent of aircraft procurement was now spent under negotiated mostly cost-plus contracts rather than competitive bidding, and that millions were being wasted because no basic cost principles had been worked out, and procurement-auditing practices were chaotic. It said that in the field of missiles, a costlier project than the atom bomb, evaluations "have consisted of briefings or presentations by directly interested groups, principally contractors' representatives and representatives of the sponsoring Services." It found that rivalry among the Services in the development of missiles, on which billions are being spent, "is getting completely out of control" and leading to great waste, with each of the three Services "striving to acquire an arsenal of weapons complete in itself to carry out any and all possible missions." It criticized the inflated and alarmist intelligence estimates of Soviet power which were used last year to "sell" Congress an accelerated big bomber program since scaled down as admittedly based on false information.

But this did not come from liberal critics. It came from a House Appropriations Subcommittee headed by Congressman Mahon of Texas. A report by liberals on the budget, put out last weekend by the Conference on Economic Progress, treated the military budget quite differently. This report, by a group in which Reuther and Leon Keyserling are the guiding spirits, had much of value to contribute in the sphere of social welfare spending but in the field of defense spending it offered not one word of critical analysis. Its projected ideal budget figured actual security spending in 1956 as forty billions and proposed by 1960 to raise this to forty-four billion dollars. It gave aid and comfort to the Pentagon by estimating that military spending as a percentage of total national production had actually fallen in the past four years "from about 14 percent of total national production to about 9.6 percent—a decline of 31 percent" and it asks "whether we are risking our lives by these slashes." Is this liberalism?

The two liberal statements, one by the ADA'ers, the other by the Conference on Economic Progress, made headlines as liberal support of the President on the budget. And on education and social welfare Eisenhower does deserve and need support against the economy bloc in Congress. But can these necessary expenditures be saved by uncritically accepting the military estimates? By treating the Pentagon as a sacred cow, is not the way prepared for appeasing the economy bloc by cutting everything else but the military? How can there possibly be wise and adequate expenditure in the field of social welfare if the military are allowed a blank check, a blank check they fill in every year with ever larger amounts?

At page 94 of the Mahon committee report (which was accepted as the full House committee report), there is a separate section of "additional views" filed by one congressman who felt the committee did not go far enough. "I firmly believe," he wrote (though only to have his words ignored by the press), "that about 30 percent of defense spending is excessive, is causing inflation, provides no real defense, and by being built into our domestic economy constitutes a real threat to our nation." He said he had been in Russia last year and what he saw "was completely opposite to the impression we had from information furnished our subcommittee by United States military witnesses." He felt that the Russian military menace had been built up here beyond all reasonable proportions in order to scare up higher military appropriations.

This dissenter protested that defense had become a gravy train, that the eighty billions spent on war orders with the fifty leading military contractors had tripled the value of their stock in five years. He pointed out that in the case of the aircraft companies the government paid most of the cost of their facilities and gave them five-year amortization on the balance. "Yet the total profits to these aircraft companies, with little investment and practically no risk," he disclosed indignantly, "increased last year, though total sales were less than the preceding year." He said testimony taken by the subcommittee in the past three years showed "great waste" and "great duplication." He warned, "The records show we are rapidly tying our domestic economy to the military, which has always been a threat to the safety of any nation. History shows," he added, "that in

Germany and Japan and every other major country, whenever the domestic economy got tied to the military, it has led to war."

This dissenter ended by recalling that five years ago the Chief of the National Production Authority "told me privately that if he were Joe Stalin and wanted to wreck the economy of the United States, he would declare five years of peace" because the loss of military spending would create a major depression. "If that 30 percent extra effort due to war and the preparedness for defense is the basis for our material prosperity," this dissenter pleaded, "then why not continue to put forth that 30 percent extra effort, not in needless waste which leaves us a poorer country but in work that will improve our country? Why can't we put forth that extra effort in reforesting our lands, harnessing our streams for electricity, reclaiming our lands through soil conservation and in those things that make our country richer and better?"

Whose name was signed to this moving appeal? Not Walter Reuther or Upton Sinclair or Alvin Hansen or Reinhold Niebuhr or Jerry Voorhis or Arthur M. Schlesinger, Jr., or Robert R. Nathan or Max Lerner or Alex Rose or Max Zaritsky. Their names were signed to the ADA manifesto of the fifty-nine in uncritical support of the President's budget, its swollen military estimates included. The signer of this "dissent" was a Democratic congressman from benighted Mississippi, James L. Whitten, a senior member of the powerful conservative House Appropriations Committee. It is a melancholy day for American liberalism when its leading spokesmen act as a sounding board for the military budget makers while it is left to a conservative Mississippi Democrat to say what Reuther, Upton Sinclair or Alvin Hansen would have said a few years ago.

Their silence today reflects the vast and inhibiting shadow cast across American life by the sheer size of the military budget. Labor as well as capital now depends upon it, and labor leaders, too, would rather acquiesce in the arms race than risk unemployment. The colleges and a whole strata of intellectuals live off the search for ever more ingenious weapons. The race for the ultimate destroyer has created a market for brains; mathematicians and physicists are at a premium. The intellectuals, like the capitalists and the labor leaders, are loath to bite the hand that feeds them. In addition, for a liberal, who has in his time signed thirty round robins and joined a half dozen organizations long dead but now suspect, criticism of military budget and the arms race is an occupational hazard. He might be accused of being "soft on communism."

MAY 27, 1957

THE INFLATIONARY SPIRAL

Walter Reuther's campaign for lower automobile prices must be seen against the background of some economic realities neither Adam Smith nor Karl Marx expected. American capitalism, like Russian communism, bears little resemblance to its idealized image. In big organized industry, wages are now determined by a peculiar kind of competition—competition among labor leaders. Their popularity with their members and their standing in the labor hierarchy depends on how much they can get in increased wages at annual or biennial bargaining sessions with the managers of industry.

These bargaining sessions have the spurious ferocity of a wrestling match, in which the mountainous contenders make up by groan and grimace for the essential unreality of the contest. The lords of industry look forward eagerly to being pinned to the mat. Trade unionism has become their profit escalator. Every extra dollar in wages gives them an excuse for several dollars extra in price increases.

These increases are made possible because the arms race has created a cost-plus economy in which big industrialists can afford to be gentlemanly. When the leading company puts up its price, its competitors (as they are still quaintly called) put up theirs by the same amount.

This happy game of wage-and-price leapfrog in the organized sector of the economy exploits the unorganized. The consumer, the smaller businesses which have to fight for their dwindling share of his dwindling dollar, the folk who live on fixed incomes, the unorganized worker and professional man, all these are the victims of perpetual inflation.

This can no more go on forever than could that New Era of Herbert Hoover's in the twenties, but it is as hazardous for a labor leader as for a capitalist to be socially responsible. The average trade unionist, like the average investor, is interested in his own take, not in the overall effect on the economy. When Mr. Reuther in his broadside of August 29 said the prerogatives of labor and management should not be "exercised in a vacuum unrelated to the needs of the whole society," he was talking a language risky with his own rank-and-file—long hair stuff, "sort of socialistic."

The Reuther proposal for a $100 cut in the price of next season's cars was smart public relations. But his offer, however cagily worded, to take that cut into account at next year's wage-bargaining session, took courage. The average auto worker will not relish the idea that he might possibly be called on to make a contribution from his own pay envelope to the *pro bono publico* of combating inflation.

Indeed the text of the letters to the Big Three which Mr. Reuther released on August 18 seem to reflect some difficulties with his own executive board. The letters are brilliant in their analysis of the industry's economic and sales position, but a slight stammer develops when the question comes up of just what labor would do if prices *were* cut $100.

At one point Mr. Reuther speaks of submitting to impartial arbitration if "a question should arise as to whether the granting of our demands would necessitate a restoration of part or all of the $100 per car price reduction." At another he speaks of "adjusting our demands downward to the extent shown to be necessary in order to avoid a price increase." The companies might have challenged this contradiction, but only at the expense of discussing a subject they would like to avoid.

A man's size can be measured by his willingness in the public interest to take positions his own following may not like. Walter Reuther has again shown himself the one American labor leader of first rank who still has this kind of social vision and daring.

The Reuther campaign represents the kind of responsible leadership commensurate with the huge power now exercised by a great trade union. The campaign cites the plea made recently by the past president of the National Automobile Dealers Association pleading with the manufacturers to absorb increased costs in pricing new models and estimating that this might be a difference in sales of a million more cars. Since autos are our most important consumer durable industry, the effect would be felt by the whole economy.

In his original letters released on August 18, Mr. Reuther showed that the effect of a $100 price cut and a million more sales for each of the Big Three would still leave them with profit margins after taxes far above the national average for manufacturing corporations generally: 18.9 percent for GM, 13.9 percent for Ford, and

19.2 percent for Chrysler as compared with the manufacturing average of 12.1 percent.

These percentages are figured on a net worth which itself represents a vast expansion financed out of exorbitant earnings at the consumer's expense. Since 1947, as Mr. Reuther showed in his statement of August 29, GM's net worth has tripled, Ford's has gone up by two and a half times, Chrysler's has doubled. Very little of this has come from the sale of stock. Most of it represents, in Mr. Reuther's vivid phrase, a compulsory investment by the consumer.

If we had a President with a flair for leadership, he could utilize Mr. Reuther's initiative. What is true in autos is also true in steel, and in every basic industry. Walter Reuther has launched a one-man campaign to educate the labor movement and the country. Will other labor leaders join him, or will they prefer comfortably to acquiesce as junior partners (very junior) in a continuous price gouge which spells serious trouble for the future?

SEPTEMBER 9, 1957

CREEPING SOCIALISM OR STUMBLING CAPITALISM

For one who, like the writer, was an active newspaperman and editorial writer in the great depression of the thirties, the striking aspect of the panicky discussion precipitated in the capital by the current recession is the stale lack of new ideas. The conservatives in both parties, like the conservatives a generation ago, believe that a sound recovery is only possible if deflation runs its course and squeezes prices and wages down to the point where new capital investment becomes profitable again. Though no one dares express this frankly, this is the reason for the opposition to a tax cut. The rich Texans who play so dominant a role in the leadership of both parties believe "a little healthy deflation" is long overdue, and fear to encourage a new upsurge of buying before there has been a downward readjustment of production costs. So Secretary of the Treasury Anderson, Lyndon Johnson and Speaker Rayburn are linked in a bipartisan coalition to choke off tax cut pressure in Congress. The ultimate philosophy of this group, as of Herbert Hoover in the thirties, is that of the big capitalists, who can weather and even benefit by a depression—so long as it does not go too far—and who see the basic standard of governmental action as the maintenance of profitability in the economy. The way to restore profitability is to squeeze costs, particularly wages. For this purpose a margin of unemployment is "healthy."

On the other hand, the labor movement, the majority of farmers, and the smaller businessmen, for whom the Democratic party traditionally speaks, have no better remedy to offer than renewed inflation, particularly through a stepped-up arms race. No one stands back and takes a good look at our economy and tries to evaluate the striking fact that a recession of unpredictable dimensions has begun even though for ten years our economy has been leaning on the inflationary crutch of an arms budget running about forty billion dollars a year. This has been a WPA of enormous proportions, far larger than the spending FDR dared to do in the thirties. If we can have a recession despite so huge a pump-priming operation, if even this is not able to maintain full employment, then obviously we need measures more thoughtful and more thoroughgoing than a tax cut of three to six billion, and some miscellaneous public works, road building and the like. If even wasting (from an economic point of view, it *is* waste) forty billions a year on arms cannot keep this economy on an even keel, then these piddling measures cannot be expected to cure it.

The truth is that we will never know how to run our economy properly until we at least have the courage to look at it *as it is*. We Americans pride ourselves on our pragmatism, but in the field of social theory we are frozen into immobility by stereotypes which bear only a distant resemblance to reality. "Free enterprise" is a national deity none dare question. But the American economic system is not a system of free enterprise. It is a mixture of corporate enterprise, which FDR once called "private collectivism," and of public ownership and control, with some genuine private enterprise of the classic free-market type still struggling on the edges. The great corporations keep prices rigid; it is the smaller businessmen who must stand the gaff of price adjustments. The basic materials of industry are all more or less controlled by private combines. Some way to subject their prices to public control, some measures of over-all planning to maintain output, a willingness to embark on measures of public ownership and development in those areas where corporate enterprise is impotent, as in the development of the great river valleys, is necessary if we are to have a healthy and growing economy, *especially if we manage to moderate the arms race and end the drift toward war*. Then, in peaceful competition with the Soviet bloc, the future will depend on whether we can handle our economy free from shibboleths as a mixed economy, part free, part corporate, part public. If this means creeping socialism, that is far better than stumbling capitalism, to use Bishop Oxnam's vivid phrase.

MARCH 31, 1958

31: *The American Secret Police*

THE FBI INVESTIGATES ITSELF

The report of the Commission on Government Security is a monument to the inexplicable folly—we do not want to use a harsher word—of Hubert Humphrey. In the middle of the uproar two years ago over the loyalty-security "numbers racket," Senator Humphrey suddenly fathered the resolution which set up this commission. The result was to hand the Eisenhower Administration and the FBI a chance to whitewash clearance procedures just when the public was demanding investigation. The Democrats could have made a political issue of the criticism aroused by the "faceless informer" and by the confusions brought to light in such cases as those of Ladejinsky. The Democratic-controlled Senate could have set up an investigation of its own. Instead Humphrey introduced a resolution which we termed "a booby trap for liberals." It called for a commission of twelve, of whom four were to be appointed by the White House and four by Nixon, thus ensuring Republican control. In addition, as we pointed out at the time, the terms of the resolution were designed to protect the precious "confidential informant" system of the FBI from a real airing.

The commission, its staff, and its proceedings were models of how not to investigate secret police practices. Not a single liberal or even a distinguished conservative was among the twelve men named to the commission. But it included one witch hunter, Chairman Walter of the House Un-American Activities Committee. The chairman, Loyd Wright, of Los Angeles, a former president of the American Bar Association, may be judged from the interview with him in last Sunday's *Washington Star* (June 23). When the interviewer suggested that Mr. Wright seemed to entertain some fears about the Supreme Court, he replied, "Very definitely. We are in the unhappy situation where the Court is taking a license to spread ideologies rather than the cornerstone of Anglo-Saxon jurisprudence, which is precedence." Mr. Wright seems to regard the First Amendment as alien ideology.

The staff, it turns out, was carefully chosen. Mr. Wright told the House Appropriations Committee last year that the top job, that of administrative director, was filled by a Mr. D. Milton Ladd at $15,000, and the number two job by a Mr. Stanley J. Tracy at the same salary. He gave no indication whatsoever as to their background and qualifications. But anyone who now gets as far as the staff biographies on page 761 of the commission report will discover that Mr. Ladd retired in 1954 after twenty-six years as an FBI man, his last post being that of assistant to J. Edgar Hoover "in charge of all FBI intelligence and criminal investigations." Mr. Tracy, it appears, also retired from the FBI in 1954, when he held the post of assistant director. In studying FBI procedures, they were reviewing a record of which their own lifework was a part. It is not strange that while the report criticizes the military for overclassification and (surprise!) the State Department's passport division for violating due process, it finds that the "competency and fairness" of the FBI "has not been seriously questioned." The verdict was built-in.

The procedure, like the staff, was designed to give the secret police a minimum of bother. The commission must have heard many witnesses—there are occasional references to them in the report—but it heard them all in private, as if they were confidential informants. If any victims were heard, their voices could not penetrate beyond the commission's closed doors. In the eighteen months of existence, the commission never held a public hearing or a press conference, except for a final briefing session just before its report was released last week. This was significant chiefly for its demonstration of how little Mr. Wright knew about his own report. Every time a question got specific, it had to be referred to the equable and competent Mr. Ladd or to the commission's sharp general counsel, a Mr. Samuel H. Liberman of St. Louis, who reminded one strongly of Mr. Benjamin Mandel, the research director of the Senate Internal Security Committee.

Mr. Hoover maintains close liaison with the congressional witch hunt committees; he was an admirer of McCarthy and approves the exposure of radicals but his old assistants took care that there should be no similar open hearings to educate the public as to security-loyalty abuses. One would never guess from the commission's report that thousands of lives have been cruelly hurt by these abuses, nor that among the confidential informants so precious to the FBI there has turned up a most odoriferous assortment of crackpots and moochers with memories so double-jointed they might (for a fee) identify Eastland himself as a fellow Bukharinite from the Bronx. This is what might have been expected when a secret police is allowed to study its own navel in secret.

The result of these narcissistic meditations is a series of recommendations embodying everything the FBI has long wanted for Christmas: a bill to legalize wire tapping, a law to punish newspapermen who print "official secrets," an executive order to provide stricter surveillance over international organizations, a law denying suspected subversives the right to travel even in normal times, extension of security procedures to civil air transport, statutory authority for the Attorney General's list and the establishment by law of a super-duper Central Security Office which will freeze the loyalty-security mania permanently into the structure of American government.

The most sinister, though little noticed, aspect of the report is its implication that the judiciary, too, cannot be trusted but must have its personnel screened for loyalty and security by the FBI. This elicited a protest from the commission's lone dissenter, former Attorney General James P. McGranery, whose views were misrepresented in the commission's press release and hidden away behind the index. Mr. McGranery also protested the proposal for a Central Security Agency as tending "to weaken the foundations of our freedom by the building of an extravagant and false façade: a top-heavy superstructure masquerading as efficient, expedient security." Coming from Mr. Truman's last and most reactionary Attorney General, this is doubly eloquent.

Behind the smoke screen of a few procedural reforms and a spurious claim to establish the right to confront accusers, the commission would extend and make permanent what began ten years ago as an emergency program limited to government employees

Suspicion rather than trust would be the leitmotif of American life; avoidance of risk, rather than freedom, its anxiety. Plato's closed society was at least to be ruled by philosophers, not flatfeet. The commission's report would move toward a closed society ruled by the ubiquitous secret agent marking down in his little black book whatever he overhears. For the logic of this program cannot be contained. Once the premises of surveillance are accepted, it tends to widen. If messenger clerks and mailmen have to be screened, why not doctors, lawyers, and newspapermen? If the "regularly established confidential informants" of the FBI are too important to the national security to be disclosed in loyalty hearings, why should not their evidence be taken secretly in court proceedings too? And if the Bill of Rights and the Constitution provide excuse for subversive decisions by judges who perversely distrust the secret police, cannot something be done to put these venerable but dangerous documents in cold storage?

Oddly enough a point of resistance turns up in the American businessman. The one point at which the report slows down respectfully is at the factory gate. "The commission," Mr. Wright told the House Appropriations Committee last year, "has already received information indicating that industry is encountering considerable trouble and expense in handling its programs of personnel, physical and document security. . . ." The only strong protests that come through in this report are those of businessmen who feel that industrial and scientific progress is being tied up in security and secrecy knots; an example is the letter from the head of United Aircraft quoted on pages 166-7, and the criticism of the military on pages 300-1. The one point at which the commission proposes to shrink rather than expand the area of surveillance is in industry. It recommends not only that the category of "confidential" on government documents be abolished but that "industry be permitted immediately to discontinue clearance of employees for existing contracts classified confidential." It opposes the Butler bill, which would have extended loyalty-security procedures to all workers in industry, even though not engaged on military contracts. It wants the Department of Commerce Office of Strategic Information abolished; OSI's surveillance of technical publications has gotten into the hair of industry.

In response to business pressure, the report adopts the logic of the Supreme Court's Cole decision which would limit loyalty-security procedures to sensitive positions. But in dealing with government, the report would extend the procedures to every employee no matter how unimportant. The contrast in treatment is striking. The fact that the government already allows private industry to clear employees for access to confidential information "without requiring a security investigation of any sort" is regarded by the commission with approval, and as indicating that "the degree of risk to the national security is not substantial." The report says "the industrial process is such that the various phases of a confidential contract are so dispersed that it would be virtually impossible to assemble this information to the detriment of the national security." It objects that the Butler bill would "require a screening of thousands of individuals [in industry] not now subject to the security program" and explains that the investigative agencies already have "the hard-core Communists . . . well identified" and readily apprehendable for detention under the Internal Security Act "in the event of war or insurrection." It cites with approval the industrial and scientific view that "security at its best can only provide lead time in this highly technological age."

But there are whole agencies and departments of government which have much less to do with any real military secrets than many businesses today. Yet the commission on security not only proposes to blanket in every government worker but to keep him under constant surveillance. He is forever suspect. "A loyalty case," the report says, "can never be *res adjudicata,*" the legal term for a case finally settled by the courts. The employee must be subject to new check at any time "even though he may have emerged clean and clear from a score of investigations and as many hearings." The ultimate idiocy is that though cleared for "suitability" and certified for "loyalty," he may still be distrusted for sensitive jobs. As the report says, "There are certain positions in Government which are so identified with the national security interest that even though an incumbent employee may not be disloyal or unsuitable for employment generally under the recommended regulations, nevertheless his background may be such that he is unsuitable for a particular position." Apparently nobody can really be trusted except the secret police.

JULY 1, 1957

J. EDGAR HOOVER REPORTS

A feature of J. Edgar Hoover's appearance each year before the House Appropriations Committee is his annual report on Communist party members. Last year he gave the membership as 17,360, a drop of 14 percent. This year, for the first time in many years, Mr. Hoover gave no figure on party membership. Perhaps he knew it would be so small as to be ludicrous.

Instead of giving a figure, Mr. Hoover made a remark whose faith in the potency of a die-hard handful could be matched only in Moscow. "I cannot emphasize too strongly," he told the Appropriations Committee, "that the numerical strength of the Communist party means nothing." Even Lenin never kept a stiffer upper lip.

The ratio of G-men to Communists is rising sharply. The new FBI budget calls for 14,025 jobs. The number of Communist party members today is probably below 5,000—and not a few of these are themselves G-men.

Mr. Hoover nevertheless is bullish. Just around the corner he sees the Communists creating "the most devastating fifth column the world has ever known." Already its influence "reaches into almost every walk of life." It would be interesting to know what Mr. Hoover includes in that "almost." The FBI even now has "approximately 150 known or suspected Communist front and Communist infiltrated organizations under investigation." (Last year he testified the House Un-American Activities alone had listed 628 "such Communist front organizations." Are the other 478 going unwatched? Or have they disappeared in the last twelve months?)

The rousing success Mr. Hoover claims to have found on the left he blames on the courts. "Crimes and subversion have become critical challenges," he told the committee, "due to the mounting success of criminal and subversive elements in employing loopholes, technicalities and delays in the law to defeat the interests of justice."

In Mr. Hoover's vocabulary, the Bill of Rights and the due process clause seem to figure, if at all, only as "loopholes" and those who are concerned with them seem always to be put down as "pseudo-liberals." He was bitter about "certain organizations" which "hypocritically bar Communists from their membership, but seek to discredit all persons who abhor Communists and commu⸝ nism. They claim to be anti-Communist but they launch attacks against congressional legislation designed to curb communism."

It is instructive to compare this with Mr. Hoover's calm testimony on another menace—that of racism. Here he said nothing which could offend any white supremacist. "The Negro situation," he said was "being exploited" by the Communists. They are trying "to infiltrate Negro mass organizations . . . not to aid the Negroes but . . . to take advantage of all controversial issues on the racial question." Eastland wouldn't have said it differently.

Racism today is the real menace to internal security. Why does Mr. Hoover never warn against the peddlers of prejudice, or the divisive effects of those who preach race hatred? Mr. Hoover told the committee he wanted to stress the fact that "our investigative policies in civil rights matters are governed entirely by orders issued by the Department" and are conducted "in a thorough, factual and impartial manner." He was saying as plainly as he could that the civil rights work was something imposed on the FBI.

One civil rights matter in which Mr. Hoover could exercise great influence is that of police brutality against Negroes. This seems to make up the bulk of civil rights complaints. He said the FBI handled 1,289 civil rights cases during the fiscal year 1957 and that this included "1,062 cases involving 1,921 law enforcement officers." Of these 1,062 cases, he said, "1,003 had been closed and 59 remained pending." Only one officer was convicted and only twelve were under indictment. Remarkably few complaints against police officers seemed to stand up under FBI investigation.

MAY 12, 1958

THE MENACE OF CYRUS EATON

In his radio reply May 19 to Cyrus Eaton's criticism of the FBI, Richard Arens, staff director of the House Un-American Activities Committee, said that one of our checks on secret police abuses is that "FBI operations are subject to the scrutiny of the free press of this nation, the newspapers, and the radio and television media."

This is true. It is also true that the FBI and its allies, particularly the House committee, do their best to discourage such scrutiny.

An example was Arens's announcement over the radio that Chairman Walter had "signed a subpoena for Mr. Eaton's appearance before the committee."

The Eaton affair illustrates the unwillingness of the FBI and its allies to meet criticism in fair discussion. The Cleveland industrialist was interviewed by Mike Wallace over a nationwide ABC hookup May 4, under the sponsorship of the Fund for the Republic. Robert M. Hutchins, president of the Fund, invited J. Edgar Hoover to reply over the same facilities. Hoover replied rather stuffily that he would not "dignify" the charges of "one Cyrus Eaton."

The President, the Secretary of State and the Attorney General all hold press conferences; J. Edgar Hoover never. He gives interviews to favored persons but never exposes himself to critical questioning.

Instead of meeting the issue squarely the FBI chief arranged for himself to be interviewed by his friend, Representative Kenneth B. Keating on the latter's TV show, "Let's Look at Congress." Chairman Walter of the House committee demanded "equal time" of ABC to make a reply to Eaton. The result was the speech by Arens, and the announcement that Eaton would be subpoenaed. A subpoena to appear before the House committee is hardly an invitation to free and open debate. It serves notice that public criticism of the FBI is a hazardous occupation.

Honest debate would have been wholesome. In some respects Eaton overstated his case. The FBI is not a Hitler Gestapo and the snoopery that goes on in our own country is still a long way from the perpetual surveillance to which the Russian people are subjected by their own political police. But we could easily slip into such bad habits if the FBI became sacrosanct.

The mentality of political snoopers is the same the world over. All criticism to them and of them is suspect. This was evident in Hoover's sneering reference in the Keating interview to "the carpings of the professional 'do-gooders,' the pseudo-liberals and the out-and-out Communists." This associates idealism ("do-gooders") and liberals with "subversion."

Though the FBI is supposed to police crime, not political thought, Hoover seems to feel he has a broad mandate in the latter field. He made it clear he was watching not only Communists but ex-Communists whom he regards as "not dedicated to the American way of life" and others whom he sees as being "in the twilight zone who can be utilized by the Communists." This could cover a wide spectrum of political activity.

In the Keating interview, Hoover said he had only ninety wiretaps in operation and all were in internal security cases. It would be interesting to know how many other types of surveillance such as "bugging" are in use and how many of these taps and "bugs" are being utilized to check on possible violations of the law and how many in listening in on citizens whose political views Hoover distrusts.

It is clear from the Hoover interview and the Arens speech that Eaton has earned the animosity of our snoopers not merely because he dared criticize the FBI but because he has been working for peace. In their eyes, this is sinister, part of "a softening up process . . . a growing climate of opinion that we can appease, negotiate, coexist," as Arens expressed it. For the snoopers, talk of peace as well as civil liberty is subversive.

MAY 26, 1958

32: *Coexistence: Choice of Risks*

THE LATEST TREACHERY OF NIKITA KHRUSHCHEV

At the risk of not being invited to Secretary Dulles's next private dinner, we're going to tell the plain truth about the State Department's reaction to Khrushchev's latest. Mr. Dulles's astringent remark at National Airport to correspondents—"We don't get optimistic quickly about these matters"—is only half the story. It is not just that the Department (after insisting for twenty-four hours that there was "nothing new" in the Khrushchev note) is more cautious than the White House. The Department regards the new Russian offer as a most unsanitary maneuver, or dirty trick. Mr. Dulles had convinced the leading writers on the easily convinced *New York Times* that *he* was the flexible one; he had persuaded the NATO Council in Copenhagen to put the wraps on summit talk; he had come back triumphant to resume (in speeches in New Hampshire, West Berlin and Minneapolis) his old brink-of-Armageddon script, with himself as the fifth horseman of the Apocalypse. The NATO Council had "expressed the hope" in its final communiqué that the Russians by agreeing "in spite of repeated Soviet refusal, to inaugurate expert technical discussions . . . on measures necessary, for example . . . to detect nuclear explosions might go far toward demonstrating the possibility of agreement on disarmament." But no one at Copenhagen dreamt that Khrushchev, as if from ambush, would leap up treacherously and agree. It just shows how dangerous it is to say *anything* to the Russians.

Technical discussions are necessary. They can also be an easy means of delay; there's never a hair so fine it can't be split. If some people here had their way, technical talks would be dragged out until we had two atom bombs in every garage. There are also people here who believe that Mr. Dulles, bowing to possible White House readiness to negotiate a cessation of tests separately, might try to block agreement by raising the ante on inspection to the point where the Russians balk. Stassen spoke of a dozen listening posts across the U.S.S.R. There are now suggestions for as many as a hundred. If Mr. Dulles had his way he'd probably insist on a radar tower behind every hen house in the Ukraine. Without public pressure and some time limit on technical talks, they can go on forever. Yet there is little we do not already know about Russian testing, and not much technical discussion is required *if both sides want an agreement*.

MAY 19, 1958

THE CHANCE TO END NUCLEAR TESTS

It would be very unwise to assume from the Eisenhower-Khrushchev exchange on technical talks that a cessation of testing is "in the bag." The enemies of an agreement in London and Washington are powerfully entrenched. The President's letter—couched in the ugly "your side," "our side" style in which our military negotiators at Panmunjom avoided mentioning Communist China by name—specifically reserves "our respective positions on the timing and interdependence of various aspects of disarmament." But the ice pack in which humanity's hopes have been tightly imprisoned is cracking and now is the time for all good men—in every forum they can reach—to press hard for an end of testing.

The hopeful point at the moment is the composition of the team we will send to Geneva. Unlike our solidly pro-AEC delegation on the United Nations Scientific Committee on Effects of Atomic Radiation, this new three-man team reflects Admiral Strauss's waning influence. Dr. Ernest O. Lawrence, Dr. Teller's faithful comrade-in-arms, and a rightist in his political preconceptions, is securely in the Strauss camp. But Robert F. Bacher, the second member of the new team, is not. As a member of the Atomic Energy Commission from 1946 to 1949, he opposed the decision to make the H-bomb. He is as distinguished a physicist as Dr. Lawrence but quite different in his approach. The third member, Dr. James Brown Fisk, a former director of research at the AEC in 1947-48, is less well known but regarded as conservative and objective by those who worked with him. Dr. Bacher and Dr. Fisk are both members of the President's Science Advisory Committee, which has already decided by majority vote (so it is privately reported here) that a test cessation with inspection would be to this country's interest. Where Dr. Fisk stood on this is not known, but there is reason to suspect that this three-man team was picked— typical Eisenhower fashion—to keep everybody happy and that Dr. Fisk is the "neutral" whose vote may be decisive.

The danger is that technical talks on the problem of detection may distract attention from the real issues. Mr. Eisenhower's letter to Premier Khrushchev said tartly that he hoped the Soviet team would also be chosen "on the basis of special competence, so as to assure that we get scientific not political conclusions." This is snide, silly and misleading. The truth is that the issues are political, not scientific, as the UN Scientific Committee on Effects of Atomic Radiation—now preparing its final report for July 1—has discovered. In approaching the problem of radiation's dangers, as in that of inspection's efficacy, the real question is a choice of risks and this choice is determined by moral and political preconceptions. According to an exclusive story out of the United Nations by Milt Freudenheim of the *Chicago Daily News,* the UN committee has discovered that nuclear test radiation *is* harmful to world health and future generations cannot but agree on its final conclusions because these involve political considerations which some members feel is beyond its province. The truth is that no one knows just how and to what degree radiation is harmful. Those who believe in the arms race and deterrence think the risk justifiable; those who see war as the inevitable result of an arms race think we run the risk for no good reason.

This is a question the average man is as equipped to answer as the scientist. Have we a right to poison the lives of some now living and many more to be born in the future, all for the sake of carrying on an endless arms race that makes all humanity vulnerable to accident and miscalculation?

JUNE 2, 1958

33: *The Marines in Lebanon*

GUNBOAT DIPLOMACY IN THE H-BOMB AGE

Those who believed that no major power would risk a world war in the H-bomb age now have their answer. It is also the answer to those who thought that the only possible danger might be from a half-mad dictator ruling a terrorized society. Eisenhower, Nixon and Dulles ordered the Marines into action in Lebanon without consulting Congress, our allies in NATO or the UN. All three were confronted with a *fait accompli*, as if this were the world of 1900, the Lebanon a banana republic on our doorstep, and the most lethal weapon still the machine gun.

A free society is supposed to have some control over its destiny, but even those in Congress and the press who feel uneasy are impelled to take the attitude that, since the die has been cast, they have no recourse but to support the President. As before every war, it is considered patriotic to let one's country slide into catastrophe; the air is full of the old familiar—and fatal—clichés: we mustn't appease, we must call their bluff, our prestige is at stake. . . .

Only eighteen months ago when President Eisenhower asked Congress to approve the so-called Eisenhower Doctrine, he promised that if armed intervention became necessary he would first consult Congress. But only one member, Representative Reuss, a maverick Democrat from Wisconsin, had the nerve to stand up and recall that promise. His criticism was cut short by Speaker Rayburn with a rebuke: "In times like these we had better allow matters to develop rather than make remarks about them." * These "matters" may be thermonuclear.

Let us assume that the Russians will not intervene, either directly or by volunteers, though this is not at all certain, considering the unsteadiness recently apparent in Kremlin policy. Stalin could back down over Iran in 1946 without risk of losing his own job, but can Khrushchev take a comparable defeat without fear of being overwhelmed by rivals? Russia aside for the moment, what if we persist in our intervention? Where can it lead us but into a military morass, an Algeria of our own many times magnified in which oil wells and pipelines will be at the mercy of guerrillas? The fact that we were taken by surprise in Iraq is not to be read merely as the failure of CIA spies to learn about a conspiracy. It is to be read as reflecting our political failure correctly to assess the realities of an allied Arab country in which we had a large military mission. The Iraqi Army we had given $45,000,000 in military supplies turned against us. Obviously it had been solidly and secretly against us for some time, since this uprising of which we had no inkling was not an overnight improvisation. If we did so badly in Iraq, what makes us think we can police the whole Arab world?

In the atmosphere of demonology created by the State Department, it has become dangerous to suggest that maybe there may be social revolutions in the Middle East, as in Iraq (all parties had been outlawed and a free press long banned in that oil company utopia), or a great big Saturday night family brawl as in the Lebanon, without its necessarily being the handiwork of Big Devil in Moscow or Little Devil in Cairo. We are being blinded by our own propaganda. The right of the Arabs to a place of respect in the world is something we must recognize, and the sooner we recognize it, incidentally, the better for Israel. The landing of the

---

* The Speaker edited his rebuke out of the *Congressional Record* but it was reported by the Associated Press and the *New York Times*. His interjection, according to the latter (July 16), "effectively cut off any further House discussion." Next day, when Celler of New York rose to ask unanimous consent for a one-minute speech, Rayburn wanted first to know if it were on foreign policy and refused consent when told that it was—until Celler explained that he wanted to support the sending of troops to Lebanon, when he was allowed to proceed. The Speaker made it clear that no further discussion of foreign policy would be allowed. This, in a representative assembly!

Marines in Beirut is calculated to unite the whole Arab world against us. The clumsy baldness with which we did it has cost us much among smaller friendly powers in the UN.

JULY 21, 1958

KHRUSHCHEV BREAKS OUT OF CONTAINMENT

We landed the Marines in Lebanon, and (as this is being written early on the morning of July 24) it looks as if Nikita Khrushchev in turn is about to land in New York. This would seem to be an authentic case of Divine Retribution, but has badly shaken the faith of Washington's foremost Presbyterian. The news that Khrushchev was coming burst on this capital yesterday in a way which showed that the Russians simply cannot be trusted. All day and into the late afternoon editions, banner headlines based on a sour editorial in *Izvestia* blared comfortingly that Khrushchev was about to spurn Ike's queasy invitation to a conference at the UN. At 3:20 P.M. the UPI ticker even carried a statement from the usually silent Soviet embassy, saying that "well-qualified Russian sources" in Washington had predicted that the Kremlin would reject the Western offer "as a complete evasion." At 3:21 P.M., one minute later, there was a flash from Moscow that the Soviet Foreign Office would soon issue an important announcement. At 4:04 P.M. the ticker spelled out that Khrushchev had accepted. Had a sputnik fallen on the White House putting green, it could not have created more panic.

This has been a swift period of anticlimax, collapsing suddenly into low comedy. Last Monday, a week after the Iraq revolt, the President met congressional leaders at the White House with the exalted calm of a man who was ready for Armageddon. But our Marines had hardly embarked in Beirut on what seemed to be a major departure of policy well past the point of no return than the Administration began nervously semaphoring that it wanted out. Suddenly we became a fervent member of the UN again and after several days it appeared that we would accept observer teams in Lebanon armed only with paper and pencil if Mr. Hammarskjöld would get us off the hook, and allow us gracefully to get the Marines away from all those soda pop vendors on the Beirut beaches. While Mr. Lodge, desperate for repartee, accused Mr. Sobolev and the Soviet Union of violating the Sherman Anti-Trust Act, the hectic weekend at the UN was marked by wistful efforts to water down the Japanese resolution to the point where Moscow might vote for it and allow an enlarged UN observer team to save face for the withdrawing Marines. And now the summit conference Mr. Dulles and Mr. Eisenhower have tried so hard to avoid for two years seems suddenly upon them; the ebullient Khrushchev might drop in at any moment. How the White House wishes there were still some last-minute way to stop him, perhaps by refusing him a visa for having been a member of the Ukrainian YCL in 1921, or by getting the bacteriological warfare corps to infect the White House with mumps. Across the dismal confusion at Hagerty's office last night was scrawled all too plainly, even before the visitor arrived, *Khrushchev go home.*

Perfidious Albion had led Mr. Eisenhower and Mr. Dulles into a trap, revenging itself for the Suez affair. The British had assured them that they could safely suggest a UN meeting in reply to Khrushchev's new call for a summit conference. Hadn't the Russians over and over again complained of a "mechanical majority" against them at the UN? Would Khrushchev ever consent to sit down with Chiang Kai-shek? Even so the draft of our reply, as communicated last Sunday night to favored correspondents, was pure cold war diatribe suggesting only that "it lies open to any of us to enlarge the scope of the Security Council considerations." It was Macmillan who widened this microscopic loophole to the point where the bulky Khrushchev came climbing through. First, under pressure from London, the United States added the two fatal sentences about Heads of Government being allowed to attend Council meetings and our being ready "if such a meeting were generally desired" to "join in following that orderly procedure." Then Macmillan translated these nebulous phrases into his own message to Khrushchev, "I would certainly be ready to go to New York for such a meeting . . . and I take it . . . that you would." And Khrushchev, before you could say Jack Dmitrievich Robinson, did.

Now the nightmare that haunts Washington is what happens when Ike finishes his prepared text and has to think up a swiftie under the TV cameras for one of those *moujik* anecdotes Khrushchev always seems to have up his sleeve. If there must be a face-to-face encounter, Washington would rather have it in some far-off place like, say, Khabarovsk, where the networks can't operate. Of course, in a diplomatic sense, as de Gaulle objected, nothing can possibly happen at a summit conference amid the crowds on the East River. But in another, public relations sense, much will if the meeting comes off. For the Russians have us over a barrel in the Middle East, and in Khrushchev they have a star performer, a shrewd comic, a natural-born vaudevillian, eager to appear at last on Broadway, where he will be the biggest hit of its kind since Fatty Arbuckle played the Palace. Mr. Dulles's cold war will never be the same again once Nikita hits town.

JULY 28, 1958

34: *Racial Equality in Crisis*

THE LINE OUTSIDE THE COURT

Nothing said within the crowded Supreme Court chamber during the Little Rock appeal was as moving as the line which waited outside. Within, except for certain deeper reverberations in the solicitor general's argument, the tone of the pleadings was conversational, almost casual; the transcript (so enterprisingly published next day by the *New York Times*) had an almost bumbling formlessness. The eloquence was in the quiet line outside. It began to form at 3:30 A.M. when a local Negro lawyer, with a name of tragic memory, Matthew Till, began the long wait in the dark at the top of the broad white marble stairs. He was joined a half-hour later by a local Negro preacher, the Reverend Samuel W. Clark. The third in line, the first white man, appeared at 5:30 A.M. He was Leo Roos, a lawyer from New Orleans, who told me he was for integration. The fourth to arrive was a Negro timid about giving his name. The fifth and sixth in line were from Arkansas, white, two young men, students at the State University in Fayetteville, from the northwestern hill country of the state, and both for integration. By 7 A.M. there were fifty people waiting. By 11 A.M., when the doors of the courtroom were finally opened to admit a scant fifty, there were almost six hundred in line, somewhat more than half Negro. Though the police kept telling them it was hopeless to wait, at least two hundred were still standing there at 2 P.M. They stayed on as if their mere presence might, as lawyers say, pray the court. It was a grave assemblage, and one felt shy in looking it over, knowing what was in the heart of every Negro there, and most of the whites. It was as if we all waited for the final promulgation of a new emancipation, this time for children and from a no less cruel bondage, that they might no longer be made to feel ashamed, from that very first day on the way to school, separate from others and unequal, irrevocably less than other men.

Mr. Thurgood Marshall complained to the Supreme Court that you don't deal with bank robberies by closing down the banks. The most striking sections of the government's brief were those which showed how few, how easily identifiable and how readily jailed were the "robbers" of the public peace inside and outside the Central High School in Little Rock. The solicitor general argued that while it might be true that there was "deep-seated popular opposition" to integration in Little Rock, the active instigators of trouble were a handful of individuals and organizations. They were named by the School Board in response to interrogatories in the district court and could be dealt with by injunction and contempt proceedings as were similar elements earlier when integration was successfully enforced in Hoxie, Arkansas. In the same way, the government's brief points out, evidence in the lower court shows it was a small group of no more than twenty-five students who caused the trouble within the school. Only two of these troublemakers were expelled. "There is not the slightest suggestion," the brief said, "that the colored children did anything to incite violence or disorderly conduct." The proper remedy within and without the school "was one directed at the obstructionists, not in their favor." What the government's brief did not say was that the federal government might have moved in boldly and tamed the mob by punishing the ringleaders for interfering with the orders of a federal court. To say that would have been to indict Mr. Rogers and Mr. Eisenhower. That would be too much to ask even of the bravest solicitor general.

We read with close attention the brief filed in the Supreme Court by Senator Fulbright, who has the unhappy role of being an Oxford-educated intellectual representing a southern state. We wondered what he would say in asking the Court to grant Little Rock more delay. His brief was literate and scholarly, almost eloquent in its counsel of despair. He warned against the "congenital optimism" with which Americans generally confront social problems. He emphasized the irrationality and "certain pathological aspects" in the southern situation, pictured both races as prisoners (though he did not say, of course, that only one is imprisoned in inferior status) and quoted the philosopher Morris Cohen on the foolishness of Cato who "would adhere to the law though the Republic be thereby destroyed." He thought the problem of integration "more likely to yield to the slow conversion of the human heart." The underdog, in short, must go on being patient until his masters have miraculously been converted; the oppressed must walk softly because the oppressor, if disturbed, becomes violent and irrational.

SEPTEMBER 8, 1958

CIVIL RIGHTS AND CIVIL LIBERTIES

Wherever white men struggle to deny colored men equal rights, whether in South Africa, Algeria or our own South, a common pattern appears. The fight to prevent other races from enjoying equality of rights ends by undermining the civil liberties of the dominant whites themselves. Police states shape up, Fascist ideologies and movements spread. Denial of justice to the black undermines freedom for the white.

The invasion of the South by the witch hunt committees, first Eastland's Senate Internal Security Subcommittee and now the House Un-American Activities Committee, is in this pattern: a means of terrorizing white moderates and liberals, recalling the two decades before the Civil War when all antislavery views in the South were suppressed and an overt anti-Jeffersonianism created a philosophy congenial to a society dominated by a slaveholding minority. The South, where family, class and money have long been the basis of oligarchic rule, is in this sense "un-American," a Whig and racist survival in an America otherwise steadily more egalitarian. But this is not the kind of un-Americanism the committee was scheduled to investigate July 29, 30 and 31 in its first southern hearings, at Atlanta.

The new hearings, like Eastland's earlier incursions, are intended to frighten into conformity those few southern whites who believe in integration and the larger minority who are ready to obey the law. So far as could be learned on the eve of the hearings, no Negroes have been subpoenaed, only whites, among them Anne and Carl Braden (her book, *The Wall Between,* gives an account of the fight for racial equality that made them the central figures in Kentucky's famous sedition trial). They have also subpoenaed Perry Cartwright and Gene Feldman, editors of the *Southern Newsletter,* and Frank Wilkinson, of the Emergency Civil Liberties Committee, who was served with a subpoena when he arrived in Atlanta last week as an observer.

A striking aspect of the new hearings is the release of a protest by 150 leading southern Negroes to the House of Representatives. This was coordinated by the Southern Conference Educational Fund, the last militant interracial group still operating in the South. The protest represents a new and heartening development. This is the first time in years a leading group of Negroes has recognized the close connection between their fight for civil rights and the fight of dissenting white elements against the witch hunt.

In the South the dissenting white is more isolated and helpless than the Negro; he has no community to sustain him; he is walled in between the contempt of white racists and the often equally racist distrust of the Negro whose rights he would champion. In this context, it was an act of courage and human solidarity for these southern Negro leaders to risk the committee's ire by a public protest.

AUGUST 4, 1958

THE WALL BETWEEN

Anne Braden grew up in the South on the right side of the tracks. She came, as they say in the South, of a good family. Very early she began to feel there was something wrong in the relations between the races. Her family was always kind to the Negro family who worked for them. "But something happened to me," Mrs. Braden writes in her book, *The Wall Between* (Monthly Review Press), "each time I looked at the Negro girl who always inherited my clothes. . . . She would sit in a straight chair in our kitchen waiting for her mother. . . . She would sit there looking uncomfortable, my old faded dress binding her at the waist and throat. And some way I knew that this was not what Jesus meant when he said to clothe the naked."

Anne became a newspaperwoman and married a fellow reporter, Carl, who came most decidedly from the *other* side of the tracks. His family was Catholic, the father an agnostic and Socialist

who lost his job in the 1922 railway shopmen's strike. The family
had known poverty ever since. Carl, at the age of thirteen, went
into a pro-seminary to prepare for the priesthood but at sixteen
decided it was not for him. He became a newspaperman in Louisville, Kentucky. "A police reporter," he once told his wife, "has to
become one of three things—a drunk, a cynic, or a reformer." Carl
chose the third course, and it led him in 1954 to agree when a
Negro veteran, Andrew Wade, asked the Bradens to buy a house
for him in a new white neighborhood in Louisville. The house was
dynamited, and the state authorities, instead of prosecuting the
dynamiters, indicted the Bradens and five other residents of Louisville for sedition. Braden, first to be tried, was sent to jail for fifteen
years, and saved only by the miracle of the Supreme Court's Steve
Nelson decision.

Anne Braden has told the whole story in her book, *The Wall
Between,* and told it with the depth and objectivity of a first-rate
novel. All that is happening elsewhere in the integration crisis is lit
up for us by this story of what that attack on housing segregation
did in and to liberal Louisville. Mrs. Braden writes with compassion
for the prisons in which men seal themselves up. She sees the
"paralyzed liberals" of Louisville, like its cross burners, as "trapped
men." She even tried, in one of the most memorable episodes of the
book, to understand her fellow southerner, the prosecutor, Scott
Hamilton, who was trying his best to send her and her husband to
prison on trumped-up charges he himself had come to believe. "If
circumstances," she asked herself, "somewhere in the past of both
our lives had been different, would I perhaps have been on his
side of this battle or he on mine?" This was the same young woman
who could firmly refuse to answer questions about the books she
read and the organizations to which she belonged. "I think we have
enough McCarthys in this country," she said defiantly when taken
before a judge, "without the grand jury turning into one."

The Bradens walked through the valley of the shadow of the
witch hunt. An FBI informer perjured herself to call Braden a
Communist; he denied it under oath. The House Un-American
Committee sent down agents to frighten Andrew Wade, the Negro
they had risked so much to help, and got him to say things one
only says about a man and a woman one does not trust. The transcript of what Wade said in a moment of weakness gave Anne
Braden the most terrible moment of the whole experience, one in

which she felt "that the things we had been working for—a world without segregation, a world of understanding and brotherhood— had turned to dust in my hand." But the moment passed. Both Wade and the Bradens recovered from it. Her book is a worthy record of a great experience, the warming story of a heroic couple's abiding faith.

SEPTEMBER 15, 1958

THE EVASIONS OF EISENHOWER

I fear the President at press conference today did our country a grave harm. Southern resistance will be invigorated by his failure unequivocally to deny the report that he wishes the Supreme Court had never handed down the school decision and by his admission that *Newsweek* may have been correct in saying that he told friends he thinks integration should proceed more slowly. (If it proceeds any more slowly they'll soon be *de*-integrating in Clinton, Tennessee, as well as in Little Rock.) The headline, "Ike Hints He Thinks School Integration Is Moving too Fast," will reverberate like a rebel yell through the South. After years of refusing to express an opinion on the subject, Mr. Eisenhower let slip a remark which shows he is at best lukewarm on integration, and regards it as another of those bothers which are the bane of the presidency. On the eve of the Supreme Court's special session on Little Rock, Mr. Eisenhower had disassociated himself from the Court and helped further to weaken and isolate it in the most fateful hour it has known since Dred Scott sued for freedom.

Mr. Eisenhower was asked seven questions about integration at today's press conference and managed, in his woolly-minded but self-protective way, to undermine the Court and the cause of integration in every answer. He made it clear that the Attorney General was filing a brief *amicus* in the Little Rock appeal only because the Court's invitation was a command, and because he was an officer of the Court. "I don't think that I would instruct them to argue one way or another," Mr. Eisenhower said. "As lawyers, as an officer of the Court, they have to voice their honest convictions." Would the brief be applicable to other situations? "Well, I think that you are making some unwarranted assumptions," Mr. Eisenhower replied. "The Justice Department has been ordered to file a brief on one particular decision by the appellate court, and I don't think it has anything to do with the rest of the problem." It was almost as if Mr. Eisenhower were telling the South, "I, too, am a victim of the Court's coercion." Over and over again he emphasized that the brief *amicus* was none of his doing, although "I would assume that any decision would certainly—I mean any brief would try to reflect the views of all of us, so far as I know, have held from the beginning." No one ventured to ask what those views were.

The power of headlines to distort is visible tonight in one newspaper which screams across page one, "President Hits School Closings as 'Terrible.'" I am afraid this will be typical. It hardly gives the true flavor of what Mr. Eisenhower actually said. When asked about state laws to close schools rather than integrate, the President first "didn't understand" the question and then said, "This, of course, would be a very terrible outcome." But, he suggested, hopefully passing the buck to the courts again, that this would cause a lot of litigation. (What would people do, sue their legislature?) Then he was sure "there would be great pressure to open the schools" but was careful to add, lest it be thought that he meant to open them on an integrated basis, "under whatever circumstances the inhabitants believed would be best." This is tailor-made for Faubus.

A Washington reporter pointed out that across the river in Arlington, Virginia, integrated schools would be deprived of state funds as a penalty for obeying the law. The reporter wanted to know whether in such cases federal funds might be made available. Mr. Eisenhower, after a lot of palaver about not shooting from the hip, indicated he didn't think this would be fair and equal treatment. (One thought it a pity, listening to him, that there were no tape recordings of Eisenhower at staff conferences in his Army days. Did he ever risk a clear opinion?)

When Mr. Eisenhower was asked whether the brief *amicus* in the Supreme Court would express his personal views, he said his own had been expressed "succinctly" in the prepared statement he gave out at his preceding conference. Succinct is a strange adjective for a statement eight paragraphs long in which one cannot find either the word "school" or the word "Negro" much less any opinion on integration. Any craggy question finds this man as sure-footed as a mountain goat. Even his Attorney General, William P. Rogers, Senator Eastland's friend, in his speech today before the American Bar Association in Los Angeles, made it clear that integration was not just "the law" because this perverse Supreme Court happened to read Gunnar Myrdal but because "For a nation which stands for full equality under law—which solemnly believes that all men are equal before the law, regardless of race, religion, or place of national origin—the result undoubtedly is permanent . . . the law of the land for today, tomorrow and I am convinced for the future—for all regions and for all people." Is Mr. Eisenhower incapable of speaking up in some such fashion? It is tragic that just when another irrepressible crisis looms ahead there should be such a nobody in the White House.

SEPTEMBER 1, 1958

35: *Little Rock: A Piece of Foreign Correspondence*

WHEN THE BOURBON FLOWED

We took the first plane out of Washington for Little Rock after hearing Chief Justice Warren read a tense and crowded courtroom the order that integration proceed. The plane's first stop was at Nashville, and passengers came aboard carrying its evening newspaper, the *Banner*. A black headline across page one indicated that we had reached the South. It said, with White Citizens Council objectivity, "Mix Now, Little Rock Told." On the editorial page, under the caption "Education Be Hanged!" there was a cartoon which pictured the Chief Justice as a burly man leaning arrogantly on a huge gavel. Behind him was a blackboard on which he had triumphantly crossed out the word "deliberate" in the phrase, "all deliberate speed," and written in the word "breakneck." A page one Associated Press bulletin claimed that a "jubilant" Mrs. Daisy Bates, local leader of the NAACP, had "hinted" that she expected "more mixing" soon, though I was later to learn that Mrs. Bates in Little Rock was harder to reach than the Secretary of State on Duck Island and twice as cautious and that any such "hint" must have been deduced by the AP man from the way she said "no comment." A staff correspondent in Little Rock quoted the Reverend Wesley Pruden, the segregationist leader, as saying, "The South will not accept this outrage, which a Communist-dominated government is trying to lay on us." This was my introduction to a regional journalism which prints such statements matter-of-factly.

We sat forward on one of four seats. Two of them, facing each other, were occupied by a gray-haired elderly white woman and a middle-aged colored woman who seemed to be traveling together. Though the former, from her accent, did not appear to be southern, she turned out to be a gentlewoman returning from a summer in Massachusetts to her plantation home below Memphis with her Negro maid. When the maid, a sturdy woman, went to the rest room, the white lady told us her maid had been with her for twenty-five years and that she had given the maid a $2500 gift on the twenty-fifth anniversary of her coming to work for her. This was to illustrate her point that there were good relations in the South between the races. "There is real love between us," the white woman said of the Negroes who grew up on her plantation. She blamed the trouble in the South on "white riffraff." She said her great-grandfather had tried to free his slaves before "the war" but they pleaded with him that they would not know how to make their way in the world. (Later that evening in Little Rock I was to meet another woman who told me that her great-grandfather had tried to free his slaves but that they begged him not to. I began almost to believe that in the slaveholding South no one was a slaveholder by choice but only out of devotion to the welfare of their black wards.) Our gentlewoman friend told us how the "cream of the crop" on her plantation in her father's time and her husband's had been sent to college, and of the eminent positions they later reached in the Negro community. Though a Democrat, she had never once voted for Roosevelt, of whom she obviously disapproved. She voted for Eisenhower twice, but no longer felt the same way about him. She spoke with gentle cynicism of the machine politicians and senators she had known in Tennessee, as a well-bred lady discussing rather vulgar retainers. She and the maid got off the plane in Memphis, leaving behind an authentic whiff of the old regime.

Below us, in the deepening dusk on leaving Memphis, was the dirty, gray, serpentine Mississippi. At Little Rock, in its modern new airport, flash bulbs popped as Virgil Blossom, the school superintendent, got off the plane ahead of us looking heavy and tired, and said a few noncommittal words for the TV reporters.

Little Rock, its main street lit up with green and red neon lights, its J. C. Penney Store and its big 5-and-10, seemed like any small Midwestern city, except for the "colored" sign in the rear as one passed the bus station. The one pleasantly different touch were the old-fashioned gas lamps on the streets, like those in Philadelphia a generation ago. On the way to the Sam Peck Hotel, we caught a glimpse of the haberdashery run by the Syrian, Karam, so prominent behind the mob scenes last year. The bellboy had that look of simulated imbecility Negroes often wear like a protective cloak in the South. The elevator was run by a pretty Negro girl.

A British newspaperman and myself were invited out that night to a party in a country home cluttered with heirlooms and good modern prints. Courtesy and political discretion forbid too close a description but after a night with a group of tortured southern liberals one acquired a new view of Tennessee Williams; he began to seem a camera-like realist. As with Negro intellectuals, all their talk came back obsessively and painfully to the race problem. These off-beat members of old families know their own political impotence and feel like aliens despite their family trees. Their self-deprecatory jokes are bitter; their talk often builds up to a kind of anguish. At moments they make one think of the nineteenth-century Russian intelligentsia distressed by the abyss between them and the people. Many of the women at least take their Christianity with deep seriousness and are torn by guilt. They are appalled by the race hatred which spills over from apparently civilized people they have known all their lives. They are despairing over those who know better but say, "Let it take its course," the "it" being the mob. They feel themselves a natural elite gone to seed, caught between the rabble (that's how most upper-class southerners think of common white people) and the rabble-rousers like Faubus, whom they despise. Yet as the bourbon flows more freely their whole environment draws them into compulsive imitation; they begin to say "niggers" and "coons" with the obscene pleasure of an adolescent using dirty words. One feels that the Negro doesn't just live in the South, he haunts it.

A liberal Little Rock newspaperman came to breakfast at the hotel next morning to give us a fill-in on the local situation. His most revealing remark, it seemed to me, came when I asked him what Negroes were thinking. "I just don't know," he said. The Little Rock story is covered almost entirely from the white side. In an

effort to get the Negro side, I went to a white lawyer, Edward Dunaway, a Columbia graduate, who is head of the Urban League, which
may seem stuffily respectable in the North but is regarded as downright radical in the South. "People ask me if I am a Yankee,"
Dunaway said with some bitterness. "One side of my family came
here from Virginia in 1820 and the other from Kentucky in 1830."
One of his grandfathers was governor of Arkansas and Senator Joe
Robinson was a cousin. Dunaway's father, also a lawyer, ran unsuc-
cessfully for Congress on an anti-Ku Klux Klan platform in the
twenties and defended Negroes condemned to death after the
Elaine, Arkansas, race riots of 1919. These began when a deputy
sheriff put in an appearance at the meeting of a union being formed
by Negro sharecroppers. Several white men and more than one
hundred Negroes were killed; eighty-seven Negroes were sentenced
to jail and twelve to the electric chair. The latter were saved by a
Supreme Court decision reversing their convictions. "I remember as
a boy visiting the condemned with my father in the penitentiary,"
Dunaway related. "They had been put to work building and painting
their own coffins. They showed us the black boxes and then sang
hymns." It left a deep impression.

Dunaway made a date for us to talk later in the afternoon
with a Negro doctor, and took us off for lunch to the Little Rock
Club, a mausoleum-like building which might have been taken for
a large undertaking establishment. We sat around with a group
having drinks, in a kind of neutral zone, the talk coming around
only slowly to The Question. A visiting Texas reporter said Dallas,
when ordered to integrate, would make Little Rock "look like a
picnic." Another man said, "Well our whole problem might be
summed up by saying that Orval Faubus just didn't want to go
back to Huntsville, and if you've ever seen Huntsville it is hard to
blame him." It was interesting to see the different ways in which
members spoke to the Negro waiters. Some addressed the waiters
with unostentatious politeness. There were others who ordered
drinks with the cold look and lordly manner that seemed to reflect
an idealized image of themselves as members of a superior race,
disposing of vast acres and accustomed to handling *nigra* servitors.
As one watched these men, one thought, "So this is the wine that
goes to the white man's head in the South."

We took a cab after lunch to Little Rock's Harlem along Ninth
Street, a district of dingy bars, dilapidated stores and hand-me-down

houses. My companion was a British reporter and we hoped the combination of his accent and mine would make it easier to get people to talk with us. But we drew a complete blank. A blind woman beggar said in a cultivated voice that she did not know what she could say that might not hurt her hereafter since she was on public assistance. "I will say this," she said, picking her words slowly, "everyone likes a good thing," meaning presumably better schools. Her son, also blind, also in a cultivated voice, said he was studying music. Farther down the street we got a less friendly reception: "White man takes what you say and uses it against you." On a side street, alongside a long unpainted barnlike building which turned out to be the upper class dorm of Philander Smith College, a Negro Methodist school, there were a number of Negro boys playing ball. They wouldn't talk either. We went inside the college, which seemed more like a run-down old high school, and were told politely but firmly by the young woman who handles publicity that the college was keeping strictly "out of it" and that nobody would comment. "No, the students even among themselves do not discuss the question." One got the feeling of extraordinary restraint and discipline, as of a community which felt itself besieged. No one even used the word "school" or "segregation" or "integration." We also had the feeling of a new educated generation, not at all the "darkies" of white stereotypes. The silence as it piled up seemed more eloquent than anything which might have been said.

We did a little better with a white pawnbroker who said he had been there twenty years. He understood the silence which had greeted us. "People don't say anything," he told us. "They're polite and friendly but never discuss it." But Negroes had been buying guns and knives and laying them away. "You get arrested if you carry them on the street," he explained, "but if you wrap them up in paper and carry them home for self-protection it's legal." The only other white man we had seen in our walk around the neighborhood came in and turned out to be the manager of the local Negro movie. "Business usually falls off just before school opens," he told us. "But I've never seen anything as bad as this year. Ever since the court in St. Louis overruled Judge Lemley people have stopped coming out on the streets at night. They keep their children home." The pawnbroker said his business was bad, too. There was a lot of unemployment in the Negro section. "People don't have anything left to pawn." But the Negroes weren't the only ones not talking. He owned six duplexes inhabited by whites and when he went around to collect the rent he found the same unwillingness to discuss schools or integration. "People on both sides just ain't talkin'." The pawnbroker summed up his own philosophy: "You gotta keep the nigger in his place or he'll run all over you." He had a permit and carried a gun. Even the Negro cops, as we had noticed, went on their patrols in pairs.

We went into a white bar near the Negro section for a beer on our way back downtown. The place was crowded and we sat down at a table with two ducktail haircut characters, one handsome and friendly, the other with flattish face and slow of speech but anxious to talk. He asked my British friend whether rock-and-roll had reached England and when assured that it had, confessed to us one of the painful experiences of his life. Elvis Presley had once been in Little Rock before he became famous and our new friend had never gone to hear him! He told us this was the worst skid row bar in town and recommended a better place uptown. He said he used to be a Methodist but was now a member of the Christian Church. He told us that about twenty years ago a Negro had assaulted a white girl and "they" had set him afire and dragged his burning body down Ninth Street and "they haven't forgotten." When we asked who he meant by "they," he said "the white folks" and repeated the story again, in the same melancholy tone. Then he told it a third time, as if it were a portent of things to come. What did he think of school integration, we ventured to ask. "It's coming," he said, shaking his head. "It'll be here in about ten years, and then as the Bible says, 'there will be wars, and rumors of wars' and war between the nations and the races." He did not speak with hatred but with a kind of dispassionate fatalism. He shook hands as we left, but his friend looked on coldly, as if he weren't going to be taken in by any furriners.

The Negro neighborhood to which we went for our appointment with the doctor was quite different from Little Rock's Harlem. He lived in a modest but well-painted frame house, set on a wide lawn. The homes and yards all looked well cared for. A Negro neighbor was cutting his grass nearby, and there was a scamper of feet and a burst of giggles within when we rang the bell. Two sets of pigtails with hair ribbons ran into the rear of the house when the doctor's wife, a tall, handsome dark woman, opened the door. She asked us to sit down in the parlor and said her husband would be home in a few minutes. There was a piano and a hi-fi set in the living room. She said her oldest boy who had just graduated from junior high was one of the new applicants for Central High. "My husband and I tried to dissuade him. We told him it would mean giving up his saxophone." Apparently the school band at Central High is not integrated. "But he insisted." The boy himself came in before going out to serve his paper route. He was a slim, shy, gangling youth. Why did he want to go to Central High? "The science facilities there are better and I want to be a doctor. I'd get a better education and I'd be paving the way for others." (It is a strange world and time in which the future of a race depends on the pioneering courage and steadiness of its children.)

The doctor, when he arrived, turned out to be a pleasant young man, conforming to neither Negro nor southern stereotypes. We asked what was the feeling in the Negro community. "I can only speak for myself," he replied. "We feel apprehensive but hopeful. We hope everybody will come to their senses." He smiled when we told him of the silence which had greeted us in Little Rock's Harlem. "That's not exactly new," he said. "Even at the best there was never much communication between us." We asked whether any of his patients were white. He said about twenty percent. He said there were Negro dentists in the plantation country whose practice was eighty-five percent white. Were any of his white patients segregationists? He supposed most of them were, but that didn't make any difference when it came to choosing a doctor. There were six Negro doctors and about one hundred white in Little Rock and both sides had a racially mixed practice. The Medical Society had been integrated for five or six years and there had been Negro students in the Little Rock medical school since 1948. "The doctors meet together but not the wives," his wife interjected. Both said it was impossible to find any consistency in racial patterns. "In a store downtown," the wife said, "I will be standing near a white woman and she will talk to me pleasantly and long. But a few minutes later when I see her again outside at the bus stop where she is with white friends, she will look straight through me." She said there were no facilities in the stores for Negro shoppers, no rest rooms, no place to get a bite to eat.

Were there interracial groups in Little Rock? There was the Arkansas Council on Human Relations, a Thursday-morning mixed prayer group, a Fellowship of Reconciliation chapter, a Bahai group, all small. All met at a Negro community center or in a Negro church. The previous Thursday, the day the Supreme Court heard final argument on the school case, there was an eighteen-hour mixed prayer vigil in a Negro Methodist Church, beginning at 6 A.M. and ending at midnight. (Later another reporter told me that a cameraman outside the prayer meeting asked a white minister going in, "Are you a nigger lover?" The minister replied, "I love God. God loves niggers. I guess that makes me a nigger lover, too." "Will you repeat that for the camera?" said the cameraman.) "Why do white people here come to interracial groups?" I asked the doctor. "Some have a guilt complex, I suppose," he answered. "They feel they and their forebears haven't treated Negroes right. Others just have deeply Christian feelings and want some way to express them."

On Sunday, with two British correspondents, I drove down to the delta country. Arkansas is half southern, half western. The mountainous country north and west of Little Rock has few Negroes; the people and the mentality of the area is more like Oklahoma and mountain Missouri. South and east of Little Rock is black country, "delta" in the sense that it gets an overflow from the Mississippi and from its tributary White and Arkansas Rivers. The land and the mentality here is southern. We decided to visit Helena, the state's only "seaport," a river town of which Mark Twain wrote in his *Life on the Mississippi*. The Negro boy who brought the rented car to the hotel for the trip and drove me back to the car rental office was friendly and said he came from that area. He followed us into the office to show us the best way to get there and the manager found him there marking the map with me. "Mandy Lee," he said, "you're getting out of your place when you come into this office." I explained it was all my fault and Mandy Lee stood aside, with a properly contrite expression. "Now, my friend," said the manager. "You're going down to nigger country. This is where they raise rice and cotton and niggers." He showed me the points of interest I would pass. "Right here," he said, "a Yankee gunboat came up the river and shelled a Confederate hospital." I thanked him and left thinking of the wondrous way in which all enemies in all wars always manage with unerring aim to hit hospitals.

The country is flat and not too interesting. We passed two Negro baptismals on the way; the women in bright Sunday clothes; many cars parked nearby, and some brother in a white gown being dipped in the water. We thought it would be rude to stop and watch, that a white man's presence would be disturbing and resented. But we did after several attempts and suspicious greetings manage to talk with one old Negro farm couple on their ramshackle porch with chickens running about in the yard. The old man said he had farmed there for sixty-eight years and the white folks thereabouts had always treated him right "and with respect." He had no complaint, the price of cotton was good but the price of victuals went up with it. "We work like oxes," said the fierce-looking old lady, his wife. Shrewd eyes looked out of her worn black African face. Their children were gone to St. Louis and Chicago, all except one daughter who sat there shyly reading in a hymn book. Good manners and journalism struggled but the latter won when we asked whether we might see the inside of their house. "It's just a poor man's house," the old man objected with dignity. "There's a sick person in there." We apologized. The old lady said, "Are things going to get better for black folks?" and later, "I hope we're not going to have a war over there in China." It turned out that she was the only person, black or white, who asked us about the Far Eastern crisis in our three days in Arkansas.

SEPTEMBER 22, 1958

IN THE DELTA COUNTRY

Helena, to our disappointment, turned out to be no more picturesque than Little Rock. We drove through the commonplace main street—"Cherry Street"—of a small river town, asleep in the Sabbath sun, with no sign of ante-bellum grandeur. We went through the "gate" in the high levee, across the Missouri Pacific tracks and down to the muddy waters of the broad and unlovely stream where cars waited for the ferry to the Mississippi side. Willows grew thick on a long mudbank island near the Arkansas side. Except for the ferry pier there was nothing to suggest the "seaport" Helena likes to call itself. We turned back disenchanted to "Nick's," a Greek restaurant at the foot of Cherry Street, and while waiting for lunch telephoned the editor of the local daily. He wasn't in but I reached his father, its publisher, and told him I had two visiting British reporters with me and we wondered whether we could talk to him or his son while we were in town. Within a few minutes both father and son turned up at Nick's to make us welcome.

They were most hospitable. Both were widely traveled; a map across one wall of the dining room in their comfortable home on the outskirts of town had red buttons pinned on it to show the places they had visited. There were red buttons all over Europe and all around the periphery of Asia, including Taipeh and Bangkok. The father recalled that he had been a guest in London at a dinner given by the publisher of the paper one of my friends represented, and insisted that we be his guests at dinner. We were taken for a ride on a small cabin cruiser on the Mississippi, and then the younger man in his convertible showed us the town, including its own ante-bellum mansion, and the old Confederate cemetery high up on a bluff where a few Yankees who fell in the Battle of Helena are also buried. We saw the local synagogue ("Jews began to come here with their slaves from Kentucky before the war," our friend told us). The town also has a large colony of Lebanese. Helena used to be three-fourths Negro and is now 60 percent black. In the back streets we saw row after row of unpainted shacks, much like those of a mining town, where Negroes lived. "They wouldn't live in better houses if you gave it to them," our friend assured us. Helena is as much "deep South" as neighboring Mississippi and Louisiana. Like them it has no school integration problem because no Negro dares file suit. But our friend said, almost boastingly, that Negroes had forced the town by litigation to provide a modern Negro high school.

At the Helena country club where other members of the family gathered for drinks and dinner with us everybody said "nigger" as a matter of course. "Our better class of niggers have left," one lady told us. There was a steady stream of migration northward. But to believe the ancedotes one would think the long distance wires from St. Louis, Chicago and New York were clogged with calls collect from homesick migrants to their white "folks" asking them to please send fare to come home. So-and-so had gotten such a call only recently and simply refused to take it; the tone implied that the gates of paradise had been shut forever on the faithless one. We were told a story about the hungry southern Negro who went for help from door to door in Chicago in vain until at one door he heard a voice yell, "You black bastard get around to the back" and sighed with relief, "Ah's found friends at last." Such are the folk tales with which the white South comforts itself.

There was hardly anyone who did not assure us at some point in the conversation that some of their best friends were niggers. The publisher told us he was sending a nigger boy through medical school in Chicago; the boy recently asked one hundred dollars for books and he had sent it to the student. When a British reporter suggested that the Negro must be a brilliant boy, he seemed to have hit a jarring note. "He'll get along," his benefactor said grudgingly. He told us a story of a local Negro who had gone to Little Rock and phoned him from there (much to the surprise of his Negro friends) to ask for ten dollars, which was sent and duly repaid. This was related as another instance of the generous way in which Negroes were treated. One woman said she couldn't have a better neighbor than the Negro woman who lived across the backyard from her home. "There isn't anything I wouldn't do for her or she wouldn't do for me," she said. "But of course I wouldn't think of asking her into my parlor. It would only embarrass both of us."

One man told us that Negroes were a problem because they just couldn't control themselves sexually, and related a story of a Negro paternity case in which four Negroes each offered to pay a share toward the support of an illegitimate child since all four felt they had been partly responsible for its birth. "Sure our niggers vote," said another man gleefully. "We paid their poll taxes and lined 'em up to vote for the liquor interests in a recent local option election." A younger woman, a nurse, said she had been working among the Negroes "by choice" for the local health service. Why? "They're so grateful." Like all these people, she seemed quite sure she knew what Negroes were really thinking. "They've been a little belligerent lately, since this school trouble started," she said. "But they change when they see you're friendly." She seemed a warm-hearted and most capable person. But she was sure that "all the trouble" in the South had been caused by a few white persons in the North who "put the NAACP up to it."

Both the gray-haired father of the family and his wife, a kindly and motherly woman, felt that integration "has got to come" but pleaded "only you've got to give us more time." When I asked the father whether most of the people in his generation and class felt that way, he said they did. But his wife was noncommittal, said she was "out of things" and didn't know. It was disappointing to read in that same day's paper two short editorials the elderly man had written. One blamed the latest Supreme Court school decision on Chief Justice Warren's wish to fulfill "the desires of his old political buddy, Harry Bridges, who wants to and does stir up all the trouble he can in the United States in the interests of his beloved Communist Russia." The other said, "Mrs. Eleanor Roosevelt has gone to Moscow. Moscow is a good place for Old Big Mouth and we hope she stays there." The portrait of these people would be incomplete without noting that they shared the upper-class southerner's contempt for his own poorer white brethren. "Why some of them are so low," one lady told us at dinner, "that niggers won't associate with them." All of our new friends in Helena were strong supporters of Governor Faubus.

SEPTEMBER 29, 1958

36: *Freedom of Thought, Here and There*

BORIS PASTERNAK

I read Boris Pasternak's *Doctor Zhivago* with joy and admiration. In its sensitive pages one is back in the wonderful world of the nineteenth-century Russian novelists. He is a fine writer, and a brave man; there are passages which, read against the background of Soviet realities, are of a sublime courage.

But I find myself more and more annoyed by the chorus of Pasternak's admirers in this country. I do not remember that *Life* magazine, which glorifies Pasternak, ever showed itself any different from the *Pravda-Kommunist* crowd in dealing with our own Pasternaks. I do not recall that *Life* defended Howard Fast for receiving the Stalin award or deplored the venomous political hostility which drove Charlie Chaplin and more recently Paul Robeson into exile.

Only a few years ago Arthur Miller, an American writer much less critical of our society than Pasternak is of his, was summoned before the House Un-American Activities Committee, submitted to humiliating interrogation, and threatened covertly with perjury charges unless he recanted his past political views. Even today the one movie house in Washington which has revived the old Chaplin classics runs an apologetic note in its advertising.

It is easier for a critic of capitalism and the cold war to live in this country than for a critic of communism to live in Russia. But an unofficial blacklist still bars some of our best artists and actors and directors in Hollywood and from radio-TV work.

The closest analogue to Pasternak is Howard Fast, and until he broke with the Communists he was forced to publish his own books. All of us who are more or less heretical in our society are forced to live on its margin, grateful that we are able to speak (at the cost of abnormal exertions) to a small audience.

Pasternak has universal meaning, for he embodies the fight the artist and the seeker after truth must wage everywhere against official dogma and conformist pressures. Not a few of our intellectuals in Hollywood and elsewhere on their psychoanalysts' couches may say the very words Pasternak puts into the mouth of Dr. Zhivago.

"The great majority of us," he protests, "are required to live a life of constant, systematic duplicity. Your health is bound to be affected if, day after day, you say the opposite of what you feel, if you grovel before what you dislike and rejoice at what brings you nothing but misfortune. Our nervous system isn't just a fiction, it's a part of our physical body, and our soul exists in space and is inside us, like the teeth in our mouth. It can't be forever violated with impunity."

In another passage Dr. Zhivago tells his beloved, "The main misfortune, the root of all evil to come, was the loss of confidence in the value of one's own opinion. People imagined it was out of date to follow their own moral sense, that they must all sing in chorus, and live by other people's notions, notions that were being crammed down everybody's throat." This applies equally to present-day America.

Unlike Ehrenburg's pedestrian *The Thaw* and Dudinstev's wooden *Not by Bread Alone,* the other protest novels of the post-Stalin period, *Doctor Zhivago* is a work of art. Giving it the Nobel prize was a political act in the best sense of the word, for it put world pressure behind the struggle of Russia's writers for greater freedom. If the masters of the Kremlin were wise they would have let Pasternak go to Stockholm and they would publish his book in Russian; such magnanimity and the book's complete negativism about the Revolution would have been a telling answer to its thesis and their critics. Bigness, obviously, is beyond them.

Whatever their folly, let us examine the mote in our own eye and remember that an American Pasternak who accepted a Soviet prize would be hauled up before the Un-American Activities Committee and blacklisted in Hollywood and on Madison Avenue. And few, *very few,* of those who are now praising Pasternak would then say one word in defense of the right to a free conscience.

NOVEMBER 3, 1958

DELICACY IN JOURNALISM

The *New York Times* managed three days in succession to run a news story, a background personality sketch and an editorial about William H. Meyer, the first Democrat to be elected to Congress from Vermont in several generations, without mentioning that he was active in the American Civil Liberties Union and campaigned for an end of nuclear tests, for banning the H-bomb and for recognition of Red China.

NOVEMBER 24, 1958

THE *DAILY WORKER*

We regret the demise of the *Daily Worker*. It leaves the United States the only one of the great world democracies without a Communist daily. The ultimate cause of its disappearance is a witch hunt which frightened away readers as it frightened people out of the party. Basically, the land of Jefferson slipped behind Britain, France and Italy. Our government took steps to make it dangerous to read a Communist paper. Aliens found themselves deported; foreign-born citizens, denaturalized; citizens, blacklisted, on the basis of allegations which often included the reading of the *Daily Worker*. In this respect all of us who believe in free traditions must blush for its passing. Freedom of the press proved less real here than in Western Europe.

The more immediate cause of the *Worker's* passing is to be found in Moscow. It would have taken no more than the barest hint from the Kremlin to make it clear to the Foster Old Guard that Moscow welcomed the appearance in the Communist world of a paper which was independent. Instead Moscow signaled by attack in its own press that it did not like the independent line which the *Worker* under John Gates had been pursuing since the Twentieth Congress. The Gates faction believes that the Old Guard thereupon shut down the *Worker* as its own way of purging the paper and that in the not too far distant future the *Daily* will be revived, but under subservient editorship.

In so acting the Khrushchev regime in our opinion missed a chance to make a contribution to peace. A *Daily Worker* independent enough to criticize Moscow itself, as the *Daily* did in the Hungarian uprising, would have been proof that the Communists are not just stooges of Moscow, that they can think and speak for themselves. It would have been a sign that de-Stalinization was continuing and thus an aid in the fight for peaceful coexistence. For it must be admitted that the existence of Communist parties which act as mere appendages of Moscow makes the fight for peaceful coexistence more difficult.

And now in justice to the *Daily Worker,* it must also be added that in thirty-four years of existence—amid much that was foolish, sectarian and cheaply slanderous (like George Morris's final piece coupling Howard Fast with Howard Rushmore)—it served many good purposes and good causes. It published much that did not see the light elsewhere. It fought for the Negro and the underprivileged; it played an honorable role in the thirties, when it contributed to the mass organization of labor and the reforms of the New Deal period. Its underpaid and overworked staff carried on under heartbreaking difficulties. In their paper's passing, they deserve a newspaperman's salute for their devotion.

JANUARY 20, 1958

37: *The Pentagon, the Moon, and Pugwash*

A NIFTY RETALIATION BASE

The Pentagon press office was busy giving out background releases on the lunar probe all day Saturday and a panel of experts held a news conference Sunday afternoon at the National Academy of Sciences. But none touched on the motivations which lead our military to spend millions on the problem of reaching the moon, and not just the moon alone. For with the lunar releases was one announcing that the Navy would soon send a manned balloon eighty thousand feet up to take a close look at Mars in order to determine its water vapor content. Perhaps if there is enough water on Mars to float a boat, the Navy will claim jurisdiction. The services are staking out the planets; the Air Force has its eye on Venus.

We'd like to call attention to two briefings behind closed doors on Capitol Hill earlier this year which have gone unnoticed. They show that the military men behind these space projects approach the new scientific wonders with the minds of comic strip characters, ready like Buck Rogers to carry out among the far stars only the same small boy savageries and cold war hates. One briefing was by Lieutenant General Donald L. Putt, Deputy Chief of Staff (Research and Development), United States Air Force, before the House Committee on Armed Services, February 25. The other was by Richard E. Horner, Assistant Secretary of the Air Force for Research and Development, before the House Appropriations Committee on March 11. An unclassified version of what General Putt said may be found at pages 4911-23 of the armed services hearings. Horner's testimony was printed in the hearings on the Air Force budget for fiscal 1959. We recommend them to anybody running short of nightmares.

The General disclosed that the Air Force's ultimate objective was to establish a missile base on the moon, and outlined its usefulness. General Putt said that since there was no atmosphere and little gravity on the moon, less energy would be required "to shoot a warhead from the moon to the earth" than from the earth to the moon. "Warheads," he explained, "could be catapulted from shafts sunk deep into the moon's surface." General Putt declared the moon "might provide a retaliation base of considerable advantage over earthbound nations," using the term with condescension, as if *we* were on the moon already.

General Putt said that if we had missile bases on the moon "an enemy would have to launch an overwhelming nuclear attack against those bases one to two days prior to attacking the continental United States." Otherwise the moon bases, observing an attack on the United States, could retaliate by destroying the attacker.

Even if the enemy destroyed us by surprise attack, our moon bases would destroy him. On the other hand, if the enemy attacked our moon bases first to make such retaliation impossible, the attack would be observed from earth and give us warning. Thus the strategy of mutual deterrence would be given a new lunar dimension.

Lest anyone think General Putt had merely stopped off to testify on his way to a long quiet stay at a good rest home, this can be checked against the Horner testimony. The Assistant Secretary of the Air Force said one advantage of a missile base on the moon is that the flight of the missile could be observed "all the way from the moon's surface to the target, which is something which cannot be done from one point on the earth to another far distant point on the earth." Mr. Horner thought that moon bases might some day break a stalemate of terror between the United States and the U.S.S.R. when "we have developed such a capability to obliterate Russia and presumably they have developed a similar capability to obliterate us" that neither side dares fire. If we could then establish a missile base on the moon, we would again gain the initiative. When our high brass sees visions and dreams dreams, this is what they see. When their heavens open, missiles *wham*.

And what if the Russians acquire moon bases, too? And a stalemate of terror develops on the moon as well as on the earth? For the answer to these questions, we must turn back to General Putt's secret briefing. "We should not regard control of the moon," he said, "as the ultimate means of insuring peace among earth nations." (Note how all these murderous monstrosities are represented as means of "insuring peace.") This would be only "a first step toward stations on planets far more distant, from which control over the moon might then be exercised." A missile base on, let us say, Mars could break a stalemate on the moon. Even if the Russians destroyed *both* the United States and its moon base in one swift surprise attack, our base on Mars could then destroy *both* their moon base and their country. The advantage would hold presumably until they had established a similar missile base on Mars or some other planet, only to be checked again by the next move, which would perhaps set up artillery outside the solar system altogether. Thus, as the Pentagon maps it, peace by mutual terror would spread outward toward the far stars.

This seems to us a good time to recall the Latin word for

moon, which is of course *luna,* and to suggest that before service rivalry explodes all over the skies we establish a fourth branch of the defense establishment for space warfare and call it the Department of Lunacy.

OCTOBER 20, 1958

MODERN SANHEDRIN

The ancient Sanhedrin which met in the Temple at Jerusalem as the highest rabbinic court was made up of seventy-one learned men. Exactly the same number signed the manifesto with which the third Pugwash conference of nuclear scientists ended their meeting in September at Kitzbühel, in Austria. This was a Sanhedrin of mankind's most learned and of some who are among its most wise. Bertrand Russell was there from England, Bhabha from India, Ogawa from Japan, Oliphant from Australia, Leopold Infeld from Poland, Topchiev from the Soviet Union and men like Linus Pauling and H. J. Muller from our own country. Nobel prize-winners were a commonplace among them. They transcended the current glowering divisions of the earth. The Western bloc, the Soviet States and the neutrals, including Yugoslavia, were represented. Yet the gravely considered warning which they issued at the end of their meeting has nowhere been made available to the general public. The newspapers, as full of chatter as a monkey cage, found no space for their conclusions; the meeting itself—made possible by the initiative and bounty of Cyrus Eaton—was barely noticed; indeed it was not quite respectable, since its sponsor, though a multimillionaire capitalist, has rendered himself controversial by questioning an exalted figure, the head of our secret police, Mr. J. Edgar Hoover. It is a commentary on our times that a little paper like our own can have the honor of printing the text of the Pugwash declaration.

The Pugwash declaration contains bad news. The arms race, as it picks up speed, passes one point of no return after another. The scientists warn that "a completely reliable system of controls for far-reaching nuclear disarmament" has become "extremely difficult, perhaps impossible." They warn that even though negotiation eliminated all nuclear weapons, the knowledge of how to make them remains "for all time, a potential threat to mankind." Should war come, any major industrial power could produce them within a year. The scientists regard the Pentagon dream of limited wars as a delusion. They see no alternative to peace. They see no substitute for the restoration of trust among men. They ask us to stop glorifying war and violence. They protest that science, harnessed everywhere to the arms race, has been diverted "from its true purpose." They call for an end of secrecy, and they affirm that science "can best serve mankind if it is free from interference by any dogma imposed from the outside, and if it exercises its right to question all postulates, including its own." This—to which sixteen Soviet bloc scientists appended their names—is not Marxism-Leninism; neither is it the milder plastic-packaged conformism of Madison Avenue; in our Orwellian world, these are words which Big Brother will not like on either side. But unless we can get people to heed these words soon, it will be too late. Thermonuclear war, reducing the remnants of mankind to a cancerous savagery, may come in our lifetime. Geneva may well be our last chance.

As before World War I and World War II, prolonged talks on disarmament are accompanied by a rising tempo of arms accumulation. This year's relatively successful negotiation toward a test ban has been accompanied by the highest level of testing yet reached; the Russians, by resuming, place supposed military over moral advantages just as we do, though both sides in this crazy contest already have more than enough monsters in stock to destroy the other. The General Staffs on both sides, now as before the other wars, work in covert and contrapuntal harmony to drown out the voices which plead the hard case of reason against the easy incitements of fear and hate. Every human being who cares must do now what he can to bring pressure on his own government. We must pressure ours at least as a starter to offer more at Geneva than a one-year ban on testing. This is no more than the quick breather required to try out new horrors, from bombs with dirtier fall-out to devices so cute they can almost make the popgun nuclear, too.

NOVEMBER 3, 1958

38: *China: Fantasy and Reality*

THE CHINESE 7th FLEET IN LONG ISLAND SOUND

China's first line of defense is on Long Island. We are honor bound to support on that island the only legitimate American government, that of Herbert Hoover, who was forced from the mainland by Democratic subversion in 1932.

Staten Island admittedly is in a different category. Our Congress, in authorizing war at any time in defense of Long Island, wisely left it to the discretion of the President to determine at the time of any attack whether it was also in our interest to defend Staten Island and Martha's Vineyard.

Since that declaration by Congress both offshore islands have become more important to the defense of Long Island and to Mr. Hoover's hope of reconquering the mainland where his picture is said to be displayed openly at the Banker's Club, the Union League and other popular rallying places.

Mr. Hoover's Republicans have deployed about a third of their strength on Staten Island and Martha's Vineyard. From the former they have cut off almost all shipping into the Port of New York while the forces on Martha's Vineyard harass the Port of Boston.

The unfriendly nature of the Democratic regime has been demonstrated by its response to these developments. The Voice of America has been threatening Long Island. Staten Island has been bombarded from the mainland.

Wars have often occurred in the past because great powers failed to make clear the point at which they would fight. We have put the regime in Washington on notice that any attack on Long Island would be an attack on China.

At the same time we have no intention of making Washington's military planning easier by letting it know in advance what we will do if the Americans try to seize the offshore islands. We are also going to keep them guessing as to whether American aggression against Staten Island will bring massive atomic retaliation against

New York. Some nervousness in other countries is we suppose natural but the free world may rest assured that all these questions will be answered in good time by our great leader, who is keeping in close touch with the situation from the Peking golf links.

In the process of determining its policy toward the United States, China has taken into account the various statements and arguments advanced by proponents of extending diplomatic recognition to Washington.* One of the most commonly advanced reasons for recognition is that reality must be "recognized" and 170,000,000 people cannot be "ignored."

While superficially appealing, both statements themselves overlook the realities of the situation. Chinese policy is, of course, based on full appreciation of the fact that the American Democratic regime is currently in control of the mainland.

Our attitude toward the people of the United States remains what it historically has been, one of sympathetic understanding; our Confucian missionaries long labored among them and are ready to return any time they overturn their present godless and materialistic regime. It is an earnest of our enduring friendship that Long Island sits on the Security Council of the United Nations, wielding a veto as one of the five great powers of the earth.

Moreover, the People's Republic of China is convinced that the American Democratic regime does not represent the true will of the American people but the fruit of a conspiracy by Franklin D. Roosevelt and his successors; our intelligence agents, who watch events in the interior closely, tell us that guerrilla forces of the NAACP led by a Negro named Faubus have already seized control of Arkansas.

Thus our policy of withholding recognition is in actuality in the ultimate interests of the American people. China holds the view that Democracy's rule in the United States is not permanent and that it one day will pass.

By withholding recognition from Washington, and keeping our Embassy in Mr. Hoover's splendid capital in Rockville Centre, we hope to hasten that passing.

SEPTEMBER 8, 1958

* Any resemblance between what follows and the wording of the United States policy statement on non-recognition of Communist China (August 9) is not purely coincidental.

DULLES AND THE DECLINE OF ANCESTOR WORSHIP

Working up toward the climax of his speech in San Francisco on why we ought never—yes, never—to recognize Communist China, Mr. Dulles touched on the danger it represented to traditional Chinese culture. "The venerated graves of ancestors," said the Secretary of State, with an almost Confucian indignation, "are everywhere being desecrated." We are sorry he did not continue in this vein. It is not only ancestor worship which is declining. Marriages are being contracted in China without casting the horoscopes of bride and groom, and houses are being built without testing the site for malevolent spirits. Such defiance of Heaven must sooner or later bring the regime's downfall.

Mr. Dulles spoke of the horrors being visited on the Chinese. "Individuality and personality are brutally suppressed," Mr. Dulles said. In the good old days, the poorest coolie or rickshaw boy, after his day's work in Shanghai, could shop around according to individual taste (as his counterparts still do in Cairo and Calcutta) before deciding which doorway or gutter he would sleep in that night. Personality flowered. "Children," Mr. Dulles went on with his description of the new commune system, "are placed in wholesale nurseries, so that the women can also be part of the slave labor." In the good old days, there were no "wholesale"—or even private, retail—nurseries; children were not separated from their mothers; both worked.

The good old days still exist in Hong Kong. A few days after Mr. Dulles spoke, Peggy Durdin provided a description in the *New York Times Magazine* of conditions in that city. "In some families," Miss Durdin wrote of the more fortunate, "the father has a permanent job, perhaps at piecework ten hours a day seven days a week in a Chinese factory; his wife embroiders at home while looking after three undernourished children."

Even into this paradise, the serpent of social reform has been creeping. Miss Durdin wrote of a new regulation to limit the hours of working women and children—but not men—to ten hours a day and six days a week. She quoted a leading Hong Kong paper, the *South China Morning Post,* as warning that the city must "make gradual, not revolutionary progress in this type of social reform." A few more years of godless propaganda and the male workers of Hong Kong will be demanding Sunday off, too.

"Few Hong Kong residents," Miss Durdin wrote, "face the ugly possibility that hundreds of thousands of people, without the elementary right to work, in daily view of luxury and plenty, repress resentments that might one day tragically explode into violence." When it comes we may expect Mr. Dulles to attribute the outbreak to indirect aggression, subversive propaganda and the lack of sound religious training. In Hong Kong's better circles, Miss Durdin wrote, "it is just not chic" to talk of the surrounding misery. This, too, is reminiscent of the good old days everywhere in Asia.

Hong Kong teems, of course, with refugees from the Communist mainland and their flight—like that of others coming across Soviet borders—testifies to much that is wrong with the new regimes. But we had better not lean back with smug satisfaction. The misery of the China mainland is the misery of a people struggling hard with bare hands to make a leap forward out of poverty; it holds a promise for the future not to be found in the slums of Hong Kong, i.e., in the good old days. We are being blinded by hateful propaganda to the immense strides forward of the new China.

A giant is awakening, dragging itself up by its bootstraps out of poverty. It is not wise to shut our eyes to this progress. It is not charitable for a people as rich and well favored as our own to survey the scene with the self-righteous distortions of Mr. Dulles. The day may come when the new China, too, will have ample means to look after the tombs of its ancestors.

DECEMBER 15, 1958

39: *Dulles: Cold, Arrogant, Ruthless*

A mixture of identification and superstition, humanity and cant, leads critics to offer the tributes Mr. Dulles has been receiving in his illness. That primitive fear lest the departed come back and take vengeance leads men to say nothing but good not only of the dead but of those who might be dying. The chorus is swelled by the courtier-like tendency of officials and journalists to demonstrate their own sense of propriety and deference to fashion by repeating the clichés of the moment. The labored articles on the Secretary's indispensability which fill the newspaper pages are an up-to-date version of the whispers that filled royal courts when a dominant Minister lay stricken. This deafening buzz-buzz stupefies the public mind.

It is noteworthy that even in this chorus one note is missing. No one pretends that in his six years at State Department Mr. Dulles has won affection. The Department knows the Secretary as a cold, arrogant and ruthless man who has been exhausting himself running around the world because he really trusts no one. Since the world each man inhabits is his own mirror, the man who thinks no one is to be trusted is the man who concludes from observation of himself that others, too, are not what they seem. Indeed no man in our time has so succeeded in creating an image of himself which he must know to be false. A lifelong servant of the most materialistic forces in our society, a Big Lawyer for the Big Money, a prewar apologist for Japanese aggression and Nazi expansion, an exponent of Machiavellianism so long as the Axis was winning, an advocate of a Christian peace as soon as its defeat was foreseen, Mr. Dulles by his constant invocation of Christianity and freedom has succeeded in making these ideals suspect in the minds of uncommitted millions who hear in them only the tom-toms beating for a new war.

It is a commentary on the limitation of men's imagination that one elderly man's struggle with a terrible illness evokes sympathy even from those who dislike all he stands for, but his proclaimed readiness to plunge the world into war over Berlin evokes no protesting image of the countless human beings he would thus consign to agony. How often this man who clings so fiercely to life has been ready to plunge the world into death! Ever since that first Indo-Chinese crisis in 1954, he has shown a heady readiness to gamble the lives of all of us. A psychologist looking at the pattern would infer self-destructive tendencies unwholesome in a Secretary of State. The same sense of humanity which leads one to wish Mr. Dulles well in his personal struggle must also lead one to hope that he will not return to office. His retirement might make possible a shift toward wiser policies.

FEBRUARY 23, 1959

40: *The Revival of Germany*

THERE IS NO ANGUISH IN THEM

Bonn

In Frankfurt, in the spring of 1946, I could still smell the unburied bodies in the massive ruins around the main railroad station. The scene, as one stepped into it then, was a nightmarish backdrop for a Wellsian movie of war between the worlds. In the Park Hotel nearby, where American journalists were quartered, shell holes made it hazardous to go to the bathroom at night.

Now, thirteen years later, one would hardly know there had been a war. The railroad square is lined with luxurious shops and high office buildings. The streets and trams are full of rosy-cheeked people, ponderously well-fed. The Park Hotel has acquired a full contingent of obsequious and resplendent flunkies.

Driving out of the city, on a lovely spring Saturday, the roads are filled with autos, scooters, motorcycles and bikes headed for the sports stadiums. Small black cars which remind one of tin lizzies, with *"Polizei"* painted in white on their hoods, are perched on the grassy edges of the roads, ready to swoop down on lawbreakers. Police guards in pairs stand at the stadium entrances with benevolent mien and military bearing. At one point a mounted police commander sits his steed with the grace of a cavalry officer.

Farther north in the Rhineland next day, in Düsseldorf where two thirds of the city was destroyed, the rebuilt streets are full of promenaders enjoying a springtime Sunday. The Königsallee, the Champs Élysées Napoleon created when he rebuilt Düsseldorf as a French bridgehead on the Rhine, is as lovely as ever. Traveling up and down the intensely battered Rhineland, it is only occasionally, near the railroad stations, a special target, that one can still see a bit of ruins. The war has left few scars on the German landscape, and even fewer perhaps on the German soul.

It is not difficult to like the Germans again—there are so many nice people among them—but it is hard not to end by being bored with them. They make dull fare. They have many virtues but there is no anguish in them. It is not an accident that they never produced a Dostoyevsky. Though their future may depend on learning from their past, the problem of How it Happened—of how a civilized people could be organized to the point of shoveling other peoples into gas furnaces—is a problem nice people don't talk about in Germany. In some extraordinary way the whole nation has acquired a warmly comforting amnesia, like a German feather bed. Often in talking with Germans, one has the feeling that the years between 1933 and 1945 were a blank through which, like Rip Van Winkle, they slept to awaken untouched and unchanged.

My first traveling companion turned out to be a Frankfurt leather merchant, a good man. He had been a prisoner of war in England and liked the English. He was against rearmament of Germany. When I asked whether there were any Jews now in his native Frankfurt, he said a part had come back, but people had little to do with them. The Jews themselves were "reserved" and kept apart. He said there was some feeling against the Jews; they were more clever than Germans in business. The few Jews who were bad hurt the reputation of the rest. There was also animosity because of restitution; Jews who sold a house in 1934 or 1937 or 1938 now came and got the houses back. This caused ill feeling. There was no mention of *why* they had to sell the houses, no reference to persecution. When he said only part of the Jews had come back, he explained that some of course had passed away. One would never have gathered from a word he said that there were any special reasons for their mortality. Nazism, of course, was never mentioned.

Not all Germans are like that. I met some who are still haunted by those terrible years, though often they turned out to be men with Jewish or Polish wives whose own children suffered in the storm. I met a young student of law who, to the question "But what if Hitler had won?" answered with deep feeling, "I would rather have died than live on in such a world." But Germans of that kind, far from being typical, often tell you they do not feel at home in their own country. The mood of the Bundesrepublik is content, self satisfied, wholly materialistic; snug and smug.

Lucifer is a tragic hero in *Paradise Lost,* but this is not a nation of Lucifers. It is capable of committing the most grandiose crimes in the most commonplace spirit. One begins to feel, in talking with them, that there are among the Germans large numbers of people capable of putting on various kinds of uniforms and committing the most awful crimes in an unimaginative, bureaucratic and paper-shuffling way and then going home and taking off their uniforms and becoming good fathers and good neighbors again and being not only surprised but offended if someone later has the bad taste to bring the matter up. The prevailing mood in Germany today when the question of Nazism comes up is that somehow they are being unjustly persecuted about matters which (1) never happened, but (2) were no different from what happens in every war and anyway (3) they were only doing their duty.

Duty—*Pflicht*—is a word which represents an important component in the German's idealized image of himself. The word has a special flavor. Mme. de Staël, who admired the Germans, but wondered more than a century ago at the contrast between their boldness in philosophy and their submissiveness in politics, observed that they obeyed their superiors *"comme si tout ordre était un devoir"*—as if every order was a duty. I heard many anecdotes about this conception of duty. A schoolmaster who was also the Nazi leader in a small town led his little Storm Troop to battle when a demonstration against the Jews was ordered. The daughter of one of the local Jews was his favorite pupil. She opened the door when the Nazis arrived. The schoolmaster leader patted her affectionately on the head and said comfortingly, "Don't be upset, we are only doing our duty." He then proceeded conscientiously to beat up her father. A Jewess, baptized at birth, who managed to live through the Third Reich because she had an influential Aryan husband told me this anecdote. She said it epitomized the Hitler years, that a kind of moral imbecility was more characteristic than sadism or hate.

This conception of duty is especially strong when it comes to serving as a soldier, an almost sacred profession in German eyes even now, as illustrated by the Niemoeller affair. Niemoeller comes closest in contemporary Germany to being a heroic spiritual figure, and a characteristically German one at that, since he first appeared on the national scene as a U-boat commander in the First World War, winning Germany's highest decoration. Then he became a pastor. Though a man of the nationalist right, he fought the Nazi attempt to take over the Protestant Church and he opposed persecution of the Jews. He was sent to a concentration camp, from which —again characteristically—he tried to volunteer as a soldier and do his *duty* when war began. Since the war, he has opposed the rearmament of Germany and seems to have become a pacifist.

Several months ago Defense Minister Strauss declared that anyone who opposed the rearmament of Germany was a potential war criminal. Pastor Niemoeller replied with a speech in which he said that the army, in training commanders and commandos, was producing the next crop of war criminals. The Defense Ministry thereupon instituted a legal proceeding against the pastor for "insulting" the armed forces. This prosecution of Niemoeller aroused only mild protest; Niemoeller had to back down and insist that he meant only *commandos* and not commanders. Then a few days ago, President Heuss, who is supposed to be a great German liberal, made a speech at the Bundeswehr training academy in which, without naming Niemoeller, he warned the cadets of the academy against "demagogy clad as Christian."

"Why do you Americans give them arms?" a German woman doctor asked me indignantly. It is the rearmament of Germany which more than any other single factor is facilitating the rebirth of the old submissive Reich. Just after the war, among the youth, there was a real yearning for a new way; among the older people *"Ohne mich"*—"without us," i.e., count us out of the next war—reflected the dominant mood. The most dangerous thing about German rearmament is its effect, internally, upon the German people. If there is to be an army, it must have officers. If there is again to be an officer class, it must be obeyed and respected. Soldiering must become an honored occupation again. Just how easily the youth can slip back into the old ways was illustrated for me by a young man in his middle twenties who called himself a pacifist and a follower of Niemoeller. Yet he had a deep respect for the German officer class. He saw no internal danger in its rebirth. The fact that these cultivated aristocrats had been disloyal to the Republic from the start and had connived in the coming to power of the Nazi rabble (as they considered them to be) had never occurred to him. This same young man told me that while his age group was still hostile to military service, the younger group between seventeen and the early twenties had begun to feel it would not be *"anständig"* (becoming, decorous, proper) for Germans not to share in NATO's defense of Germany. This is the new propaganda line, and it has caught on. The era of *"Ohne mich,"* as President Heuss proclaimed in that same address recently to the Bundeswehr officer academy, is over.

It is as if an old comedy is being replayed here, but at a much swifter tempo. The comedy is the rebuilding of a "republican" German army by "good European" liberals. Stresemann in the twenties was the "good European" liberal as Heuss and Adenauer are now. Papers seized by our troops in Germany after the war have revealed the double game Stresemann played in the secret rearmament of Germany behind the backs of his Anglo-French colleagues. It is useful to recall the Reichstag debates in the twenties when men like Chancellor Marx assured the Socialists that the officers and men recruited for the Reichswehr were being carefully screened to insure that the new army would be loyally republican. Adenauer and Heuss may not be Stresemanns but thanks to rearmament they have provided a façade behind which reactionary elements and real Nazis (not just opportunists) have infiltrated the armed forces and the government to the point where they could easily take it over if an economic depression or an international crisis required a change of policy. The Nazis are especially numerous in the Foreign Office.

At present, all goes well. The masses are content with the republic since they have jobs and bread. The leadership has only one real fear, an agreement between East and West over the heads of the Germans. The prospect that peaceful reunification is impossible does not alarm the leadership; on the contrary this is essential to their plans. Unlike the Americans, the German leadership has never felt that war was imminent and does not think so today; Bonn is far more relaxed than Washington. This estimate of the international situation plus the desire to extort political concessions explains why the leadership has moved so slowly in re-creating a new German army. It did not want to rush into the creation of a mass army with obsolete weapons. It wants to wait and develop a small army with maximum nuclear striking power. If it thought war at all likely, it would not have proceeded so slowly.

An urgent immediate objective is to block any agreement for denuclearization of Central Europe. By the time Adenauer was through with Macmillan, mutual withdrawal of forces had been changed not only to "thinning out" and possibly merely to a freezing of the military status quo, but qualified by the promise that an agreement would not "discriminate against any particular kind of weapons or any nation." The German army wants to be sure of having nuclear arms. If Adenauer were the "good European" he claims to be, if he were as distrustful of his own people as he says he is whenever reunification is discussed privately, he would hardly be so anxious to give them such dangerous weapons to play with.

There is something precarious, unreal and "un-German" about the antiseptic white Bundeshaus from which Germany is now governed. It looks more like a modern gymnasium in Tel Aviv than a German Parliament. It bears no relationship to the dominant style of this lovely little Rhineland university town. In the corridors of the Bundeshaus, the deputies do not look at all like the natural rulers of the Reich. The military bearing, the *schmiss,* the arrogance, are completely lacking. The deputies look like out-of-work Shakespearian actors or slightly shady Balkan traveling salesmen as they rush by with their bulging briefcases. Their clothes are ill-fitting, their overcoats shapeless, their lack of style painful. Their hairdos tend to be those of German professors, a nimbus of unkempt hair around a balding brow. Many are returned exiles; there is about them all an air of not quite belonging. One feels that when comes *der Tag* again they will easily be swept away.

I was at the press conference at which the Socialist leaders, Carlo Schmid and Fritz Erler, reported on their unhappy mission to Moscow. The press conference was held in the modernistic assembly hall in the SPD (German Socialist Party) wing of the Bundeshaus. It was like a big classroom, adorned with one picture, that of the lean-faced Schumacher. Their melancholy report was music to the ears of Adenauer. Khrushchev's indifference to reunification was emphasized even more strongly in private (so a Socialist deputy told me) by Zorin who said flatly, "We *want* Germany divided." This was the end of the hope to which the Opposition had so long clung that maybe Moscow would agree to free elections, i.e., to relinquish East Germany, if Germany were denuclearized and out of NATO. The Adenauer crowd felt that Khrushchev had destroyed the Opposition for them. When the Socialists shortly afterward issued their elaborate step-by-step plan for German reunification no one took it very seriously. A few years ago, it might have been possible. Now it seems to be too late.

The whole Adenauer policy of "containing" Russia until Moscow surrendered East Germany on Western terms is also in ruins, but it has been a long time since those on the inside believed in it. Its purpose was to anchor Germany securely to the United States and prevent a Moscow-Washington entente. What the Socialists fear is that the right will soon be saying that "democracy" failed to re-unite Germany. The Socialists fear that when the army is fully grown, the right will look for a deal with Russia, and that an anti-democratic regime will ally itself for reasons of power and commercial expansion with Moscow.

But all this is still in the future. At the moment the placid German folk aren't very interested in anything. They are capable of wild moods of enthusiasm but rarely for republics, and their lack of fervor today extends even to national questions. I found no one who thought the West German people were very concerned about the "fate of their brothers" in the East or would be ready, if asked, to accept a lower standard of living for a while to liberate them. It may be different in Berlin, but here in the West the Germans never cared less.

MARCH 30, 1959

BERLIN: DIVIDED CITY IN A DIVIDED WORLD

Berlin

To go from capitalist West Berlin to Communist East Berlin and back only costs twenty pfennigs each way on the subway or the elevated, and is as easy as going from Manhattan to Brooklyn, but this swift and unimpeded transit is deceptive. The subway or elevated rider, unlike the motorist or pedestrian who goes by way of the Brandenburger Tor, does not even have to pass a border guard. Indeed the stranger does not know whether he is getting off in West or East Berlin. The same people, the same faces, are on both sides of the border, and there is a constant coming and going among them. The huge MGM theatre on the Kurfürstendamm in West Berlin, where *Die Katze auf dem heissen Blechdach* (Cat on a Hot Tin Roof) is now playing, advertises "Ostbesucher 1:1" in huge letters. This means that MGM is offering to take East Berlin marks at 1-to-1 parity with West Marks from East Berliners buying admission tickets, a bargain rate since the West City mark is worth three and a half times the East Berlin Mark on the free market. But then the Berlin crisis has hurt the tourist business and West Berlin is glad to get East Berlin trade even at a discount. Yet though communication is easy, the cleft between them is nonetheless very real.

Flying into Berlin from Bonn, looking down upon the city at night for the first time, West Berlin is festive with light, East Berlin is ill-lit and dark. The Kurfürstendamm, the shiny front West Berlin puts on to the world, is as bright with advertising signs as Broadway, and as invitingly lined with cafés and shops as the Champs Élysées. At one end one sees the dark hulk of the ruined *Gedächtniskirche,* the Memorial Church from which the Kurfürstendamm radiates outward as the Champs Élysées does from the Étoile in Paris. A bell tolls the hours from the ruined tower. Far down toward the other end, high against the night sky, is the familiar Bayer Aspirin sign in blue and under it Agfa in red; the church may have taken a beating but I. G. Farben's main products flourish again. In between, around the walls and atop the buildings along this broad avenue, the great capitalist concerns of the world proclaim their wares, here on the city border, deep within the East Zone, as if in defiance of that Communist world which stretches from the Elbe to the far Pacific. Here is Ford and GM's Opel, Ufa and MGM, Philips and Telefunken, Lufthansa and Pan Am, Esso and Veedol, Mercedes-Benz and Bosch, Siemens and Olivetti, AEG and Janssen. The great German banks and insurance companies light up the night sky with them. In the shop windows, the stroller may see the latest cars and rich furs, fine foods and fruits from all over the world, jewels and champagnes, the sausages and hams Germans love, and delicacies like asparagus at 7.50 DM a jar, or about $1.75. The window shopper is never far from the black and white display with which the giant Deutsche Bank in every few blocks supplies that day's quotations for every stock on the Berlin bourse. The capitalist who takes a *Spaziergang* here may stop often to study and reflect on the state of his investments. The Kurfürstendamm says to the glowering East, "Look how rich capitalism is. How can you ever hope to equal this?" It is a system and an ideology that all this electric power advertises.

The guide in the rubberneck bus which took us around both Berlins early Palm Sunday morning referred ironically to the Kurfürstendamm as the "Propagandastrasse." Only a block off this dazzling thoroughfare, the scenes are less impressive. There is hardly a back street without its ruins, though these are not as shocking as in the East where the tourist is introduced to the grimier back streets and to the untouched wreckage and rubble of Wilhelm's empire and Hitler's along the Wilhelmstrasse. We saw the block of rubble where Hitler killed himself in his bunker. We saw the memorial garden for the Russian war dead built with the stones from his Chancellery. We saw Russian soldiers, many of whom looked like young boys just off the farm, wandering about, taking each other's pictures in front of the touching statue of Mother Russia mourning her sons; the face is the worn and tender face of an old *babushka*. We saw the tablet which says in Russian and German, *"Die Heimat Wird Ihre Helden Nicht Vergessen"* (the homeland will never forget her heroes). The streets of East Berlin seemed deserted, bare and unprepossessing after the Kurfürstendamm. But when another American newspaperman and I came back after lunch to look around on our own, we found the showplace streets of East Berlin, the Stalinallee and Unter den Linden, full of promenaders. Children were playing with hoops. A boom business was being done in Eskimo pies by street vendors. The Budapest café was full and we found a dance building doing a rush business, a top floor with waltzes for the elderly and a lower floor for the younger set.

That Sunday afternoon and a prowl about East Berlin on my own next day showed how much our own propaganda has oversold us on how bad things are in East Berlin. The people look well dressed and well fed, more so than the crowds I saw in Moscow and Warsaw three years ago. Along the Stalinallee and Unter den Linden, the Soviet world has its own propaganda show. There are rich shops with tasteful displays showing luxury goods, clothing, foodstuffs, jewelry, candies, books and toys. The Ministry of Light Industry had an Easter display that was as lovely as anything in the West. I saw Hungarian champagnes, orange juice bottled by the China National Fruit Export Corporation, Bulgarian fruits and Russian preserves in jars. The prices were obviously beyond those of ordinary workers in the East City, but then ordinary workers in West Berlin don't buy ten-dollar shirts or five-dollar ties either. Visitors from other Soviet countries were not only impressed, I was told, but even a little jealous of what the Germans were getting. By Soviet standards, Stalinallee is as striking a display of luxury as the Kurfürstendamm. A young man who attached himself to us Sunday afternoon said only police officials, higher party bureaucrats and specialists could afford these luxuries. In any society such luxury helps to solidify the ruling class, whether capitalist or bureaucratic, and to assuage the conscience and maintain the loyalty of the intellectuals. Like the rest of the Soviet world, East Germany has its own bourgeoisic.

The two Germanies and the two Berlins have one thing in common—they are the pets of the occupation powers. Competition between East and West for the Germans is reflected on the Soviet side as well as on ours. Much reconstruction is under way in East Berlin. I saw many new apartment house developments for workers. The presence of West Berlin inside the German Democratic Republic, and the open frontier within the divided city, have made the East Berlin regime milder than that which exists in the East Zone beyond the closely guarded frontier around all Berlin. The East Zone regime itself has been the beneficiary of favored treatment. Just as West Germany has made a dominant place for itself in Western Europe through the Common Market, Euratom and similar agreements, so East Germany has become the most important industrial area of the Soviet world outside the Soviet Union itself. German know-how, German *Fleissigkeit* (diligence) is paying off on both sides. East Germany is the world's largest producer of soft coal, and this is being utilized as the basis for a huge chemical industry, with all this makes possible in variegated plastics and synthetics. So important is this becoming that the wasteful use of soft coal for synthetic gasoline is being tapered off and a pipeline built to bring gasoline from the Urals so the soft coal can be used for more economic purposes. Division of labor is making itself felt in the Soviet bloc and East Germany is becoming the most important source for the products of special skills. The standard of living is rising; the people are off a bread diet; I visited huge food stores well stocked with meats, fruits, fish and much frozen food—the last seems to be a Bulgarian specialty. The new economic relations which bind each part of Germany so profitably to its respective bloc make reunification less and less likely as the years go on. This is a factor as important as the political.

We have been oversold on the "slavery" of East Berlin and East Germany. In the former at least people speak rather freely and critically on the streets. The chief complaint, oddly enough, is the high cost and poor quality of the coffee. Intellectually, the Iron Curtain exists. The government-owned kiosks sell only Communist papers, including papers from China and Albania; no Western literature is on sale. An intellectual with whom I struck up a conversation on the street said he brought newspapers in from West Berlin regularly by hiding them inside his socks and that they were passed from hand to hand. He said things were easier in East Berlin than in the rest of the East Zone; there people were constantly under "observation." He said he worked in the theatre, that the public was bored with worker plays ("We see workers all day long, at night we want to see well-dressed people on the stage" is the public reaction) and with plays about the Russian Revolution. At a theatre ticket agency nearby I saw *The Diary of Anne Frank* and Synge's *Playboy of the Western World* advertised. Thought control is real here, tempered by the presence of West Berlin so close by. The German Democratic Republic is not at all democratic but the picture of the East as "slave" is silly and dangerous. We only blind ourselves with our own oversimplifications when careful negotiation and thought are so necessary.

APRIL 6, 1959

SOCIALISM AND COMMUNISM

Berlin

In the two Berlins I have had the privilege of interviewing two men who typify the two mentalities which clash here. Both men lived in exile in America. Both men are Jewish, a fact which in Germany makes me fearful for both of them. Both returned to important positions. One was the lifelong Communist, Gerhart Eisler, a German Old Bolshevik, now vice-president of the radio and television broadcasting service of the German Democratic Republic. The other was Dr. Paul Hertz, West Berlin's Senator, i.e., Cabinet Minister, for Economics and Credit, a Socialist since his youth. When one considers their respective backgrounds, one despairs of ever getting such men to work together. Indeed neither thinks they can, neither even pays much lip service to reunification. Eisler is a Communist who has stuck with the party through all the terrible turns and twists of party line since the early twenties; he was with the International Brigade in Spain as a kind of commissar. The last time I saw him was before the House Un-American Activities Committee a decade ago when his sister, who broke with the party in the early twenties, accused him of being a Comintern agent. He later fled America while his sentence for contempt of the committee was being appealed. He asked me to lunch at the rather dingy press club on Friedrichstrasse in East Berlin; he looked older but well, and he spoke with that assurance and lack of party line cant one encounters in Communist circles only among officials securely near the top. His wife, Hilda, who joined us for a few minutes, edits a periodical called *Magazin* which is said to be the only publication between the Elbe and the Pacific which publishes pictures of pin-up girls, a daring innovation in Soviet journalism which wins no laurels for liveliness.

Hertz received me next day in his big office overlooking the lovely little park and fountain near West Berlin's old-fashioned Rathaus. The Senator is a living link with the greatest days and names of German socialism. With Karl Kautsky, he left the party to oppose the First World War. He boasts that Kautsky, who had three sons of his own, called Hertz his "fourth son." With Hilferding, Hertz helped to edit the famous Socialist organ *Freiheit*. Martov, the grand old man of Russian Social Democracy, took refuge with Hertz in Berlin after fleeing the Soviet Union. From 1919 to 1933, Hertz was a Social Democratic deputy and general secretary of the Social Democratic faction in the Reichstag. He left in 1933 with the party executive committee, which settled down for five years in Prague and then one year in Paris before the war broke out. He lived in the United States from 1939 to 1949, becoming an American citizen in 1946 and earning his living as economic adviser to a small brokerage house in New York. His two children, one of them a psychology professor at Ohio State, stayed behind when in 1949 his old friend, Mayor Ernst Reuter of Berlin, persuaded him to come back. In 1951 he became a German citizen again. He was the "Erhard" of West Berlin, the chief director of its amazing economic recovery and reconstruction since the war and the blockade. Now seventy-one, he has an energy, forcefulness and zest that belie his years, but he has moved from the left to the right of the Socialist movement.

These two able old men see the world from extraordinarily different points of view; the conflict between their philosophies is deeper than between Communist and capitalist. They share the same Marxist tradition up to the point where the Russian Revolution split the Marxist movement into two wings with that deep mutual hatred only the fraternal feel for each other. These feelings have been made more intense because they are Germans, and share the peculiar German experience. For Eisler the lesson of German history between 1919 and 1933 is that the weakness of the Social Democrats was criminal, that a ruthless purge of reactionary elements, Russian style, shortly after World War I and a Bolshevik dictatorship in Germany would have nipped Hitlerism at its roots and prevented a world war. For men like Eisler, Social Democracy merely provided a façade behind which the forces of reaction were able to reconstitute themselves after the fall of the Hohenzollerns.

For men like Hertz, on the other hand, Eisler represents a force which helped to undermine the prewar Republic, which joined hands often with the Nazis in specific situations against the Social Democrats, which divided the left until it was too late, and which turned the Socialist dream in Russia into a dictatorial horror, a kind of Red fascism, extinguishing all liberty.

These two men share a common tendency—they see the only hope of rebuilding a decent Germany in close reliance upon a foreign power, Eisler on Russia, Hertz on America. Both, in consequence, really favor its continued division. Both are typical, the former of the East Zone German mentality which tends in faithful imitation to be more rigid even than the Russians, the latter of the Berlin type of socialism—pragmatic, Americanized in its distrust of old-fashioned Socialist ideology, indeed rather New Dealish than socialistic, and primarily concerned with the city's defense against the East.

Hertz is also a Berliner. For Berliners, Berlin is not just the center of the world; it is the world. So I was not surprised (after hints dropped to me by Socialists in Bonn) at the opinions Senator Hertz expressed. Like most of the West Berlin Socialists, he does not like the step-by-step plan for reunification put forward last week by the West German Socialist party. "If that plan leads to reunification at all," Senator Hertz said, "it would be the kind of reunification we saw in Poland and Czechoslovakia where the Communist party ended by swallowing up the Socialist party." Senator Hertz sees a parallel with Munich. "Weakness," Hertz said, "is not the way to peace." He says Khrushchev's purpose is to make all Germany Communist. He says the solution of the German problem depends upon a world settlement. But when I suggested that the German question in turn blocked a world settlement, creating a really vicious circle, he replied in a typically Berlin way. He said if the Allies only stood firm and insisted on their rights to access, then Berlin would grow and prosper. He pictured with pride the success already achieved. In 1950 there were 350,000 jobless and only 550,000 at work; today there are only 60,000 jobless and 900,000 at work. He spoke gratefully of United States counterpart funds which supplied the capital for this development and emphasized the fact that the city government had forced the private businessmen to whom it loaned this capital to pay interest and amortization in a normal banking way. "In 1950 we could pay for only half our imports," Senator Hertz said. "Today we can pay for 86 percent. Give us a few more years and we will wholly pay our way." The crisis has not caused a flight of capital. The Berliners were standing firm. For him, as for an ancient Greek, it was the City which counted; he spoke with satisfaction of the fact that one day he addressed the metal workers union, the next day the Chamber of Commerce. Civic patriotism rather than ideology or class feeling was reflected in all he said.

The Berlin point of view colored his attitude toward West German developments. In this, he resembled the dominant American point of view far more than the West German Socialist. He is not afraid of German rearmament; he thinks the German people have changed; he thinks they have learned their lesson and will never try again for world domination. "I know," he told me, "this is what the outside world fears a Germany dominated again by the Hitler clique and of course we have to be careful. No member of the Berlin government ever had anything to do with the Nazis. That's not true of Federal Germany. They have some among their officers and in their courts." This was putting it more mildly than the Socialists do in Bonn; there I was told that 65 percent of the Foreign Office was staffed by Nazis—not just opportunists but convinced Nazis. In the same way, Hertz disparaged the danger of anti-Semitism. "The fact is," he said, "that the Nazis have had no success whatever at the polls." Sure there was some anti-Semitism; it would take years to get rid of it all. But he and Mayor Brandt's press officer and the head of the white collar workers' union in Berlin were all Jews returned from exile; never had a single anti-Semitic word been said against them. Was this, perhaps, I asked, peculiar to Berlin? Here municipal pride broke through again and he agreed. "Berlin never gave in to Hitler," the Senator said proudly.

I got quite a different picture on the other side of the line in East Berlin. "We know the Germans," Eisler said. "We know what they're thinking in the West. The old military crowd is saying, 'We lost the last war because we had poor allies—the Italians and the Japanese. Now we have a good ally, the United States. This time we can win.' To let matters slide, to let the rearmament of West Germany go on, particularly in atomic weapons, is for both sides to lose all control over the situation. People like the West German Defense Minister, Strauss, will determine the course of events. We have raised the question of Berlin as a warning bell. The question of Berlin itself is easy to settle. We have no designs on West Berlin. We have no desire to conquer it or to interfere in it. We already control 99 percent of the traffic between West Germany and West Berlin. We're not going to interfere with the rest. We're not crazy. We don't want trouble. We want a peaceful life. We believe we can build a new kind of Germany here—a Germany without militarism. We're prepared to join in all kinds of international guarantees for West Berlin. Neutral troops could be stationed there, but we don't want to see occupation troops—using the city as a bridgehead for a future war. We want to get rid of the forces which right here in the middle of the German Democratic Republic exploit West Berlin for trouble-making, preparing for *der Tag*. We want to liquidate the centers of provocative action but we're not worried about people fleeing. Many are beginning to come back. We're going to solve the refugee problem by social improvement. But don't forget that a few thousand people in West Berlin can start serious trouble; we were close to it when a mob formed at the Brandenburger Tor during the Hungarian uprising, ready to march in and storm the Soviet Embassy. If they had marched, we would have had to shoot and the consequences would have been serious. Anywhere else a demonstration is a minor matter but here it could start a world war."

When I asked about the rearmament in East Germany and its social dangers, Eisler said, "We're developing a new kind of army. Our officers are carefully screened. Our commanding general and Minister of Defense, Willi Stoph, is a bricklayer by trade and was in the underground against Hitler. His second-in-command, General Heinz Hoffman, fought in the International Brigade in Spain. Another general, Heinz Kessler, was a Luftwaffe flight sergeant who held up his pilot with a gun during the war and forced him to land behind the Russian lines. We're not using the old-time officers of the Free German Committee. All our officers are politically tested. Our militia groups in the factory are made up only of selected class-conscious workers. We have no mass militia. We have no general conscription. It's too expensive. We need the labor."

Unlike the East German press, which greeted the new Socialist reunification plan with hostility, Eisler spoke of it as constructive but it was evident that he did not put much faith in the possibility of reunification. I asked whether he thought the Russians might agree to real reunification if Washington made large credits available for the Soviet bloc. "Not even for ten billions," Eisler said. "A new world war would cost many times more than that and a Germany reunified under Bonn would mean a new war."

Eisler spoke with warmth and sincerity, but for all his affability and intelligence, he has the familiar Communist mentality. He really cannot understand why Socialists in the West distrust the promises of the East. The swallowing up of Socialist parties seems a natural development to him; the Hungarian Revolution, a simple case of counterrevolution crushed. "I know," he said fiercely, "how a counterrevolution should be dealt with." Was it not difficult, I asked, to have coexistence when the Soviet bloc, by ostracizing the Yugoslavs again, dramatized their renewed belief that there was only one way—theirs—to socialism? Eisler could not see the point. Like the Russians, Eisler will admit "mistakes," but like the Russians, too, he draws few conclusions from them except within his own inflexible frame of reference. I understand the East German Communist fears of developments in West Germany—many Socialists in West Germany share them—but I also understand West German Socialist distrust of Communist promises. I see no way to get them to work together. Yet failure here in Berlin may be catastrophic for all of us. I see no immediate crisis but I see trouble later, when the East Germans are stronger and the West Germans have atomic arms. Berlin is a slow fuse which some day could detonate the world.

APRIL 6, 1959

PARTNERSHIP WITH KRUPP

Those who recall the revelations made by Thurman Arnold before the Truman committee after Pearl Harbor on the secret agreements between I. G. Farben and Standard Oil which hobbled United States defense production will take very seriously the news from Bonn, "U. S. Arms Makers Are Pouring Capital into West Germany." All too familiar names like Krupp's appear in the reports of new armament alliances between United States and German firms. Their agreements, like many of the cartel pacts which the

Truman committee exposed, may well contain clauses contrary to American interests, and some steps ought to be taken by Congress at least to force the filing of all such agreements with the United States government, particularly the antitrust division of Justice. The men who made and survived Hitler are not the most trustworthy of partners. It was bad enough to give the signal for rearmament of the Reich. It is a new and worse step to allow the development of a private arms business in partnership with American arms makers like General Dynamics and the aircraft companies. This will create vested interests in international trouble to maintain a market for their arms. Of course, Germany is now our ally against communism. But it is well to remember that she was our "bulwark against bolshevism" then, too.

The emergence of powerful German-American combines in the arms business is made the more serious by the campaign developing for further amendment of the Atomic Energy Act to permit us to engage in the nuclear rearmament of Germany. The ax of German nuclear rearmament is again ground in a report made on contract to the Senate Foreign Relations Committee by something called the Foreign Policy Research Institute of the University of Pennsylvania, another of those mechanisms by which cold war intellectuals can climb on the gravy train of the arms program, providing high-class rationalizations for the Pentagon and other official agencies. Having consulted among others with Dr. Henry A. Kissinger, the limited nuclear war sage on the Rockefeller Brothers Fund payroll, the report rehashes the argument for giving nuclear arms to our allies, the nightmare dreamed up in his latter years by John Foster Dulles. The notion that the world will be made a safer and saner place by spreading deadly weapons more widely requires for its defense intellectual contortions so arduous that they deserve to be well paid, though we don't see why the Senate Foreign Relations Committee should pay for what General Dynamics or the Rockefeller Brothers Fund would otherwise finance. Who deserves contempt more than intellectuals who choose to serve the forces of destruction? The next step after a nuclear rearmed Germany will be a private German atomic arms industry (Krupp already has an interest in the first German reactor). The industrial genuises to whom we owe the crematorium will then be able to apply their talents more widely.

OCTOBER 26, 1959

THE WARNING ON THE SYNAGOGUE WALLS

Ever since the defeat of Hitler, the problem of creating a new Germany has been frustrated by focusing attention on small-fry Nazis while the big offenders went free. The pattern is still with us in the current furor over the synagogue scrawlings in West Germany. The wrath of the law is coming down on a few screwball nobodies while attention is diverted from the extent to which Adenauer's new Germany is run by the same men who ran Hitler's. Hans Globke, the Chancellor's right-hand man, wrote the official commentaries on Hitler's barbaric racial laws. Adenauer's Minister of the Interior, Gerhard Schroeder, the Reich's highest police official, is a former Hitler Storm Trooper. The Minister of Refugees, Theodor Oberlaender, was an SS captain assigned to those renegade Russian troops known as the Vlasov Army which was soon demoralized by the Nazi attitude toward Slavs as *Untermenschen*. Accusations that he took part in a massacre of Polish Jews when Lvov was occupied in 1941 are now being sifted by a tribunal at the Hague. A third member of the Adenauer Cabinet, Minister of Justice Fritz Schaeffer, made a scandalously irresponsible attack on the program of restitution to victims of Nazism. This lags badly while Nazis get their pensions and a convicted war criminal like Dr. Schlegelberger, once Minister of Justice under Hitler, lives in comfort on a pension of more than $5,000 a year. The Chancellor himself has admitted that two out of three officials in the German Foreign Office served under Hitler. Here in Washington the Ambassador, Grewe, was a member of the lawyers' and university professors' group of the Nazi party. The German judiciary is packed with men who had no difficulty in serving the Nazis. Industrialists like Krupp and Flick, who built fortunes on Nazi plunder and slave labor, have been allowed to rebuild their empires.

It is not that these men retain their Nazi convictions. It is, if anything, worse. It is that these ruling strata of Germans are composed of men who have no real convictions other than a smug faith in their own cleverness. Had Hitler won, they would have been sitting pretty. Once Hitler fell, they managed to get themselves out from under. Then they were Nazis. Today they are "democrats." Tomorrow they will be whatever best advances their private careers and fortunes. Like Hitler before them, they curried favor with the

West and won their absolution by harping on the Red menace. Like Hitler, they are quite capable of making their pact with Moscow when they feel that would best serve their interests. The example they set German youth is a cynical one, and the government they run manages, typically, to remain authoritarian in spirit though democratic in form. Dr. Adenauer, *der Alte,* is an irascible and high-handed practitioner of one-man rule who pays as little attention to his own party subordinates as he does to the opposition. This is hardly the way to train the Germans in self-government. It must not be forgotten that this republic has shallower roots than Weimar's; in 1918 the German people overthrew the Kaiser and made peace. There was no such revolution against Hitler; there were no German partisans fighting him as there were Italian partisans fighting Mussolini. The majority of the population was not only content but enthusiastic with the booty and the slave labor Hitler made available until he made the mistake of losing the war. Yet this is the unstable and unreliable state which has more and more become the main partner of American foreign policy since the war, vetoing every attempt at an East-West settlement until Germany with nuclear arms and West Europe's largest army can negotiate its own deal from a situation of strength with the Russians.

Like the writing on the wall in the Book of Daniel, the synagogue scrawlings in Germany and elsewhere are a prophetic warning. The paranoia Hitler exploited for German nationalism lives on underground and could cost mankind dearly again. The lesson is to stop before we take the fatal step of placing the new nuclear and thermonuclear weapons in the hands of those who served Hitler. In our tug-of-war with Russia we have been conjuring up and arming a monster. The men we have enlisted have already proven themselves deaf to human suffering and devoted only to self and national aggrandizement.

JANUARY 18, 1960

41: *The Khrushchev Visit*

ARRIVAL OF A WIZARD

When I got to the Rochambeau monument at the corner of Lafayette Square which is nearest Blair House, the ropes were up along Pennsylvania Avenue but there were few people waiting. It was 9:30 A.M. Two photographers squatted outside Blair House. Three eager beaver students, one in a bright red shirt, were sitting on the curb. There were half a dozen cops on the corner in the sunshine. The air was crisp and autumnal. Four poorly dressed Negroes had anticipated me in finding vantage points around the high base of the monument from which to see Khrushchev arrive.

What one noticed first was that there were no displays of flags along Pennsylvania Avenue; every bantamweight visiting dictator from Latin America sees his flag hung from the lampposts between the Capitol and the White House but there were no hammer-and-sickles in sight. What one noticed next, as the morning wore on and the streets slowly filled, was how vigilantly the police were weeding out hostile banners. An Army sergeant came striding angrily across from the White House and pointed out to police a soldier with a mourning arm-band and a black skull-and-crossbones flag. He was quickly hauled away to await the arrival of MP's, and could be heard muttering indignantly about "a thug like Khrushchev." A stout shapeless woman in blue who tried to unfurl a banner reading "Khrushchev Not Welcome Here" got similar treatment.

The State Department had long planned "a muted welcome," and government employees had not been released from work to swell out the crowds as is usual when foreign potentates are expected. Lafayette Square filled up slowly. There were many tourists, recognizable by cameras carried on shoulder straps; the kind of white-haired ladies who still go faithfully to peace rallies; a sprinkling of students and a high proportion of Negroes. The latter were guarded and noncommittal. The sidewalks did not fill out until the lunch hour, and the crowds were oddly quiet. Nobody seemed to speak to his neighbor; there was no joking; one felt that both the hostile and the friendly were afraid to be heard. The miasma of the loyalty-security program may have affected the latter while new immigrants like the Hungarians brought police-state fears with them. A crowd in Moscow in Stalin's day might have been just this unsure about how to welcome a foreign visitor.

It was not so much a cold as a confused and inhibited crowd which stood waiting to see the Soviet Premier. For days in advance, it had been warned that his would be a malignant, almost occult, presence. The Most Reverend Patrick A. O'Boyle, Archbishop of Washington, had publicly requested that Catholic priests and members of religious orders stay away from Khrushchev during his visit, as if something hypnotic in his very gaze might impel priests to sign up for private lessons in Marxism-Leninism. The newspapers were full of ads warning against the ill effects of the visit. One intrepid fellow named Leon Ackerman inserted a full page subversively bearing the quotation "Love Thy Neighbor as Thyself" in the *Evening Star* the night before Khrushchev's arrival but dared not openly suggest that this might apply to our Soviet neighbors. Cardinal Spellman astutely prescribed three extra Hail Mary's daily in the parochial schools to protect children during the visit from ideological fall-out. No visiting wizard ever had a bigger advance build-up.

When a loud-speaker finally announced the arrival at Andrews Field, a white streak appeared in the cloudless heavens overhead and then a second white streak turned it into a cross, as if to ward off maleficence. Anti-Communists had hired a skywriting plane. As Khrushchev's unexpectedly pleasant voice and soft Russian began to come over the amplifier, a lone policeman appeared high up on the roof of the rococo old State Department building and stood with folded arms against the sky. When the translation brought across Khrushchev's little joke about the earth being several hundred kilograms lighter and the moon that much heavier, there was no chuckle in the crowd. But there was an angry rumble, the first and only reaction I heard, as Khrushchev went on to say that when the United States pennant reached the moon it would be greeted by the Soviet pennant "as an old resident." A bright-eyed lady nearby answered the indignant "heys" of the crowd by saying tongue-in-cheek, "He thinks we have a sense of humor." It began to look as if this were another of Khrushchev's misconceptions about the United States.

When the parade started past, there was a burst of applause for the mounted police, riding a troop of horses as graceful as ballet dancers. But there was only light applause and a few timid cheers for the ebullient Khrushchev when he swept by, waving his black homburg above his shiny bald head. Ike, seated between him and the motherly-looking Mrs. K., did not seem at all happy, and indeed on the TV screens later that night it began to look as if the CIA had advised him to keep his famous smile carefully hidden lest the visiting Old Bolshevik expropriate it. Ike will get a heartier reception in Moscow. Our capital was lovelier than ever in the bright sun but its bewildered people must have seemed cold. Moscow will be dark, gloomy and chill but its people's welcome will be warm. The Russians must remember that peace has long been regarded as a suspect word here; that these visits represent a sharp turn of policy; and that only Ike could have gotten away with this first ice-breaking prelude to what so many of us hope will be a thaw. The cold war has too long kept our minds in deep freeze.

SEPTEMBER 21, 1959

THE SALESMANSHIP OF K.

Writing midway in the Khrushchev visit, while he is en route to Iowa, I would say that the net effect of his tour will be about the same as the effect on Americans of a visit to Russia.

Those Americans who go to Russia with right-of-center preconceptions tend to come back with a more friendly, more human conception of it; the Soviet Union, they can see, is not the "slave society" of State Department rhetoric. On the other hand most of those Americans who go to Russia with left-of-center preconceptions tend to come back appalled by its dinginess, its low living standards, its stuffy atmosphere of conformity; the Soviet Union, they can see, is hardly the "workers' paradise" of Communist propaganda.

The visit, unless there is some striking change before this issue appears, is likely to have a similar effect. Mr. Khrushchev's sense of humor, his gusto, his very failings, cannot help but break up some hostile stereotypes. On the other hand, for those of us who believe deeply in peace and coexistence, the Soviet Premier has focused attention on aspects of his character which make us realize with a pungent immediacy that negotiation with him will not be easy, nor a really peaceful coexistence readily achieved.

In some ways Mr. Khrushchev has turned out surprisingly to be a poor salesman. The most elementary rule of salesmanship is not to offend the customers. Mr. Khrushchev has hardly arrived in a new city before he is telling the Mayor or the reception committee that ours will soon be a second-rate or third-rate country. This is no way to make friends.

Mr. Khrushchev is also wiping out good first impressions in another way. He is constantly talking of what a plain-spoken and undiplomatic man he is. But when people speak to him plainly, he flies off the handle. If he wanted to be reserved and dignified, people would be reserved and dignified with him. But since he affects the breezy and democratic, he cannot fall back huffily on his dignity when discussion becomes straightforward. Mr. Khrushchev is creating the impression that he likes to dish it out, but he can't take it.

Part of this thin-skinned quality is a product of the Soviet system. Mr. Khrushchev has grown up in a society where the rulers have lost the habit of persuasion. For many years, except in the highest and innermost councils, the "line" has been determined from above and ladled out uniformly by a completely controlled press. "They" decide how much the people shall know and what the people shall think. The Russians are a very democratic people in their manners, their instincts and their approach to life but their government is a hierarchical bureaucracy in which each echelon expects the one below it to obey orders without question. This does not make them easy to get along with, except on their own terms.

We had been told that Mr. Khrushchev was a formidable debater, but he seems to be more adept at evading than at meeting issues. This is particularly striking on the question of censorship. In his speech to the Economics Club in New York he protested against the view "that the policy of coexistence we are offering to you means in effect the establishment of a 'disunited world.'" Mr. Khrushchev said that "in reality it is exactly the opposite that we want to achieve." Peaceful coexistence, he declared, "implies ever increasing economic and cultural intercourse between peoples." But when he was asked afterward why his government did not allow foreign magazines and newspapers to be distributed freely in the Soviet Union, and why it censored "the dispatches of American correspondents in the Soviet Union," he complained that he was a guest of the President, that this was interference in internal affairs, that he was an old sparrow and could not be muddled, that we also engaged in "jamming" and that we had not allowed Paul Robeson to sing abroad. This series of *non sequiturs* does not add to Mr. Khrushchev's luster as a debater. How does one have "cultural intercourse" without exchanging ideas?

Mr. Khrushchev on closer inspection has showed himself to be both a conceited and a limited man. He reminds me in some ways of Mr. Truman. Mr. Truman is also a self-made man whose earlier humility soon turned into a vast conceit. Both men show that a little knowledge is a dangerous thing. Both are inordinately proud of their half-baked history. Mr. Khrushchev's constant references to how capitalism replaced feudalism recall Mr. Truman's appeals to history in their ostentation and their callow oversimplification. The stereotypes in Mr. Khrushchev's mind are those of a kind of schoolboy third-grade Marxism, and their variance from reality has hurt his mission and endangers the cause of coexistence.

I first felt this on listening to his address before the Economics Club in New York. This was an arrogant speech which made enemies when he might so easily have made friends. Here were a group of leading American capitalists gathered to treat him as an honored guest. Their dinner demonstrated their readiness for coexistence. In arranging it, they had shown themselves quite different from the leaders of the American labor movement, who either flatly refused to sit down with him or arranged a meeting only in order to lecture him. Mr. Khrushchev, by turning on his charm, could easily have won that Economics Club audience. Instead he read a cold, boastful and unfriendly speech.

This speech had inferiority complex written all over it. It also showed the effects of Communist stereotypes. Mr. Khrushchev seems to have felt that he was facing an audience of capitalist monsters. He told them he had no horns, but he could not shake off the Communist demonology which put horns on *them*. His message sounded like a warning that they had better be friendly to Russia while there was yet time because they would soon be beaten. This engaging theme was topped off by a patronizing prediction. "Although I do not claim to be a prophet," Mr. Khrushchev said smugly, "I can say that some [businessmen] apparently will have a few bitter moments when they realize that they have incorrectly assessed the situation and erred in their calculations. If they are business-like and clever people, then, as the experience of the Socialist countries has shown, after the transition to the new social system, the American people will give them an opportunity to apply their knowledge, their energy and their abilities." This left a bad taste, especially since many of the capitalists at that dinner represented the only forces which have been pressuring the White House for relaxation of international tension and a slowdown in the arms race. It is unfortunately true that the only class which is striving at all against the arms race in America today is that section of the capitalist class which is (1) concerned with fiscal solvency and (2) much too confident of its own ability in mass production and distribution to be afraid of peaceful competition with the Soviet Union. The trade union movement, by contrast, is afraid that any letup in the arms race will bring unemployment. The worried worker, not the bloodthirsty capitalist, is the big political obstacle. This reality, so unlike Marxist stereotypes, has yet to get across to Mr. Khrushchev.

There is a second and more fundamental stereotype which blocks peaceful coexistence. This is related to the formula of different roads to socialism which Mr. Khrushchev seemed ready to accept in 1956. If one conceives of the world in terms of black-and-white, here something called "capitalism" and there something called "socialism," two diametrically opposed systems, then peaceful coexistence between them is really only possible on the rather unfriendly basis of a world split in two, with the "Socialist" world quarantined off against the "bad" ideas coming from the "capitalist" world. But if one recognizes that "creeping socialism" is the hallmark of our time, that socialism has been advancing everywhere, that all countries are moving toward it in their own way, in accordance with their own past and traditions, then instead of a sharply contrasted world of black-and-white we have a medley of systems in which peaceful coexistence and mutual borrowing of ideas between countries becomes easy. But Mr. Khrushchev seems to be as afraid to say anything good about capitalism as the average politician in this country is to say anything good about communism. Indeed it was curious to notice how often, as if with one eye nervously on the Politburo, Mr. Khrushchev assured his various audiences that he could not be converted to capitalism.

Mr. Khrushchev went out to Hyde Park to pay tribute to the memory of Franklin D. Roosevelt. But if he had the foggiest notion of what FDR represents in American history, Mr. Khrushchev could hardly have said at the luncheon given him in New York that he could see no difference between present-day American capitalism and the capitalism described by Marx. To see our present society as no different from the ugly horror of mid-Victorian industrialism described in *Das Kapital* can lead to all kinds of Communist delusions: of an American working class living in increasing misery, of an American capitalist class forced desperately into widening imperialist adventure to make up for the dwindling market at home. Something like this is served up in the Soviet press and Mr. Khrushchev seems to be affected by it. The American worker today has a lot more than his chains to lose. To recognize this would smooth the path of peaceful coexistence.

SEPTEMBER 28, 1959

PEACE IS BECOMING RESPECTABLE

What we have been seeing is an extraordinary example of leadership in its most elementary form. We had been marching in one direction and we are now marching in another. With Mr. Eisenhower at our head we had been proceeding on the assumption that the world was menaced by a diabolic conspiracy run from Moscow, and that our own safety lay in piling up an ever larger supply of ever more destructive arms. With Mr. Eisenhower at our head we have now executed an about face and are proceeding on the assumption that the Russians want peace as much as we do, and that we must slowly by patient negotiation disentangle the issues which hinder peaceful coexistence. Quite suddenly peace has become a respectable word again.

This momentous change is the more striking inasmuch as in other ways nothing has changed at all. One searches the joint communiqué which ended the Eisenhower-Khrushchev visit in vain for any sign of any agreement on any specific question. On disarmament, all the American President and the Soviet Premier could agree on was a pledge "to make every effort to achieve a constructive solution"; on Germany, "the positions of both sides were expounded"; on Berlin, they will resume negotiations; on trade, there were discussions but they drew a blank; with respect to "an exchange of persons and ideas" certain agreements are "expected" (as they had been for some time) "in the near future." Of nuclear matters, either with respect to cessation of testing or cooperation for peaceful purposes, there was no mention. There was agreement only that "all outstanding international questions should be settled not by the application of force but by peaceful means through negotiation." Beyond this generality they were unable to go.

But the atmosphere miraculously has been changed. Before, they were rigidly hostile. Now they are, so to speak, rigidly friendly.

The rigidity extends so far that Mr. Khrushchev really did not go beyond Mr. Gromyko's previous assurances at Geneva that in reopening the Berlin question, Moscow was in no sense laying down an ultimatum, or setting a fixed deadline. The President had hoped to get Khrushchev to agree that Allied rights in Berlin would continue until a change could be negotiated. All he got and this not until the final talks on Sunday was an oral agreement allowing Mr. Eisenhower to state that there was no fixed time limit on the talks. Even on this there was a subtle but unmistakable difference in emphasis between the way the President stated this agreement at press conference and the way the Soviet Premier confirmed it next day in Moscow. Mr. Eisenhower said they agreed that while negotiations on Berlin "should not be prolonged indefinitely . . . there could be no fixed time limit on them." In Moscow, where Tass dutifully omitted this from its summary of the Eisenhower press conference until it could check with the boss, Mr. Khrushchev said they agreed that in resuming negotiations "a restricted period of time cannot be given but that on the other hand they must not be drawn out indefinitely." One emphasized the lack of a time limit, the other that the talks must not be dragged out indefinitely. This still leaves it clear that if no new status for West Berlin is negotiated, the Soviet Union intends to take action on its own in a separate treaty with East Germany. The carrot is small and the stick almost invisible but still there. Neither side really budged.

Certainly on the crucial question of Germany, Mr. Khrushchev differs little if any from Mr. Molotov, and Mr. Eisenhower little if any from Mr. Truman. The difference is that both men emerged from Camp David not only smiling but apparently in genuine friendliness—and the vast propaganda apparatus at the command of both men in their respective countries is signaling friendship. This is to the good, but signals can be reversed if the better atmosphere does not yield concrete agreements.

What gives one hope is that this signal finds a willing audience on both sides. In a sense Mr. Khrushchev by his whistle-stop tour of America won an election in Russia. His trip here, his reception, the build-up in the Soviet press, solidified his position at home. We have made him unmistakably Moscow's number one man at last. Peace is popular in the Soviet Union, and in this he embodies the deepest longings of the Soviet people. The picture here is not so simple. There exist pressure groups here advancing policies which could lead only to war, yet the Gallup poll showed that only 19 percent of our people disapproved of the Khrushchev visit and there is political timing in postponing Mr. Eisenhower's return trip until next May or June, on the threshold of the 1960 elections. It was the cutest press agentry in years to blame this postponement on the grandchildren; they may not grow up under communism, as Khrushchev predicted, but it looks as if they may live four more years under Republicanism.

Coexistence has moved so far along in recent weeks that each side's political campaigns suddenly seem now to be waged on the other's territory. Just as Khrushchev solidified himself at home by his successful tour here, so Eisenhower is likely to win the United States election by barnstorming the Soviet Union next spring. Even if the results again are mainly atmospheric, they will sharpen the image of his party as the party of peace and prosperity. While the Communists here still want to work within the Democratic party, Mr. Khrushchev is going to make it very difficult for the Democrats to win next year. Such, his comrades may well muse, is the mysterious way the dialectic moves its wonders to perform.

The exchange of visits, that ice-breaking for which we are thankful to both men, will reshape our politics in many ways if no upset intervenes. It will make Nixon the candidate of the Republicans as the heir of Eisenhower and his advance scout in Moscow. It will smother the hopes of Rockefeller, who belongs with George Meany, Cardinal Spellman and the cold war Democrats. It may make Adlai Stevenson, the only top echelon Democrat to welcome Khrushchev and support Eisenhower, the Democratic nominee again. For the Democrats will need a man who can compete as a symbol of peace and who has broken with the stale stereotypes of Truman and Acheson. Humphrey is the only other choice in this respect, but Adlai outranks him in age and fame and the promise of being able to carry the conservatives of the party along with him.

If Ike, who began by making peace in Korea, ends by making peace with Russia, the Democrats must change their cold war tune. A worthy new score could be composed, if they have the courage to sing it. Only a conservative and a general could really make a settlement with Russia; this much is true. But once that peace is made only a liberal Democrat, in the tradition of FDR, can do the job of successfully substituting plowshares production for armament. Only the Democrats can move toward that pragmatic combination of free enterprise with economic planning which is essential to assure America's growth in coming years.

Each side, in the great Russo-American race, fears what is genuine in the other. Our Republicans fear economic planning. Russia's stuffy new managerial class with its bourgeois outlook fears the fresh winds of free ideas. For all foxy Grandpa Khrushchev's boasting in that glamorized farewell TV version of the Soviet system, they're so unsure of themselves they're frightened of free competition in ideas. The printed word is still the weapon they fear most. Their workers' state gives the worker very little in the way of rights against his bosses; they fear uncensored comparison. I have seen the Soviet Union and—peace to the shade of Lincoln Steffens—it is *not* the future. Our Republicans, on the other hand, showed their bankruptcy in the thirties when FDR demonstrated that we could make democracy work to satisfy the aspirations of worker and farmer. We have nothing to fear from peaceful coexistence, but the road to it will bring a similar challenge and in meeting it we can again demonstrate our country's greatness.

OCTOBER 5, 1959

42: *On the Economic Front*

LAGGING LABOR LEADERS

The important point to observe about the steel strike is that the steel companies have not suffered from it. On the contrary, they benefited by it, and invited it. Early this year they told their customers to stock up in expectation of a strike, and on the basis of the advance orders so accumulated, the steel companies enjoyed a boom in business during the first half of the year, turning out a record-breaking 64 million tons and working the mills on the average nearly 90 percent of capacity. By the time the walkout began on July 14, the steel companies had produced enough in six months to keep the economy going for ten; in mid-September, according to Secretary of Labor Mitchell, most steel-using industries were still working off supplies built up before the strike. It was much more profitable for the steel companies to run the mills at a high rate of capacity for six months than to keep them working at a lower rate for ten, and it was, of course, far cheaper to have the workers out on strike than to lay some of them off and have to pay them supplementary unemployment benefits. During the first six months of this year, U. S. Steel earned 16.7 percent after taxes on net worth, enough to give it a respectable return for the year even if the mills don't reopen until 1960. The workers, not the companies, were hurt.

Organized labor in steel has lost a great deal of its bargaining power. There was a time when steel labor leadership could think in the same public-be-damned terms as the steel magnates, pushing up wages without concern for the fact that wage increases might be paid for several times over by the public in exorbitant price increases. The big organized industries and the big organized unions could benefit within this inflationary spiral at the expense of the smaller competitive industries, the weaker unions, the unorganized and the people living on fixed incomes. Even as late as last February, when Senator Kefauver suggested it would be wise policy for the steel workers to limit their wage demands to the increase in labor productivity on condition that the companies make no further increase in price, David McDonald of the United Steel Workers retorted that he wished the Senator would "keep his nose out of my business." (No doubt Roger Blough, chairman of U. S. Steel, to whom the Senator also addressed this proposal, felt the same way but he was wise enough not to say so.)

Not only is the steel price-wage structure very much the public's business but McDonald's union is soon going to need the public's help and good will. The situation which confronts the steel workers can no longer be met by conventional trade union tactics.

The steel industry, confronted with a steady decline in demand,* has met the situation in a way that spells trouble for labor. Instead of cutting costs and seeking new markets, the industry has raised prices to the point where it can break even below 35 percent of capacity, and U. S. Steel perhaps below 30. This means steel can get along with fewer workers, and an annual strike of several months a year would be a great convenience.

In this changing situation the steel workers are going to need something different from the tough guy postures of an uninspired AFL-CIO leadership. Ever since the merger, efforts to think in terms of social policy have been suspect. What the steel workers and the rest of us are up against is a kind of economic planning. Steel and a number of basic industries are the scene of successful experiments in private socialism—their masters have long freed themselves from the bracing rigors of the free market and plan for profitable pricing at a comfortable level of output well below capacity. While the market for steel declines, the price goes steadily up; testimony by Gardiner C. Means and John Kenneth Galbraith before the Kefauver monopoly subcommittee hearings on Administered Prices last March showed that the price of steel is now doubling every ten years. This profitably managed under-utilization in the production of modern industry's basic material puts a drag on economic growth and—with the spread of automation—could add every year to the ranks of the permanently unemployed in steel and other basic industries. At the same time the labor movement is being weakened by a parallel development: the increased ratio of white collar, technical and supervisory employees to industrial workers. The former are harder to organize and non-proletarian in outlook. The foundations of the labor movement as we knew it are slipping.

The labor movement now has a common interest with the general public in working out new mechanisms to check the inflationary spiral fed by monopolistic and administered prices in basic industries controlled by a managerial few, and a common interest in making public welfare and development the standards of eco-

---

* Its old mainstay, the railroads, are virtually going out of business; armament has switched from steel to aircraft, newer metals and electronics; a glut of oil has reduced the demand for oil well equipment and the decline in farm income has cut into farm equipment sales.

nomic planning in these industries. But when in April and May, hearings were held by the Kefauver subcommittee on the first tentative step in that direction—legislation to require price notification hearings in such controlled industries as steel—McDonald though aware of the broader issues opposed it and Walter Reuther was the only labor leader who turned up in support.

OCTOBER 19, 1959

THE MYTHS THAT MENACE AMERICA'S FUTURE

Most Americans would be surprised to hear that they had an ideology. It sounds so foreign. But you can have an ideology without knowing it, and even your best friends may be afraid to tell you. An ideology is a kind of secular religion. It is a triumph of cherished faith over observed fact. It is a collection of venerable myths it is not respectable to question, though we all really know that they are untrue. The American ideology is a belief that our economy is somehow a triumph of free enterprise—individualistic, private and competitive. Just as the most devout among us know that Colonel Glenn was in no danger of running into God or colliding with stray angels Up There, so the most staunchly conservative among us know the pious picture of free enterprise bears little resemblance to the realities of money-making. But few say so out loud.

There is one vital difference, however, between our religious and our secular faiths. We take the latter much more seriously. No political figure would dare suggest that the Air Force stop testing nuclear missiles in the stratosphere lest it somehow disturb the heavenly choir. But in the realm of economic and social policy, ideology dominates common sense. It takes a bold politician to question the hallowed superstitions of free enterprise. This was vividly demonstrated again on May 3 when the House of Representatives after less than four hours of debate passed the Communications Satellite Bill by a lopsided vote of 354 to 9. This bill, if it now passes the Senate, will be the first Big Steal in outer space. It will hand over communications satellites, with all their enormous potential in communication, entertainment, education and propaganda, to dominance by one giant corporation, American Telephone & Telegraph, with a big financial stake in slowing up this new breakthrough in technology in order to protect its investments in older, obsolete facilities.

In examining the myths that determined the action of the House, one can see in just what an unreal world most Americans live and most governmental decisions are made. There is first of all the myth that equates A.T. & T. with private ownership. It is, on the contrary, collective property, but under private control. Its 223,000,000 shares outstanding are owned by more than 2,000,000 shareholders. But they have little if any voice in what is done with their property. The officers and directors who actually control it own, as of record in February of this year, only 18,149 shares, or less than one-hundredth of one percent. The men who own it don't control it. The men who control it don't own it. This disposes also of the related myth that wide public distribution of shares somehow protects the public interest, and creates what our propagandists call a "people's capitalism." The owners of these huge collective enterprises are only a helpless and anonymous herd. The wider the shareholdings the easier for the inside clique of bankers, managers and big investors.

Then there is the myth that A.T. & T. embodies the virtues of free enterprise. Its record, on the contrary, is technologically backward, as Congressman William Fitts Ryan of New York pointed out, in leading a lonely fight against the bill in the House. Expert testimony before Senator Russell Long's investigating subcommittee in the Senate provided many examples, including "one-piece telephones, modern switching equipment, and the dial phone, which were not placed on the market for years after they had been developed" in order to protect investment in obsolete equipment. For those aware that A.T. & T. is a monopoly, there is the myth that it is safely subject to public regulation. Summarizing his painstaking years of antitrust investigation. Congressman Emanuel Celler showed how ignominiously the Federal Communications Commission has failed in its regulatory task, how easily A.T. & T. has been able to overcharge long-distance users alone a billion dollars in the past seven years.

There is the myth, taught in our country almost from the first grade in school, that anything public ownership does is bad, everything private ownership does is good. This survives the observed fact that in the fresh and recent past a whole series of technological breakthroughs of the most momentous kind—from the unlocking of atomic energy to the placing of satellites in orbit—were only made possible by governmental action under public ownership. Whether in capitalist America or Communist Russia, in Britain or France, only government has had the resources for such giant accomplishments, only government could take the vast financial risks involved. Under cover of this myth, private interest only grabs what public money has developed. Mr. Kowalski of Connecticut, one of the brave handful who supported Mr. Ryan's crusade in the House for a publicly-owned space communications authority, pointed out that some twenty-five billion dollars of tax moneys had been spent in opening up the possibilities of space and that half a billion has been spent on communications satellite research alone. Yet a special committee of interested companies organized by A.T. & T. has been able to put through the House a bill which will give them control of the fruits in communications. For them, Mr. Smith's dreaded Rules Committee acted swiftly and favorably, reporting the bill without question. For them, both party leaderships joined forces in a burst of mutual self-congratulation on the House floor that was the most nauseating part of the spectacle. To watch this bipartisan response was to see that when the big moneyed men want action, the two-party system becomes a myth too.

Three basic considerations were trampled down in this rush to do A.T. & T.'s bidding. The first two concern the genuine private enterprise which still exists in the interstices and on the margins of our economy. Only through a publicly-owned space authority could all communications concerns be assured of a chance to use these revolutionary new facilities. Only through such an authority could the smaller independent manufacturers hope to prevent this huge potential market for equipment from being pre-empted by A.T. & T.'s own wholly owned equipment subsidiary, Western Electric, and its allies. Here the myth of free enterprise is being used to destroy its reality. The new communications satellite corporation created by the House will be a legalized cartel.

A third basic consideration is in the sphere of foreign relations. These satellite systems require international agreements. Their negotiation interlocks with many other aspects of public policy. The responsibility for these should be in the hands of the government.

The original bill proposed by the Administration kept the conduct of these negotiations in the State Department. The bill, as rewritten in response to A.T. & T. pressure and weakly accepted by the Kennedy Administration, merely provides that the State Department be "advised." Congressman Celler offered an amendment from the floor giving the President the same veto power over this new communications corporation that he has over the Civil Aeronautics Board in so far as international transportation is concerned. This was brushed aside. To all such sobering considerations there was a continuous mythical refrain. "This," as Congressman Roudebush said in a paean of support for this giveaway bill, "is the free enterprise way; this is the capitalistic way; this is the profit system way; and this is the American way." This equates Big Steals by Big Corporations with "the American way." No satirist could top that one.

The reason for rushing the bill now is to give the monopolists the inside track in this first great peacetime space venture. This is really a New Frontier, but in confronting it the Kennedy Administration shows its incapacity to think in terms which fit the phrase, the very banner it has chosen. Mr. Kennedy gave up the battle in his letter last February 7 to those other two pioneering pillars of this Administration, Vice-President Johnson and Speaker McCormack, when he said space communications was a subject "which, by nature, is essentially private enterprise in character." From this patent fallacy flowed the surrender to A.T. & T. Communications have long been notoriously monopolistic on earth. The whole idea of handing over communications in space to the same private monopolists will strike other nations as absurdly anachronistic.

The only chance to block this steal now is in the Senate where seven senators led by Kefauver are proposing that a publicly-owned Communications Satellite Authority be established to guarantee technological progress and the public interest in the skies. An even more fundamental issue is involved. It is whether our country can, on great occasions other than the making and preparing for war, mobilize its full strength free from doctrinaire considerations, whether it can operate in the pragmatic way which is supposed to be our best tradition. In the years to come, in competition with the forced draft industrial expansion of the Socialist countries, our country's future growth and greatness will depend on its ability to plan in a big way, and to carry through vast enterprises under public direction, for peaceful purposes. The issue is not public vs. private enterprise. The problem is to free real enterprise, public and private, from shortsighted private monopolies. This is the full magnitude of the issue soon to come before the Senate.

MAY 14, 1962

43: *The Supreme Court Retreats*

THE BALANCING DOCTRINE OF FELIX FRANKFURTER

A new majority on the United States Supreme Court is beating a hasty retreat from the liberal decisions of the last few years on fundamental liberties and Negro rights. Two 5-to-4 decisions handed down last Monday give the signal for resumption of the witch hunt by congressional committees and their "little un-American" imitators in the states. A third decision indicated to the South that the Court is being softened up on the race issue. The Barenblatt decision gives the House Un-American Activities Committee judicial approval beyond Walter's dreams. The Uphaus decision, written by Tom Clark, not only grants a similar amplitude of authority to state witch hunts but spells out sharply the limits of the *Nelson* case, indicating point by point all the states may do to harass radicals. This will be read in the South as a mandate for white supremacists. The Virginia NAACP case abdicates the special jurisdiction of the federal courts in civil rights cases and makes easier the South's strategy of nullification by prolonged litigation. Monday, June 8, was a black day in the history of the Court.

The sharp shift rightward occurred when the supposedly liberal Frankfurter and the conservative Harlan abandoned the position they took in the Watkins case two years ago and carried the two new judges, Whittaker and Stewart, with them. When the Court ruled 7-1 against the House committee in the Watkins case, Clark was the only dissenter. Whittaker did not participate; Stewart was not yet on the Court. Frankfurter concurred in a separate opinion. Now the Court, in upholding the Barenblatt conviction, is 5-to-4 the other way. It is Frankfurter who deserves most to be criticized for the shift. In deserting the liberals more openly than at any other time in his tortuous judicial course, Frankfurter provided not only the swing vote but the philosophy for the victorious reaction.

The new majority does not deny that the law establishing the Un-American Committee abridges basic freedoms. But it says that where First Amendment rights are asserted "resolution of the issue always involves a balancing by the courts of the competing private and public interests at stake."

This "balancing" theory is Frankfurter's pernicious contribution to constitutional law. It cuts the heart out of the First Amendment. "To apply the Court's balancing test under such circumstances," Mr. Justice Black protested for the minority, "is to read the First Amendment to say, 'Congress shall make no law abridging freedom of speech, press, assembly and petition, unless Congress and the Supreme Court reach the joint conclusion that on balance the interest of the government in stifling these freedoms is greater than the interest of the people in having them exercised.' " It is Frankfurter, with his reputation as a liberal and a scholar, who has recruited a new rightist majority by winning Harlan and the two newer judges over to this doctrine. Felix Frankfurter betrayed the cause of liberty in America last Monday.

The new syllogism starts with the Frankfurter thesis that abridgment is constitutional if reasonable and proceeds to the minor premise that regulation is reasonable if it is aimed at Communists. The conclusion is that the witch hunters may do pretty much as they please so long as they claim to be hunting Communists. The effect is to outlaw the Communist party, a step (as Black points out) which Congress has several times refused to take, and to declare unlawful ideas which may be regarded as communistic. Harlan for the majority bases this on the "right of self-preservation," that oldest and mangiest crotchet of despotic government. "That notion," Black points out in a dissent which will rank as a classic in the literature of freedom, "rests on the unarticulated premise that this nation's security hangs upon its power to punish people because of what they think, speak or write about, or because of those with whom they associate for political purposes. The government in its brief virtually admits this position when it speaks of the 'communication of unlawful ideas.' I challenge this premise, and deny that ideas can be proscribed under our Constitution."

By now, after the experience of the McCarthy years, few will be naïve enough to suppose that the outlawry of the Communists is of importance only to that broken little faction of elderly sectarians. The fear of being suspected of sympathy with them has cast a pall on public discussion of all the most momentous issues before us as a people. A whole generation of intellectuals has moved into a sterile suburbia and abdicated its rights and duties in order to escape the witch hunt. The mild recovery which followed on the censure of McCarthy and the liberal decisions of the Warren court is now jeopardized. The test is the test of the people. The Congress has been afraid to vote against the House committee and Eastland's Senate counterpart on internal security. Many in Congress hoped the Court would dispose of these odoriferous vehicles for crypto-fascism. Now the Court has surrendered, too. Almost two centuries ago, Alexander Hamilton, defending in the Federalist Papers (Number LXXXIV) the absence of a Bill of Rights in the original draft of the Constitution, warned that the most explicit guarantee of speech and press could be twisted by legalistic exegesis into authority for the very restrictions it forbade. The Frankfurter doctrine fulfills the Hamiltonian prophecy. Hamilton also argued that basic liberties depend ultimately on "the general spirit of the people." If their concern for freedom decays, he wrote, no Bill of Rights can preserve it.

This, then, is the challenge to ourselves and our neighbors. Will there be sufficient intelligence and courage to preserve what an earlier generation established with so much insight and sacrifice? We urge the widest possible circulation in discussion groups of the Black dissent in *Barenblatt* and the Brennan dissent in *Uphaus*. We urge support for all victims of the witch hunt. We urge a national emergency conference to defend the First Amendment. We believe the fight can be won despite cowardice in Congress and betrayal in the Supreme Court if enough people bestir themselves. The fight for peace cannot be won if the fight for free discussion is lost.

JUNE 15, 1959

SEX UPSETS THE COURT

Three decisions Monday showed that the liberals are not yet permanently in a minority of four. Justice Potter Stewart tipped the scales by joining Warren, Black, Douglas and Brennan in ruling against the use of "faceless informers" in loyalty-security cases, in reversing the suspension from practice imposed on defense counsel in the Hawaii Smith Act trials, and in finding a clear First Amendment issue in the censoring of the film *Lady Chatterley's Lover,* where the Court was unanimous in upholding the film but bitterly split and even fragmented in charting the legal route to the agreed result. The most important of these three cases was the decision in *Greene v. McElroy,* which involved an appeal from an engineer whose career in industry had been ruined by anonymous accusation in a typical industrial security procedure.

The Greene case is another example of the way in which the cold war, with the enhanced power it gives the military and the secret police, is eating away the foundations of our free society. Justice Clark, who sees the world very much as does J. Edgar Hoover, protested in his lone dissent that no one has a constitutional right of access "to the government's military secrets." But that is not the real issue. The real issue must be seen in the context of a situation in which the category of government secrets is spreading all over the bureaucratic and industrial landscape; our military mania for secrecy is beginning to approach Russian proportions. Some three million workers in industry are directly affected by industrial clearance procedures. Ordinary clearance alone does not means access to top secrets, and top secret clearance is hedged about by need-to-know regulations which require even the most politically purified and homogenized to show special need for specific information. In this context can the government set up what purports to be a fair trial procedure for clearance and ruin a man as disloyal without giving him a chance to confront and cross-examine his accusers? A man does not have a right to see military secrets but he does have a right to protect his reputation and livelihood from kangaroo court destruction by faceless informers. The government may arbitrarily shut off access to secrets. But when it pretends to try a man, may it do so unfairly? This is the issue.

The situation is made worse when the screening is in the hands of a secret police network which regards any liberal or do-gooder as *prima facie* suspect. The test of political reliability here, as the facts in the Greene case again demonstrate, is a stodgy conformity, just as in the Soviet Union. Any contact with Russians—like any Russian contact with Americans in Moscow—puts a damning stain on a man's reputation no amount of evidence can later erase. Attending social functions at the Russian Embassy in Washington 1944-47 and meeting at that time with Russian officials were among the counts against Greene, though top-level executives of his company "whose right to clearance [the Court says] was never challenged" corroborated his testimony that he was trying to sell his company's products. Another count against Greene was that in 1947 he attended the Third Annual Dinner of the Southern Conference for Human Welfare. "This dinner," says a footnote to the decision, "was also attended by many Washington notables, including several members of this Court." The weight attached to the scuttlebutt collected by the FBI from unknown informants seems to have varied with the atmosphere. Clearance was three times given Greene *before* the Korean War (top secret in February, 1950) and then revoked in November, 1951. It was restored in 1952 after a hearing but revoked again in 1953 when McCarthy's shadow fell across the Pentagon.

The determination of loyalty is obviously far from being a science. The value of allowing confrontation and cross-examination is that, as in any other proceeding, they are the best method we have for sifting out error, mistaken identity, false accusation and malice. Though these cases are usually discussed as if only the accused had an interest in the outcome, the public has an interest in keeping the atmosphere of free discussion from being poisoned by fear of informers, and the government has an interest in keeping the services of valuable people like Greene, who had done good work for the Navy in the fields of electronics and rocket launchers. If informers are kept anonymous, irresponsible gossip is encouraged and, among the so-called "professional informers," psychopathic liars are long shielded from view, as has now been demonstrated in a number of proceedings where notorious FBI undercover spies had to stand up in the witness box.

The divisions in the Court are nowhere more evident than in the way it agreed unanimously—in six separate opinions—that the film, *Lady Chatterley's Lover*, was not obscene. Justice Frankfurter quoted D. H. Lawrence in favor of censoring pornography and used the film as a peg on which to expound his theory of regulation under the First Amendment. Justice Potter Stewart, for a five-man majority, declared in full-blown Holmes-Brandeis accents that the First Amendment protects advocacy of adultery as well as socialism. Black joined in that opinion, in a separate opinion by Douglas opposing all censorship as prior restraint and in a third opinion of his own (as the only Justice who had not seen the film) objecting that precedent would require the Court to "appraise each movie, on a case by case method." We have rarely seen the Court so overheated. Sex seems to be worse even than communism for judicial composure.

JULY 6, 1959

UNDERCUTTING THE FIRST AMENDMENT

The deep cleft within the Supreme Court on First Amendment rights was again visible in the California obscenity case decided last week. On one side, Mr. Justice Black believes that the First Amendment means what it says, that Congress shall make "no law . . . abridging the freedom of speech or of the press" and that the word "liberty" in the Fourteenth Amendment, which binds the state legislatures, must be read almost as strictly. On the other side, Mr. Justice Frankfurter would blur the clear mandate of the First Amendment by reading it as if it said that the interest in free expression can be balanced against other interests of the community.

The "balancing" doctrine invites exceptions. The exceptions as they accumulate undermine fundamental safeguards. Sometimes the motives may seem good or bad, but the net effect is the same. Mr. Justice Frankfurter's first major success was the Beauharnais case in 1952. With Jackson, Black, Douglas and Reed dissenting, Frankfurter wrote a 5-4 decision upholding an Illinois racial libel law. There he balanced the interest in free speech against the interest in racial peace. Two years ago, on the issue of obscene literature, he won over the otherwise liberal Mr. Justice Brennan to the "balancing" doctrine in the Roth case. There the interest in a free press was balanced against a public interest in suppressing pornographic literature.

In the California case, the Court was unanimous in agreeing that the California obscene literature statute was unconstitutional, but the court split five ways in reaching the result. The position most favorable to censorship was taken by Mr. Justice Frankfurter, who insists on interpreting the First Amendment in the light of the eighteenth-century common law though the purpose of the Amendment was to make sure that the English law's restrictive doctrines in politics, morality and religion would not be applicable to speech and press in this country. Mr. Justice Brennan held the California law void on a thin technicality easily remedied by those who want censorship. In the very act of opposing censorship in this case, the majority repeated the "balancing" doctrine which opens the way to it in others. Mr. Justice Brennan quoted the words he used two years ago in the Roth decision saying "the door barring federal and state intrusion" into the area of free speech and press "must be kept tightly closed and opened only the slightest crack necessary to prevent encroachment upon more important interests."

It is these "slight cracks" which Mr. Justice Black fears. "What," he asks, "are the 'more important' interests for the protection of which constitutional freedoms of speech and press must be given second place?" He wants to know what is the standard "by which one can determine when abridgment of speech and press goes 'too far.' " He sees censorship as "the deadly enemy of freedom and progress" and protests, "the plain language of the Constitution forbids it." He warns, "While it is 'obscenity and indecency' before us today, the experience of mankind—both ancient and modern— shows that this type of elastic phrase can, and most likely will, be synonymous with the political, and maybe with the religious unorthodoxy of tomorrow."

The "balancing" theory has already borne bitter fruit in the political field. The Barenblatt and Uphaus decisions were based on the view that the right of Congress or the states to investigate supposed Communist conspiracy overbalanced the inhibitory effect of witch hunt investigations on First Amendment freedoms. The day the Court handed down the California decision, Dr. Willard Uphaus was sentenced to one year in jail in New Hampshire for refusing to hand over to a Red-hunting Attorney General a list of guests at his "peace fellowship" camp in that state. Some thirty others are headed for jail under the interpretation of the First Amendment applied in the Barenblatt and Uphaus decisions. In the case of one of them, Carl Braden, the Fifth Circuit Court of Appeals in Atlanta a few days before showed how effective a weapon this placed in the hands of Southern white racists. (The same circuit has since upheld the conviction of Frank Wilkinson.)

The Fifth Circuit upheld Mr. Braden's conviction for contempt of the Un-American Activities Committee. He had refused on First Amendment grounds to answer questions about his activities on behalf of racial justice in the South. The Court ruled that "Legislative purposes might be furthered by a determination of whether organizations ostensibly active in championing timely objectives, such as integration and civil rights, are in fact being used for the spread of the propaganda of a foreign-dominated Communist organization with subversive designs. . . . One who is known or believed to be a Communist and is suspected of being engaged in un-American activities does not acquire immunity by adopting the role of a racial integrationist."

This, which applies the "balancing" doctrine as embodied in *Barenblatt,* is made to order for southern bigots who see the struggle of the Negro for full emancipation as a Red plot. They can use congressional and state witch hunt committees to pillory every man, white or black, who fights for racial justice.

DECEMBER 21, 1959

DAISY BATES VS. LITTLE ROCK

At first glance the Supreme Court's decision in *Daisy Bates v. Little Rock* seems to uphold the right of political privacy. The Court was unanimous in reversing the conviction of NAACP officials who refused to furnish city officials the names of their members. The Court upheld their plea "that the public disclosure of our members and contributors might lead to their harassment, economic reprisals, and even bodily harm." Mr. Justice Stewart for the Court said it was now "beyond dispute that freedom of association for the purpose of advancing ideas and airing grievances is protected by the due process clause of the Fourteenth Amendment from invasion by the states." He quoted from the similar case of *NAACP v. Alabama* two years ago: "Inviolability of privacy in group association may in many circumstances be indispensable to preservation of freedom of association, particularly where a group espouses dissident beliefs." On its face this appears to reaffirm traditional liberties.

But more closely examined what the Court really said is that it will uphold the right of privacy to protect dissident groups only when they are not too dissident for the taste of the majority. The meaning of the decision becomes clearer if one turns to the concurring opinion by Black and Douglas. They felt that the Arkansas ordinances "violate freedom of speech and assembly guaranteed by the First Amendment which the Court has many times held was made applicable to the states by the Fourteenth." They argued "that First Amendment rights are beyond abridgment either by legislation that directly restrains their exercise or by suppression or impairment through harassment, humiliation, or exposure by government."

The majority approach was different. It proceeded not from the clear words of the First Amendment but from the "balancing" doctrine of Mr. Justice Frankfurter. As Mr. Justice Stewart said, "Where there is a significant encroachment upon personal liberty, the state may prevail only upon showing a subordinating interest which is compelling." When basic freedoms are threatened, Mr. Justice Stewart said, "it becomes the duty of this Court to determine whether the action bears a reasonable relationship to the achievement of the governmental purposes asserted as its justification." The Court did not think these asserted purposes sufficient to outweigh the NAACP's rights.

This is the fourth case in four years which has dealt with the right of the states to intrude on political privacy. They provide an illuminating pattern. In June, 1957, the Court held (Clark dissenting) that the state of New Hampshire could not send Paul Sweezy to jail for refusing to answer questions about his associates in the Progressive party. In June, 1958, Mr. Justice Harlan held that the NAACP could not be punished for contempt because it refused to obey an Alabama judge's order to disclose its members. Pointedly, he based his decision on his own concurring opinion (with Frankfurter) in *Sweezy* where Harlan made much of the fact that Sweezy had not refused to answer questions about his relations with the Communist party, but only with the (supposedly less subversive) Progressive party. Then last June, Harlan and Frankfurter joined in the 5-to-4 decision by Mr. Justice Clark which upheld a year's sentence on Dr. Willard Uphaus for refusing to give New Hampshire a list of the guests at his Peace Fellowship camp. Here the majority held that First Amendment rights were outweighed by the state's need "to determine whether there were subversive persons in New Hampshire."

This implies that the First Amendment does not apply to "subversives" and the test is what five judges consider as falling within that vague witch hunter's category. In the South today the NAACP is the number one subversive organization and the Arkansas Supreme Court in that climate found it easy to uphold the Little Rock ordinances. A United States Supreme Court with a Dixiecrat majority would have found it just as easy by using the Frankfurter doctrine to balance away the NAACP's liberties. This doctrine substitutes the political prejudices and fears of a shifting majority for the unambiguous mandate of the First Amendment. Presently it allows political privacy, but only to those views not considered too dangerous.

FEBRUARY 29, 1960

BALANCING AWAY THE FIFTH AMENDMENT

The Supreme Court has chosen an ill-timed moment to throw new victims to the House Un-American Activities Committee. The lost appeals of the two social workers in *Nelson and Globe* v. *California* come just when Chairman Walter and his colleagues, by attacking the National Council of Churches in the affair of the Air Force manual, have been demonstrating how closely their activities duplicate McCarthy's. The implication that the armed forces are soft on communism, and our country's largest Protestant organization suspect for subversion, seems a replay of the McCarthy era. At such a time, when the menace of the committee, its ignorance and arrogance, are clearer than ever, the Supreme Court has in effect reversed the Slochower decision, reducing the area of protection afforded witnesses by the Fifth Amendment.

In *Slochower* four years ago, Mr. Justice Clark said in a 5-to-4 decision (with Harlan, Reed, Burton and Minton dissenting) that the privilege against self-incrimination "would be reduced to a hollow mockery" if regarded as a confession of guilt and made the basis for discharge. Now in the case of Arthur Globe (with Black, Douglas and Brennan dissenting; Warren abstaining), Mr. Justice Clark says Globe was fired not for taking the Fifth but for "insubordination," since he had been instructed by Los Angeles authorities under state law to answer questions asked him by the committee. This deserves a place in the primers of logic. You cannot fire a man for taking the Fifth but you can fire him for disobeying an order *not* to take the Fifth! No matter how you slice it this still comes out as punishing a man for using a privilege given him by the Constitution. It is another step in the whittling away process begun in 1958 when two Justices who had dissented in *Slochower* won Clark and Frankfurter to their side with ingenious subterfuges for circumventing that decision, and tipped the Court 5-to-4 the other way. Mr. Justice Harlan in *Lerner* v. *Casey* upheld the dismissal of a New York subway guard on the ground that while he had a right to take the Fifth this showed "lack of candor." Similarly Mr. Justice Burton in *Beilan* v. *Board of Education* upheld the dismissal of a Philadelphia schoolteacher on the ground that taking the Fifth proved "incompetency" as a teacher. These holdings enrich the literature of sophistry.

In the Slochower case, Mr. Justice Clark began with a statement of the Frankfurter "balancing" theory. The problem, Clark said, lay in "balancing the state's interest in the loyalty of those in its service" against the "traditional safeguards of individual rights." He decided that Professor Harry Slochower's invocation of the Fifth Amendment was not proper grounds for discharge because the questions asked him by the Senate Internal Security Committee bore no relation to his duties as a teacher and because his membership in the Communist party twelve years earlier had long been disclosed to the New York City Board of Education. The facts in the case of the Los Angeles social workers remarkably parallel those of *Slochower*. California, like New York City, has a law making refusal to answer, grounds for dismissal from public employment. The questions asked the social workers by the Un-American Activities Committee bore no relation to their duties. The dark spots in their political past were known to their employers. They had been investigated, had taken loyalty oaths and could have been prosecuted if the House committee had any new evidence. Their hearing, like Slochower's, sensationally exploited the rehash of stale material in a context where witnesses may have feared that if they did not take the Fifth on all political questions they might be held to have waived their privilege and been called upon to name others. A careful review of the record indicates that Mr. Globe's skeleton-in-the-closet was association with the John Reed Club (misspelt John *Reid* in the Court's opinion as in the committee records) when he was in college. Mr. Nelson's was membership in the United Public Workers from 1942 to 1944. Neither is exactly a crime.

These cases illustrate the unpredictable mysteries of the "balancing" process. Why, when the facts were so alike, did the shifting majority balance the scales so differently in 1960 from 1956? What were the Justices, in fact, balancing? No question of security was involved for California. On a genuine balance, the country's need for curbing the committee outweighs risks far more real than those disclosed in these new appeals. Were Frankfurter, Harlan and Clark really balancing their own conception of what is politic, their desire to appease rightist critics of the Court, against the urgent necessity to stop the steady erosion of constitutional safeguards?

MARCH 7, 1960

THE INTERNAL SECURITY ACT UPHELD

The heart of the intricate and savage Internal Security Act lies in the registration provisions which the Supreme Court upheld 5-to-4 last Monday. These rest in turn, to a considerable degree, on proof by parallelism. That is to say, the Subversive Activities Control Board set up by the act, in determining which organizations must register with it as communistic, studies the extent to which they follow party line. This is what led President Truman in vetoing the measure on September 22, 1950 to say:

"Obviously, if this law were on the statute books, the part of prudence would be to avoid saying anything that might be construed by someone as not deviating sufficiently from the current Communist propaganda line. And since no one could be sure in advance what views were safe to express, the inevitable tendency would be to express no views on controversial subjects."

A Congress afraid to vote against anything labeled anti-Communist passed it over Truman's veto. Among those voting to override in the House were Nixon and Kennedy, the former a sponsor of this measure, long known as the Mundt-Nixon bill.

The Supreme Court's decision will hurt the best interests of the United States in three ways. The first and most important was that indicated by the Truman veto message. The decision will tend to inhibit political discussion and activity. The inhibitory potential of the Act takes on formidable outlines as one examines its ingeniously interlocked provisions. Its area of jurisdiction, like Dante's Hell, is divided into various degrees of damnation. Three categories of organizations are made subject to the inquisitorial eye of the Subversive Activities Control Board—the very name would make Jefferson wince. The condemned are divided into Communist "action," Communist "front" and Communist "infiltrated" organizations. All three are required to wear the scarlet letter; they are forbidden to mail any publication or other communication or make any radio or TV broadcast without plainly labeling it as "disseminated by [name], a Communist organization." The first two categories must register, and on registering their members lose the right to travel (even *application* for a passport becomes a crime), to work in defense facilities, or to hold government jobs; they are, in short, reduced to second-class citizens. Communist "action" organizations, though not the other two categories, must register their members as well as their officers, and failure to register is punishable by Draconian penalties: a fine of $10,000 *and* a prison sentence of five years may be imposed for *each day* of failure to register. A delay of 30 days could mean a fine of $300,000 and 150 years in jail; longevity will henceforth be a prime requirement for American radicals. Such sanctions will not encourage marching in May Day parades.

The second way in which the Supreme Court hurt our country was in defacing its "image" abroad. Even in the most despotic country, every citizen is free to *agree* with the government. The test is freedom to oppose it, and to oppose it fundamentally. Just as there will be no freedom in the Soviet bloc until there is freedom to be *anti*-Communist, so the measure of freedom here is the freedom to *be* Communist.

"If there be any among us," Jefferson said in his first Inaugural, "who would wish to dissolve this Union or to change its Republican form of government, let them stand undisturbed as monuments of the safety with which error of opinion may be tolerated where reason is left free to combat it." If there be any such among us today they'd better hurry down and register. Mr. Justice Frankfurter and his four colleagues no longer have that same faith in reason. We are participants in a slow degeneration from the faith that once made America a shining light in the eyes of mankind. In a country where freedom of the press was regarded as a foundation stone of liberty, we now have an act which requires of all registered organizations the "listing, in such form and detail as the Attorney General shall by regulation prescribe, of all printing presses and machines including but not limited to rotary presses . . . offsets . . . ditto machines . . . or any mechanical devices . . . capable of being used to produce or publish printed matter or material."

One would have to go to the statute books of the Franco or Salazar regimes to match this meticulous frenzy in fear of the printed word. Is this America?

JUNE 12, 1961

44: *Debut of the New Frontier*

IF ONLY JOHN F. KENNEDY WERE IN HANS CHRISTIAN ANDERSEN

The new President and the lovely new young First Lady are as charming as any Prince and Princess out of a childhood book of fairy tales. How could one's heart help but warm to them and to wish them well? There is a divinity that doth hedge Presidents as well as Kings, and there must be few of us who do not hope deep down that by some magic this new monarch's wand will wave away our ills. The primitive superstition close beneath the surface of our selves suffuses the beginning of a new reign or Administration with an almost religious festivity; the bands play, the troops march; past errors are wiped away, the country is reborn for a fresh start.

Eight years ago the country could place its reliance on the father image of an old soldier. Now our talisman is a youthful St. George, who can slay the dragon or charm him away. The mood was deepened by the brisk but elevated tone, the brief but comprehensive sweep, of his Inaugural Message, above all by the unmistakable zest of his "I do not shrink from this responsibility—I welcome it." And there he was—the eager beaver—at the White House early and on time next morning, fresh after only a few hours sleep, a young man determined to make good in a new job. He didn't even take his Sunday off. This young man should go far. After a part-time President, away on sick leave or vacation much of the time, this *was* a change.

In the euphoric post-Inaugural atmosphere sober reflection seems sacrilegious. Right and left, there is applause for the Inaugural Address. How could it please such diverse people? The secret lies both in the new President and in ourselves. The Inaugural Message had something in it for everybody. At one point it seemed to promise a step up in the cold war, at another an intensified search for peace.

At one point there was cheer for those who want greater arms expenditures—"only when our arms are sufficient beyond doubt" (more billions?) "can we be certain beyond doubt that they will never be employed." But the very next paragraph offered cheer to the advocates of disarmament—"both sides overburdened by the cost of modern weapons, both rightly alarmed by the steady spread of the deadly atom, yet both racing to alter that uncertain balance of terror that stays the hand of mankind's final war." But how can arms be made sufficient beyond doubt when both sides are racing to alter an uncertain balance of terror? Logically these propositions cancel each other out. But each of us assumes that the proposition with which we disagree was put in as eyewash for our adversaries. So wishful thinking shuts off the inner ear, and it does not register what we do not wish to hear.

A little sleight-of-hand, a certain modicum of chicanery, are inseparable from the governance of men. Mr. Kennedy was after all the nominee of the Democratic party; he was not elected by acclamation at a convention of idealists and pacifists; he must keep very disparate elements happy, though perhaps only happily deceived, if he is to achieve a sufficient common denominator in the party and the country for effective action. He is a President, not a dictator, and any man as either is still a prisoner of the habitual; men can only be moved a little way beyond the familiar. Mr. Kennedy gives every indication of being the greatest master of manipulative politics since FDR, no mean man at razzle-dazzle. It is a necessary quality, and we must be patient. But in being patient there is no reason to shut our eyes to realities. Mr. Kennedy, for all his activism, seems to be a rather cautious perhaps even conventional man. He will grow; he reads; he can be reached; he has potentials of sympathy and of vision. But at the outset of his Administration the key posts are occupied by much the same types representing much the same forces as under Mr. Eisenhower. Mr. Kennedy as a politician in his dealings with Congress, the military bureaucracy and the moneyed powers of the country instinctively looks for the winning combination, the line of least resistance. This is not good enough to cope with an increasingly unstable world, long and ludicrously outgrown its nation-state diapers, menaced by the religious fanaticism of competing, oversimplified and delusive ideologies. Only unconventional measures can possibly get mankind away from the brink.

To see how little signs there are of these unconventional measures one has only to ask what was the meaning of Mr. Kennedy's declaration that "we shall pay any price . . . to assure the survival and the success of liberty." Does this mean that we are prepared to pay the price of giving up sugar, banana or oil interests in Latin America to show our neighbors how they can end poverty within the framework of a free society? Above all are we ready to pay the price of adopting those wide measures of social reconstruction to replace the arms race and save liberty from the garrison state? Or will we find ourselves ultimately asked to bear the burden of piling up more arms in the fallacious search for that new delusion, a balanced nuclear deterrent?

JANUARY 30, 1961

45: *No Way to Hide*

ALMOST AS SAFE AS IVORY SOAP IS PURE?

Crisis is piling on crisis, instabilities mount in an unstable world, frustration is added to frustration. At such a time it is dangerous to spread the illusion that thermonuclear war may be a way out, a cleansing thunderstorm in the planet's humid summer, or a cathartic that would magically purge our ills, if only we are ready to spend a cramped week or two in underground shelters, emerging on a world from which communism had happily disappeared but where free enterprise was all set to go again. As if orchestrated out of Washington, mass circulation media are beginning to condition the public mind for nuclear war. The *Saturday Evening Post* inaugurates a new department, "The Voice of Dissent," with a piece by that favorite iconoclast of the Air Force, Herman Kahn. The Associated Press sends out a series of interviews with Dr. Edward Teller on how exaggerated are fears of thermonuclear war. *U.S. News & World Report* runs a cheerful cover piece, "If Bombs Do Fall," *

* "What about money? asks *U.S. News & World Report*. Instead of destroying all old bills that are taken out of circulation, the Government is storing money away in strongboxes around the country. Enough $1 bills have been saved to last 8 months. . . . Bank accounts safe? Plans are being worked

with a side story from Japan on how well the survivors of Hiroshima
and Nagasaki are doing. *Life* magazine puts a civilian in a reddish
fallout suit looking like a partially boiled lobster on its cover, with
the glad tidings, "How You Can Survive Fallout. 97 Out of 100
People Can Be Saved. . . ."

No doubt the purpose is to make our threat of going to war
over Berlin credible to Khrushchev, as indeed it should. Our ultimate weapon, Madison Avenue, may be able to sell anything to the
American people, even the notion—why fool around with aspirin?
—that one little bullet through the head and that headache will
disappear. Some years back, the Pentagon and popular magazines
were advertising how many Russian cities we could "take out" if
necessary. Now the same moral imbecility is being applied to our
own cities. "About five million people," *Life* says lightly, "less than
3% of the population, would die." It adds hastily, to anticipate any
vestigial humane twinges, "This in itself is a ghastly number. But
you have to look at it coldly. . . ." *Life* has been telling us right-
eously that the godless Chinese Reds put little value on human life.
Mao is willing to see millions die to wipe out capitalism but Henry
Luce is willing to see millions die to wipe out communism. Kennedy, like Khrushchev, prepares the public mind to gamble all, if
necessary, on Berlin. This is the real mobilization. Our moral
scruples and our good sense must first be conscripted.

Worse than the horror is the levity, the transparent mendacity
and the eager commercialism. A happy family with three children
is shown by *Life* in their well-stocked, assemble-it-yourself, pre-
fabricated steel shelter, only seven hundred dollars from the Kelsey-
Hayes Company (and soon to be marketed by Sears, Roebuck). A
picture shows a girl laughingly talking on the phone from an underground shelter, as if to her beau, who is presumably in his own
shelter and ready to take her to the latest movie as soon as the all
clear sounds. Grandmother's old-fashioned remedies turn out to be
best after all even in thermonuclear war. "The best first aid for
radiation sickness," *Life* advises, "is to take hot tea or a solution of
baking soda." Suddenly thermonuclear war is made to seem familiar, almost cozy. All you need is a shelter, a well-stocked pantry,
some new gadgets like Geiger counters. The budding boom in these

out to enable you to write checks on your bank account—even if the bank
itself were destroyed."

products promises to stimulate badly lagging magazine linage. *Life's* editorial hopes Khrushchev notices "our spontaneous boom in shelter-building" and concludes euphorically, "He cannot doubt our ability to wage nuclear war, or to erase his cities." Aren't we getting our people ready to accept the erasure of ours? We used to think thermonuclear war likely only if lunatics came to power. Well, here they are.

I am not arguing for surrender, a runout on Berlin, dishonor, national cowardice, appeasement or better-red-than-dead. I am trying to say that when a nation faces problems as complex as those which now face ours in Germany, the United Nations, the Congo, Laos and the resumption of nuclear testing, there is a duty on every publisher and every writer to help inculcate sobriety and the need for reflection. The President's power to maneuver and negotiate is not helped by piling delusion upon hysteria, by making people feel not only that we face a simple choice of death-or-surrender but that most of us won't die anyway—so why bother to negotiate?

Why should President Kennedy lend his name to *Life's* wicked stunt? Nowhere does *Life* tell us what level and kind of attack it assumes which need kill only 3 percent of our people. The latest Rand study in the new Holifield committee hearings shows 3 percent dead as the result of "a very small attack delivering 300 megatons" on military targets exclusively. Even this small attack, if aimed at our cities, would put inescapable death (with everyone in some shelter) up to 35 percent. The same study (p. 216, House Government Operations, Civil Defense, August, 1961) shows a 3,000-megaton attack on cities would put inescapable deaths up to 80 percent. The new Holifield report on these hearings says than an attack half this size, as assumed by Secretary McNamara, would kill fifty million Americans and seriously injury twenty million more. The report warns that the existing basement space on which the Secretary relies to save ten to fifteen million lives won't do. "All deaths from fallout can be prevented," the report says, "but not in existing buildings, even when improved. Nation-wide, the largest number of structures do not afford even the bare minimum factor considered necessary to bring the radiation hazard down to tolerable levels."

Stewart Alsop's "Report Card" on Kennedy in the *Saturday Evening Post* September 16 disclosed that the President told congressional leaders a new war would cost 70,000,000 dead Americans. Even Dr. Teller did not go beyond saying that 90 percent of our population could be saved. Where did *Life* get that 97 percent? Was it a copywriter's bright flash? Just as Ivory Soap is sold as 99 percent pure, is thermonuclear war to be sold as 97 percent safe?

SEPTEMBER 25, 1961

IS THIS HOW KENNEDY WAGES A PEACE RACE?

The new Defense Department pamphlet on fallout protection begins with what might be termed a commercial. "The purpose of this booklet," it says, "is to help save lives if a nuclear attack should ever come to America. The foreign and defense policies of your Government make such an attack unlikely, and to keep it unlikely is their most important aim. It is for this reason that we have devoted so large an effort to creating and maintaining our deterrent forces." This is smooth press agentry for the military, but it hardly fits the testimony in the daily headlines. Our foreign policies keep us on the brink of war in a half-dozen far places from Vietnam to Berlin. Our military policies are based upon a nuclear arms race which even many military men agree must lead to a nuclear war. The effect of the pamphlet is to condition the public mind for the disaster these policies make inevitable. In the name of civil defense, our brains are being washed.

Even a paper as firmly enlisted in the cold war as the *Baltimore Sun* (January 2) finds that "the tone of the whole booklet, whatever it may say specifically, is to suggest that safety in a nuclear attack is really rather easy and quite neat." The times call for the widest public discussion of the need to end the arms race and create a new world order. Only a few months ago the President was talking of a "peace race." Instead all the facilities of the Defense Department for molding public opinion—it has energetic branches which suggest and arrange stories for TV, the radio, the films, magazines and newspapers—have been put to work since last spring selling the shelter delusion. It is appalling to learn from the *New York Times* (December 31) that the preparation of this fallout pamphlet was originally entrusted to a team from Time, Inc., headed by Edward Thompson, managing editor of *Life* magazine, which last September 15 published (with an approving letter from Mr. Kennedy) that Pied Piperish sensation "How You Can Survive Fallout. 97 Out of 100 People Can Be Saved." The *Time-Life* crowd is notoriously unreliable as to facts: the home office's capacity for distorting the news it gets from the field is an open journalistic scandal; Henry Luce's crusade for brinksmanship, notably in the Far East, is an old story. It is bad enough that this one man should control so large a sector of American mass communications; it is worse that he is invited in to run a major propaganda campaign for the government.

It is true that the pamphlet prepared by the *Time-Life* team proved to be more than Secretary of Defense McNamara could stomach. It must have been pretty bad if this pamphlet is adjudged a more moderate version. It would be fascinating to know how the skilled *Time-Life* men made more palatable the suggestions in this pamphlet that "the water in toilet flush tanks . . . is drinkable" and that "in an emergency most canned and packaged animal foods can be eaten by humans without harm." Or to see the euphemisms with which they originally veiled the report's lame admission that while "many" of the supposed fifty million shelter spaces to be marked by the National Shelter Survey in existing buildings are in central areas "exposed to destruction by blast and fire in the event of a nuclear attack," this "space is immediately available and the cost of identification, marking and stocking is less than four dollars per space." In other words, not worth much but cheap.

From every post office the government will now be giving out this pamphlet by the millions. What needs to be driven deep into public consciousness is that there is now no alternative to peace, and that peace requires an end of international anarchy, limitations on national sovereignty and establishment of world law. This pamphlet strives on the contrary to hide from public awareness that war is now obsolete. It admits in passing that "the details of a Civil Defense Program may change with changes in the kinds of missiles that might be used against us," but it never honestly faces up to the implications. The steady growth in the size and number of nuclear missiles may soon make even the best shelter in the most distant area useless for survival. The booklet assumes a 5-megaton weapon when the Russians have already detonated a monster more than ten times that size, and claim to have 100-MT bombs. The booklet assumes a fallout-producing ground burst when it is quite possible to maximize blast and fire effects and eliminate local fallout by exploding bombs at high altitudes. A 100-MT bomb (as *Consumer Reports* for January points out) would then set afire an area as large as Vermont, and a 1,000-MT bomb would "easily do the same for an area equivalent to the states of New York, New Jersey and Pennsylvania all put together."

Even elaborate shelters with their own air and water supplies, sealed off from fire, deep enough to survive blast, somehow able to guarantee exit from under tons of rubble, would still be unable to guarantee survival in the permanently scarred and poisoned landscape that thermonuclear weapons are able to create. Harrison Brown at Denver last week estimated that United States and Russian stock piles now contain 60,000 megatons of TNT equivalent. Ralph Lapp estimated last year that an attack which dropped little more than one-tenth this amount on the United States could hopelessly poison our croplands. The Soviet farmlands are equally vulnerable. Dr. Lapp calculated an attack of 7,500 megatons (40 percent of it fission products) would render the United States unlivable. There is an upper limit of attack beyond which no civil defense is possible because the earth itself would be too poisoned radioactively to feed those left to live upon it. This level of attack is below the amounts in stock pile and within the delivery power on both sides.

During the holidays there was a burst of self-righteous indignation over India's forcible reconquest of Goa. But the real lesson has not sunk in. Each nation, in a world without law, is a law unto itself. For each the end justifies the means. Wherever an evil seems insufferably bad, the right to resort to war against it is taken for granted. We criticize India and the Afro-Asians generally for feeling that way about colonialism. But we feel and act the same way about communism, and the Soviet states react likewise when confronted by what they call capitalist imperialism. What Nehru did in Goa was less reprehensible than the secret conniving at war against Cuba by our government which has just been disclosed by the President of Guatemala. If Nehru doesn't practice what he preaches neither do we and neither does the Kremlin. The truth is that, as in civil life, the welfare of the world community demands the elimination of the habit of taking the law into one's own hands. No evil is so great as to justify resort to war, for war may mean the end of all civilization. No dispute is so sacred that it should not be subjected to arbitration by independent organs of the world community. As Bertrand Russell said in his latest book, *Has Man a Future?*, "War has so long been a part of human life that it is difficult for our feelings and our imaginations to grasp that the present anarchic national freedoms are likely to result in freedom only for corpses." It is this exercise in objectivity, it is this conditioning for universal perspectives, that our people need if our country and the world is to be saved, not a pamphlet propagating the delusion that we can play with thermonuclear fire and survive as a nation.

JANUARY 8, 1962

THE MYTHOLOGY OF THE ANTI-MISSILE MISSILE

The anti-missile missile, which has become the excuse for resumption of nuclear testing, may usefully be examined from the standpoint of mythology, as a relic of belief in the supernatural. The anti-missile missile is only the latest of those ultimate weapons on which our hopes have rested for a military miracle, in this case for something like the invisible and impenetrable cloak which enables the hero in the fairy tale to emerge victoriously unscathed from amid enemy swords and lances. This belief in an ultimate magical weapon, like other superstitions, survives all demonstration to the contrary. We had the atom bomb years before the Russians and they had both the H-bomb and the ICBM before we did, but none of these earlier ultimate weapons enabled one side to force the surrender of the other. To the delusions of the irresistible offensive is now added the delusion of the insuperable defense. We think of the anti-missile missile in terms of Buck Rogers. We see the tense comic strip panel in which our side (or theirs) says, "Their (or our) missiles are landing but our (or their) missiles have been halted in mid-flight by some mysterious new anti-missile device. There is nothing left to do but phone Khrushchev (or Kennedy) to surrender. Capitalism (or communism) has conquered the world."

This delusion reflects a faith in science which has nothing to do with a faith in the methods of experiment and reason. It is a faith in the magical potency of science, and thus little different from any primitive tribesman's belief in his witch doctor. We believe our wonder workers, if only given ample funds, will come up with some new weapon that will once and for all smash our enemies. From a sober military point of view, this faith in any one weapon is ludicrous. As General Bradley said in that speech at St. Alban's here in Washington November 5, 1957, which was so hastily buried by our opinion makers, "Missiles will bring anti-missiles, and anti-missiles will bring anti-anti-missiles. But inevitably this whole electronic house of cards will reach a point where it can be constructed no higher." The hope of an anti-missile rests on the fact that the ballistic missile follows a fixed trajectory. The hope of an anti-anti-missile rests on the possibility of changing that trajectory in mid-flight. The hope of both rests on the experience that for any weapon of war there is always a counter weapon to be found, and so on ad infinitum, that is, if the human race lasts.

All this is worth a closer explanation because the business of arranging a meeting in mid-air between a missile and an anti-missile is more complex even than arranging a meeting of minds between the White House and the Kremlin. This is how you start to construct an anti-missile. You know the missile follows a fixed curve. Therefore once it rises far enough above the radar horizon to enable you to map the beginning of the curve, you can determine the rest of the curve. The problem is to build an electronic device capable of computing this in the few minutes available, and automatically aiming your anti-missile to some intermediate point on that curve where it can hit the oncoming enemy missile before it reaches your territory. It is, as has been said crudely, like hitting a bullet with a bullet. This problem is hard enough. The real problem of the anti-missile however is much harder. It is the problem of designing an electronic network of anti-missile batteries which can cope not with one missile but with a flood of missiles accompanied by several times as many decoys, distinguishing the real from the false, and determining in split seconds which of your anti-missiles is going to be aimed at which missile.

Nobody knows whether this belongs in the realm of electronics or in Grimm's Fairy Tales as revised by General Dynamics. Dr. Hans Bethe, in that speech at Cornell on January 5 which set the arms race crowd gunning for him, said he did not think "any really effective" anti-missile was possible. "It is not very difficult," he said, "to design a defensive missile which will come close enough to an ICBM to destroy it by means of an atomic explosion. There is also no problem about providing atomic warheads for anti-missiles. But the offense can send decoys along with their missiles which are almost impossible to distinguish from the missiles, and they can send many missiles simultaneously which saturate the radars of the defense. Thus I think the AICBM [anti intercontinental ballistic missile] virtually hopeless." It is for this heresy, which threatens the biggest military boondoggle ever dangled before the electronic industry, that Dr. Bethe is under attack. The development of the Nike-Zeus anti-missile system would provide from fifteen to twenty billion dollars' worth of business. Who cares that it might be rendered obsolete before its completion by the next development, a means to change the trajectory of the missile in mid-flight, which would frustrate all the intricate computing and targeting mechanisms of Nike-Zeus?

It is in the perfection of these targeting and computing mechanisms, not in the warhead, that the secret of an anti-missile system lies. The warhead is essentially no different from the warhead of the missile. This is what makes doubly nonsensical the reports being leaked out of evidence that the Russians were testing an anti-missile. First, there is no way to determine from the debris or waves set off by a bomb whether it was being tested for missile or anti-missile purposes. Secondly, the testing of a warhead does not mean that either we or the Russians have solved the enormously intricate problem of targeting and computing for an anti-missile system. The explanations leaked out to the United States and British press are so varied as to create doubt. As in a criminal trial, too many alibis are worse than none. An accused who claims to have been (1) home in bed, (2) at a night club, and (3) only accidentally passing the scene of the crime when it happened is obviously a liar. One paper (the London *Sunday Times,* February 11) says "suspicions [i.e., of an anti-missile] have increased since the discovery that two of the Russian tests on Novaya Zemlya appear to have involved relatively small nuclear weapons above the atmosphere" while another paper (the London Sunday *Observer,* February 11) says the evidence of a Soviet anti-missile is "circumstantial." Since the United States last December successfully got a Nike-Zeus anti-missile to hit a Nike-Hercules missile "high above the White Sands proving ground in New Mexico" it is assumed (the *Observer* reports) that the Russians can do likewise!

The truth is that this anti-missile excuse for resuming testing is, as one scientist phrased it privately to us, "a publicity gimmick." The real rationale for test resumption was expressed by Assistant Secretary of State Harlan Cleveland on February 10 at Rollins College, Florida. "Given the technology of nuclear weapons," Mr. Cleveland said, "the first requisite of orderly change is to prevent our Soviet rivals from getting ahead, or thinking they can get ahead, in the hidden and costly game of nuclear deterrence." The logic is the mutually disastrous logic of any arms race. If each side aims to show the other it can never get ahead, this must push both into ever bigger arms expenditure and further along the way to garrison states; Russia, back toward Stalinism; we toward a parallel revival of paranoid suspicion and repression. But this Administration, like the Democratic party as a whole, remains committed to the arms race as the line of least resistance, as a grandiose WPA for perpetual prosperity until the bombs go off. This is what lies behind the President's impossible new condition that we will enter no new moratorium without a means to detect Russian *preparations* for new tests. (Would we be prepared to open *our* laboratories for surveillance?) We fear any proposal which might interfere with another round of testing now that the Russians have had theirs. This has to stop somewhere but we don't really want the arms race to stop. This explains the press briefings immediately held here to make sure that the release of Powers was not interpreted as an improvement in Soviet relations, and the near panic visible in the wake of Khrushchev's suggestion that the top leaders meet on disarmament. All that talk about our waging a peace race is blarney, a gift with which Mr. Kennedy is richly endowed. It is not a Russian anti-missile that the dominant alliance of the military and arms industry fears. It is their old enemy, relaxation of tension.

FEBRUARY 19, 1962

ONE WISTFUL HOPE ON A BLEAK HORIZON

Geneva

It is time the anthropologists took over, and recognized the disarmament conference as a form of religious ritual engaged in by humanity between its world wars. Not long before the last one, a disarmament conference here was within sight of unanimous agreement on a treaty to ban the bombing plane; now another is as seriously—but no more or less—discussing the abolition of the ballistic missile. This city which gave mankind palliatives as diverse as Esperanto and the Red Cross, is the Mecca of the disarmers. Of the twenty-five Swiss cantons, Geneva, true to its tradition of inextinguishable hope, was one of the four which voted yesterday forever to bar atomic arms from Swiss territory. The Catholic, conservative and German-speaking cantons, however, swamped the socialistic French-speaking Protestant areas and the initiative was rejected almost two to one. The delegates, reconvening this morning for the third week of the current disarmament conference, read in their morning Swiss papers not one but two disheartening messages. The more obvious was the dwindling chance of preventing the spread of nuclear weapons; the Swiss too want to reserve the possibility of an independent nuclear deterrent, as the British call it. Just around the corner is the prospect of an international trade in second-hand, last-year's-model nuclear arms for the smaller and poorer Powers. The other, less obvious message, is that here, too, apathy reigns; barely half the Swiss bothered to vote at all. In Geneva canton, little more than a third went to the polls; the idealists marshaled, the hotel keepers strolled in the sun. Mont Blanc, after several days of rain, was majestically visible beyond the blue Lake; few cared to notice, a little further off, the mushroom cloud shaping up.

The setting for the conference at the *Palais des Nations* is as familiar as the libretto; weapons change but not disarmament tactics. These have become almost as stylized as the classical ballet. The *Palais* is deceptively severe in its architecture. The atmosphere in its offices is relaxed; the problems may be urgent but they are also perpetual and the staffs are in no hurry. This is a place of frequent and extended coffee breaks where idealists—like the fat peacocks on the wide well-kept lawns—may safely be let out to graze. Amid the neatly labeled cubbyhole offices one may find men engaged in the lifelong production of shocking but harmless documents on all kinds of nefarious human trades and habits, from those of narcotics to those of armament and war. One feels oneself among lotus eaters in a land of perpetual though gentle motion; here, as it were, God proposes and Satan disposes. As in a richly endowed temple, the bells ring and the rites are celebrated; mystic anguish subsides with the years into leisurely priesthood; evil goes on in the outside world but one's pension rights accumulate. The case against sin is voluminously documented but with discreet deference for the Powers whence, after all, the annual budgets are met. This deplorable world is made as pleasant for oneself as possible while waiting piously for the next. As I write, a planeload of go-getter, women's strike-for-peace delegates have just arrived from America to grasp these officials working on disarmament firmly by the lapel, and to set the statesmen straight. I wish I could tap the conversations between these passionate women militants and these gracefully reconciled idealists who will be appalled to hear again all they know

so well, and indeed earn their livelihood by repeating, though with
no real hope that it will make any difference. How many moribund
consciences these women will twinge!

The Foreign Ministers have left and the real work of the
conference, as they say, has begun. This is true in the sense but
only in the sense that the "real work" of the conference is to disentangle from one's pledges and try to put the blame for failure on
the other side. From another, and more realistic sense, the conference
may already be over. The disarmament conference, from this point
of view, was an elaborate façade for the settlement of more important business. There seems to be a general though perhaps too
optimistic feeling that the way was cleared between Rusk and
Gromyko for a Berlin settlement which will be unveiled at a summit
meeting in the latter part of May. On nuclear testing, there seems
to be a tacit agreement between Washington and Moscow to take
up the subject again only after another round of testing; the neutrals, desperate and frustrated, were to make one more grand effort
behind closed doors this morning to stop them but the outlook was
not promising. In Washington, one felt that all those well-publicized
weeks of agonizing indecision was a fraud, that the decision to
resume had already been made by the kind of political necessities
to which Mr. Kennedy was most responsive. Here, in Geneva, one
gets the impression that on the Soviet side, too, there is an almost
smug readiness for another round, a complacent assurance that
negotiation will be possible after it's over. The Russians could easily
have put us on the spot by accepting neutral inspection if a neutral
seismographic network turned up with objective indicators of a
hidden nuclear test. But they, like us, seem afraid to risk even
propaganda gestures lest they interfere with another series of tests.

The press has been encouraged by the United States information officers, as they are euphemistically called, to dwell on the
unusually polite and non-acrimonious tone of the proceedings so
far, as if it were a positive achievement for Mr. Zorin and Mr. Dean
to meet without any attempt at mayhem. It would be tempting but
untrue to attribute this improvement in tone to the tacit agreement
of the great Powers to give themselves just one more round of
testing before, as it were, joining atomics anonymous. The real
reason for the restrained language seems to be the presence of the
neutrals, for in the subcommittee on nuclear testing, where the
nuclear Powers confront each other without neutral witnesses, the

transcripts reveal an acridly polemical tone which recalls the best days of Vishinsky and Dulles. In the lower ranks of the more or less permanent delegations on disarmament, these conferences are a form of gamesmanship; only a rare few dedicated souls take the work seriously. But among the leaders of the delegations, the momentum of combat in one Geneva conference after another has worked emotions to such a pitch that it would only take the slightest blip on the radar screens to get Mr. Dean to let fly with an H-bomb at Mr. Tsarapkin; after prolonged and repetitive bargaining sessions each side seems to regard the other as a pack of swindlers. Intimacy has not flowered into love.

The exasperation is as great on general and complete disarmament as on nuclear testing, but the situation is the reverse. On nuclear testing the two big Powers disagree violently in public on basic principles but agree privately in practice on resumption of testing. On general and complete disarmament, they agree publicly on basic principles but disagree violently in private as soon as the question arises of putting them into practice. The United States delegation is deeply annoyed—indeed regards it as a blow below the belt—that the Russians turned up with a detailed draft treaty on general and complete disarmament and tabled this as a basis for discussion. For a moment, last Thursday, the neutrals thought the sun was breaking through the angry clouds when the innocuous preamble of the Soviet draft with two United States amendments was almost adopted. It looked that night as if mankind were on the verge at least of a general and complete preamble to a disarmament treaty. But somehow—the details are not clear—the happy event was delayed and on Friday when Article 1 came up, heavy fighting broke out. While the preamble is merely against sin, Article 1 talks sweepingly of closing down all dens of military iniquity within four years. Though Mr. Kennedy's program of general and complete disarmament, as presented to the United Nations last September, is in principle as sweeping as the Russian and Mr. Zorin was able to defend the general declarations of Article 1 by quoting chapter and verse from the United States plan, the Western side shied away violently. Mr. Godber of the United Kingdom didn't know why the two sides couldn't get together instead on such projects as a joint study of how best to verify the elimination of nuclear weapons stock piles. Mr. Dean protested that the Russians were trying to build a house without a blueprint; they replied that their treaty *was* a blueprint, and that the other side was free point by point to amend or change that blueprint. To the outside observer it seemed that what was missing was not a blueprint but a willingness on the United States side to be drawn into discussion of how to build the house of disarmament at all. On Friday, the very first day on which the plenary committee tackled the specifics of disarmament, the divergence grew so wide that Senator de Mello-Franco of Brazil spoke despairingly of "an impasse" though he rose later to explain tactfully that all he meant was that the conferees had arrived at a crossroads.

It is the old and familiar crossroads. On the United States side we want absolute guaranties against violation of any treaty while the Russians want absolute guaranties that a treaty cannot be used to map their bases for attack before complete and general disarmament has been achieved. Neither side is prepared to recognize that while they talk of absolute security in either sense, technological changes are destroying it. The risk of sudden attack by a few planes or rockets hidden from inspectors is less than the risk of unleashing monsters of destruction through the probability of accident as these weapons pile up and grow more complex. On the other side, the Russian fear that inspectors may spot their bases for attack begins to seem ludicrous as we learn more and more about the surveillance to which they were subjected by U-2 and are being subjected by its successor satellite spy systems. These neuroses again block agreement. The key to resolution of the difficulty seems to lie in the time limit. If the process is long drawn out, then the Russians can reasonably fear that after much inspection and little disarmament, we may break off the process and be in a better position to attack. On the other hand, given the will to agree, if the time limit is short, verification should be negotiable, especially if sampling and zonal systems are applied. But the Russians cannot expect to get a treaty under which we would have no way to verify the forces which remained on their side after cuts were made.

The reader will note that after the pessimism I brought with me from the Washington scene I am beginning to take the details of negotiation seriously, as if all this were real. The neutral hope is that by a similar process maybe the West can be drawn so inextricably into discussion that it will be unable to back out. The United States must soon, if only to compete with the Russians, present something like a draft treaty of its own. In principle it cannot be too different. What happens when the two are put to-gether? If a man doesn't want to marry a girl, he had best not enter into a theoretical discussion with her father, mother and brothers on when, where and how they would be wed if he finally made up his mind to wed her. Such theoretical discussions are perilous for bachelorhood. So the neutrals hold their breath and hope.

APRIL 9, 1962

THE HIDDEN TRUTH ABOUT THE NUCLEAR ARMS RACE

The most revealing portion of the President's speech announc-ing the resumption of atmospheric testing lay in that passage where he said the leaders of the Soviet Union were watching and "should we fail to follow the dictates of our own security, they will chalk it up not to good will, but to a failure of will—not to our confidence in Western superiority, but to our fear of world opinion, the very world opinion for which they showed such contempt. They could well be encouraged by such signs of weakness. . . ."

This was not the sober analysis of military or technological need. It was gamesmanship. It declared that we were acting out of fear—fear of what the Russians might think. It also implied that disregard for the opinion of mankind was, or could be regarded, as a sign of strength. These are psychological and political considera-tions yet they came immediately after a passage in which Mr. Kennedy had assured the country and the world that his decision to test in the atmosphere was not based on "political or psycho-logical reasons."

This is very different from following "the dictates of our own security." It is following the persistent but primitive concept that the way to deal with a tough guy is to show him you're as tough as he is. A decision of this character required no patient sifting of radioactive particles gathered by airborne intelligence patrols. This is the familiar strategy of every schoolyard quarrel and barroom brawl. Suppose the scientific experts had decided that "the dictates of our own security" required no testing. In such a case which considerations would determine the decision—the real needs of our security or the fear of not looking tough enough?

In this realm of secrecy and disingenuous government state-ment, no one can be sure of the facts. But I believe that in this case "the dictates of our own security" called for a decision *not* to resume tests and to negotiate a new moratorium with the Russians instead. I believe this decision was rejected not because of what the *Russians might think we thought they'd think* (the two governments have a pretty clear idea of their relative strength; only the peoples are in the dark) but because of what the American people might think. Such a decision would be too hard to explain at home. It would require a kind of bold leadership for which Mr. Kennedy has shown neither taste nor capacity.

Mr. Kennedy's speech was most striking in what it did not say. It did not say the Russians have forged ahead or even caught up with us in nuclear weapons technology. It did not fall back on the myth that an anti-missile weapon may be just around the corner that could dramatically change the world balance of power. These would have been falsehoods. Let us look at what Mr. Kennedy did say:

"In short, last fall's tests, in and by themselves, did not give the Soviet Union superiority in nuclear power. They did, however, provide the Soviet laboratories with a mass of data and experience on which, over the next two or three years, they can base significant analyses, experiments and extrapolations, preparing for the next test series which would confirm or advance their findings. And I must report to you that further Soviet series, in the absence of further Western progress, could well provide the Soviet Union with a nuclear attack and defense capability so powerful as to encourage offensive designs."

This implies that the Soviets do not yet have a nuclear arsenal sufficient to encourage offensive designs; apparently all they have now is a retaliatory capacity. It also implies that if testing goes on they *will* acquire such an arsenal.

The fallacious part of the paragraph we quoted lies in the phrase, "in the absence of further Western progress." This embodies a delusion of semantic origin arising from the picture created by the term "arms race." In a race, if one side puts on a fresh spurt, the other side must do so, too, to keep up or stay ahead. But the facts of the nuclear arms race do not fit this metaphor. Nuclear weapons technology is not an infinite body of knowledge. As Dr. Hans Bethe said in his famous speech at Cornell January 5,

"The value of tests has been grossly exaggerated. We already know so much about atomic weapons that there is very little more to learn. We have weapons of all sizes for all reasonable military purposes. Only relatively minor improvements can be made in the yield of weapons for a given weight."

He spoke of the "extensive Russian tests" as an attempt to "catch up to our technology." In this kind of "race," it is to the advantage of the one ahead to call it off before the one behind catches up. The longer this kind of race goes on, the more the two sides draw abreast.

If, as Mr. Kennedy said, "further Soviet series," after two or three years of digesting new data, "could well provide the Soviet Union with a nuclear attack and defense capability so powerful as to encourage offensive designs," then it is to our national interest to prevent new Soviet test series from taking place. These, as our own experience and decision shows, must take place in the atmosphere where they are open to long-range detection without any special system of international surveillance. Underground tests have proven of limited value; indeed their chief effect has been to provide the Teller-military-AEC combination with a way to confuse the public and to hamper the test ban negotiations. An agreement with moderate inspection might have been reached if inspection requirements had not been pitched so high as to make the Russians fear our real purpose was military intelligence. Thus the talks broke down and now our resumption of atmospheric testing will give the Russians the excuse they want for that new series of tests which may end our nuclear superiority.

Time will reveal that those who campaigned for a nuclear test ban were acting in the best interests of United States security while those who opposed it, and built up so many nightmares to frighten the public away from it, as Dr. Edward Teller and the AEC-Pentagon crowd did, were acting against our country's best interest. A test ban would have frozen the nuclear arms race at a point of clear United States technological superiority. It still could, for we are still ahead. But this would require courageous leadership—in explaining the true nature of the nuclear arms race to the public, in freeing ourselves from the notion that only an elaborate system of surveillance within Russia could police a new ban, and in defying those interests which are opposed to any kind of halt for very different reasons. The arms industry crowd wants new tests to provide new models, or "generations," of missiles to maintain sales as they maintain sales of automobiles—with new gadget improvements every year.

To assess Mr. Kennedy's test resumption message one must clear away the fog of propaganda. An obstacle to any new test cessation agreement is the charge that the Russians broke the last one. But is this quite true? How many Americans remember that on December 29, 1959, President Eisenhower announced that we no longer considered ourselves bound by the test moratorium and declared ourselves "free to resume nuclear testing" at any time we chose to do so? Mr. Eisenhower said that in the meantime the United States "will continue its active program of weapon research development." The Russians may justly be condemned for starting up first, but it can hardly be said that they broke an agreement. Mr. Eisenhower had publicly abrogated it a year and a half earlier.

A second factor which needs evaluation is the part played by the U-2 incident six months after Eisenhower's declaration. Few Americans are aware of the extent to which we had been "inspecting" Russia via the U-2 or its consequences for Russian security. Thanks to the recent indiscretion of Colonel Barney Oldfield, chief press officer of the North American Defense Command, we now have a very clear view of how effective this aerial surveillance was. Colonel Oldfield was accused of violating security by telling a space writers conference at Fort Worth, Texas, that we knew of Soviet space failures because our U-2 showed Soviet launching pads with rockets in place and then scorched earth at the same sites. Obviously we had been getting a pretty close look behind that Iron Curtain.

A few days later Colonel Oldfield gave an interview to the Canadian press (*New York Herald-Tribune,* February 24) which left less to inference: "Colonel Oldfield said the photographs taken by the U-2 planes over a period of four years gave the United States a great deal of information on Soviet military power, including the location of missile and atomic sites, aircraft and submarine production and rocket developments." Then Colonel Oldfield added that although the U-2 flights were called off in May, 1960, after they had wrecked the summit, "this didn't leave us exactly paralyzed on getting Soviet intelligence." Colonel Oldfield, Canadian press said, did not elaborate on this hint.

There is reason to believe that we have reconnaissance satellites which have taken over the photography tasks of the U-2. Thus an Associated Press dispatch from Washington January 5 (*New York Post,* same day) quoted "United States intelligence specialists" as saying that the Soviets were lagging in the ICBM race. "The most recent intelligence evaluations, sources said," according to the AP, "credit the Russians with what were termed 'startlingly few' liquid-fuel ICBM's in place. They said the Russians have three or four fewer than the United States which has emplaced forty-five liquid-fuel Atlas ICBM's." Obviously, U-2 or no U-2, we are still getting close enough looks at Russia to count missiles in place.

It would appear that while the public has been told about the impossibility of disarmament without inspection, and the Soviets have been denounced for unwillingness to "open up," the Soviet Union has been subjected to very thorough inspection. The truth about this did not begin to come out until after the U-2 incident; a month later, in June, 1960, then CIA Director Allen Dulles first gave the Senate preparedness subcommittee a secret briefing in which he was able to disclose that there was no missile gap.

Both Dr. Ralph Lapp in the *Bulletin of the Atomic Scientists* and Dr. Bethe in his Cornell speech declared the U-2 had much to do with the resumption of Soviet nuclear testing. "Soviet secrecy as to their strategic bases," Dr. Lapp wrote (p. 288, BAS, September, 1961), "was a priceless asset and must have given the Kremlin a great sense of security. This position of security was undermined by the U-2 affair. Generals in the U.S.S.R. must have viewed their fixed ICBM bases as highly vulnerable to a United States first strike or pre-emptive attack. To redress this loss of security, there must have arisen a strong military demand for solid-fueled, mobile, ballistic missiles of intercontinental range." Dr. Bethe expressed similar views. He said that as long as the Soviet missiles were above ground "we could destroy them by a surprise attack if we knew their exact locations." The discovery of their missile bases by the U-2's meant that the Russians had to learn how to make "solid-fuel missiles similar to our Minutemen which could be put in hardened sites," i.e., underground. Dr. Bethe said that most of the Russian tests were in the one- to five-megaton range. This range, according to Dr. Bethe, is "just the range" for the development of such missiles.[*]

To this extent at least the Soviet tests may be regarded as defensive and an attempt to catch up with our technology in order

[*] The AP dispatch cited above quoted the same intelligence specialists as reporting that the Soviets would "trail the United States by about half a year in getting an advanced ICBM ready for combat." Our solid-fuel Minuteman is supposed to become "operational" this summer but the first Russian missile of the same type not until early 1963.

to hide their missiles underground. By putting their missiles underground as a secure second-strike retaliatory force they would cut down the temptation of a first strike against them, the so-called counterforce strategy of the Air Force. As Dr. Bethe said, "The major part of their test series, therefore, may well have reduced rather than increased the danger of war." The whole idea of a stabilized nuclear deterrent is that each side shall possess roughly equal missile forces so well hidden that they cannot be destroyed in a first strike. This means that neither can hit the other without the certainty of devastating retaliation.

But the whole idea of a stabilized nuclear deterrent is being abandoned. This is hidden from public view in Mr. Kennedy's message which gives the appearance of candor without the reality. Its tantalizingly opaque phrases hide more than they disclose. Nowhere, for example, does it touch on the question of overkill. How much is enough? The House majority leader, Carl Albert of Oklahoma, a man not given to reckless utterance, told a Jefferson-Jackson Day dinner in Richmond, Virginia, recently, "We have five times the atomic capability of the Soviet Union." (*Washington Star,* February 18). Are we trying to preserve or widen so huge a margin? Dr. Bethe's speech, as we reported in our issue of January 15, disclosed that we can deliver 20,000 megatons—20,000 *million tons of TNT equivalent!*—in 1,500 long-range bombers alone without counting the 150 missiles (50 ICBM's, 100 Polarises) we have already. How do you divide 50 or at most 100 prime targets in the Soviet Union among 1,500 planes and 150 missiles? "The Russians," Dr. Bethe said, "have smaller numbers but still enough to destroy us many times over." How much more do both sides require before they sit down to negotiate?

What purpose does new testing on our part serve in this picture? How much is determined by military and how much by muscle-flexing considerations? Does the clue here lie in the new propaganda campaign launched with a speech last October 21 by Deputy Secretary of Defense Gilpatric? This reflected, as the *U.S. News & World Report* said November 6, "a decision by the White House to counter propaganda—which suddenly has taken hold around the world—that the United States is weak, Russia strong." The armament lobby in its bomber gap and missile gap campaigns had pictured the Russians as ten feet tall in order to get bigger appropriations out of Congress. Now our answer to Khrushchev's 100-megaton monster was to picture them as three feet small. The *U.S. News & World Report* in the wake of Gilpatric's speech said that the ICBM missile gap was three to one in our favor (150 ICBM's and Polarises against less than 50 ICBM's on the Russian side). In long-range bombers our edge was given at ten to one (some 1,500 to only 150 for the Russians).

If these figures were correct, or anywhere near correct, two contradictory conclusions could be drawn from them. One was that with this overwhelming lead we could well afford to negotiate arms control, reduction and disarmament. The other was that with a lead this overwhelming we ought to be able to dictate terms. The latter has become the premise of policy. Its corollary is to speed up the arms race in order to maintain overwhelming superiority. The increase of almost ten billions or nearly 25 percent in the Kennedy arms budget over Eisenhower's—and now the decision to resume testing—seem designed, as Assistant Secretary of State Harlan Cleveland said at Rollins College, Florida, February 10 "to prevent our Soviet rivals from getting ahead, or thinking they can get ahead, in the hidden and costly game of nuclear deterrence." This policy, of course, is made to order for the military-industrial complex which lives on the arms race. Just how it can be reconciled with Mr. Kennedy's "peace race" was demonstrated in agile fashion by Arthur Schlesinger, Jr., the President's assistant, when he told the Young Democrats in San Diego January 6, "To persist in piling up the weapons of mass destruction is a tragic choice. But we live in a world of tragic choices; and there is no point in kidding ourselves that painful problems have painless solutions. It is an irony of our times that the arms race offers the only road to arms control. . . ." This neatly accommodates the Kennedy policy of running an arms race and a peace race at the same time, though even Professor Schlesinger only speaks of this as a way to arms control, not disarmament. The dream is of an arms control in which we are so strong that we can do the controlling. This is a variant of the old Acheson-Dulles belief that if only we build up overwhelming power we can dictate an unconditional surrender. But behind these rationalizations lies a simple policy, the policy of following the line of least resistance, which is the arms race.

The line of least resistance is the only grand design visible in the Kennedy Administration. A man who will not put up a real fight even for adequate aid to education is unlikely to put up a real fight for disarmament. Mr. Kennedy, to judge from the eloquent words he utters on the subject from time to time, is aware of the deadly danger, but like Eisenhower he is too anxious to remain popular with everybody to do anything much about it; to be that popular one must reign instead of rule. In the absence of effective presidential leadership to the contrary, the White House is pulled along in the wake of the powerful industrial and bureaucratic interests which would be doubly hurt by disarmament, first in the profits they draw from it, and second in the reorientation of national energies to fill the armament gap. Reconstruction at home and abroad would not require so many generals and it would not be the same luxurious cost plus operation as building missiles.

I regard the stories about Mr. Kennedy's agonizing over the decision to resume testing with jaundiced eye. I do not mean to imply that Mr. Kennedy may not have been agonized personally. But no one who has watched this Administration can believe that any other decision was likely. *It would have been too hard to explain.* It would have meant a fight. It would have been too out of character. I do not mean to say that Mr. Kennedy, a clever man with clever advisers, will not seek to find ways to do enough, or seem to do enough, about disarmament to keep the peace people happy, too, along with the arms people. But that only means that Mr. Kennedy, in going with the tide, will do it cleverly.

The arms race undertow is substituting for nuclear deterrence a much more adventurous policy in which we hope to make the Russians feel that, if they provoke us too far, we are strong enough to make a first strike. This is why, despite the discovery that there is no missile gap, we plan to build up a force of some 1,600 missiles by 1965. Even hardened underground solid-fuel missile bases are not invulnerable if one side can afford to aim half a dozen ICBM's at each ICBM of the other. It is against this background that one can better understand that passage in Mr. Kennedy's message where he said we must test in order to "enable us to add to our missiles certain penetration aids and decoys, and to make those missiles effective at high-altitude detonations, in order to render ineffective any anti-missile or interceptor system an enemy might some day develop." This smacks of first strike, and it is already planning for the *anti*-anti-missile. The direction in which all this leads on the military plane was indicated in Secretary McNamara's speech at Chicago February 17 when he pictured a situation in which we would be so strong that we could knock out the enemy's bases and still have enough power left to use it "as a bargaining weapon—by threatening further attack. . . . Our large reserve of protected fire-power would give an enemy an incentive to avoid our cities and to stop a war." This is the first public appearance of a new "counterforce" policy favored by the Air Force under which we could smash enemy bases but leave his cities as "hostages" to prevent retaliation against ours. Here the limited-war fallacy emerges in giant dimensions. This is a new kind of "pause," a pause after a nuclear attack. It expects the Russians, after the horror of a nuclear attack, to exercise a rationality and restraint hardly to be expected from a colony of Christian saints. It also assumes that they, too, will build so many missiles they also will always have a reserve, perhaps in some Siberian deep-freeze. How stop such lunacy when Mr. Kennedy himself talks in his resumption message as if new tests would somehow make it possible to win and survive a thermonuclear war?

MARCH 12, 1962

46: *Our Feud with Fidel*

OUR AIR OF INJURED INNOCENCE OVER CUBA

On one plane of our national consciousness, it is assumed with approval that our government is doing all in its power short of war to overthrow the Castro government in Cuba. On another and separate plane, we take it as an affront when the Cuban regime accuses us of aggressive intent. Like the respectable *bourgeois* in a French farce who has a mistress stashed away in another part of town, we manage at one and the same time to enjoy illicit pleasure and righteous indignation. The average American reads with satisfaction in our daily press and weekly picture magazines of the Cubans being trained on our soil and in a growing number of Central American hide-outs for an invasion of Cuba. The Sunday supplements treat the CIA and its operatives like a real-life comic-strip adventure story; we get a vicarious satisfaction from its cloak-and-dagger exploits; we thrill at the broad hints of its adeptness in setting conflagrations, getting rid of dangerous characters in governments we do not like, and buying up men of the lesser breeds on our borders. But let the Castro regime complain of such activities and we at once take the complaint as further evidence of its unregenerate character and perverse unfriendliness.

It is true that the Castro government often gets its facts mixed up. But we in our turn seize on any minor error of accusation to work up a fine protective lather of injured innocence. When Castro, after a growing number of terrorist incidents, including the bombing of a department store in Havana, accused the United States Embassy of acting as director and paymaster for such activities, and demanded that we cut its staff to eleven men, he may have been foolish to take a step which invited a break in relations—and he may have been wrong in some of his accusations. But why the sudden pretense on our part that CIA operatives only spend their time translating *Pravda*? If terrorism broke out in our country after the Cuban press had been boasting of a secret agency for such activities, would we wait for affidavits before taking action to stop it?

Those more thoughtful Americans who can manage to get the transcript of the Security Council debate earlier this month on the Cuban charge of imminent aggression will blush to see this process in full operation. The Cuban government was silly and overwrought in accusing the United States of being "about to perpetrate within a few hours direct military aggression." But much of Mr. Roa's indictment was based on material published in our own press about the way United States government agencies and big businesses have been helping to train Cubans and American adventurers for infiltration and invasion of Cuba. Mr. Wadsworth dismissed all this as "a welter of photographs" and newspaper clippings.

Such activities are in plain violation of international law and of our neutrality statutes. It is not true that in this regard and in regard to swiftly-built new air bases in Guatemala "the United States"—as Mr. Wadsworth indignantly exclaimed—"has nothing to hide." Much *is* hidden.

The charge by Mr. Roa which most called for rebuttal, because most pregnant with future trouble, was his charge that men trained in the camps of Miami, Orlando, Homestead, Fort Lauderdale and Fort Myers, Florida, were being moved in American planes to Swan Island in the Caribbean and then in groups of 150 to Guantánamo. This was not supported by American press clippings but it was evident from Mr. Roa's speech that the Cubans have an extensive intelligence service, and it is dangerous if they really believe—true or untrue—that Guantánamo is being used for such a purpose. This could spark off war, and there may be forces, Cuban or American, which would like Castro to believe this in order to provoke trouble. We think more responsible United States agencies should make sure that this is not true, or if true that the practice of so using Guantánamo is ended, and that assurances to this effect are given the Cuban government.

We are moving toward something far more fateful than a minor colonial police operation in our relations with Cuba. It is indicative of a kind of giddy arrogance that the very day Mr. Wadsworth on January 4 was assuring the Security Council that our intentions were pure as driven snow, correspondents were being given a background not-for-attribution briefing on our plans to choke off the Castro regime with a sea and air blockade. This was the common source of all those stories in the papers of January 5 on our plans to "isolate" Castro. Our hope for such a blockade also explains our sudden action on January 4 in voting limited economic sanctions at the OAS against the Dominican Republic, a move Castro could not avoid supporting but which is intended to win Venezuela's vote later for similar sanctions against Cuba. To blockade Cuba would be to risk international complications and a hemispheric chain reaction. The countries which stand with us in breaking relations and which might support stronger action are provocative symbols of all the Latin American masses hate. Five of the six represent the remaining dictatorships in the hemisphere: the Dominican Republic, Haiti, Nicaragua, Guatemala and Paraguay. The sixth, our most recent acquisition as an ally against Castro is Peru, a country ruled by a small oligarchy. Except for El Salvador, nowhere in Latin America is there a deeper gulf between haves and have-nots than in Peru. We couldn't have less attractive recruits than these six for a crusade against a popular hero like Castro.

This is a made-to-order recipe for a hemispheric civil war. We see Castro as a pawn in our global struggle with the U.S.S.R. The Latin American masses see him as their first honest champion since the Mexican Revolution and a man who dared defy American oil and sugar firms. The Latins couldn't care less about our cold war. To drift into open aggression against Cuba is to run the risk of tearing the hemisphere apart. The road to the restoration of hemispheric solidarity runs through Havana. The sooner we restore good relations with Castro the sooner we can channel the volcanic forces of Latin American resentment into orderly and peaceful change. A new President provides a chance for a fresh start.

JANUARY 16, 1961

TWO MONTHS BEFORE THE BAY OF PIGS

My first morning in Havana I bought all the papers and went to work on them after breakfast with my Spanish-English dictionary. The most promising item seemed to be a two-column editorial on the front page of the Communist paper *Hoy* with a heading in large type, "The Worst Enemy." I expected a diatribe against the CIA, Guatemala, American imperialism or those wicked ones in Miami. Instead it turned out to be an attack on careless driving and automobile accidents. "The counterrevolutionary enemies with all their attacks, crimes and sabotage," *Hoy* complained, "have caused us fewer deaths than these accidents." There are people who will find it discouraging to learn that reckless driving can still be a main topic of concern in Havana.

Outwardly at least, in the warm February sunshine, Havana seemed to have changed little from the city as I saw it last August. Lines of taxicabs and limousines still waited outside the hotels for the tourists who weren't there. More buildings seemed to have one or two soldiers on guard in front of them. But there was little indication either of siege or of unrest. The only visible remains of the great January invasion scare were tattered posters saying, "Death to the Invader," with a tongue-in-cheek quotation from Fidel, "We know that we are not alone and that an attack on Cuba will lead to its own destruction. But, nevertheless, we don't want them to commit suicide on our coast." In the early morning sunshine, the white trucks marked Limpieza de Calle (Street Cleaning) were already sprinkling the Prado while platoons of white wings swept and washed the square behind them. There was no sign of a gasoline shortage; traffic was heavy. Except for two new Soviet magazines, *Union Sovietica* and *China Reconstruye,* and the absence of the *New York Times,* the newsstands seemed unchanged. There was no sign of inflation in the prices marked in the shop windows, nor of rationing in the restaurants. Only once, during a week's stay, was I to be accosted by a moneychanger, though the peso on the black market is supposed to be less than half the legal rate of one-to-one for the dollar. The Castro regime seemed very much a going concern.

Despite the breaking off of relations, a stray American encountered no signs of hostility. On the contrary he was made to feel by the friendly welcome in the streets that it was a positive morale builder to see an American. Sloppy Joe's was still the emptiest and most mournful-looking bar in town, and the big news was that Castro and his entire Cabinet were going out to cut sugar cane Sunday. Some 112,000 had already volunteered to cut cane with them, and the papers, along with instructions on where to mobilize, were warning volunteers to bring along their own lunches. The newest crop of wall posters proclaimed this the year of the struggle against illiteracy; Cuba hopes in one year to do what UNESCO says would take ten: to teach everyone to read and write. Small armies of teachers are going out into the countryside; housemaids go to special night classes in the towns; signs proclaim, "Make every home a school."

In official circles, and among supporters of the regime, there is an atmosphere of revolutionary euphoria which strikes even a sympathetic visitor as dangerously unrealistic. If ever a little country was giddy with success, it is Castro's Cuba. My purpose in going down to Cuba was to see what changes had taken place since my last visit in August and to explore the possibilities of a peaceful settlement between the United States and Cuba. The euphoria—and the demagogy—appalled me. I set off to Cuba in a mood of optimism. I found myself returning, not in despair, but in that mood of awed and helpless wonder with which one looks on at the unfolding of a heroic tragedy. The gulf between Washington and Havana is deeper even than that between Washington and Moscow. The Fidelistas are living in a dream world, a world which revolves around Cuba, but as they see it, it also contains that big weakling to the north, the United States, and that distant but doting foster parent, the Soviet Union, which is ready on notice from Havana to plunge the whole world into atomic war if Uncle Sam misbehaves. There were moments when a visitor was made to feel that if we North Americans are not careful, Cuba might annex the United States and liberate its suffering people from the yoke of monopoly capitalism. Castro's Cuba is the Don Quixote in the world family of nations today.

My own mission was perhaps a little Quixotic, too. I had hoped to come back with news and interviews to show how easily and painlessly peace could be achieved between Washington and Havana. I am afraid I had it all figured out in advance. I expected the Cuban leaders to see that it was impractical to create a completely socialized state just off the shores of the United States of America; to learn from the fate of Nagy in Hungary that a revolutionary regime has to be circumspect in dealing with a big powerful neighbor; to be ready, as similarly-placed regimes have been, to avoid the provocative and to work out a *modus vivendi* within these political realities.

I felt that the Castro regime could save the agrarian reform and the industrialization program on a basis of socialism if it was willing to settle for a mixed society, to negotiate some compensation for United States properties, and to restore some. Obviously it could not give up the sugar and cattle *latifundia* without giving up its *raison d'être,* and it could not give up the industrialization program which is the counterpart of agrarian reform. But in between there were possibilities of face-saving concessions which would do the Cubans no harm. There was no reason why such concerns as F. W. Woolworth should not be allowed to resume business, or that room could not be found within the area of industrialization for some cooperation with foreign firms, as has been done in Ghana and Guinea.

In the political realm—I might as well make a clean breast of this—I envisaged a declaration of ultimate free elections and ultimate restoration of fundamental political liberties. I felt that Cuba would have to end the situation in which the Communist party was the only legally existing party in Cuba, perhaps by merging it in a united revolutionary party led by the Fidelistas. I could see the United States adjusting to a one-party regime in Cuba of the kind which has led revolutions from Mexico to Ghana. But I could see no possibility of a peaceful settlement if Cuba allowed the Communists alone to operate outside the framework of the July 26 movement. In other words I felt that Cuba might save the achievements of the Revolution if it offered some face-saving compromises to Washington and assurance that Cuba would not become a Soviet base in this hemisphere. By this last, I do not necessarily mean a military base, but a political base.

Starting with this all-too-neat blueprint, I found a whole series of negative factors in Havana. There was a misconception of the United States fully as distorted as our view of Cuba. There was a heady youthful recklessness which can lead this regime very easily to overplay its hand. There was an attitude toward the Soviet bloc which can only be described as a naïve kind of infantile leftism. There was a daring conception of Cuba as the leader of a hemispheric upsurge against Yanqui imperialism which portends bad relations not only with the United States but with the more cautious regimes to the south of Cuba. It is a pity Khrushchev does not visit Havana. He would get as big a scare in Havana as he probably does in Peking.

In short, your wistful pilgrim found himself face to face in Havana with a full-fledged revolution, in all its creative folly and self-deceptive enthusiasm. To ask it to be sensible was like asking a volcano to take it easy. Nothing could be harder for an observer from a rich status quo society than to understand a group of desperate idealists striving within a short time to remake a poor colonial society in the shadow of a hostile great power. Perhaps it could be attempted only by smoking a little political marijuana to keep up their courage. Every Cuban effort for reform during the last half century has met warnings—usually true, as it turned out—that the United States would never allow it. I must have seemed another in that mournful procession of warning liberals.

Walking the streets, trying hard to digest the experience, one had to recognize that in this case what United States policy would *not* allow were moderate, mixed-society solutions. These are possible only where countries are still able to deal with both sides in the East-West struggle. But by our oil and sugar policies, we have made Cuba completely dependent on the Soviet bloc; one might as well ask for a mixed society in Outer Mongolia. Our oil embargo would have brought Cuban economic life to a standstill within a few weeks but for Soviet oil and Soviet tankers. Our refusal to buy Cuban sugar would have been as disastrous for the Cuban economy if the Soviet bloc had not come to Castro's rescue. Once the ties with the United States had been broken, it was easier to barter sugar for equipment from the Soviet bloc and set out to industrialize the island on a socialist basis than to try the long drawn-out process of luring capitalist investment from other Western countries which would hesitate to allow it in the face of United States hostility. What France did in Guinea, we did in Cuba. Castro, like Sekou

Touré, was left with no alternative. Indeed Castro's position is worse. Guinea is still bush country. Cuba is not; its sugar mills, its transport, its electric power, depend on imported oil. Castro's oil supply, his sugar market and now his industrialization program depend entirely on the good will of the Soviet bloc. Like the fallen maiden in the melodrama, Castro may well cry out to Washington, "You made me what I am today."

With this economic and political dependence have come ideological changes. For the first time, in talking with Fidelista intellectuals, I felt that Cuba was on its way to becoming a Soviet-style Popular Democracy. Again for this the United States shares responsibility. A combination of factors is pushing Cuba in this direction. On the one side is gratitude toward the Soviet bloc, dependence on its good will, a desire to flatter by imitating its methods. On the other hand is repulsion for the United States, and fear of the interventionist groups we are supporting. The familiar chain reaction of counterrevolution is at work, stirring suspicion, strengthening the secret police and arbitrary legal methods; these in turn create new hostility to the regime. A general tightening up of controls is in progress, though the only visible signs of opposition in Havana are religious. There are placards in many shop windows asking, "Will your child be a believer or an atheist?" and announcing that March 5 will be Catechism Day. The night I arrived a band of youths in ragged procession were marching down the Prado shouting the Catholic slogan, "Cuba, si; Rusia, no."

It is to Castro's credit that there are few signs of a cult of personality, but the press is completely Fidelista. While the bookstores are still full of heretical anti-Communist works, there has been a steady infection of totalitarian ideas. This is evident when one brings up the question of a free press and of ultimate free elections. On the former, one encounters vague Rousseauean ideas, and no very clear answers are elicited. There seems to be an oversimplified notion that so long as the press is freed from the influence of big business monopolies, there is no longer a problem. The press —so goes this populist mysticism—then expresses the will of the majority, or of the working class or of the people's state. The idea that a free press, with the right of the individual to express dissenting views, has a role to play in any society, capitalist or socialist, begins to seem as counterrevolutionary in Cuba as in East Germany or Hungary. As for free elections, I was told that once the economic problems of a society are solved, there was no need for politics; all problems would then merely be technical, and could be handled by technicians!

It is difficult, against the background of Latin American misery and United States relations, for an American liberal to talk with his Cuban opposite numbers of free press, free elections and the rule of law. These ideals have been so dirtied in practice; Latin Americans have known so little of them; we ourselves have so far abandoned them; that it is very hard to make Latin Americans see any reality behind the rhetoric. On a wall in Havana I saw a poster which quoted Bolívar as saying, "The United States seems destined by Providence to plague America with miseries in the name of liberty." It was not pleasant to hear Fidel in a rather demagogic speech the Saturday night after my arrival taunt the United States for putting down an iron curtain around Cuba and forbidding its citizens to travel there. "What do they confess with this?" Castro asked. "Their failure and their fear of the example and of the truth, and of the influence that Cuba has not only in Latin America but in the United States itself." How can an American liberal argue convincingly in Cuba for a free press and against arbitrary government when we ourselves set up barriers to free communication?

I had no way of really judging how serious are the interventionist guerrillas dropped in the Escambray hills and perhaps elsewhere. But I am inclined to suspect that these activities give the Castro regime a shot in the arm, a danger with which to energize and mobilize the people, costly in terms of militiamen withdrawn from production but perhaps worth the cost. The effect is to give the regime an excuse further to tighten its controls. The logic of the struggle is to destroy the moderates. It is as if the United States felt that it could effectively fight Castroism in Latin America only by pushing Cuba into the Soviet bloc and into an internal struggle with the Catholic Church. On the other hand, within Cuba, the hostility of the United States has strengthened the radicals and left the regime with little alternative but to seize more properties in order to obtain revenue, to wipe out middle-class opposition and to press forward while it can on the industrialization of Cuba. At the same time, our effort to mobilize Latin America against Castro, forces his regime to take countermeasures and raise the Latin American masses against us. Thus the stage is being set for a hemispheric struggle unless a settlement between Washington and Moscow can bring as its corollary a settlement between Washington and Havana.

When Washington clamped down on Castro's oil, he could turn to Moscow. If Moscow were now to bring pressure, he has nowhere to go. If China had an excess of petroleum and a fleet of tankers, Castro would still have an alternative. Indeed, the Cuban problem illustrates what the Kremlin will be up against when China is a major industrial power. The Cuban leaders admire the Russians, but lean toward Peking. There is a curious economic reason visible in the comprehensive report Major Ernesto Guevara made over the Cuban TV January 6 on his return from the Soviet bloc. Except for China, no other country in the Soviet bloc really needs Cuba's one export commodity—sugar. The Soviet Union, as Major Guevara explained, "is at present the world's largest sugar producer. Exactly two years ago the Soviet Union beat Cuba's output and is now the largest producer as a result of its execution of a vast sugar development plan." East Europe has its own beet sugar.

All the East European satellites together only promise to take 300,000 tons of Cuban sugar while smaller token amounts, as gestures of good will, were taken by the Asian satellites: North Korea, 20,000 tons; North Vietnam, 5,000 tons and Outer Mongolia, 1,000 tons. The biggest contract, naturally, was with the Soviet Union, but this contained a curious proviso. "The Soviet Union," Major Guevara said, "undertakes to buy 2,700,000 tons of sugar in the event that the United States fails to buy sugar, an event which seems most likely." This proviso seems to reflect two premises, one economic and the other political. The first is that the Soviet Union does not need sugar. The second is that it is not disposed to shut the door on a resumption of normal trade relations between the United States and Cuba. The Russians could shut that door simply by a firm contract to take over the bulk of the Cuban sugar crop. By leaving the door open, they also leave the door open to negotiations with Washington in which Cuba may figure. In this connection, it should be noted that if the summit conference hadn't broken down last year, the Russians would have been much less ready to step in when the oil embargo was imposed on Cuba last July. The Cubans may fear a rapprochement between Washington and Moscow.

In this, their position is similar to that of China, which also fears being isolated by a Russo-American understanding. China's economics, like China's politics, fit those of the Castro regime. China is buying 1,000,000 tons of sugar. "With the Peoples Republic of China," as Major Guevara said in his radio report, "the problems are entirely different because sugar is very scarce in China. Our agreement with China for a credit of 100 million pesos and our contract to supply China with 1,000,000 tons of sugar will be implemented without difficulty." Indeed China's potential market could easily make Cuba independent of the United States sugar market. Major Guevara pointed out that China "is a country with less than two kilograms per capita annual consumption of sugar while in Cuba the figure is around forty kilograms and in industrialized countries between thirty and forty kilograms per capita. Were China to raise that consumption to ten kilograms, still a low figure per capita per annum, it would demand Cuba's entire crop of 7,000,000 tons, or a lot more than our present annual output of 6,000,000 tons."

Like China, Cuba is a revolutionary power with a revolutionary mentality, and a revolutionary attitude toward war, even in the atomic age. The attitude of the Castro regime is indicated in another section of the Guevara broadcast where he said:

"Cuba is engaged in an economic war and nearly, but not quite, in a kind of warfare which is not simply economic, against a mighty power and with the support of another mighty power. We of Cuba must do our part because we are not onlookers in this struggle between two colossi over Cuba; we are a very important, a most important part in that struggle. We must maintain the unity of our people and the spirit of our people, their capacity for sacrifice, present and expandable. This capacity of our people for sacrifice must be expanded far more than it is now because it is a fact known to one familiar with the history of all of the socialist countries that here in Cuba we have had practically no experience of suffering. Here in Cuba we mention the figure of twenty thousand dead but over there in China they put the figure at twenty million dead. . . . China and the Soviet Union know the vast loss of millions of their citizens. They love peace deeply. The Soviet Union and its citizens are impregnated with the thought of peace and the conviction that they can win all of their goals by peaceful means. Yet, they are ready to go to the destruction of all they have in a war characterized by the use of atomic weaponry and unimaginable destruction of lives simply for the sake of maintaining their principle and protecting Cuba."

Major Guevara is the least demagogic and the most sober,

though perhaps also the most revolutionary, of all the Cuban leaders. It is to be doubted whether the Chinese, much less the Russians, are quite that ready to die for Cuba; the real danger is that step by step both sides in the East-West struggle may be drawn into positions over Cuba where they can no longer draw back. I found most Fidelistas quite light-headed in their attitude toward war, and in their faith that the Soviet Union would cheerfully risk its existence to support Cuba. Little Cuba is in fact turning against us the whole idea of massive deterrence—the idea that the nation which is ready to risk bringing the planet down in nuclear suicide holds the winning hand. In this, too, the Cuban psychology is like the Chinese rather than the Russians, and though no one said so, I suspect that like Peking the Cubans too consider us a "paper tiger." The oil and sugar companies, by forcing us into an intransigent attitude toward the Cuban Revolution, have created a problem of formidable proportions on our doorstep.

FEBRUARY 27, 1961

THE DEED WAS DONE QUICKLY, BUT IT'S MACBETH WHO'S DEAD

Here in Washington, and earlier at the UN in New York, it was being whispered that if the Cuban deed were to be done, it would be best if it were done quickly. And so, it seems, these Shakespearian prayers have been granted, except that it is Macbeth not the King who lies slain. The rebel invasion of Cuba, as this is being written, seems to have been crushed. There is an atmosphere of deep gloom at the State Department. The President, due to "the press of business," has just announced that he will be unable to witness that weekend naval training exercise off the Florida coast, and the Navy followed this a few minutes later by canceling the exercise altogether, though it was supposed to have been routine. Several hours before the news came over the UPI ticker that rebel headquarters had lost all contact with the troops on the beachhead in Las Villas ("Do you want me to evacuate you?" seems to have been the last words transmitted to them by the commander of an offshore supply vessel), the AP's State Department correspondent John M. Hightower had already filed a dispatch saying that the rebel invasion "was reported on excellent authority today" to have failed to set off "the political defections and uprisings" on which the expedition had counted. The failure was a failure of Intelligence, and it is being said jokingly in the State Department press room that after the U-2 incident and the debacle in Laos, the Cuban defeat is the third strike against the CIA, and on three strikes it should be out. Fidel Castro will have done us a favor if his cleanup of the invasion also leads to a cleanup of Allen Dulles and the CIA. They have again demonstrated their incompetence.

The shattering of the invasion hopes may also shatter the Kennedy honeymoon. The post-mortems had begun before the defeat was confirmed. On the hill, a Senate Internal Security sub-committee under Dodd of Connecticut has been holding executive sessions today to hear complaints from the wilder right wing of the Cuban emigration against the Miro Cardona coalition. A preview was provided in last night's *Washington Star* where its right-wing columnist Constantine Brown attacked the Miro Cardona coalition as too far left, and predicted on the basis of earlier hearings by Internal Security "should the present counterrevolution succeed, there will not be much change in the totalitarian policies of Castro." On the other hand, the left wing of the emigration had already begun to grumble bitterly about Kennedy. Those who had hoped for a new Fidelism without Fidel were disappointed on two scores. The first is that they had been forced to accept an economic and social program tailored to the moderate right and inconsistent, in their view, with the hopes aroused by the *Alianza para el progreso*. The second is with the invasion itself, in which they had had little hope from the beginning.

One of the key points to watch, I had been told earlier, was the choice of military leader for the invasion forces. There were two candidates. The candidate of the anti-Castro left led by Manolo Ray was Colonel Ramón Barquin, the most respected military figure in the emigration, an army officer who had been imprisoned by Batista for revolting against him. Colonel Barquin was named military commander of Havana by Fidel and defected last summer. Colonel Barquin was against any large-scale invasion, predicting that it would be disastrous if attempted because the time for it was not ripe; he is reported to have said that it would be militarily difficult and psychologically bad, uniting the Cuban people behind Castro against what would inevitably appear to be a foreign-inspired invasion. He was in favor of infiltrating small groups and working from within. The candidate of the right-wingers was Captain Manuel Artimé, a young man in his late twenties, a member of the *Agrup-*

ción Católica, who had served for a month or two with Castro in the Sierra Maestra. He was described to me as "the pinup boy of the CIA" and the darling of the right-wing *Diario de la Marina,* which only last Saturday appealed for a new government which would exclude all who had ever served with Castro.

Captain Artimé was, however, to be forgiven his short stay under Fidel's banner and it was Captain Artimé who was chosen to command the invasion. The right wanted a man of its own in charge of the troops, and a man who shared its objective. This was not a new popular uprising but a beachhead on which a provisional government could quickly be established and then appeal for American arms and American military support. The paymasters of the counterrevolution, the big sugar and oil and other companies which helped finance the invasion, didn't invest their money to buy themselves a new revolution.

No doubt the defeat will be disguised as a lack of materiel. I have never seen a military force equipped so quickly with tanks and jets, at least in the headlines. A few days ago it was being leaked by the CIA that we had to mount an invasion quickly before Soviet MIGs arrived. They seem to have been supplied more quickly than anyone expected by the Lem Jones firm, which was hired to polish up public relations for the rebel forces. On Tuesday afternoon, Lem Jones put out a bulletin saying that Soviet tanks and MIGs had destroyed "sizeable amounts of medical supplies and equipment" on the Matanzas beachhead, "humanitarian supplies . . . destined for the Cuban freedom fighters who are shedding their blood to overthrow the shackles of Communism." Thanks to this communiqué, the headlines in this morning's papers were full of Soviet tanks and jets, although smaller, more sober stories buried inside the *New York Times,* the *Herald-Tribune* and the *Washington Star* explained that heavy tanks would be useless on that swampy terrain, questioned whether Fidel had MIGs and pointed out that these planes would be of dubious value against small bodies of troops with mountain-forest cover. These side stories, which seemed to originate from responsible sources in the Pentagon, said the fighting was essentially a small arms operation but in the headlines the Soviet tanks and MIGs fought on undeterred.

On the stock market Monday, the stocks of American firms which lost property in Cuba rose hopefully but wiser estimates were already available. Albert M. Colegrove in the Scripps-Howard papers said most businessmen operating in Latin America disagreed with the rosy hopes of the rebels and quoted one United States businessman from Panama as saying, "Why don't you folks up there in Florida stop kidding yourselves? Sure Castro has lost some support among the middle-class people who still remain in Cuba, but most of the peasants, who comprise the great bulk of the Cuban population, still think he's great." These businessmen seemed to have a more realistic view than such liberals as the editors of the *Washington Post,* the *New Republic* and Max Lerner who lined up so quickly—and as it turns out so prematurely—with the war crowd. Now it is difficult to see what the anti-Castro forces can do. With no bridgehead, there can be no provisional government and it is too late for direct action by the Marines. This is not 1917.

At the United Nations earlier this week, one felt that the Cuban invasion was destroying Adlai Stevenson and the United States morally. How defend the indefensible and deny the undeniable? But the defeat of the rebel forces has suddenly turned high tragedy into low comedy. The Latins who spoke so bitterly in private and were so conspicuously silent in public will now laugh at the United States. It is better that the defeat came now and quickly before the flames could spread. I hope we are not going to try and retrieve our prestige by jumping into a jungle war in Laos, and that the bigger Latin countries will rescue us by firmly pressing for negotiations between Washington and Havana. We're lucky if we can liquidate this David and Goliath affair with no more than this minor bloody nose. It is too bad that our own folly gave Khrushchev a cheap and easy chance to win a victory of prestige, but that is an irretrievable error. Let's not compound it with greater folly by continuing our vendetta against Castro.

APRIL 21, 1961

TIME, THE MONROE DOCTRINE AND WAR ON CUBA

Time magazine calls for war against Cuba in a special cover article about the Monroe Doctrine. Its suggestion of "a direct U.S. invasion of Cuba, carried out with sufficient force to get the job done with surgical speed and efficiency"; its dismissal of inter-American pacts against intervention as "multilateral flypaper"; and its distortions of the Monroe Doctrine to lay a basis for such action will hurt our country deeply in this hemisphere and beyond it. It recalls how another lord of the press, William Randolph Hearst, helped pressure another unwilling but wavering President, McKinley, into war. To see how the Monroe Doctrine looks to our neighbors is now a necessity.

No Monroe Doctrine freed Latin America. "Our brothers of the north," Bolívar said, "have been apathetic bystanders in our struggle." Latin America owed its successful revolt to the weakening of Spain by the Napoleonic invasion. From that point on, Britain and the United States became rivals for the hemisphere. Both preferred to leave a weakened Spain in control. Britain wanted a Spain strong enough to counterbalance France but too weak to stop British trade with Spanish America. Once we had taken Florida, we preferred Spanish rule in Cuba and Puerto Rico rather than their liberation by the antislavery Spanish-American revolutionists or their annexation by Britain.

The Holy Alliance of Russia, Austria and Prussia, with France, when it threatened reconquest of the Spanish colonies, was a threat to England's trade and power. The joint declaration suggested to us by the British Foreign Minister, Canning, in August, 1823, was a subtle effort to block American expansion as well, by getting us to join England in declaring, "We aim not at the possession of any portion of them [i.e., the former Spanish colonies] ourselves." In the Cabinet discussion which preceded the Monroe Doctrine, "Mr. John Quincy Adams thought that Canning wanted some public pledge from the United States not only against the forcible intervention of the Holy Alliance in Spanish America but also especially against the acquisition by the United States of any part of those countries" (p. 100, J. Reuben Clark's Memorandum on the Monroe Doctrine, State Department, 1930). The shape of things to come may be seen in the same record's notation that Calhoun was prepared for such a declaration "even if it should pledge the United States not to take Cuba or Texas." Adams was against the acceptance of any such self-denying pledge. The Monroe Doctrine as declared in December, 1823, warned the European powers *other than Spain* to keep *their* hands off the colonies but did not pledge us to do so.

It was American rivalry with Britain, not a fraternal desire to protect Spanish America, which bulked large behind the Monroe Doctrine. In the three years after it was made, five newly independent Latin nations, Chile, Colombia, Brazil, Mexico and the United Provinces of the Río de la Plata (as Argentina was then known)

appealed to us for aid under the Doctrine against European interference but were brushed off. The Monroe Doctrine was all but forgotten for a quarter century until Polk revived it against British and
French interference in the annexation of Texas and the war with
Mexico. We used it as a battle cry in the Oregon dispute with Britain and in protesting British designs in California, before we took it
from Mexico. The Doctrine showed itself in the Mexican war as an
instrument of our own expansion at the expense of our Latin neighbors. The hemisphere was to be our private preserve. This attitude
reached its boldest and baldest assertion in the famous message
which Secretary of State Olney sent the British in 1895 in the Venezuela dispute. "The United States is practically sovereign on this
continent," Olney informed England, "and its fiat is law upon the
subjects to which it confines its interposition. Why? It is not because
of the pure friendship or good will felt for it. . . . It is because,
in addition to all other grounds, its infinite resources combined with
its isolated position render it master of the situation and practically
invulnerable against any or all powers."

One of the simple-minded notions about the Monroe Doctrine
is that it saved Spanish America by shutting off the New World
from the quarrels of the old. This is only a partial truth. A sphere
of interest policy always places smaller neighbors at the mercy of
the sphere's dominant power, and unable to play the big powers
against each other for their own protection. One reason our Revolution succeeded is that we were able to play off France against England. American dominance was as feared by Latin America as Russian power was by the Turks, the Iranians and the Poles under similar circumstances. Stalin's insistence on Russia's right to have
"friendly neighbors" was the equivalent of our Monroe Doctrine.
The policy of the Big Stick, and Dollar Diplomacy, as practiced
under Teddy Roosevelt, Taft, Woodrow Wilson and Coolidge led
the Latins to reverse Canning's famous dictum and seek in the Old
World some way to redress the balance of the New.

The first challenge to United States supremacy was not the
Russian thermonuclear weapon, which has deprived us of what
Olney described as an "isolated position . . . invulnerable against
any and all powers." The first challenge was the rise of the Axis
under which Nazi, Fascist, and Japanese influence, abetted by
Franco's anti-American appeals to *Hispanidad,* spread widely in
Latin America. Even so anti-Fascist a country as Mexico turned

in desperation to an oil deal with the Third Reich to end the strangling embargo which followed its expropriation of the American oil companies, as Castro turned to Russian aid under similar circumstances. It was fear of Yankee hegemony which the Good Neighbor policy met; FDR at Montevideo in 1933 began the process of converting the Monroe Doctrine from an instrument of American domination to a hemispheric self-defense pact, buttressed for the first time by our pledges not to intervene in the affairs of our neighbors. These are the pledges, most clearly expressed in the 1948 Bogotá Pact, which we have been violating by our economic blockade of Cuba.

For the Latin Americans the longer-range issue in Cuba is their right to carry on trade and diplomatic relations with the Soviet Union as a counterpoise to the United States. Our hostile policy toward Cuba raises the question for them—at what point will the United States interfere with their Soviet relations if Cuba is crushed? When they buy cheaper oil? For us Americans, the situation is a challenge to our maturity, wisdom and patience. Let us stop talking about the Monroe Doctrine, as if it came down from Mt. Sinai; the Latins hate it. Let us think instead in terms of true national interests. We are the beneficiaries of the policies it cloaked; our great country, from sea to sea, is the fruit of conquest and expansion. It is not to our interest to have Russian bases in this hemisphere, though it be only a taste of the same medicine we give them by our bases in Turkey and Iran. But as in the thirties we must see that to preserve a friendly hemisphere we must adopt policies of equality and partnership with our Latin neighbors.

War against Cuba would stir up hateful memories and split the hemisphere apart. Resumption of Cuban relations, honoring those treaties in which we gave up the Big Stick, would win us friends and enable us to dislodge Russian influence. To resume unilateral policies of force would be to invite disaster in the hemisphere, even if the Russians do nothing here or elsewhere. For it would revive fears of Yankee imperialism, destroy the middle of the road elements on which the Alliance for Progress depends and turn a Cuban war into a hemispheric civil war. Our country's greatness and its security depend now more than ever on our ability to look at this Cuban situation with eyes neither clouded by myths about the Monroe Doctrine nor blinded by frustration that we can no longer always and completely have our own way.

SEPTEMBER 21, 1962

NOT EASY TO BE A REPORTER—*AT LARGE*—IN HAVANA

"It's a long time since I've made out a ticket to Havana," said the girl at the airline ticket counter in Washington. On the plane for New Orleans, when it looked as if we were going to be late, I explained to the stewardess that I was anxious to make the connection for Mexico City because I had to catch a plane for Cuba next day. "Going to *Cuba?*" the stewardess repeated incredulously. After dinner she came back and asked, "Aren't you afraid?" In New Orleans the Mexico City connection had left and several of us were routed through Houston. When a mink-clad fellow traveler—if she will pardon the phrase—heard I was going on to Havana, she screamed with surprise. "You going to Cuba? I didn't know anybody went there any more." I began to feel as if I were headed for the moon.

The day before I left Washington, Mr. Kennedy at press conference had announced he would soon be imposing new restrictions on other nations' shipping to Cuba. On the way to the airport, I read an editorial in the *Washington Daily News* saying "failure of the Soviet Union to live up to its agreement with Cuba is on the whole a good break for the United States" because otherwise "President Kennedy's rather vague promises against invasion might have proved embarrassing." These seemed a poor prelude to a mission of peace, even by one well-meaning Yankee journalist, slightly overweight, traveling to an island neighbor on which his government's blockade was imposing hunger.

In Mexico City, there was the same sensation of traveling to a land cut off, besieged, rendered unfamiliar. The taxi driver, on our way in from the airport, assured me when asked how people there felt about Castro that they were good Catholics, implying that as such they were naturally hostile to all sons of Satan. The well-stocked bookstores of the Mexican metropolis, two years ago full of works about and by Castro, were now swept clean of such literature. The only place I encountered sympathy for Cuba was in a Mexico City pharmacy. I had with me a list of medicines urgently needed in Havana and I had decided to buy what I could in Mexico. When I explained my purpose, I was given warm and friendly attention, helped with my selections and offered a 10 percent discount on my one hundred dollars in purchases. I took the discount in extra medical supplies. "Those poor people," said the clerk in Spanish, of the Cubans, as she wrapped my package in holiday gift paper.

At the airport next day, it was clear that the Mexican government did not look on visits to Cuba with any such sentimental eye. As we cleared the last immigration barrier, every visitor leaving for Cuba was photographed, close up, by a police photographer. Then a long wait began. First the Cubana Air Lines plane was late in arriving and then it was late in leaving. A rumor spread that an incoming American on board had been arrested by the Cubans, forbidden permission to land, and ordered back to Cuba. Then it turned out that the Mexican government, which is trying to make travel to Cuba as difficult as possible for North Americans, was refusing to let two Canadians and an American get off the plane because they lacked transit visas. Fortunately the American was married to a Belgian woman. Among the Havana-bound passengers waiting (mostly diplomats) was the Belgian Ambassador. He finally loosened the noose of hostile Mexican regulations and obtained permission for the American and the Canadians to land in transit and thus release our plane for the return flight.

We set off at last, elated but hungry, all of us wondering whether the Cuban starvation rations we had read about would begin on the trip. But our fears proved unfounded, and Cubana Air Lines served us an excellent dinner. There was even a chess set on board with which I and a Dutch businessman were able to make the flight of almost four hours pass swiftly. But the ordeal of entry into the strange new world of Cuba was not yet over. We landed a little after midnight, and the familiar airport seemed less festive than on earlier occasions. There was no band to serenade us. The only banner in evidence said, "We are thankful for the fraternal aid of the Socialist countries." It was soon evident that this gratitude did not extend to visiting United States journalists. We all passed the health officer quickly and together, but every time I moved up to the immigration barrier I was waved back while others were cleared through. The immigration officer in charge had a lean and hungry look. I could not catch his eye and I had a vague feeling that I was going to have trouble.

Everybody else had been cleared through. The airport was empty of all but officials and porters when my case was finally taken up. My money was changed, down to the last penny, at the official peso-for-dollar rate. My bags were gone through carefully and the medicines I had brought were taken from me. I protested that they were urgently needed and showed a letter from the Medical Aid for Cuba Committee giving me, at my request, a list of the medicines most in short supply and the name of a doctor at a Havana hospital to contact on my arrival. I said I was afraid they might be lost around the airport. An angry young militant shouted furiously at me that under the Revolution nothing was lost! I was tired and cross and rather relished the idea of a good fight and shouted back at him not to give me that line of hooey, or words to that effect. The militant thereupon insisted that I be given a receipt, item for item, and a customs ticket with which the hospital could retrieve the medicines. (A doctor from the hospital picked up the receipt from me two days later and went to the airport where he was given forms to fill out and told to return next day. I never did find out for sure whether the medicines got through). But I had clearly marked myself in his Jacobinical eye as a counterrevolutionary element. While he looked on glaring, another agent started through a zipper portfolio I was carrying. When I assured him there was nothing in it but *"periodicos"* (papers and magazines), he ruled that these could not enter Cuba but must be left at the airport where I could pick them up on leaving. I pulled out a recent issue of *The New Yorker* in protest to show him I was not carrying dangerous literature, though I afterward thought nothing could be more subversive to morale under the austerities of socialism than those glittering ads it carried. I don't know how the argument would have ended if an officer had not interrupted to tell me that I would have to go with him to the immigration office in Havana for questioning. Two militiamen with him picked up the portfolio along with my two other bags and hustled me out to a car waiting in the darkness outside.

So at two in the morning, I started off for Havana in an automobile with two militiamen and the immigration officer, none of whom could—or would—speak English. When I tried to find out what was up, they would shout, *"Habla español,"* as if the mere attempt to speak in English was an affront to Cuba's newly-found nationalist dignity. My papers were in order. I had a United States passport cleared for travel to Cuba and I had a visa issued by the Cubans through the Czech Embassy in Washington. Apparently these documents merely demonstrated how clever imperialist agents could be. We seemed to be short of gas and kept stopping along the darkened roads at gas stations only to find them closed. I had a vision of us running out of gas and of making the long march into Havana with my captors and my bags on foot. But luckily we found a gas station open, filled our tank and reached a police station on a narrow street in the old city of Havana. There my captors were greeted with warm revolutionary *abrazos,* and no doubt felicitated on their fine catch. They disappeared into a combination police dormitory and jail in the rear of the station. I found myself with two new guards. They refused to let me phone the hotel at which I was supposed to have reservations and told me I was being held incommunicado to await the arrival of an immigration officer in the morning. I refused to go to sleep on a cot set up for me in the rear just outside the jail cells and spent the rest of the night alternately dozing in a chair and roaming around the police station.

It was dingy and it smelled like police stations do all over the world. It differed only in its pictures and in its books. The pictures on the wall were those of José Marti and of Camille Cienfuegos, the latter a *barbudo* of Christlike beauty, one of the early heroes and martyrs of the Revolution. The only picture of Fidel Castro was one torn out of a newspaper and pinned to the bulletin board along with an article about Maceo, the Negro general who was one of the leaders in the revolt against Spain. On the blackboard was written an invitation to comrades of the police to attend the wedding of one of them.

The tattered volumes on the bookshelves were unlike those to be found in the police stations of any other country in the world. There was Plato's *Republic* and, of course, *Don Quixote.* There was a two-volume history of the Platt Amendment we imposed on Cuba after the war with Spain. There was Liu Shao-chi's *How to Be a Good Communist* and Lenin's *Bankruptcy of the Second International.* There was Trotsky's famous attack on Stalinism, *Their Morals and Ours.* There was also his *Permanent Revolution* and his *Last Testament of Lenin.* There were several examples of the inexpensive Marxist books the Soviet Union exports in large quantities like Kostantinov's *Fundamentals of Marxist Philosophy* and there were large stacks of back numbers of the *Peking Review.*

I was poorly guarded and could have run away if I had known where I was. But this would have meant leaving my bags behind and risking a shot from the pistols of my guards. In any case, it was much too interesting an experience to run away from. Of the two guards, both young, the one in charge was as implacable as the well-bred revolutionist should be when dealing with a counterrevolutionary suspect; my repeated efforts to argue him into making a phone call were of no avail. His assistant, who seemed to be studying an introductory book on aeronautical engineering during the night, was friendly. He told me he was a *campesino,* that he had gone through only five grades of school at the time of the Revolution and he waxed eloquent on its benefits, though much of his Spanish I could not understand. As we were standing outside the station talking, a newsboy came along with the paper *Hoy,* organ of the Cuban Communist party. He bought me a copy and we settled down to read a document not to be found in Communist papers anywhere else in the Soviet world except Albania and North Korea and perhaps North Vietnam—a partial text several columns long as distributed by the Chinese News Agency of the editorial, "Proletarians of All Countries, Unite in Order to Fight Against Our Common Enemy" with which the *People's Daily* of Peking, December 15, had replied to Khrushchev's defense a few days earlier of his policy on Cuba. The Castro regime supplied the Cuban public impartially with the full text of what both sides in the Soviet world, the Russian and the Chinese, had said in their bitter dispute over Cuba, thermonuclear war and policy toward the United States.

At 6 A.M. my *campesino* friend went out and returned with two long loaves of bread and a large can of coffee. The two guards settled down to their breakfast and waved me to join them. I was allowed to wash up in the lavatory behind the police barracks, which seemed to be full of police sleeping in bunks piled three tiers high. The guards broke off huge slabs of bread which we dunked in small cans of coffee. The bread and coffee tasted good and I settled down afterward to sleep in a swivel chair. But when I awoke and saw it was past nine o'clock and there was no sign of a hearing officer I began to get restless. When a new shift of guards came on and I heard my case being discussed with the night shift, I renewed my efforts at a phone call. In my rudimentary Spanish, using the fingers of one hand to make my point, I said there were probably three or four *periodistas* (newspapermen) in the United States still friendly to the Cuban Revolution, that I was one of them, that I had brought scarce medicines as a present to Cuba, and that here I was being held a prisoner. I said Che Guevara, Roa, Dorticos and other top leaders knew me and all they had to do was telephone to check my identity. "Look," I said, as a clincher, "didn't Fidel himself in a recent speech attack *bureaucracia* and isn't this an example of bureaucracy at work?" My words seemed to make an impression on one of the new guards. He went off down the street—to make a phone call, I hoped. In the meantime, when ten o'clock came with no action, I thought I had better raise a tantrum. I began kicking chairs around the police station and demanding that someone who spoke English be summoned. This brought angry and sleepy guards pouring out of the barracks and finally I was taken inside, and a policeman awakened who spoke English.

There was a furious torrent of Spanish from the guard to the policeman who spoke English, and then I had an unpleasant surprise. At intervals, through the night, when I tried to make a phone call, I was assured that an immigration officer would be there at nine o'clock, and it was implied that then my difficulties would be over. But now I was informed by the English-speaking policeman that nothing could be done for me because it was not an immigration matter at all, but was in the hands of the security police. With this, as if to dramatize the hopelessness of further discussion, he turned over in his bunk and went back to sleep again.

It had been a comfort to remember, during the night, that Professor Samuel Shapiro told me before I left the States that he had twice been arrested in Cuba, once on arrival, again on departure, for incautious remarks at the airport. But with the news that the security police were in charge of my case, I began to feel real alarm. I suddenly remembered the fate of my good friend, Mordecai Oren. An Israeli Left Zionist newspaperman, he had been arrested by the Czechs on a visit to Prague and framed for espionage in connection with the Slansky affair and imprisoned for four years. I recalled that when I met him at the Belgrade conference in September, 1961, he told me of the methods used to extract a false confession from him. He had given me a copy of his book, as translated from the Hebrew and published in France under Jean-Paul Sartre's aegis (M. Oren: *Prisonnier politique à Prague;* Les Temps Modernes: Julliard, 1960), in which he told the story. I wondered whether a similar fate might be in store for me. I had said to my wife on leaving in high spirits that if I were locked up in Cuba she was to send me oatmeal cookies. Now it looked as if this might turn out to be a prophetic joke!

I decided I had better calm down and rest up for a possible ordeal. I came out of the police dormitory and stretched out on two chairs in the rear of the police station to get some sleep. My audience was a ragged collection of two dozen juvenile delinquents picked up off the streets and locked up for the night. They had poured out of their cells for breakfast during my tantrum and now their chatter ceased and they looked on in wonder at this unexpected diversion with their bread and coffee.

I shut my eyes and tried to sleep. The thought crossed my mind that if I were to have a prolonged stay in a Cuban jail, I could grow a beard and emerge a *barbudo*. I must have slept a short while. When I opened my eyes again, there in the doorway of the police station was the guard who had seemed to be impressed with my story, and had gone off—I hoped, to make a phone call. He signaled with one hand, the five fingers outstretched, and formed *"Cinco minutos"* with his lips. It sounded as if he had indeed gotten help for me. I closed my eyes again. Then I heard a typewriter. Within a few minutes I was given a one-page document in quintuplicate for signature. I could see that it was a release but I refused on principle to sign until it had been translated into English. Now the guards seemed to be anxious to get rid of me as soon as possible. They awakened the same English-speaking policeman in the barracks and brought him out immediately. It was an unconditional release which involved no concessions on my part, though there was still no explanation of why I had been detained in the first place. I signed all five copies, took one for myself and asked that a taxi be summoned. My anonymous friend among the guards found one for me. He and a plain-clothes man helped me with my bags. They had not been searched or examined again. I shook hands warmly with the guard I suspected of having made a phone call for me and thanked him again. I was free. It was almost noon on a warm sunny Sunday in Havana.

Finding a hotel was a problem. No reservations had been made for me. All the hotels I phoned seemed to be jammed. I managed to reach an old friend in the Cuban Foreign Ministry. He arranged to meet me at the Havana Riviera, and apologized profusely for my detention, but he was as mystified as I was as to why I had been held. I had the feeling that in Cuba the vagaries of the secret police were accepted as one might accept elsewhere the vagaries of the weather. To make up for what happened he got me a room at the Havana Riviera. This huge luxury hotel, built by a Las Vegas group, I believe, is now a Foreign Ministry hostel for visiting VIPs. The bedroom assigned me was palatial. Its huge mirror windows looked out on a baby-blue sea and the great curve of the *Malecon*. The place was spotless, the only sign of the revolution being an ash tray on which was imprinted an appeal to the proletariat to unite. I had made it from jail to gilded palace, as the Chinese might say, in one great leap forward.

I had a shave and a hot bath and a short nap and then set forth, as befits a loyal American, to celebrate my freedom with a nostalgic pilgrimage to Sloppy Joe's, the bar which was for so many years the Mecca of thirsty or lonesome fellow American tourists. Strangely enough the cab driver—and this itself struck me as a sign of how times have changed—had never heard of Sloppy Joe's! I directed him to go to the Prado. There I got out. I walked past the familiar but now boarded up curio shops and the equally familiar but still open bars like Dirty Dick's, and there, miraculously, was Sloppy Joe's, open too and still in business. I felt as if I were on *terra firma* at last.

There were only six patrons—two of them shooting dice—at the long mahogany bar, probably one of the world's longest. The walls were still lined with pictures of American celebrities taken on past visits to Havana—bygone worthies from a bygone past, from Joe Lewis to Joan Blondell and Willie Pep to Carole Landis. I ordered a daiquiri, which cost only ninety cents and was first-rate. Despite Marxism-Leninism, Cuba's daiquiris remain the world's best. The bartender observed me discreetly but curiously. "You English?" he asked. "No," I said, "American." He looked at me warily, as if I were a phantom. "Any other Americans here?" I asked him. "No," said the bartender, "in Cuba, Americans *feen eesh*." He said it with a sweeping gesture, neither sadly nor triumphantly but objectively and with finality, as of an unalterable fact. I felt like the last Yankee imperialist, unwelcome and no longer at home.

JANUARY 7, 1963

CASTRO'S OWN BRAND OF MARXISM-LENINISM

Cuba, seen from within, looks very different than from without. Food may be poor and lacking in variety, but there is enough to eat and no sign whatever of starvation; indeed one Latin American reporter, who had been all over the country in the past few months, told me he thought the poor people of Cuba were better fed today than in any other country of Latin America. I had been led by the United States press to expect to see a city slowly being strangled by blockade; instead the streets were lively, taxis plentiful and the number of private cars surprising for a country so dependent for its oil on a distant source of supply. The *guaguas* (buses) seemed decrepit and were terribly overcrowded in the evening rush hour—but that is hardly a condition peculiar to underdeveloped or Socialist countries; bus commuters of the world everywhere are ready to unite. Finally, neither in the streets nor at the university, in the shops or restaurants, nor in their homes, do the Cubans seem a people cowed. The notion that Russian troops may be in Cuba to help Fidel hold his people down is the silliest delusion the United States government and press have ever encouraged. I saw no Russian soldiers and only an occasional Russian civilian in Havana, a city where everyone seems to be carrying a pistol, a sten gun or a machine gun. If the Cuban people and the Fidelistas were as permeated by discontent as Washington seems to think, they could shoot the place up and mow any stray Russians down any time they wanted to. Nowhere in the Soviet bloc are the people themselves armed as in Cuba.

Cuba, only ninety miles away, is today unmistakably a part of the Soviet world, and Havana is a Soviet capital. The newsstands carry only Soviet publications. The bookstores no longer display the works of heretical Communists like Victor Serge; the objective or hostile accounts of communism one could still buy there two years ago have disappeared from the shelves. The young Cuban studying English, even when he wants to read *Huckleberry Finn* or *Moby Dick,* reads them in inexpensive Soviet editions I saw in bookstore windows. The movies show the same *Our Nikita* film as in Moscow; Polish, Bulgarian, and Chinese films have replaced Hollywood's. Partly this is our own fault. We have made dollar exchange available abroad in many countries for the import of American magazines and books; we have been trying for years to get American publications into Moscow. But in Cuba we shut off the export of American publications and films by our trade embargo policies long before Cuba had become Sovietized culturally. If we think it would be good for United States policy and for better understanding to have the *New York Times* on sale in Moscow, why not in Havana? If we negotiate the entry of American films into the Soviet Union, why not into Cuba? Alfredo Guevara, head of the Cuban Institute of Art and Movie Industries, in a speech to the First National Congress of Culture, held in Havana while I was there, said, "We are not the enemies of the artistic works of any country," and expressed a hope for North American films.

The policy of pulling down an iron curtain of our own on Cuba, of nonintercourse and embargo, has fostered Sovietization in culture as in other realms. It has speeded up the liquidation of the American presence and of American influence in this lovely neighboring isle. A more self-defeating policy would be difficult to imagine. I am not speaking only in abstract terms. I suddenly felt jealous as an American to see none of our films advertised outside the movie houses. And I felt disturbed to notice the changed attitude toward Americans. I went out of my way everywhere to say I was an American, to see what the response would be. For the first time, the response was a chill. I was not treated rudely—the Cubans are too gentle a people for that—but nobody opened up to me, and the announcement tended not to encourage but to stop conversation. We have succeeded in making ourselves unpopular in one of the few places in Latin America where North Americans were genuinely liked in the past, even by those critical of us politically.

To say that Cuba is now part of the Soviet world is no longer the end but merely the beginning of political analysis. For the Soviet world is no longer monolithic and securely centralized as in the days of Stalin. In Cuba, one is at the very heart of the growing struggle between Moscow and Peking, a struggle as fierce but of far larger dimensions than that between Stalin and Trotzky. Then the instrument of state power was securely in the hands of one faction. Now each has its capital and a mighty country at its disposal. Of all the schisms that have rent world communism since 1917, this is the most momentous, for there are huge armies and resources—and fundamental national conflicts—on both sides. But Cuba is no mere passive bone of contention between these two giant rivals. On the contrary, just as Fidel Castro by sheer uncompromising verve and nerve has made this little island of less than seven million people the catalytic factor in the relations of two continents, of Anglo-Saxon North America and its Latin neighbors to the south, so he has made Cuba a positive and independent factor in internal Soviet bloc politics.

The split between Moscow and Peking, Khrushchev and Mao, is only the most obvious and sensational of the turbulent convulsions today in a Soviet world coming alive again from its Stalinist Ice Age. Less sensational but in many ways more important for the future is the tough rear-guard action being fought by the "dogmatists"—the hard-liners—against a youth whose appetite for freedom has only been whetted by the zigzags of the Khrushchevite thaw. These liberal forces find their inspiration in Cuba. "The Albanians," one shrewd Soviet bloc observer told me, "are only tribal gangsters. They carry no weight elsewhere in the bloc. But the Cubans are another story. They are like early Christians. The honesty, the selflessness, the revolutionary purity of the leadership centered around Fidel Castro represent a new and thrilling phenomena for Soviet youth. They grew up in the stuffy atmosphere of bureaucracy and repression. They have never seen a revolution in its first and marvelous phase. A new and inspiring wind blows out of Cuba, and Fidel and Cuba are immensely popular everywhere in the bloc. For Khrushchev, China is a foreign policy matter. But Cuba is in a curious way a domestic matter. Mikoyan, you will notice, did not spend twenty-three days in China. He spent them in Cuba. This is a measure of its importance." Khrushchev cannot ignore Cuba's popularity at home in the Soviet Union because Fidel is popular with the same forces which see in Khrushchev their best hope of winning and widening the fight against neo-Stalinist dogmatism.

Interlocked with these divergent views on foreign and domestic policy are those controversies which center about "different roads to socialism"—the question of how much freedom shall be granted the various Soviet regimes and the various Communist parties in the non-Communist world. One reason for the convulsions shaking the bloc is that considerable freedom and considerable polycentricism has developed; life stirs again in the bureaucratized corpse of Marxism-Leninism. Cuba, on the far periphery of the Soviet world geographically, not even fully accepted as genuinely "Marxist-Leninist" much less as a member of the Warsaw Pact, has become in a paradoxical way the crossroads of Sovietism ideologically. Cuba is at the very center of its decisive battles.

Cuba is the one nation in the Soviet world which is still not securely either in the Russian or the Chinese camp. It is the only place in the Soviet world where the full texts of both Khrushchev and Mao are regularly and impartially published. Castro, though dependent on Russia and the Russian bloc, said not a single word in praise of Khrushchev in his January 2 speech on the fourth anniversary of the Cuban Revolution. On the contrary, he said very coolly, "The Soviet government, in search of peace, arrived at certain agreements with the North American government, but this does not mean that we have renounced this right, the right to possess the weapons we deem pertinent as a sovereign country. And for that reason we do not accept the unilateral inspection that they wanted to establish here with the only purpose, of the imperialists, to humble us. And there was no inspection and there will be no inspection. And if they want inspection, let them permit us to inspect them." This, in the Cuban context and atmosphere, was not just telling off Kennedy. It was also telling off Khrushchev.

American official propaganda comforts itself with the idea that Castro lost prestige in the missile affair. But as seen from Havana, it is not Castro who has lost prestige in recent weeks. It is Kennedy and Khrushchev who have lost prestige. Castro's answer to the missiles removal agreement was his Five Points and his refusal to permit inspection. Castro explained privately according to one account that a big power could place and remove missiles without loss of prestige, but that for Cuba prestige was an almost material thing it could not afford to lose. So in his darkest recent hour, with the news that Khrushchev over his head had negotiated removal of the missiles with Kennedy, Castro sat down and wrote his Five Points, among them in return of Guantánamo, and made Khrushchev accept them! It was Russia and America which had to give way on inspection, not Cuba. On the heels of that, Castro made Kennedy pay the full $62,000,000 fine imposed on the exiles who attempted the Bay of Pigs invasion. When the cash and freight costs are added to the $53,000,000 in food and medicine, Castro got every last dollar of that fine. Months ago he would have ransomed them for $28,000,000. We refused and ended up by paying $62,000,000. Can the Fidelistas be blamed if they feel that Castro emerged with *increased,* Kennedy and Khrushchev with *diminished,* prestige? One of the smallest countries on earth made the two giants of the planet accept its terms. Is it any wonder if some Cubans go beyond even the Chinese and regard both the United States and the U.S.S.R. as paper tigers?

Some European Communists regard Cuba as under Chinese influence. This is a gross oversimplification. Fidel's Marxism-Leninism is a *compote* all his own. In foreign policy, it is true, he is close to the Chinese viewpoint, for both Cuba and China are treated as outcasts and enemies by United States policy. He also shares China's hostility to Yugoslavia, since Tito is a beneficiary of United States aid—but internally Castroism is more Titoist than Tito himself. No country in the bloc is so surely pursuing its own different road to socialism. In press relations with Western correspondents, Cuba is almost Stalinist. In dealing with the arts, the students and internal discussion, Cuba has passed safely through a brief Socialist-Realist phase and is now by Soviet standards *avant-garde*. For Cuba, as seen from the West, has lost considerable intellectual freedom. But Cuba, as seen from the Soviet East, now has more artistic and intellectual freedom than any other member of the bloc except perhaps Poland. In some ways Cuba is Trotzkyist without knowing it—here the revolution is *permanent,* the foreign policy revolutionary rather than collaborationist but the domestic policy in the arts and thought freer.

Indeed as seen from within, the island often seems to be anarchist, and hard to fit into the conventional lineaments of Marxism-Leninism altogether. It was a revolution made without a party and is today in many ways a government without a state. There are organs of administration but no legislature, not even of the Communist rubber stamp variety; no visible local or provincial governments. Fidel roams the island, his own inspector general, in constant touch with popular feeling, carrying on the government under his hat. Celia Sanchez, secretary to the offices of both President and Prime Minister, is said to be the one firm central organ of government which can be located with certainty in one appointed spot. The term Popular Democracy is Orwellian double talk in Eastern Europe, for its bureaucratic police regimes are neither popular nor democratic. But Cuba in its own peculiar way *is* a Popular Democracy, a kind of continuous town meeting under a popular dictator, very much like the demagogues (the word in Greek merely means leaders of the *demos,* or people) who led the poor against the rich in the Greek city-states. Marx and Lenin would be delighted perhaps but certainly a little confused by what goes on in Cuba today in their name.

For one thing, Cuba is the one Soviet State in which the Communist party not only does not rule but is on notice that it had better behave itself. In this tropical island, everything grows fast, even ideologies, and few Americans are aware of the swift ideological changes which have been occurring in Cuba. In December 1961, Fidel made his famous speech declaring himself a Marxist-Leninist. Three months later he made his first anti-Communist speech, driving a Communist leader into exile and purging his followers from the government. In the intricate maneuvers which went on between the Fidelistas and the Communists, the latter thought they could take over the new revolutionary organization (ORI) into which Fidel sought to merge his July 26 movement, the Thirteenth of March Revolutionary Directorate and the Popular Socialist Party (as the Communists call themselves). A Communist, Anibal Escalante, was made general secretary of the ORI and sought by tactics like Stalin's to take over, putting his men into key positions and making Communist party loyalty the first qualification for membership.

In addition, according to Fidel's speech of March 26, 1962, which drove Escalante into exile, a whispering campaign was begun "against the prestige of certain well-known and very valuable comrades" who were regarded as too independent of the CP clique. Che Guevara is reported to have been one of their targets, for he fought this tendency to "sectarianism" in filling the key posts of government and industry. Some Communists seem to have made the mistake, among others, of regarding Fidel as a *petit bourgeois,* perhaps even a sort of Cuban Kerensky, who could be replaced by them as the revolution proceeded. This was how they regarded him when he was up in the hills fighting Batista and some of the same attitude seems to have survived. For in the speech Castro complained that some people "after having skimmed a little Marxist book" went around saying that his famous 1953 speech, *History Will Absolve Me,* "was a reactionary document." Castro admitted that this speech "was not yet the expression of a Marxist mind, but it was the expression of a young man who was leaning toward Marxism and who was beginning to act like a Marxist." But he said its value lay not in "its theoretical, economic and political content" but in the fact that it was a denunciation of the Batista dictatorship "made in the midst of the bayonets of a hundred soldiers . . . a task a bit more difficult than that of posing as a revolutionary now." Wounded pride is not the least important element visible in this speech, a turning point in Cuba's internal politics.

Seen in perspective, Fidel's "I am a Marxist-Leninist" speech outflanked the Communists and made it possible for him to attack them three months later without seeming to be engaged in a rightist maneuver. The strangest part of the whole affair is that the Chinese, everywhere else, complain that the Russians help bourgeois nationalists in the colonial world rather than Communists, but in Cuba they support Fidel rather than the Cuban CP. More gently but as unmistakably as in Ben Bella's Algeria, the Communists are being liquidated as an independent political force. Fidel is constructing a new party, as Tito did, and when that job of organization is accomplished he will have not only full command at home but greater maneuvering power in foreign policy. No ruler ever managed to exercise more political independence in a situation more intrinsically dependent than Fidel's, for his is the only Soviet bloc country which is almost entirely shut off from trade with the non-Soviet world. As in his original landing against Batista, Fidel's main resource is nerve, and we will never be able to think straight about Cuba until we abandon the notion that this soldier-statesman is a puppet, a fool or a "nut."

In attempting, however imperfectly, to sketch in some of the nuances of Cuba's position, I do not want to leave the impression that I think Fidel Castro is in any way an American style anti-Communist. In reading the I-am-a-Marxist-Leninist speech and in revisiting Cuba, I felt that this speech had been doubly distorted in the United States. The right-wingers seized on it to say, "You see, Fidel was a Communist all along." Persons like myself, friendly to Cuba, and with a lifelong acquaintance with Communists, simply could not see Fidel Castro as a Marxist-Leninist and interpreted the speech as some kind of maneuver to assure Soviet support. I no longer think this true. I think the speech is to be read as a truthful statement. Castro in his own mind has become a Marxist-Leninist. He sees the one-party Socialist state as a swift means of development. He believes the Cuban Revolution would have been crushed without Soviet aid and orientation. He may also regard Marxism-Leninism as the philosophy furthest removed from the

United States and therefore most likely to keep his revolutionary youth from contamination by the United States. But at the same time, for him, Marxism-Leninism is not the same as accepting dictation either by the Cuban Communist party or by the Soviet bloc. This is *his* revolution. He wouldn't have made it if he had gone by the Marxist-Leninist book, and he won't let theory stand in the way of any action needed to preserve it. Under the surface of their oversimplified—often downright "infantile left"—theories, these Cuban "Marxist-Leninists" are pragmatic. When Che Guevara told the students, "If we're Marxists, we got there our own way," he was giving us a basic insight into the Fidelista movement.

An equally pragmatic United States foreign policy could come to terms with Cuba if it were willing to accept the basic aims of the Castro revolution. On that basis, in my opinion, the problem of compensation could be solved and the fear of a Soviet base on our doorstep dissipated. Time is on Fidel's side; his problems and Cuba's are minor. We exaggerate the burden on the Soviet bloc; it can easily provide the machine tools and technicians to make a success in so small and rich an island. All they need to do is to make a showplace for 6,500,000 Cubans and we will be on the spot with the 200,000,000 in the rest of Latin America.

JANUARY 14, 1963

FRESH LIGHT ON THE MYSTERY OF THE MISSILES

The only top leader I saw in my ten days in Havana was Armando Hart, the Minister of Education. But this energetic and devoted young man spoke only of the successful campaign against illiteracy and his mounting problems as more and more Cubans began to go to school, and to stay there for a higher education, all safely nonpolitical topics. I did not succeed in talking with Prime Minister Castro or any other top leader capable of discussing foreign policy questions. Knowledgeable persons told me Fidel was going through an agonizing reappraisal in the wake of the missiles affair, that until he spoke on January 2 no one knew what the new line would be, and that lesser men would hesitate to discuss such delicate matters. I found my old friends in Havana asking the same question about the missiles affair that I heard in Washington: Why did Khrushchev put them into Cuba in the first place if he was so ready to take them out again? The consensus among reporters with whom I spoke—and these included men from Soviet bloc, uncommitted and Latin American countries—was that Khrushchev had made a mistake. Nobody spelled this out but obviously the mistake was to believe that he could get away with placing nuclear missiles in Cuba.

The removal of the missiles stirred anger among the Fidelistas, and I was told that Fidel had gone several times to the University to appeal to the students to be quiet. Cubans made up a little poem which went like this:

> *Nikita, Nikita,*
> *Lo que se da,*
> *No se quita*

i.e., Nikita, Nikita, what you gave, you can't take back. In the eyes of the Fidelistas, the purpose of the missiles was simply to deter an American attack; they turned against us our own favorite theory of deterrence. But if I had had a chance to talk with top leaders I could have raised the questions which did not occur to the ordinary Fidelista: Did the Cubans realize that these missiles could be quickly observed, that theirs would be soft bases which could fairly easily be put out of commission by conventional attack, that their presence in Cuba would make Cuba a first target in the event of war between the United States and the U.S.S.R., that the missiles would raise tension and increase risk? The political questions were as delicate as the military. The Russians had agreed to remove the missiles without consulting Castro. For a man—and a people—as sensitive about their national dignity, this was an affront. An island besieged by the United States, and so dependent on the U.S.S.R., could hardly afford open discussion of such questions.

Now that Castro has made his long-awaited speech of January 2 and discussed the missiles affair, some illumination can be found by comparing the three versions now available, the Russian, the Chinese and the Cuban. Khrushchev's version, as set forth in his foreign policy address to the Supreme Soviet December 12, was that the missiles were placed there at Cuba's request, for "exclusively humanitarian motives." Khrushchev said, "Our aim was only to defend Cuba." The United States, he said, was trying "to export counterrevolution" and threatening Cuba with invasion. "We were confident," he said, "that this step," i.e., placing the missiles, "would bring the aggressors to their senses." Realizing "that Cuba was not defenseless," they would be "compelled to change their plans" and "then the need for retaining rockets in Cuba would naturally disappear."

This was the kindergarten version. What if the United States, once the missiles were removed, changed its plans again and invaded? If the Cubans were satisfied with this version, they would hardly have published the full text of Khrushchev in their press only to follow it up a few days later by printing first a partial and then the full text of the reply made by the Chinese in the Peking *People's Daily*, December 15.

The Chinese were anxious to answer Khrushchev's charge that theirs was a policy of adventurism which might well plunge the whole world into thermonuclear war. The Chinese replied that while they were opposed to "the imperialist policy of nuclear blackmail," they also saw no need whatsoever for Socialist countries to use nuclear weapons as chips in gambling or as a means of intimidation." This implied that the missiles were emplaced by the Russians as "chips" in a strategic game. "To do this," the Chinese said, "would really be committing the error of adventurism." They went on to say that "if one has blind faith in nuclear weapons" and "becomes scared out of one's wits by imperialist nuclear blackmail, one may possibly jump from one extreme to the other and commit the error of capitulationism." The Chinese said the Cubans had committed neither but implied the Russians were guilty of both. They quoted with approval Castro's statement that the way to peace "is not the way of sacrificing or infringing upon people's rights," a sideswipe at Khrushchev, and praised the Cubans because "far from being frightened by United States nuclear blackmail, they insisted on their five just demands."

This must have been music to Fidelista ears. The Chinese went on to make a puzzling remark. "The whole world knows," the Chinese said, "that we neither requested the introduction of nuclear weapons into Cuba nor obstructed the withdrawal of 'offensive' weapons from the country."

The Chinese have an influential Embassy in Havana. To say that they did not obstruct the removal of the missiles is to say that they did not advise the Cubans to resist the removal. That much seems clear. But why should they feel it necessary to say that they had never "requested" the placing of nuclear missiles in Cuba? No one assumed that they did. Castro's speech of January 2 throws some light on this. He suggested that the emplacing of the missiles in Cuba had been requested by the Russians. "We agreed with the Soviet Union on the weapons which were set up here," Fidel said, "because we understood that we were fulfilling two obligations: one toward the country, fortifying its defenses in view of imperialist threats, and one obligation toward the peoples of the Socialist camp." This contradicted Khrushchev's account. It implied that Castro allowed the missiles to be set up in Cuba not only to deter United States attack but also because he was persuaded that in doing so he would be fulfilling an obligation to the Soviet bloc. Was it to help right the Soviet missile gap by placing IRBM's in Cuba? Castro did not say. But this reference in his speech would help to explain what the Chinese meant when they said *they* had not requested the placing of missiles in Cuba, and then went on to call the emplacement "adventurism" and the swift removal "capitulationism."

Castro in his speech of January 2 had no word of praise for Khrushchev. Castro did not say, as Khrushchev did, that with the United States no-invasion pledge, there was no further need of missiles to deter a United States attack. On the contrary Castro said that while "the Soviet government, in search of peace, arrived at certain agreements with the North American government" this did not mean that Cuba had renounced "the right to possess the weapons we deem proper and to take the international steps we deem pertinent as a sovereign country." He said over and over again that he did not believe United States pledges and he would not allow inspection. The Kremlin is not accustomed to such coolly independent language.

As for the Sino-Soviet struggle, Castro alone of all the Soviet leaders declared his neutrality between Moscow and Peking. This, too, is unheard of in the bloc. There personal rivalries have always taken on doctrinal forms, and questions of doctrine in turn have been debated in the intransigent tones of medieval theological dispute, in which the loser was doomed to be outcast as a heretic. Castro stood aside from this *furor theologicus*. In his January 2 speech the Cuban spoke of the split with sorrow. He said Cuba was forced to carry on its struggle for economic development in "a bitter situation" amid "discrepancies in the bosom of the Socialist family." The very word chosen must raise eyebrows in Moscow *and* Peking. Castro could hardly have picked a weaker word than "discrepancies" for what they regard as a mortal quarrel. He said, "We see with clarity here, from this trench ninety miles from the Yankee empire, how much cause for concern these discrepancies can be, how much unity is needed, how much all the strength of the entire Socialist camp is needed to face up to these enemies." He announced that "the line of our people" was to be "to struggle for unity" in the Socialist camp so that it could present "a united front to the imperialists." Unity "inside and outside" was his watchword. This neutralism in the Soviet cold war will be as unpalatable to Moscow and Peking as India's neutralism in our cold war has been to us.

There is no better place than Havana to listen in on the controversies shaking the bloc. I did not speak with Chinese but I did speak with Russians, Poles and Yugoslavs. They cannot dismiss the Sino-Soviet struggle as easily as Castro. For Castro the problem is to save unity so he can get help from both sides in his struggle against American strangulation. For these others the problem is more complex. "The Cubans wanted to join the bloc," one Yugoslav said bitterly, "to have its advantages but then did not wish to accept its obligations." He thought it sheer madness for the Cubans to expect the Russians to risk a thermonuclear conflict on their behalf. From the Yugoslav and Polish points of view, Castro fails to see that a Chinese victory would be the end of "different roads to socialism," and that Castro would be the first to find this unbearable. For Poles and Russians, the Cubans seem not to understand that while Khrushchev may be too cautious for their taste, his downfall would threaten the greater freedom within the Soviet bloc which followed the death of Stalin and the defeat of the Old Guard. In their opinion the very same Fidelistas who cheer China's "paper tiger" line would be the first to rebel if Chinese-style thought control were to be imposed on Cuba. As for the Russians, their friendliness for Cuba in no way interferes with their obvious desire for friendlier relations with the United States.

These talks in Havana showed me that wherever American policy was to some degree flexible and pragmatic, rather than rigidly ideological, this paid off. The Yugoslavs, the Poles, the Russians—none took as dark a view of the possibilities of peaceful coexistence as the Cubans or the Chinese. This difference does not have its origin in theory but in experience. We treat communism as negotiable—everywhere but in Cuba and China. We have diplomatic relations with most of the bloc. We do some business with them. We have cultural exchanges. We even extend aid to two Communist countries, Yugoslavia and Poland. But China and Cuba are outside the pale. Is it any wonder that they, knowing only our rigid hostility, are rigidly hostile in return?

One way to look at the recent crisis is that we were brought to the brink of thermonuclear war because we had driven an island neighbor so far into fear and enmity that it was willing to emplace nuclear missiles against us. We can be back on the brink again very easily by misjudging our relations with Cuba. From all I could learn, the events of that awful weekend when the world came so close to destruction brought Castro new support from among his own people, as the Russian threat once evoked support for Tito. People who had never volunteered before came out for militia service. Those foreign observers who were in the front-line trenches when a United States attack was expected at any moment said they had never seen anything like it in their experience of war. "The sense of the people's courage," said one East European observer, "was a physical, tangible thing. You felt it in your skin and in your spine." Of course, he added, the Cubans have no conception of what a modern war, even a "conventional" one, would be like. "Everybody was running around with pistols, as in the Wild West," he said. "They did not realize that in a real war they might never see the enemy at all, much less engage in hand-to-hand combat with him." The Cubans are a brave people with a great tradition, fighting after a half century to complete a revolution we twice thwarted before, once after they defeated the Spaniards at the beginning of the century and again in 1933 after they overthrew Machado.

A visit to Havana for any foreigner today is both frustrating and inspiring. Red tape and inefficiency are suffocating, and in the middle echelons of the bureaucracy—the worst echelons everywhere —one meets officials who seem to arrive late and leave early and devote themselves in between to keeping up the morale of the cigar industry by smoking their way gloriously through the Revolution. Appointments are made and broken in the most maddening fashion. Petty officials drag out the simplest tasks to magnify their own sense of importance. One finds in oneself a sudden sympathy with the "imperialists" who have to do business in these Latin lands of a *mañana* that rarely comes. But then one encounters a very different type of official, some young guerrilla soldier turned administrator, whose sobriety and devotion are at once apparent. I was often reminded at such moments of the best *chaverim* (comrades) whom I had known in Israel in the greatest days of its struggle. Indeed Castro's Cuba often recalled Israel, in the courage of its people in the face of such great odds, and in the spirit of the Fidelistas. There is no way of knowing what portion of the Cuban people are with Fidel but everyone with whom I spoke felt that his support was substantial. The spirit of the Fidelistas is difficult to explain to persons like ourselves who live in a stable society, indeed a society which often seems stalemated at dead center. For the Fidelistas—and they are particularly strong among the youth and the Negroes—the Revolution is still in its first uncorrupted phase. For them the experience is like love. They live in a springtime of mankind when words which have grown overblown and empty elsewhere become meaningful—love of country, devotion, selflessness, readiness to sacrifice one's life for others, the joy of struggling to end misery and to build a better society. How speak of these things to the jaded intellectuals of Washington?

Elsewhere youth has turned beatnik in the shadow of the mushroom cloud. In Cuba the same youth still *believes*. A whole new generation of technicians, scientists, doctors and engineers are being developed from them to replace those who have fled. The best and most promising youth are being brought in as *becados*—50,000 of them—given scholarships (*becas*) and stipends to make it possible for them to study. It was the holiday season and I was unable to talk with them. But a girl who is teaching some of the premedical students English spoke glowingly of their enthusiasm and devotion.

Without hope, faith and charity, Castro's Cuba cannot be understood. We underestimate its grass roots strength and we overestimate its difficulties. A Britisher who had gone through the London blitz, a Pole who had seen his country forced to make a revolution in a land leveled by war and depopulated by Nazism, a Yugoslav who knew at first hand what the Partisans went through, a Russian who had seen war in all its appalling fury—such observers told me they regarded the Cuban Revolution as a de luxe affair, the standard of living as extraordinarily high, the food supply as phenomenal for a country undergoing so fundamental a revolution against the will of so powerful a neighbor. It is, thanks to the kind of buildings we Yankee imperialists left behind, the world's first air-conditioned revolution. They keep the air conditioning on even in December when it is hardly needed. It is also, thanks to the existence of a huge Soviet bloc, getting a level of aid from abroad such as no other revolution has ever enjoyed. An American engineer who spent a lifetime in the automotive industry in Detroit and is now running a Cuban government laboratory for products research and automation told me the machine tools being supplied by the bloc are of very good quality. He said even a country like North Korea, so recently leveled by war, is sending Cuba first-class milling machinery. "They may be short of consumer goods," he told me, "but the task of supplying capital equipment and technicians for a country as small as this one is 'chicken feed' for the Soviet bloc." He is very optimistic about the future. He thinks Cuba will be growing its own food needs in three or four years and he says a geological survey has found not only many valuable metals like cobalt but petroleum. If Cuba can supply its own oil and food, it will really be independent.

The true Fidelistas are a pleasure to talk with. One of them was the young soldier in charge of the new fishing port. When I told him the United States fears this will be a Soviet naval base, he said, "We are building this port in Havana. We are building a re-frigerating plant, a canning plant, a fileting plant. You will be able to see for yourself that our purpose is fishing." Traditionally Cubans have paid little attention to the food potential of the seas around them. In other quarters I was told that Cuba hopes also to fish the little-touched South Atlantic, that the Russians can fish the North Atlantic from their own bases but that for South Atlantic fisheries it will be advantageous to them to have fish-processing and ship-repair facilities in Cuba. Others spoke of the plans going forward for automation in the sugar fields. Part of the Revolution's problems arises from its success rather than its failure. Labor is growing short. The hard work of cane cutting is not popular and peasants are no longer forced by hunger and misery to take on such back-breaking tasks. They are also eating more, and supplying the cities with less. My own impression in the shops was that price control and rationing were working fairly well, and there was more avail-able than I had been led to believe. In everything the children come first. Milk was impossible to get in Havana's best hotels but a Mexican reporter told me of visiting a fishing village in Oriente where every morning a truck came over bad roads to deliver twenty-eight liters of milk for the twenty-eight babies. Those people in Havana with babies all told me they got their milk ration regularly. If Havana is poorer, the countryside is richer. And in the hotels at night one sees a whole new class of Negroes and mulattoes, the men in dinner jackets, the girls in new-style half-bustle dresses, enjoying themselves where hitherto only the rich and the foreigner played. The sense of full racial equality and ease is one of the most pleasant experiences for the guilt-burdened white American in Castro's Cuba.

It was my sixth visit to Cuba—three times before and three times since the Revolution. I did not encounter enemies of the regime. I did not visit the prisons, or study the workings of the bloc system which is supposed to give the Castroites eyes and ears everywhere against the threat of sabotage and our CIA, but must work some injustice too. The Cuba I picture is a Cuba as it appears through friendly eyes. This, of course, is not the whole truth. A revolution is a complex phenomena, a tragic struggle to be fully grasped only when seen from many points of view with compassion for the exiles as well as the victors. But I believe it is dangerously misleading to make policy and form opinion, as we do back home, almost exclusively on the basis of hostile views. To look at Castro's Cuba only through the eyes of those who have fled, to concentrate on the negative aspects as our press does, to exaggerate these and even to falsify, is to make it almost impossible to fashion flexible and wise policy. For years we read in our press that the Russian Revolution and then the Chinese was on the verge of collapse. Every time we are confronted with a new revolution we take to the opium pipes of our own propaganda. Those who try to be objective or friendly are dismissed as dupes, and sometimes—as the Stalin years demonstrate—they were. But events have also shown that in the long run the dupes prove less misleading than the doped.

JANUARY 21, 1963

47: *Epilogue*

WORDS TO BE ENGRAVED ON A NEW ROSETTA STONE

The Berlin crisis brings forcibly to attention that the capitalist and Communist systems have one charming characteristic in common. Neither asks its people whether they want to risk the suicide of the human race in a quarrel over access to one city; or indeed whether they want to go to war at all. Over there, where the workers and peasants have been freed from the heavy yoke of monopoly capitalism, a worried Russian can't even write a letter to *Pravda,* or go to a peace meeting. Over here, where such channels of protest are still open to a few, these are too few to count. Congress is locked in fierce contention over such momentous issues as whether aid to education shall include parochial schools, but it hardly looks up to notice that war clouds are gathering which could mean the end of our species. The Russians and the Americans resemble two huge herds moving toward possible conflict, too closely packed to struggle successfully against their fate. The helplessness of human kind is the dominant feature of the planetary landscape as the crisis approaches.

The next feature which the broad view turns up is that the problems of American-Russian relations are not really soluble in the existing frame of reference. By this I mean the system which divides the planet into sovereign nation-states knowing no law but their own will and no protection but their own strength. Man may be on the verge of visiting the stars but he still lives in a jungle. Armies, spies, and the constant need for keeping people mobilized with fear and hatred, are the pillars of the nation-state system. Can Russia trust us and our allies not to spy out her secrets, or we trust them not to spy out ours? Can X trust Y not to cheat if he can get away with it, since Y regards X as the embodiment of all evil and against such evil the end justifies the means—and X regards Y in exactly the same way? How can we stop testing and devising new monsters of destruction lest *he* steal a march on us and come up with some new whooper-dooper? Given such a world, how can the rest of mankind expect to make effective protest if Americans and

Russians again pollute the skies, the seas and the earth with radioactivity, or chew up huge quantities of basic metals on vast military and spatial toys while millions of fellow creatures are lucky to have a wooden plow?

Woven into the crisis are other human ways that help to make it difficult to resolve. The leader of the herd must consider not only the welfare of the herd but his own prestige; this lost, the leadership may pass to someone else; indeed he may be trampled down by those behind him. Neither leader is a madman and neither leader wants war, but both are getting themselves into a position where one must back down or slink away and lose face unless he calls the other's bluff. The stake is suffering beyond imagination for millions. This is more or less realized, but the realization makes little difference just as it turns out to make little difference that for many months the leaders on both sides have been saying that war is now impossible. Suddenly it is quite possible. The two leaders have met. They have made clear to each other that they are prepared to go to war unless the other backs down. Worse than war by miscalculation is war by cold calculation. We are prepared to call the other side's bluff and blow everybody's brains out, our own included, rather than give in.

Another odd feature of the human landscape in these climactic years is that both sides claim to be moved by the purest impulses of human brotherhood. On our side are the Christians or the Judaeo-Christians, who believe—or think they believe—in human brotherhood. On the other side are the heirs of Marx, who founded another creed of brotherhood. Both creeds are brotherhoods of the oppressed, dedicated to building a better world for all mankind, in the here and/or the hereafter. Among allies on both sides are subsidiary creeds like Mohammedanism, which also postulate human brotherhood, not to mention the nineteenth-century creed of free markets and free enterprise as the only true road to the greatest good of the greatest number. Everybody is intent on building a better world in which all men will be brothers but no one is really willing to start out by being fraternal in the world as it is. The unspoken corollary of all these brotherly creeds is that the millennium can only be ushered in by a vast brotherly blood bath. So on both sides men are devotedly ready, if ordered, to press the button.

Which of the contending creeds is the true one? Solomon found the true mother by watching which woman preferred to give up the baby rather than have it cut in half. Here both contenders prefer the death of the world to its loss to the other. Clearly both are false and neither deserves the love of mankind. On one side is a caricature of socialism, on the other a caricature of freedom. How free are men who can be blown off the map at any moment without their permission?

Some crisis was bound to arise. For many months men have talked of coexistence. But the leadership on both sides has envisaged coexistence as a deplorable and distasteful necessity, arising from a technological misfortune: it was no longer possible to destroy others without destroying ourselves. It naturally flowed from this that coexistence was not really to be peace, a lying down of the lion with the lamb, but only a new form of struggle, more insidious, more protracted, leading by safer means to the extinction of the other. No one said, we must learn to live together, we must stress our similarities not our differences, we must think of ourselves as one species on a small planet, as indeed sometimes we notice that we are. *They* spoke of coexistence as only a new and more intensified form of class struggle while we saw in it only a way by other means to spread our own system. No one saw it as a breathing spell, in the shadow of monsters neither side wished to unleash, a breathing spell in which to learn that—as the Gospel says— we are all parts of one another.

Should the war come, those who survive will be a long, long time rebuilding. They may be helped to build something better if somehow the memory can be preserved of how poorly the world was organized and the species conditioned. Should the crisis pass, it is by a study of this landscape that we may possibly find our way out of peril to something more stable. The sovereign state is our enemy. Only if it dies can humanity live.

JUNE 21, 1961

INDEX

About the Author

Born in 1907, I. F. Stone has been a working newspaperman since the age of fourteen when, during his sophomore year at a small-town high school, he launched a monthly, *The Progress*, which supported — among other causes — the League of Nations and Gandhi's first efforts at freedom for India.

While at school and college, he worked for daily newspapers in Camden, New Jersey, Philadelphia, and New York.

Since 1940 he has served in succession as a Washington correspondent and commentator for *The Nation*, the newspaper *PM*, the *New York Post*, and the *Daily Compass*. In 1953 he launched *I. F. Stone's Weekly*, a legendary venture in independent, one-man journalism, which he edited and published for nineteen years. He has written extensively for the *New York Review of Books* and long served as a contributing editor. He writes a Washington column at irregular intervals for *The Nation* and many daily papers at home and abroad, including the *Philadelphia Inquirer*, on which he worked while he was in college.

In semiretirement Mr. Stone returned to the philosophy and classical history he had studied in college. He taught himself ancient Greek and wrote *The Trial of Socrates*, a controversial probe of the most famous free-speech case of all time, widely acclaimed on publication in 1988.

Mr. Stone and his wife, Esther, live in Washington. They have three married children.